Volume 5

Minnesota Monographs in the Humanities

Gerhard Weiss, founding editor

Leonard Unger, editor

MILTON'S

EARTHLY PARADISE

✿✿✿✿✿✿✿✿✿✿✿✿✿✿✿

A Historical Study of Eden

JOSEPH E. DUNCAN

UNIVERSITY OF MINNESOTA PRESS, MINNEAPOLIS

Library of Congress Catalog Card Number: 71-187167

ISBN 0-8166-0633-1

To My Colleagues in English
at the University of Minnesota, Duluth

ACKNOWLEDGMENTS

I find that I owe many debts, both for aid in research and in writing and for financial assistance. I owe this first kind of debt to books, to libraries, and to individuals. I was led to my own study by such works as Don Cameron Allen's *The Legend of Noah*, Ernest Lee Tuveson's *Millennium and Utopia*, and Watson Kirkconnell's *The Celestial Cycle*. I have received valuable guidance from Sister Mary Irma Corcoran's *Milton's Paradise with Reference to the Hexameral Background*, A. Bartlett Giamatti's *The Earthly Paradise and the Renaissance Epic*, and Arnold Williams's *The Common Expositor*. I am aware of an immense debt to numerous other works which have proved most helpful to me in writing this book.

I want particularly to acknowledge the assistance given me by the librarians of the Union Theological Seminary Library, where I did the greater part of my research. I am also deeply grateful to the librarians of both the Duluth and Minneapolis campuses of the University of Minnesota and to those of the Columbia University Library, the Harvard University Library, the New York Public Library, the Newberry Library, and the British Museum Library.

When I first became interested in my subject, I received encouragement and valuable suggestions from Professor Marjorie

Nicolson, who had guided my study at Columbia University, and from Professor Don Cameron Allen. While working on this study, I have consistently profited from the knowledge and interest of Professor James F. Maclear of the Department of History of the University of Minnesota, Duluth. I have also received help from colleagues in English and languages. My mother, Mrs. Joseph L. Duncan, has assisted in proofreading. Michael Cruikshank has helped a great deal through his work on the index.

I am grateful to the University of Minnesota for granting me two sabbatical leaves and a single-quarter leave, and to the University Graduate School for two grants-in-aid. I also wish to thank the American Council of Learned Societies for a grant-in-aid.

J. E. D.

CONTENTS

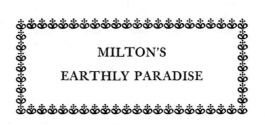

MILTON'S
EARTHLY PARADISE

HISTORIA
SACRA
PARADISI TERRESTRIS
ET SANCTISSIMI INNOCENTIAE STATVS

IN QVA

Primo. Paradiſus Terrenus . *Secundo* . Vita beatiſ-
ſima Adami, & Euæ in Horto . *Tertio* . Status
fæliciſſimus ſuorum Poſterum; ſi Originalis
ſtetiſſet Iuſtitia . *Quarto.* Tentatio ; Pecca-
tum; Iudicium ; ac Pœna Prothoparen-
tum. *Vltimo.* Vita ærumnoſa eorum-
dem; quã ab exilio vſque ad dor-
mitionem diù, & miſere duxe-
re ; deſcribitur .

IN HAC SACRA HISTORIA

Ex Scripturis, Concilijs, Patribus, Theologis, Expoſitoribus, Rabi-
nis, Hiſtoricis, Annaliſtis, Chronologis , & Geographis mira-
bilis ſacra eruditio decerpitur; concinnè diſponitur; ac fa-
matiſſimus Duplex ille Humanæ Naturæ Status
Naturæ Integræ , & Naturæ Corruptæ
breuiſſime exponitur.

AVCTORE

AVGVSTINO INVEGES
SACERDOTE. SICVLO. SACCENSI.

Panormi , Ex Typographia Petri de Iſola **1649.**

Impr. Saler. V. G.   Impr. pro Sp. Dr Iopp. F. P. Franciſc. Meroldus

INTRODUCTION

∴ THE EARTHLY PARADISE, so variously interpreted from primitive myth to modern psychology, is at the heart of much of the thought and literature of the sixteenth and seventeenth centuries. The ideas of the earthly paradise held by Milton and his contemporaries reflected many centuries of acceptance, rejection, and interpretation of earlier myth, theology, and literature. Today, we can look forward through the history of these changing conceptions of paradise to *Paradise Lost* and beyond, or we can look back to the beginnings of this paradise tradition from the perspective provided by *Paradise Lost*.

The twofold purpose of this book is to provide a brief history of the idea of the true earthly paradise — the garden in Eden — in Western thought, and to contribute to the understanding of some of the literary works which have dealt with the story of the lost paradise, including the most complex of these, Milton's *Paradise Lost*. This study approaches *Paradise Lost* by examining the changing ideas of the nature, meaning, and importance of the Edenic paradise through the centuries. It attempts to consider the relation of Milton's Paradise to this paradise tradition and to show in what ways so much of this earlier tradition became a part of *Paradise Lost*, while other aspects were rejected. More specifically, this work seeks to explain how Milton's conception

3

of paradise is similar to or different from the conceptions of his predecessors, contemporaries, and successors, both commentators and poets, and how Milton's Paradise fits into the framework of Renaissance conceptions of paradise. To explicate this fully, the distinctive attitudes and problems of Milton and his contemporaries in an Eden-centered age will be investigated. Commentators' efforts to explain the unique historical importance of paradise, to discover its exact site, and to understand its spiritual meaning will be examined as will the ways in which Milton and other imaginative writers interpreted the paradise story — a subject which was deemed as important for an understanding of the human condition, and yet was divorced from human experience.

The chapters on the Renaissance raise and at least in part answer the question: In what ways do the commentators' assumptions, interests, and ideas concerning the Edenic paradise appear also in *Paradise Lost*? The commentators, dealing with a historical interpretation of paradise somewhat like modern anthropologists, sought to comprehend the beginnings of man and his world — the first development of knowledge, religion, government, and marriage and the family — and to relate these beginnings to later history. Milton and other Renaissance poets writing about the paradise story would have agreed with these prose writers that the events in paradise were immensely important. Although it is often hazardous to try to show specific influences on a work like *Paradise Lost*, it is evident, first, that Milton and the prose writers shared many of the same concerns and, second, that he was affected by the cumulative influence of their approach, despite various disagreements. This is borne out by Milton's occupation with orthodox and unorthodox ideas of creation, Adam's knowledge and ability to know God aright, and the origins of family life, religion, and society founded on man's reason and liberty. This is also reflected in Milton's attention to the location of paradise, his emphasis on the natural and the rational, his account of the destruction of paradise, and his interest in the typological relationship between the terrestrial and celestial paradises,

4

since typology was closely associated with a historical interpretation of Scripture.

Milton's poetic and dramatic embodiment of these conceptions of the historical paradise is only one aspect of the harmonious complexity of *Paradise Lost*. Milton's re-creation of paradise is not only superb poetry of great allusive subtlety, drawing upon a long tradition, but it is also a penetrating account of the origins of man, involving highly complex and controversial issues. More particularly, the historical significance of the paradise story for both Milton and the commentators indicates once again the close relation between the last two books of *Paradise Lost* and the rest of the epic. Though Milton inherited the images of paradise from classical and Christian poetry, he would never have doubted that paradise was more important as history than as poetry. Yet the poetry and the history could not be divorced. Only through great and inspired poetry could the transcendent truth of the history be suggested.

Because of today's interest in comparative mythology, Old Testament origins, depth psychology, and anthropology, we inevitably view paradise from a different — and probably more dim — perspective from that of our forefathers. From our vantage point, however, we are aware that Milton wrote at a critical moment, when an infinitely rich tradition of Hebraic and Christian beliefs about paradise was available to him, and before the widespread rejection of much of this tradition would make it increasingly difficult for a poet to write a serious historical epic about the biblical paradise. Finally, through hindsight, we can discern in *Paradise Lost* the consistent fusion of mythic, theological, and literary elements into an imaginative whole.

The appeal of the paradise images through the ages has been well documented. Often the attempts to understand this appeal shed new light only to create new mystery. Early belief abounds with accounts of an earthly paradise, with its perpetual spring, trees of life and knowledge, fountains of immortality, and rivers that water the earth. The Sumerians and Babylonians envisioned the garden of Siduri and the land of Dilmun as paradise. The sacred books of India celebrate a resplendent paradise atop Mount Meru, from which fall four rivers. The Chinese crown Kuen-Lun with a paradise. In Iranian myth, the mountain Haraberezaiti links heaven and earth. The Greeks wrote of the golden age, the garden of Alcinous, the Elysian Fields, and of the sorrows brought by Pandora and Proserpina. Scandinavian legend tells of the Himinbjorg and of the paradise on Midgard, a mountain of immeasurable height in the middle of the world. Similar paradises are known in other cultures, and throughout them runs the recurrent pattern of error and fall; and the paradise is lost.

During the early Christian era and the Middle Ages, descriptions of paradise were still colored by myth and legend, as writers conceived of it as an inaccessible mountaintop, an exotic isle, or a timeless land just beyond the realm of Prester John. However, Christian writers made their most important contribution to the paradise tradition by giving form and substance and historical validity to Adam and Eve and the garden in Eden. The early Christian writers speculated about the nature and life of paradise, developed the concepts of man's original righteousness and original sin, and saw the events in paradise as the beginnings of human history. In their interpretations of the paradise story, early Christian poets provided the framework for *Paradise Lost* and other imaginative works of the Renaissance. St. Thomas Aquinas, in his realistic, logical discussion of the life of paradise, gave renewed theological importance to the Scriptural account of the lost paradise and helped to prepare the way for the humanistic commentary of the Renaissance, while Dante recaptured the spiritual perfection of the state of innocence. The aim of the rational commentary of the Renaissance was to provide a credible, detailed, and historically valid interpretation of the literal sense of the Scriptural account. Renaissance writers tried not only to determine the year and even the hour of the events in paradise, but to identify the exact site of the Edenic garden in order to demonstrate the accuracy of the opening chapters of Genesis. They also sought in paradise the origins of knowledge, law, the family, religion, and society. It was in this intellectual climate that Milton matured; this was the moment of *Paradise Lost*. In the hundred years after the publication of *Paradise Lost*, many writers openly rejected both the Scriptural account of the lost paradise and the theological doctrines founded upon it. After Milton, poets turned to Adam and Eve for diverting romance or turned away from them altogether in favor of abstract argument.

Contemporary interpretations of paradise are beyond the scope of this study, except insofar as they inescapably affect our approach to *Paradise Lost* and the earlier conceptions of paradise and perhaps also increase our understanding of the continuing tension between the powerful vision of the early paradise and its rational explanations. If the idea of paradise has lost much of its importance historically and theologically, it has gained a new importance psychologically and anthropologically. Carl Jung has regarded paradise as an unconscious archetype, related to the Mother archetype, which is associated with a longing for redemption and the fertility of garden, cave, spring, and tree. The archetype, although unperceived, makes itself felt in the fascinating power of the images it arranges, many of which have existed from the remotest times. This archetype, manifested in myth, vision, and dream, may be altered by its mode of perception and colored by the social context or the individual consciousness. Following Jung, Maud Bodkin considered paradise as an important archetypal pattern persisting amid variations. She related it also to Freud's pleasure principle offering a subjective release, and found her best examples of this pattern in the mountain garden and underground river of *Paradise Lost* and "Kubla Khan." In his far-reaching anthropological studies, Mircea Eliade has emphasized the recurrence of imitations of the celestial archetype of paradise and the continued nostalgia for a lost paradise in both primitive and modern cultures. According to Eliade, the tree of life, the fountain, and the sacred mountain linking heaven and earth appear repeatedly as part of the "symbolism of the center" through which man gains a sense of absolute reality. In his psychological history of man, Norman O. Brown interpreted Eliade in Freudian terms and summed up much of his thought in the statement that

7

"for Freud as for St. Augustine, mankind's destiny is a departure from, and an effort to regain, paradise, but in between these two terms man is at war with himself." More recently, John Armstrong has traced an "alternative" paradise tradition including a small group of masterpieces "which do not seek to represent arcadian happiness but are, essentially, severe realizations of imaginative power, and so articulate the ideal form that its strength derives from the very elements making it unsustainable." [1]

I

EASTWARD IN EDEN

∴ AT THE TIME John Milton was writing *Paradise Lost*, some ♋ European thinkers were engaged in heated controversy about the accuracy, authorship, and inspiration of the Scriptures. Despite these arguments, Milton and most of his contemporaries accepted the story of Adam and Eve and the garden in Eden as a literal and inspired historical account written by Moses. Viewing this history in the light of centuries of Christian commentary, they were prepared to defend their interpretation of Scripture to the utmost of their powers. And Milton, seeking to base his epic upon the only true account of man's origins, depended as fully as possible upon Genesis, unaware of the earlier mythic traditions and unsympathetic to the radical reinterpretation of Genesis by Christian commentators through the centuries. Yet, by the end of the seventeenth century, there were numerous challenges to the biblical account of man's beginnings. Today, biblical scholars say that the Eden material was rooted in traditions far older than Moses and that the first chapters of Genesis were derived from diverse sources and underwent many revisions. Modern commentators also feel that the Adam and Eve portrayed by the Hebrew writers were quite different from the perfect figures envisioned by Milton in accordance with the orthodox Christian tradition.

MILTON'S EARTHLY PARADISE

Myths of Paradise

Although there is no exact parallel to the Eden story in Genesis, many of its elements seem related to Sumerian, Babylonian, and Assyrian mythical material, much of which could have been transmitted from Mesopotamia to Palestine by the middle of the second millennium. Probably the eariest account of a paradise and a fall is the epic of Gilgamesh, which evidently existed in some form two or three thousand years before the composition of Genesis. In this epic the natural man Enkidu is seduced by a city harlot and rejected by the animals with whom he has lived in innocence. The king Gilgamesh, grieved by the death of Enkidu, seeks his ancestor and the lost paradise to try to unravel the enigma of mortality. After a "night journey," he visits a scorpion-guarded mountaintop paradise resplendent with gem-bearing bushes and lapis lazuli leaves hung thick with fruit. This is inhabited by the Sun, walking in the dawn, and the goddess Siduri. He then proceeds across the waters of death to Dilmun, a land without infirmity or grief, possibly situated on the Persian Gulf. He obtains a plant giving immortality, only to have it stolen by a serpent. Similarly, in a Babylonian myth, Adapa, a kind of Adam figure, loses the immortality within his grasp. He is admitted to heaven, views its secrets and obtains knowledge, and is offered food and drink bringing everlasting life, but he rejects these for he has been warned by the goddess Ea — perhaps for his own good — that they will bring death.[1] Like Adam and Eve, he gains knowledge, but through trickery loses his chance to live forever.

Several writers have speculated about the mythical elements lying behind the Genesis account. William F. Albright has listed as recurrent motifs the paradise situated at the source of four rivers, the tree of life inhabited by the serpent and guarded by griffins and whirling swords, the loss of immortality through the serpent's cunning, and the seduction of the archetypal man by the mother-goddess who induces him to eat. Robert Graves has maintained that all gardens of delight, usually complete with

10

serpents, were originally ruled by goddesses, and has associated Eve with the Sumerian love goddess Arurru or Ishtar and with the Hittite Heba. Sir James Frazer has suggested that the forbidden tree was originally a tree of death and that the serpent, as in many myths, perverted God's message, deceived man, and ate of the tree of life himself, as evidenced by the shedding of his skin. He also noted many accounts of the creation of woman from a male rib.[2]

The Garden in Eden

Genesis provides the indispensable account of the garden that would come to be known as paradise; however, some other Jewish writings also describe the garden and associate it with heaven or an abode of the blest.

Most modern biblical scholars agree that the story of the life of innocence in the garden (it would not be known as paradise for many centuries) was combined with other material by Yahwist writers about the ninth century B.C. They distinguish between this narrative in Genesis 2 and 3 and the Priestly Code of Genesis 1, written about the sixth century B.C. Paul Humbert contends that a creation myth was subordinated to a paradise myth in a new composition. The original paradise myth would have included the picture of the garden with the trees of life and of knowledge, the lack of shame in nakedness, the prohibition, the temptation, fall and expulsion while the creation of living things, the instructions to dress and keep the land, the naming of animals, and the institution of marriage would have belonged to the creation myth. In the paradise myth, man gains discernment only after the fall; in the creation myth, knowledge, including sexual knowledge, is immediate and natural. Similarly, Cuthbert A. Simpson in *The Interpreter's Bible* assumes that there was an early version of Genesis 2 depicting a carefree life in the garden without sexual consciousness. Secondary insertions introduced the tree of life, the necessity of work, and the naming of the animals. Simpson thinks that a second Yahwist writer from northern Palestine brought material from an Eden saga into the narrative.

11

Most recent exegetes regard the passage locating the garden in relation to the four rivers as one of the latest additions to the account in Genesis 2 and 3.[3]

In composing this narrative, the Yahwist writers, Milton's most important source and strikingly like Milton himself, were reworking old stories in a new interpretation that was rational, theological, and artistic. The germ not only of the setting and incidents, but also of many of the concepts and attitudes of *Paradise Lost* appear in Genesis. The story in Genesis 2–3 is made as credible as possible and is filled with spiritual truth. Man is to work, even in the garden, and the serpent remains a mortal creature of God. The central experience is not the eating from a magic tree, but the sense of guilt, the fear of death, the disordering of human relations and the alienation from God following the violation of a divine commandment.[4] In its explanation of the origin of work and marriage and of man's agricultural and nomadic life after the expulsion, Genesis anticipates more sophisticated and systematic attempts to found a whole theology, history, and social structure on the events in Eden. Similarly, the approach in Genesis to a linear, providential, universal human history, beginning in the garden, prepares for the cosmic historical sweep envisioned by Christian writers from St. Augustine to Milton. The consummate artistry of the Yahwists' narrative of the garden seems deliberate, with their effects probably the result of pruning, while Milton's were the fruits of rich elaboration within a much more complex tradition.

The passage describing the four rivers and the lands surrounding Eden (Gen. 2:10–14) brings one surprisingly into the world of nations and precise place names. This early attempt to locate the garden and to relate it to the civilized world suggests the laborious efforts of Milton's contemporaries to locate paradise precisely with map and argument. The description actually fits no place. The Hebrews at various times located paradise at Mount Saphon in Syria, at Hebron, at Jerusalem, and at the head of the Persian Gulf. With the exception of an attempt to locate paradise at the North Pole, most modern commentators have been content to try to understand where the Genesis writer thought he was locating it.[5] Most of these studies place it on or beneath the Persian Gulf or in or near the Assyrian mountains.

The aims and accomplishments of the Yahwist writers, in forming a literary masterpiece from earlier material, were closer to Milton than he could have known, and their conception of the story of the lost garden was different from Milton's in ways he could not have realized. Instead of the magnificently ordered universe of *Paradise Lost*, the early Hebrews apparently thought of the earth as a disc arising from the waters. Paradise itself was an enclosed garden, or at best a park. And, most important, in Genesis there is no original righteousness, no original sin, and no Satan. S. R. Driver in his standard commentary on Genesis has written: "The view of the high intellectual capacities of our first parents has been familiarized to many by the great poem of Milton, who represents Adam and Eve as holding discourse together in words of singular elevation, refinement, and grace. But there is nothing in the representation of Genesis to justify it; and it is opposed to everything that we know of the method of God's providence." The Adam and Eve of Genesis are great children and the knowledge they gain "of good and evil" is apparently knowledge of all things. As another well-known modern scholar, John Skinner, has said, their sin is presented as "something intelligible, not needing explanation, not a mystery." [6] The Yahwist writers did not have to face the problem of providing characterizations that would explain how two perfect creatures could fall. Moreover, the concept of an inherited original sin as the source of the world's evil would not be developed for many centuries.

Besides the account in Genesis, there are references to a paradise garden in Ezekiel, which seem to stem from a different tradition. In the first of these passages (Ezek. 28:11–19) occurs the only biblical description of the Edenic garden as atop a high mountain, as it appears in *Paradise Lost*. Here, though not in the Genesis account, it is described as "the garden of God," as it is by Milton (IV, 209). The king of Tyre, like Adam, sins and is expelled from the mountain of God by a cherub. In another passage (Ezek. 31:2–9) a cedar of Lebanon, reaching to the clouds and representing Pharaoh, is compared with the beautiful and abundantly watered trees of Eden. A third passage (Ezek. 47:1–12), which pictures the temple with four streams flowing from it, is at least one source for the idea of the Church as paradise. These descriptions in Ezekiel are closer than those in Genesis to modern conceptions of an archetypal pattern of paradise and they are related to other primitive notions of paradise too. Ezekiel's garden resembles the high, heavily jeweled garden of Siduri, the shrine of Humbaba which, with its sacred cedars and river, is also described in *Gilgamesh*, and the Babylonian sacred groves where the fruit is taboo but the animals friendly to man.[7]

With the translation of the Hebrew Scriptures into the Greek of the Septuagint in the third century B.C., the simple enclosed garden of Genesis became "paradise," with an added cluster of rich connotation. The Hebrew word for Eden, which perhaps originally meant a flatland, was associated with the Hebrew verb "to delight." The garden "in Eden" was interpreted as a garden "of delight" and was translated by the Greek word for paradise. This word, originally meaning a royal park and probably of Persian derivation, had been made familiar in Greek usage by Xenophon.[8] This idea of a pleasure garden was embodied in the Vulgate translation "paradisum voluptatis." Other Latin translations referring to a "paradisum deliciarum" are probably the ultimate source of Milton's "Delicious Paradise" (IV, 132).

An assumption of some relation between the earthly garden and a heavenly abode, common in the Renaissance, appears in early Jewish thought. According to some speculations about Jewish beliefs, the garden in Genesis with its four rivers was patterned after the Milky Way with its branches, and Ezekiel's mountain with its "garden of God" came down from heaven. The conception of the Edenic garden in Enoch, Baruch, and Esdras, suggestive of that in Ezekiel, forms a transition from the idea of the primitive home to the Talmudic and New Testament conceptions of an abode of the blest. This Jewish garden of righteousness, with its tree of wisdom, anticipates the medieval Christian idea of paradise as the home of translated souls. Also, in the Cabbala, the Zohar, and the Hebraic commentaries of the Christian era, the earthly paradise is often regarded as a model in miniature of the heavenly paradise.[9]

Milton's Use of Genesis

How much and yet how little of Milton's Paradise is based on Genesis! But these few verses telling the paradise story, accepted as divinely inspired history, were his crucial and indispensable source. Despite his heavy dependence also on the classical and Christian traditions, Milton tried deliberately to make the maximum direct use of Genesis. Scarcely a detail from Genesis is omitted, the biblical language is often retained, and some elements are either repeated several times or expanded. However, by presenting a number of episodes as an unrecorded interlude between Genesis 2 and 3 and by bringing in most of Genesis 2 by allusion and the characters' recollections, Milton achieved great flexibility in the arrangement of his narrative and in the interweaving of new strands from tradition and invention.

Milton followed Genesis closely in describing Paradise and the life of Adam and Eve. There are a number of references to the trees of life and of knowledge in the midst of the garden, to the injunction to work, and to the command not to partake of the tree of knowledge. The serpent is repeatedly described as subtle or sly. Perhaps even in Adam's and Eve's address in their morning orisons to the mists and exhalations that "wet the thirstie earth with falling showers" (V, 190), there is a reference to the mist that went up from the earth and "watered the whole face of the ground" (Gen. 2:6).[10]

Milton, however, found his greatest opportunities for dramatic and poetic development in the biblical accounts of the creation of man, the naming of the animals, the creation of woman, and the institution of marriage. Although Genesis 2 was his chief source for the description of life in Paradise before the Fall, he followed the order of creation given in Genesis 1 (plants, animals, man, woman) rather than the order in Genesis 2 (man, trees, animals, woman). The explanation in the Priestly Code of man's creation in the divine image and his dominion over the creatures is easily reconciled with the Yahwist reference to his lack of shame in nudity (IV, 288–313). The Yahwist version of man's creation is also introduced in Satan's angered contempt for "This Man of Clay" who "us the more to spite his Maker rais'd / from dust" (IX, 176–78). And after the Fall, Adam reminds Eve "that we are dust, / And thither must return and be no more" (XI, 199–200). Following the many allusions to the events of Genesis 2 in earlier books of *Paradise Lost*, Adam finally explains these events chronologically to Raphael in Book VIII. He was created outside Paradise, in accordance with the usual interpretation of Genesis 2:7–8. Upon entering Paradise, he finds the creatures already formed. He is then guided by God to the Mount of Paradise and given the commandment concerning the tree of knowledge.

In Genesis 2 God asserts that it is not good for man to be alone and promises "an help meet for him." He then presents the beasts to Adam for naming, "but for Adam there was not found an help meet for him." Many exegetes think this passage is an imperfect fusion of various strands. It has also been suggested that it is a modification of a myth of a natural man like Enkidu, who lived with and perhaps cohabited with the beasts.[11] Various Renaissance writers, including Du Bartas, made references here to unnatural unions. Milton expands this biblical account into a long dialogue between a rather playful God and a presumptuous Adam (VIII, 338–451). Adam comprehends not only the nature of each bird and beast, but how his own nature is different from theirs. He is then led to understand the rational and spiritual quality of human love. At the conclusion of Adam's narration, Raphael defines true love, explaining to Adam once more why "Among the Beasts no Mate for thee was found" (VIII, 594).

In Genesis God causes a deep sleep to fall on Adam, then forms Eve and brings her to Adam. This sleep is not meant to anesthetize Adam, but is induced to prevent him from actually observing God performing his miracles. However, to permit Adam to tell Raphael of Eve's creation, Milton narrowly avoids violation of the deeply rooted conviction of the Old Testament writers that God should not be seen "in the act." Nature brings Adam a sleep which leaves open the

> Cell
> Of Fancie my internal sight, by which
> Abstract as in a trance methought I saw. . . .
> (VIII, 460–62)

What he sees is realistic enough: "cordial spirits warme / And Life-blood streaming fresh." Adam awakes without Eve, but soon sees her approaching, guided by God's voice. Adam resumes his dialogue with God, closely paraphrasing Genesis 2:23–24, which was possibly a late textual addition. Man and woman in marriage shall be not only "one Flesh," but also "one Heart, one Soule." Evidently wishing to exploit the poetic potentialities of this episode, Milton included two other variations on the theme of the first meeting. Eve recalls that, after admiring her reflection, she heeded a voice guiding her to Adam waiting "under a Platan." Milton's Adam claims her not only as his flesh and bone but "Part of my Soul . . . My other half" (IV, 487–88). Eve, just before beginning this account of her first hours, addresses Adam as "thou for whom / And from whom I was formed flesh of thy flesh" (IV, 440–41). Again, the marriage is recalled:

> Heav'nly Quires the Hymenaean sung
> What day the genial Angel to our Sire
> Brought her in naked beauty more adorn'd,
> More lovely than *Pandora* . . . (IV, 711–14).

The verses in Genesis proclaiming the marriage of Adam and Eve may be regarded as the ultimate source of the inseparable union of love and Paradise in *Paradise Lost*, inspiring Eve's love lyric, "All seasons and thir change" (IV, 640–56), the epithalamium, "Haile wedded Love" (IV, 750–70), and the couple's evening prayer expressing gratitude for "mutual love, the Crown of all our bliss / Ordain'd by thee" (IV, 727–29). The description of Eve as "the mother of all living" (Gen. 3:20), which is also a mythic appellation, also seems to be echoed in Milton's "Mother of human Race" and "Mother of Mankind" (IV, 475; V, 388).

Milton, then, apparently sought to gain the utmost development from the brief account in Genesis. He quoted, reiterated, and expanded freely.[12] Yet the biblical story of the garden was only one of the streams that converged in Milton's Paradise.

2

"SUCH PLEASING LICENCE"

CHRISTIAN writers trying to envision and describe the Edenic paradise, told of so briefly in Genesis, repeatedly turned to the earthly "paradises" of Greek and Latin literature. Milton and his contemporaries knew and loved these classical descriptions of an imagined paradise and later descriptions influenced by them. The golden age, the Garden of Alcinous, and other classical concepts were often regarded as faded, distorted images of the true biblical Eden, and sometimes they were dismissed as altogether false. Milton was charmed by the "pleasing licence" of myth and alluded to several of these classical paradises in creating his Paradise; he could not long forget that these were "feign'd," but only the Edenic paradise was true.

Classical ideals of a happy, blessed life and of a pleasant natural setting contributed much to the Christian ideal of the life of innocence in the Edenic paradise. The temporal idea of the golden age had its spatial counterpart in the stories of various remote sites, such as the Fortunate Islands and the Gardens of the Hesperides, where the life of the golden age still existed. A. Bartlett Giamatti in *The Earthly Paradise and the Renaissance Epic* notes the tendency for all blessed places to become some kind of golden age site, and for all golden age sites to become blessed places. He explains that these accounts of a golden age existence and the many classical descriptions of gardens and landscapes provided medieval and Renaissance writers with the models, images, and motifs for their own gardens, including their depictions of the garden in Eden. Also, as Ernst Robert Curtius has shown, rhetorical patterns for describing certain ideal landscapes were formulated by classical writers and passed on to the Middle Ages and the Renaissance. From Homer came the fruitful Garden of Alcinous, the perpetual spring of Elysium, the mixed forest, the carpet of flowers, and the miniature landscape with tree, spring, and grass. Virgil's *Aeneid* crystallized the *topos* of the *locus amoenus*, or pleasance, which Curtius describes as "the principal motif of all nature description" from the Empire to the sixteenth century. To the essential tree or trees, meadow, and spring or brook might be added flowers, birdsong, and a breeze.[1] Such ideal classical landscapes became an integral part of the Christian concepts of the Edenic paradise.

Classical "Paradises"

The classical idea of the golden age, like the Hebraic story of paradise, was gradually developed from different strands.[2] In his characterization of the Elysian Fields (*Od.*, IV, 561–68), Homer pictured the ideal life that would become an essential part of descriptions of the golden age. Elysium is faraway — at the world's end, beyond Ocean. Like the lost paradise, it is removed from ordinary human life, but is an abode of the blest. The climate is perfect; there is a gentle west wind, but no snows or storms. Life is always pleasant, a "dream of ease." Hesiod in his *Works and Days* (ll. 109–20) was the first to attribute this ideal life to a "golden race" or "golden generation," and to place it in a historical perspective. Like Adam and Eve, this race lived at the beginnings of time without sorrow or pain, amidst great abundance and on friendly terms with the immortals. There was, however, no Eve — indeed no women — and no "paradise" or specified location for their life. Hesiod also first identified this golden life with the rule of Kronos, whom the Romans understood to be

Saturn, and whom in turn many Christians would understand to be Adam. Hesiod linked his account of successive races with the story of the Woman (later identified as Pandora), who brought all the evils to the world. However, according to Hesiod, there was no fall, but a gradual deterioration as the golden race was succeeded by a silver race and a bronze race; this decline, interrupted by the race of heroes, was resumed with the iron age. Nevertheless, Hesiod's heroes were rewarded with a golden age existence under the rule of Kronos, and dwelt in the "islands of the blest" located, like Homer's Elysium, at the world's end. Giamatti has found in Hesiod the seeds for the identification of the golden age existence with Elysium in Christian descriptions of the Edenic paradise. Later, in the *Phaenomena* of the Greek Stoic Aratus, Dike, the goddess of universal justice, joined Kronos in the myth of the golden age. Dike lived with the first two races, but then fled to the heavens where she was invoked as Astraea. Ovid's *Metamorphoses* (I, 89–112) wove together the strands of the myth in a poetic characterization of the ideal life which later would be adapted and reinterpreted by countless Christian writers. The men of the "golden age," naturally loving justice, lived as vegetarians from the earth's abundance, without agriculture, commerce, law, war, or women. The perfect setting was also suggested in Ovid's descriptions of the rich but unplowed fields, green oaks dripping nectar, and rivers of milk and honey. But the golden age concept found its Christian apotheosis in Virgil's *Fourth Eclogue*: Christians interpreted Virgil's heralding of a future golden age as a prophecy of the birth of Christ.

Various isolated parts of the world, particularly islands, were often thought of as exhibiting bits and pieces of the life of the golden age. In his *Olympian II* Pindar followed Hesiod in placing the afterlife of the virtuous on the Islands of the Blest ruled by Kronos. In Diodorus Siculus's history, the seven Islands of the Blest, over which the sun passed directly, were dominated by the Stoic law of nature. All the inhabitants were beautiful, healthy, and promiscuous, living in perfect concord and dying voluntarily at 150. In the *Epode XVI* of Horace, the Islands of the Blest — fruitful, clear, and temperate — became an ethical ideal: "Jupiter set apart these shores for a righteous folk, ever since with bronze he dimmed the lustre of the golden age." Ancient geographers sometimes placed these Islands of the Blest, or Fortunate Isles, together with the Gardens of the Hesperides, in the western sea or near Africa. Isidore of Seville, for instance, located them near Mauretania; but by the sixth century Christian descriptions of the Edenic paradise owed so much to the golden age and the blessed isles that Isidore felt compelled to distinguish between them and to insist that these islands were not paradise.[3]

Some of the pervasive influence of Virgil's Elysium on Christian descriptions of paradise was probably due to its association with the Islands of the Blest and other places where men enjoyed the life of the golden age. This association, however, developed only tentatively and gradually. In the *Aeneid* one may find an imaginative, though not a specific, link between Elysium and the golden age.[4] In the imagination of later writers, Virgil's Elysium (*Aeneid*, VI, 637–94) merged with Homer's Elysium and the Islands of the Blest, which had already been established as golden age sites. His description helped Claudius Marius Victor, Prudentius, and Milton envision fully the garden in Eden described briefly by the Yahwist. Virgil's Elysium, like Milton's Paradise, opens with an unending succession of groves, woods, and meadows. In Virgil's first references to the "happy places" ("locos laetos") and the "groves of the blest" ("Fortunatorum Nemorum") the happy life and the pleasant setting fuse much as they do in *Paradise Lost*. Elysium is the home in the Lower World of purified spirits, who dance and sing and engage in sports under their own sun and stars. They have no fixed abode, but live amidst a neverending variety of scented laurels, shady groves, shining fields, and surging streams. Eventually they will drink from the great Elysian river, the Lethe, which glides past its peaceful shores and rustling woods, and will return to earth.

Descriptions of various classical gardens also contributed immensely to the poetic realization of the Edenic garden. Milton's allusions to two of these gardens, the Garden of Alcinous and the Gardens of the Hesperides, suggest the indescribable beauty of the true paradise garden. Homer's Garden of Alcinous, (*Od.*, VII, 112–34), visited by Odysseus, enjoyed an eternal spring and was famed for its sensuous beauty and fertility. Some have considered the realm of Alcinous a fairyland, yet its original may have been the isle of Corcyia.[5] Here, as in Milton's Paradise, nature pours forth her bounty in unending profusion: trees bear simultaneously both blossom and fruit; and streams from a central fountain wind through orchard, arbor, and garden plot. But, although the Garden of Alcinous provided the abundance of the life of the golden age, it — unlike Milton's Paradise — remained forever uninhabited. The classical gardens drawn on most richly by Milton were the Gardens of the Hesperides. In Hesiod's *Theogony* (ll. 215–16), the Gardens of the Hesperides (meaning "in the west") were placed beyond the ocean, in the same location as Homer's Elysium and Hesiod's blessed isles. The Hesperides, daughters of Hesperus, kept orchards heavily laden with fruit and also a tree with golden apples, which was guarded by an ever wakeful dragon. Only Hercules is able to pluck these forbidden fruits. Lucan also described these island gardens. Gradually the Gardens of the Hesperides became imaginatively linked with Elysium, the Islands of the Blest, and the life of the golden age, and like the Garden in Eden, they had ancient mythic origins and were remembered for their fruit.

Other classical landscapes contributed their own loveliness to later descriptions of the Edenic paradise. A long tradition lay behind the allusions to the Proserpina story in *Paradise Lost*. From the Homeric *Hymn to Demeter* to Claudian's *De Raptu Proserpinae*, poets lavished their most alluring images on depictions of Nature in her prime. To the field of Enna, with its flowers of many kinds and hues, might be added a variety of trees, a cave, and a stream. The *Hymn to Pythian Apollo* introduced the Graces and Hours which later would dance into Milton's Paradise and the idealized pastoral settings of countless Renaissance works. The classical *topos* of the *locus amoenus*, the traditional rhetorical formula for illustrating the lovely place, also passed into medieval and Renaissance descriptions of paradise. This *topos*, as it was developed in Homer's characterization of Calypso's Grotto and in the seventh idyll of Theodritus, unites grass, shade, and water — meadow, forest, and stream — in an image that connotes rest and satisfaction, peace and harmony. It is the staple of pastoral poetry. Nature is brought into a harmonious relation both with the divine order and with man. A landscape, whose caves and spring and luxuriant growth reflects the generative power of nature, becomes the setting for human love and sexuality. This landscape would later be adapted for presenting either an idealized or ambiguous interpretation of the human love and sexuality of Adam and Eve. Another classical rhetorical pattern related to the *locus amoenus* was the picture of the mixed forest of non-fruit-bearing trees; this, too, would influence descriptions of Christian paradises. Finally, the mountaintop paradise of Dante and Milton is anticipated in the poetry of Statius and Claudian. In the *Achilleid*, Statius depicts a grove, sacred to the rites of Bacchus, which is so high that it almost reaches heaven. In the *Epithalamium de Nuptiis Honorii Augusti*, Claudian illustrates a mountaintop retreat of Venus. As in descriptions of the Edenic paradise, it is so high that it is free from frost, wind, or clouds.[6]

These classical descriptions of a golden age existence, of fruitful gardens and lovely landscapes, paralleled the Semitic accounts in some ways, but also made important new contributions to later descriptions of the paradise in Eden. Although there were comparable characterizations of an early innocence in an ideal setting, the golden race had no descendants and the inhabitants of faraway isles remained far away; the classical narratives, unlike Genesis, did not embody the beginnings of a universal, providential history. However, classical writers developed an ethical ideal of the good life and an aesthetic ideal of sensuous loveliness in relation to the paradisal setting. A golden age existence, either at the world's beginning or as an afterlife, was associated with an ideal of virtue. Unlike Genesis or Ezekiel, classical literature often presented the positive virtue of the inhabitants as the most essential feature of an earthly paradise. In the fully developed classical tradition, those enjoying the life of the golden age possessed an inherent virtue or received a reward for virtue. This image was also mirrored in the idealized conceptions of the "blameless Ethiopians," Hyperboreans, and other faraway, virtuous races. This ethical ideal harmonized with the later Christian ideal of original righteousness. Similarly, classical descriptions of the earth's abundance, of the varied scenery of Elysium, and of a pristine Arcadian landscape provided an ideal of beauty that inspired Christian poets who praised the wonder of the garden planted by God.

Christian Interpretations

Christian writers at first rejected the classical ideas of a golden age existence and of remote, blessed isles, but later considered them distorted reflections of sacred truth. "The Hortatory Address to the Greeks," attributed to Justin Martyr (100–c.165), was the turning point in the Christianization of classical myth. After indicating the inconsistency and diversity in the beliefs of classical writers, the author developed his contention that Homer had learned Hebraic doctrine in Egypt. Homer, he said, imitated the biblical account of the Creation in his description of Achilles' shield and "contrived also that the garden of Alcinous should preserve the likeness of Paradise, and through this likeness he presented it as ever-blooming and full of fruits." Justin Martyr found, too, a reference to Adam as the first man in the midst of a pagan oracle's hymn. Classical parallels to the Bible, first cautiously explained as distorted versions of revealed truth, were later eagerly sought. Clement of Alexandria (c.150–c.215) established elaborate correspondences between ancient myths and the Scriptures. The classical idea of the poet as an inspired singer of sacred truth was accepted by Lactantius (260–340) and other early Church fathers, which helped gain Christian acceptance for classical poets. The descriptions of the golden age, especially in Virgil's *Fourth Eclogue*, were felt to be full of Christian significance. Lactantius argued that the story of the golden age and its passing should be accepted as a poetic interpretation of genuine truth.[7] The various golden age sites and the Christian paradise blended together.

In *The Myth of the Golden Age in the Renaissance*, Harry Levin writes, "During the seven hundred and fifty years between the memory-haunted Boethius and the forward-looking Jean de Meun, the golden age might be said to have gone underground." Although there were many isolated references, the Church did not assimilate the Christianized interpretation of the golden age. Though the spatial concept of the *locus amoenus* was handed on from the classical era through succeeding centuries to the Renaissance, the temporal concept of the golden age "would burst forth in the Renaissance." The myth was reanimated in the thirteenth century: while Jean de Meun exploited the sexual potentialities of the golden age, Albertino Mussato, Italian poet-diplomat, praised the classical poets as Christian theologians whose myths related the events of Genesis. The life of the golden age, as freshly envisioned, provided an image for the Italian Renaissance. Its unifying concept in the Renaissance, said Levin, was pleasure; its images were projections of ideas "fostering an emphasis on free will, an ethic of hedonism, and a cult of beauty," and its scene was always the *locus amoenus*. Despite the example of Virgil's *Fourth Eclogue*, the golden age myth and pastoralism did not really converge until the Renaissance.[8] Although in the works of many Renaissance writers the classical idea of the golden age reflected the Christian aura of the Edenic paradise only rather dimly, various interpretations of the golden age contributed to descriptions of paradise or merged with these in the depiction of other ideal sites.

During the Renaissance many devoted to a rational interpretation of history continued to associate various classical concepts with Eden, while others grew skeptical and tended to dismiss the possibility that myths contained sacred truths. Despite the interrelationships between classical and Christian ideas, Renaissance writers distinguished between golden age sites, earthly paradises, and enchanted gardens; the first were classical, the second Christian, and the third, the false paradises like Spenser's Bower of Bliss, were a perverted mixture of the others.[9] The idea of the golden age enjoyed its greatest popularity in England in the late sixteenth and early seventeenth centuries but its connection to Christian history remained controversial.

At this time the golden age was best known through editions of Ovid's *Metamorphoses,* which had been given a Christian interpretation since the fourteenth century. During the first decades of the sixteenth century most editions included the allegorical commentary of Father Petrus Lavinius, who regarded the golden age as representing paradise. Arthur Golding's edition (1565–67) held that "the first foundation of [Ovid's] woorke from Moyses wrightings tooke," and of course it related the golden age and Eden. George Sandys in his edition of the *Metamorphoses* tried to clarify the historical aspects of Ovid by relating "fabulous Traditions" to "divine history." In accordance with biblical interpretation, he found Ovid's allusions to milk, honey, and nectar to symbolize plenty, felicity, and eternal youth. His edition was one source for an elaborate analogy between Saturn and Adam which apparently was convincing to many. As Saturn was the son of Coelus and Cybel, so Adam was the son of God and the earth. As Saturn was the first who reigned and the inventor of tillage, so also was Adam. Saturn was ejected from heaven and Adam from paradise. Saturn devoured his children, and Adam ruined his posterity. Saturn hid himself from Jupiter, and Adam hid himself from God.[10] Indeed, many Renaissance scholars probably took the golden age much more seriously than had Hesiod.

Other writers noted different parallels. Sir Walter Ralegh in his world history dismissed many fables, but agreed that Adam was the original of Saturn and asserted "so also was the Fiction of those Golden apples kept by a Dragon taken from the Serpent, which tempted Evah: so was Paradise itself transported out of Asia into Africa, and made the Garden of the Hesperides." In his geography, Nathanael Carpenter wrote that Homer, Orpheus, Linus, Pindar, and Hesiod spoke of the Garden of Alcinous and the Elysian Fields, "all of which derived their first invention from this description of *Paradise,* recorded from *Moses* in *Holy Scripture.*"[11]

This assumption about the relationship between classical myth and Genesis helped Renaissance writers weave together various strands of the classical and the Hebraic-Christian traditions. Under the influence of different Stoic conceptions of the natural law, the golden age had been regarded either as a time when men were virtuous through following reason and the universal law of nature or as a time when men followed their own natural instincts.[12] This first idea is reflected in Guarini's *Il Pastor Fido*, which offers a Christianized picture of the golden age. His pastoral Arcadia is the last remaining site of the golden age existence. Though making love is the chief concern of Guarini's shepherds, the official law of his golden age is "Piaccia se lice" — it is pleasing if it is permitted. There was "No happinesse but what from virtue grew" and "Husband and Lover signify'd one thing." The description closes with a prayer to the "King of Kings" to awake those who forsake "Thee, and the glory of the ancient world." Several English poets associated the golden age with a state of innocence or with paradise. Spenser's "antique Age" lived like an "innocent / In simple truth and blamelesse chastitie," and William Browne's golden age possessed "No wisdom but was mixed with simpleness." Drayton's "To the Virginian Voyage," which suggests Horace's epode on the Islands of the Blest, hails "VIRGINIA, / Earth's only paradise," where "the golden age / Still Natures lawes doth give." Yet, in other accounts, the most important value of the first age or of the Edenic paradise was sensual delight. In the *Roman de la Rose*, the Dreamer felt that the Garden of Mirth was superior to paradise.[13] In the final act of Tasso's *Aminta* the "happy golden age" is hailed not for its rivers of milk or honey-dripping trees, but for its freedom in love. The golden law is "S'ei piace, ei lice" — if it pleases, it's permitted — and Tasso's god of love grants "il suo amoroso paradiso" to all his followers. Donne in *Elegy XVII* took a mischievous delight in the opportunities offered our happy sires when women were no sooner asked than won. Finally, sexual pleasure and the paradisal life became virtually identified in John Hopkins's late seventeenth-century imitation of *Paradise Lost*. This glorification of a happy time of sexual freedom, even if it was not intended altogether seriously, contributed to the description of the enchanted gardens, or false paradises, of the Renaissance. And although such places as Spenser's Bower of Bliss and Armida's garden in Tasso's *Gerusalemme Liberata* appear to be scenes of carefree delight, they conceal real dangers in their enticements to sensual surrender.

Other writers, however, gradually undermined the popular notion the golden age was an authentic characterization of the Edenic paradise. While Machiavelli, Louis Le Roy, and others quietly assumed man's early savagery, the French historian Jean Bodin directly attacked the idea of the golden age as a false and harmful belief. Examine historians, not poets, he urged his contemporaries. Agreeing with other historians who had attempted to reconcile the early Hebrew and the classical pasts, he identified Saturn with Nimrod and estimated that the so-called golden age, occurring soon after the Flood, had lasted about 250 years. But, according to the Bible, this was actually a period of crime and abomination. He objected particularly to the belief in the decay of nature fostered by this golden dream of old men. In the "golden age," he said, "men were scattered like beasts in the fields and the woods" until gradually they were refined by custom and law. In England, Bodin was referred to by Sidney, Harvey, Nashe, Spenser, and Hobbes, and was probably read by most serious students of history. "You suppose the firsst age was the goulde age," wrote Gabriel Harvey. "It is nothinge so," but is rather now.[14] Hobbes in *The Leviathan* dealt a further blow to serious historical belief in the golden age. In his picture of early society, where there was a constant war of each against all and where there was no justice or injustice because no law, there was indeed no place for Astraea.

Classical Myth in Milton's Paradise

Milton had grown up with the various Christian interpretations of the gardens and golden age sites in classical literature, and by the time he was writing *Paradise Lost* he had seen the rejection of many of these conceptions on both rational and religious grounds. His Paradise reflects both experiences.

Milton could view the origins of the world in classical terms just as easily as in Christian ones. His early works convey three

29

allusions to Astraea, and in "On the Morning of Christ's Nativity" he envisioned the day when "Time will run back, and fetch the age of gold." But Milton was most revealing in his allusion to "golden poetic ages of such pleasing licence, as in the fabl'd reign of old Saturn." [15] Beauty was not Truth.

Although Milton's attitude toward classical myth was ambiguous, it was an indispensable strand in his creation of Paradise. Even though some of his allusions are simply common poetic language, the setting, the mood, the atmosphere, and the tempo of the life of his Paradise owe an immeasurable debt not only to particular classical ideas of an earthly paradise but to the beautiful world of classical poetry, itself a kind of paradise of pristine loveliness for Milton and many of his contemporaries. The splendor of Adam and Eve and of Paradise itself is suggested through mythical comparison. Aurora and "Aurora's fan" awaken Adam and Eve (V, 6), Hesperus ushers in the evening (IV, 605–6), and the Hours and Graces dance away the days (IV, 267). After gardening, the couple enjoy "coole Zephyr" (IV, 329), the gentle wind of the Elysian Fields. And even Adam's voice is "Milde, as when Zephyrus on Flora breathes" (V, 16). They conduct Raphael to a sylvan lodge like "Pomona's Arbour" (V, 378) and tender him with various fruits like those "where Alcinous reign'd" (V, 341). The first parents live and love among the flower-strewn lawns and banks, the shaded groves and bowers, the mixed forests, the fountains and streams, and the "umbrageous Grots and Caves" (IV, 257) of classical landscape. One of the most important functions of classical myth in Milton's Paradise is to fix, intensify, and sustain an image, to slow the tempo while the imagination seeks the unimaginable beauty of an unfallen world.

The use of "feign'd" myth in direct conjunction with the inspired paradise narrative in Genesis introduced some delicate problems. Generally, Milton omitted mythical amplification of these central Biblical events, but the classical allusion is never long absent. Through the simple, often biblical speech of Adam and Eve themselves, the epic tells of the creation of man, the giving of the commandment concerning the tree of knowledge, the

naming of the animals, the making and presentation of Eve. However, Milton's depiction of the tree of life "blooming Ambrosial
Fruit / Of vegetable Gold" (IV, 219–20) suggests the golden tree
of the Garden of the Hesperides; and rather strangely the heavenly choirs associate the presentation of Eve to Adam with the
presentation of Pandora to Epimetheus (IV, 711–19). The most
notable use of myth directly to amplify the Genesis text is the
description of the serpent before the temptation (IX, 504–10).

In Milton's invented scenes the use of myth is freer, but ambiguous. Sometimes the credibility of the myth seems assumed, but
often the myth is explicitly rejected. Apart from the description
of Adam's voice and the comparison of Adam and Eve to Jupiter
and Juno (IV, 497–502), the allusions point toward the superlative qualities of Eve, who contributes much more to the mood
and atmosphere of the garden than does Adam. As Eve advances
to meet Raphael, her image is caught and held; she is more
lovely than "the fairest Goddess feign'd / Of three that in Mount
Ida naked strove" (V, 381–82). Again, when Eve departs alone
just before the temptation, Adam gazes after her "long with ardent look" as she runs swiftly toward her meeting with Satan,
more fleet of foot than Diana and "likest" Pomona or "*Ceres* in
her Prime" (IX, 385–96). The myth is not rejected here, or in
the final comparison of the unfallen Eve to Circe (IX, 520–22).

In picturing the classical paradises, Milton sometimes seemed
to accept them as true and sometimes rejected them as "feign'd,"
but always found them less beautiful than the one true paradise.
In an attempt at least to suggest the beauty of the Edenic paradise, he drew upon the ideals of the golden age, the Gardens of
the Hesperides, the Elysian Fields and the Islands of the Blest,
the Garden of Alcinous, and other classical paradises.

Milton preferred the images of specific classical gardens or isles
to general references to the dimming golden age. Nevertheless, his
Paradise enjoys the eternal spring, the natural abundance, and
the gentle breezes of the classical dream of a golden age. Milton's
description of the state of innocence was generally consistent

with the Christianized idea of a golden age in which men were both virtuous and carefree. The embraces of Adam and Eve also suggested the paradise of love depicted by Tasso and others in their accounts of the golden age; Eve, more glorious in her nudity than Venus, was led off to amorous play in the nuptial bower as soon as she was introduced to Adam (VIII, 500–11). The allusions to "*Ceres* in her Prime" and to Pan and the Graces leading an eternal spring call to mind the pristine earth before the seasonal cycle.

Elysium and the *locus amoenus* bloom afresh in Milton's Paradise. Milton knew the *Aeneid* almost by heart, and certainly Virgil's description of Elysium formed a part of Milton's imaginative vision of his Paradise. The topography of Paradise — Adam's "various view" — with its groves, "level Downs," "palmie hilloc," "irriguous Valley," streams, and woods, is similar. Adam possesses

A happy rural seat of various view;
Groves whose rich trees wept odorous Gumms and Balme. . . .

(IV, 247–48)

This seems derived from Virgil's, "Fortunatorum Nemorum sedesque beatas" (VI, 639). A "pure now purer" or "amplior" air greets one in both. As one sees in Elysium some dancing and some chanting, in Paradise "Universal Pan / Knit with the *Graces* and the *Hours* in dance / Led on the Eternal Spring." Milton's Paradise implies an endless discovery of *loci amoeni*, but sometimes all the elements are crystallized in a few lines:

> Under a tuft of shade that on a green
> Stood whispering soft, by a fresh Fountain side
> They sat them down . . . (IV, 325–27).

Milton's Paradise, however, is more flowery, more wild, and much more fragrant than Virgil's Elysium. Flowers are suggested by metaphor, but are not specifically noted by Virgil. Milton's direct references to Elysium are always associated with flowers (for example, *Comus*, 992–97; *P.L.*, III, 358–59). Whereas Virgil's Elysium has only one scented laurel grove, sweet odors permeate Milton's Paradise (IV, 156–65; V, 348–49, 377–80). Raphael, for instance, advances through fields of an almost cloying sweetness:

> Into the blissful field, through Groves of Myrrhe,
> And flouring odours, Cassia, Nard, and Balme.
> (V, 292–93)

Milton borrowed from the landscapes of Theocritus and others— landscapes far more lush than those of Virgil's Augustan classicism — and from early Christian paradises influenced by these. He combined the fruitfulness of the Garden of Alcinous with the blessed groves of Elysium. The classical mixed forest also appears (IV, 137–42), but Milton's Paradise is wild above the rule or art of most classical landscape.

In depicting the superlative loveliness of Paradise, Milton not only followed classical example, but depended on Renaissance interpretations of golden age sites, which also became a part of his imaginative vision of Paradise. As D. T. Starnes and E. W. Talbert have argued, Milton evidently had read the discussions of Elysium and related topics in the *Mythologiae* of Natalis Comes and the *Dictionarium Historicum, Geographicum, Poeticum* of Charles Stephanus. He imitated Stephanus in identifying the Gardens of the Hesperides, his favorite golden age site, with the Islands of the Blest and Elysium. Apparently drawing on his knowledge of these Renaissance dictionaries, Milton first synthesized the ideas and details of his vision of an earthly paradise in *Comus*.[16] In the epilogue to the masque, the Attendant Spirit describes "the broad fields of the sky" to which he is ascending:

> There I suck the liquid air
> All amidst the Gardens fair
> Of *Hesperus*, and his daughters three
> That sing about the golden tree:
> Along the crisped shades and bowres
> Revels the spruce and jocond Spring,
> The Graces, and the rosie-boosm'd Howres,
> Thither all their bounties bring,
> That there eternal Summer dwels,
> And West winds, with musky wing

> About the cedar'n alleys fling
> *Nard*, and *Cassia's* balmy smels.
> *Iris* there with humid bow,
> Waters the odorous banks that blow
> Flowers of more mingled hew
> Than her purfl'd scarf can shew
> And drenches with *Elysian* dew
> (List mortals if your ears be true)
> Beds of *Hyacinth*, and Roses
> Where young *Adonis* oft reposes . . .
> (979–98)

Fusing the traditional elements of the golden age sites, Milton created in *Comus* a Christian paradise that would remain the imaginative pattern for the Paradise of *Paradise Lost*. The Hesperian gardens attracted other classical paradises into their imaginative field, offering the most specific and sensuous images of a faraway paradise of transcendent beauty. These gardens, with their golden apples and dragon, also could most easily be conceived of as a distorted reflection of the true lost paradise of Genesis. In Milton's vision of Paradise, these various classical gardens, as they were explained in dictionaries and transformed in *Comus*, become one with each other and with the Edenic paradise. Milton's Paradise holds trees with "Blossoms and Fruits at once of golden hue" (IV, 148), and

> Others whose fruit burnisht with Golden Rinde
> Hung amiable, *Hesperian* Fables true,
> If true, here only, and of delicious taste.
> (IV, 249–51)

Even though the Hesperian trees become a part of the true paradise, Milton reveals his ambiguous attitude toward the "Fables true": if they were true, the underlying basis of their truth was the true paradise (and this possibility is the basis for including the golden fruit in Paradise), but the "if true" indicates a reluctant skepticism about the belief that the Hesperian gardens and other golden age sites were reflections of the Edenic paradise. Other aspects of the description in *Paradise Lost* were in keeping with Renaissance accounts of classical paradises. Starnes and Talbert have maintained that there was more than coincidence in some close similarities between *Paradise Lost* and the Renaissance dictionaries: "pure now purer air" (IV, 153), and Stephanus's "ubi iam aer purior est"; "now gentle Gales / Fanning their odoriferous wings" (IV, 156–57), and Comes's "atque ventos ibi plurimum suaves et odoriferos leniter spirare." Milton's "native perfumes" and "balmy spoils" as well as illustrations like those of the "blissful fields" through which Raphael strides may also owe something to these Renaissance accounts of scented fields of roses, violets, and hyacinths, and groves of laurel and myrtle.

In striving to express the inexpressible beauty of the true paradise, Milton twice unrolled resounding catalogues of classical paradises:

> Not that faire field
> Of *Enna*, where *Proserpin* gathering flours
> Her self a fairer Floure by gloomie *Dis*
> Was gatherd, which cost *Ceres* all that pain
> To seek her through the world; nor that sweet Grove
> Of *Daphne* by *Orontes*, and th' inspired
> *Castalian* Spring, might with this Paradise
> Of *Eden* strive; nor that *Nyseian* Ile
> Girt with the River *Triton*, where old *Cham*,
> Whom Gentiles *Ammon* call and *Lybian Jove*,
> Hid *Amalthea* and her Florid Son
> Young *Bacchus* from his Stepdame *Rhea*'s eye.
>
> (IV, 268–79)

This passage continues with a description of Mount Amara probably based on Renaissance travel literature. Here again Milton compares the true paradise to classical gardens:

> Spot more delicious than those Gardens feign'd
> Or of reviv'd *Adonis*, or renowned
> *Alcinous*, host of old *Laertes* Son,
> Or that, not mystic, where the Sapient King
> Held dalliance with his faire *Egyptian* Spouse.
>
> (IX, 439–43)

These two passages, occurring just before the first appearance of Adam and Eve and just before the temptation, evoke images and feelings that may enable the fallen imagination to pause and to struggle back to the one true lost paradise. They also contain their own interest and relevant comment. These gardens had been described in works familiar to the Renaissance, and sum up ancient ideals. Ovid was the best source for the "faire field / Of Enna." In his little miniature, the flower-filled field outside Enna, bordered with a lake and wood, enjoys the eternal spring before the harshness of seasons. Ortelius and others had characterized the grove of Daphne near Antioch in Syria as dark with cypresses of infinite height which covered the whole grove, about ten miles in compass, like a roof; its oracle made it a sacred omphalos. Diodorus Siculus had depicted the craggy retreat on the beautiful isle of Nysa in Tunis.[17] The Garden of Adonis, best known in Spenser's luxuriant description, and Homer's Garden of Alcinous, offering both fruit and blossom together, had seemed pregnant with beauty and meaning for untold centuries. The final garden, "not mystic," is that portrayed in the Song of Solomon. These classic paradises are doubly lost, for they belong to a vanished world of loveliness which must also be rejected as pagan error.

Like almost all classical scenes, these paradises are inhabited. Every inhabitant is in close relationship with the gods. Each of these gardens, the joy of a nymph or a goddess, suggests a close affinity between Eve, lovely beyond all goddesses, and the garden that transcends all other gardens. But "gloomie Dis" and the threat to Bacchus cast a passing shadow over Paradise.

In these and other passages Milton employed a technique of double comparison: first, these poetic pagan gardens were more beautiful than any true, existing contemporary gardens; second, the biblical paradise is infinitely superior to the pagan gardens, because it is inconceivably beautiful and because it is true. The images of the pagan gardens, although valid, were inadequate. Milton's treatment of classical myth is persistently ambiguous: repeatedly he created a beautiful mythical world, only to dash it to pieces. No doubt was cast upon the classical gardens first compared to paradise (IV, 268–79), but those in the second comparison (IX, 439–43) were explicitly labeled as false. Only Solomon's garden was authentically recorded. Did Milton consider the gardens of Adonis and Alcinous as even allegorically true? They were "mystic" because they had long been interpreted allegorically, but there is no necessary implication that he accepted them as pagan reflections of Genesis or of the true Edenic paradise.

This technique of ambiguity and double comparison enabled Milton simultaneously to draw upon and reject the sensuous beauty of the classical world. The "pleasing licence" of myth became a large and essential portion of his great tapestry of Paradise, but its rejection helped emphasize the unique value of Christian truth. This ambiguity was a reflection of the age and of Milton's personality, but it also became a part of the aesthetic structure of *Paradise Lost*. As in "Lycidas" the "dread voice" and the mood "of a higher strain" break through the beauty of the pastoral, so in *Paradise Lost* Calliope is "an empty dreame" (VII, 39) and only Urania is true.

3

THE EARLY CHRISTIAN ERA

.:. MILTON and his age sometimes praised the early Christian
writers and sometimes scourged them, particularly for rejecting a literal interpretation of Scripture in favor of allegories;
but they generally accepted these writers' doctrines concerning
Adam's life in paradise and his sin. Although these doctrines gave
the scenes in paradise a unique theological and historical importance, the Renaissance writers turned to the early Christian period for poetry as well as for doctrine. Renaissance poets discovered that Christian poets more than a thousand years before them
had commenced the task of fusing myth, chronicle, and theology
into new artistic wholes justifying the ways of God to man.

Renaissance presses poured forth numerous editions of early
Christian writers. The hexameral literature, most of which was
unknown during the Middle Ages, became a kind of vogue. Before 1660 the commentaries of Philo Judaeus on Genesis had been
printed three times, Lactantius and St. Jerome had been published in twelve editions, and St. Augustine in nine. The hexamerons of St. Basil and St. Ambrose appeared with prefaces by
Erasmus, who ranked St. Basil with the best Greek authors. There
were eight editions of St. Ambrose before the end of the sixteenth
century, and two works attributed to St. Basil, *On Paradise* and
On the Original Nature of Man, were usually reprinted with his

works and regarded as authentic. St. Ephrem Syrus's homilies and hymns on paradise were published in three editions near the beginning of the seventeenth century, and the commentary on paradise by Moses Bar Cephas was printed three times during the century. The early Christian poets who dramatized Genesis also were enjoying a comparable popularity: a single volume brought together the work of Avitus, Cyprian, Dracontius, Hilary, and Marius Victor, and there were independent editions of Dracontius and Marius Victor.[1]

References to the fathers of the church were the staple of both commentary and controversy. Separate tracts on paradise as well as the great monumental commentaries on Genesis like that of Benedictus Pererius were filled with quotations and allusions to the early Christian writers. Studies of Milton's reading and of his use of the fathers demonstrate his thorough familiarity with these commentators and poets. Milton referred to patristic works almost as often as classical ones, and would often include at least a dozen citations from patristic writing in the discussion of any question.[2]

Paradise in Christian Thought

If early Christians had not accepted the Old Testament, the story of the lost paradise would never have become a cornerstone of Christian theology and history, and *Paradise Lost* would never have been written. Though some early Christians rejected the Old Testament and the Gnostics and the Manichaeans ridiculed it, most of the early Christian writers accepted it as a genuine revelation. The need for the Redemption was derived from the sinfulness of the Fall. The new religion that told of the Redemption recalled the messianic prophecies of the old religion. Also, the Old Testament account of the Creation and Eden assisted the new religion in meeting the claims of the Greeks, Egyptians, and Chaldeans about the antiquity of their religions. However, in interpreting the Old Testament, both the allegorical and literal commentators struggled with the dualism of the Gnostics and Manichaeans when trying to show how an omnipotent and beneficent God could permit two newly created and innocent creatures to fall into evil.[3] In explaining the first chapters of Genesis, these writers sought to elucidate both the appearance and spiritual meaning of paradise, the nature of the state of innocence, and the place of paradise in Christian history. These ideas were further developed by the medieval writers and later adapted and reinterpreted by the rational commentators and poets of the Renaissance.

In describing the wonders of paradise, the patristic commentators and poets anticipated centuries of later writers. Their conceptions of the garden were colored by accounts of the Elysian Fields and the Fortunate Isles and perhaps by Ezekiel's picture of the mountain paradise. The description of the trees and fragrances of paradise by Athanasius of Alexandria helped bring about the association of paradise with India. St. Basil's popular account of the Creation depicted the entire prelapsarian earth as a kind of paradise, while Pseudo-Basil and Moses Bar Cephas pictured a mountain paradise comparable to the Mount of Paradise in *Paradise Lost*. In the work of the early Christian poets, descriptions of the earthly paradise provide the richest, most dazzling passages. Nevertheless, for the patristic writers paradise was physically and spiritually more refined than our world, while for the men of the Renaissance it became a very real and natural garden in a specific location.

Though the Renaissance rationalists rejected vigorously any exclusively allegorical interpretation such as that of Origen, they often accepted the view of many patristic exegetes that paradise had both a literal and a symbolic meaning. Many even respected the spiritual interpretations of Philo, the first-century Alexandrian Jew. In patristic thought the Edenic paradise came to stand for the virtuous soul, Christ, the Church, and the celestial paradise. The ponderous *Book of Paradise* of Palladius (d. 425) found a provisional paradise in monasticism.

One of the most important legacies left by the fathers was their development of the idea of original righteousness — the physical, intellectual, and spiritual perfection of Adam and Eve before the Fall. In the minimal conception of the first parents' prelapsarian endowments, they were happy children, but in the maximal conception they grew to become responsible adults, endowed in body, mind, and spirit as no other humans have ever been. These minimal and maximal conceptions of Adam's endowments were closely related to minimal and maximal conceptions of his sinfulness and of the consequences of the Fall. In regarding Adam and Eve as very immature and not yet ready for the knowledge of good and evil, Theophilus, St. Irenaeus, and others absolved God of placing evil in paradise and explained how innocent creatures could disobey. Though elements of this idea remained a part of Christian thought, many later writers concluded that the sacrifice of Christ had been necessary because man had sinned greatly when he had fallen from a state of God-given perfection. As pictured by St. Basil and Gregory of Nyssa, Adam and Eve were pure, passionless, and almost angelic. To this Stoic apathy St. Ambrose added the God-given law of nature, a certain and constant guide to the first parents. Gradually the conception of the wise, intelligent, virtuous Adam which appears in *Paradise Lost* emerged. Adam's original perfection, implied in Ezekiel 28 and embroidered in pre-Christian Jewish legend, was developed into the elaborate ideas of original righteousness and original justice, which were followed after the Fall by original sin and original guilt. The most complete and influential early explanation of original righteousness appeared in the later writings of St. Augustine, who portrayed an Adam with great physical, intellectual, and spiritual endowments, an Adam more wise than the most eminent philosopher of a fallen world. However, this Adam was not an angel, but was natural and human. St. Augustine's exposition provided a solid base for the medieval doctors and Renaissance commentators who delighted in continuing to build upon this belief.

For Christians, history began in paradise. All the events that had occurred there were of unparalleled historical importance. The formulation of the doctrines of original righteousness, original sin, and redemption led to a universal, providential Christian history. Whereas many classical writers assumed the eternity of man and contended that history was cyclical, Christians saw history as an irreversible straight line marked by the Fall and the Incarnation and leading from paradise to a new heaven and a new earth. Since history was envisioned as a span of about 6000 years, paradise and surely Adam seemed within the memory of man, and the Second Coming appeared imminent. Indeed, history might be subsumed under the concepts of "paradise lost" and "paradise regained." Again, St. Augustine provided the most thorough and authoritative early account of what would have happened if man had not sinned, what had happened, and what was to happen. The historical pattern of *The City of God* became a vital part of the Christian tradition and an essential part of *Paradise Lost*.

These seminal ideas concerning paradise and Adam were gradually developed, amidst controversy and conflict, by scores of Christian writers, some of whom, first in the East and then in the West, made particularly significant and memorable contributions.

Alexandrian Allegory: Philo and Origen

In the rich culture of Alexandria, where Greek, Christian, and Jewish cultures met, biblical exegesis was fused with Platonic philosophy in a highly intellectual and allegorical interpretation of Scripture. Readings of the paradise story that would be long remembered were given by two of the Alexandrians, the cultivated Jew Philo and the unorthodox but brilliant Origen. Milton's contemporaries found some tenable concepts in Philo, but castigated Origen's allegories more consistently than any other interpretation of Scripture.

Some men of letters freely adapted to their own use the Platonized Scriptural interpretations of Philo. Henry More revived Philo's allegories in his *Conjectura Cabbalistica*. Philo's influence is also evident in most literary characterizations of Adam and Eve, including those in *Paradise Lost*. Milton, when he could refer to Philo to advantage in argument, called him "another solid authority" and "one very studious in the law of Moses." [4]

Approaching Genesis through the concepts and methods of Greek philosophy, Philo was the first to present a systematic philosophical allegory as the true meaning of Moses' inspired account of Adam and Eve in paradise. Familiar both with rabbinical allegories and with philosophical interpretations of Homer, Philo felt that Scripture had an underlying meaning comprehensible to those who had freed themselves from worldly passions. Philo rejected a literal meaning entirely only when it conflicted with the underlying truth, but he preferred allegory as the method of the initiate who could truly see and study the intelligible world and the soul rather than bodily forms.

Although Philo sometimes seemed to accept a literal reading of the paradise story, in his more deeply philosophical writings he regarded much of the account as myth and vehemently rejected any anthropomorphic conception of God. "Let not such fables as that God tills the soil and plants paradise enter our mind," for "never yet have trees of life or of understanding appeared on earth, nor is it likely that they will appear hereafter." Again he suggested that the creation of Eve "was of the nature of a myth." "For how could anyone," he asked, "admit that a woman, or a human being at all, came into existence out of a man's side?" But Philo never doubted the underlying truth and significance of Genesis. "Now these are no mythical fictions, such as poets and sophists delight in," he said, "but modes of making ideas visible, bidding us resort to allegorical interpretation guided in our renderings by what lies beneath the surface." [5]

Seeking truth in allegory, Philo viewed the story of man's creation and the life in the garden as a dramatization of the leading ideas of Greek philosophy. Platonism helped him reconcile the Yahwist and Priestly accounts. In his interpretation, Genesis 1 tells of the creation of an ideal man, sexless, incorporeal, and immortal, a kind of Platonic idea, while Genesis 2 relates the creation of a perfect corporeal and individual man. This earthly man, fashioned according to the Pythagorean laws of proportion, was truly beautiful and good, excelling any who has appeared since. His soul was made from the pattern of the divine Word, or Reason. He lived seven years in paradise, a realm of earthly wisdom and virtues, reflecting the heavenly. Only with sexual differentiation, symbolizing the relation between reason and sensation, did he enter the realm of temptation and sin.[6] Depending upon Platonic ideals, the Stoic conception of nature, and the Aristotelian idea of the priority of form, Philo contributed to the transformation of the primitive Yahwist Adam.

Particularly influential for the Christian tradition and Christian poetry was Philo's ethical and psychological interpretation of Adam and Eve. Adapting the ideas of Plato's *Timaeus*, Philo thought of the earthly man as compounded of body, a rational soul, and an irrational soul. As in Plato, this rational soul is immortal and is divinely endowed with reason and free will by which it can control the emotions and desires of the irrational soul. He associated the Edenic garden and its plants with the rational soul and its virtues. Because its trees are not earthly, Philo concluded, "We must conceive therefore that the bountiful God plants in the soul as it were a garden of virtues and of the modes of conduct corresponding to each of them, a garden that brings the soul to perfect happiness." He explained that "Moses evidently signifies by the pleasance the ruling power of the soul which is full of countless opinions, as it might be of plants, and by the tree of life he signifies reverence toward God, the greatest of the virtues," and by the tree of knowledge, moral prudence. The story of Adam and Eve, for Philo, signified the reciprocal relationship between the mind of the rational soul and the sense perception of the irrational soul, a soul drama leading to the loss of the paradise of virtues. Adam, as mind, sleeps while Eve, as active sense perception, arises to be hailed as "flesh of my flesh." Eve, introducing bodily pleasures, brings a blameworthy life. She first encounters pleasure, signified by the serpent's offer of the fruit, and offers pleasure to reason as master, who then becomes the slave.[7] Thus Philo, transforming the early myth into an ethical drama of the inner paradise, prepared the way for both the allegorical interpretations of Christian theology and the imaginative characterizations of Christian poetry.

The Alexandrine allegorical reading of Genesis, developed by Philo, Clement, and others, was crystallized in a Christian interpretation by Origen (185–253). A center of controversy in the early Christian period, Origen was a prime target of Renaissance exegetes defending a literal and historical interpretation of paradise. While Origen recommended a threefold literal, moral, and spiritual reading, corresponding to the body, soul, and spirit, he stressed the figurative interpretations. There are some similarities between Origen's and Milton's theories of exegesis, yet Milton referred to him as "the erroneous Origen" and regarded some of his ideas as heretical and ridiculous. Although Origen's philosophical interpretations were designed to meet anti-Christian ridicule, it is no wonder that they continued to outrage many Christians. He seemed himself to ridicule the Scriptural account of paradise:

And who is so silly as to believe that God, after the manner of a farmer, "planted a paradise eastward in Eden," and set in it a visible and palpable "tree of life," of such a sort that anyone who tasted its fruit with his bodily teeth would gain life; and again that one could partake "of good and evil" by masticating the fruit taken from the tree of that name? And when God is said to "walk in the paradise in the cool of the day" and Adam to hide himself behind a tree, I do not think anyone will doubt that these are figurative expressions which indicate certain mysteries through a semblance of history and not through actual events.[8]

Origen did, however, suggest that "the saints as they depart from this life will remain in some place situated on the earth, which the divine scripture calls 'paradise.'" He envisioned this as a "school for souls." These souls could later mount sphere by sphere to the heavens.[9]

Origen allegorized the paradise story as an unhistorical parable about the nature of man. Concerning paradise, he said that "the kindly disposed reader" could "see that all these things have a significant allegorical meaning." He maintained that "so also the story of Adam and his sin will be interpreted philosophically by those who know that Adam means *anthropos,* and that in speaking of Adam, Moses is speaking of the nature of man."[10] For Origen, Adam apparently was every man and Eve every woman, and the paradise drama was enacted in the life of each individual soul. This Christian union of the Hebrew narrative and Greek philosophy, depending heavily upon Plato and Philo, provided an interpretation of paradise which would remain provocative and meaningful.

The Later Eastern Fathers: The Cappadocians, St. John, and Bar Cephas

The Renaissance commentators generally found congenial the literal and historical emphasis in the interpretations of the later Eastern fathers. The Cappadocian monk St. Basil (to whom was attributed the work of his anonymous follower now known as Pseudo-Basil) and St. John of Damascus were frequently cited. Milton read both Basil and Pseudo-Basil.[11] St. Basil's brother Gregory of Nyssa and his friend Gregory Nazianzen were known, but were less popular. Although much of the tract on paradise by Moses Bar Cephas seemed more legend than history, this too appealed to an age fascinated by man's beginnings in Eden. These writers pictured a highly spiritualized Adam inhabiting a magnificent paradise which was simultaneously both physical and spiritual.

St. Basil (330–379) was best known for his *Hexameron,* a series of homilies on the wonders of the Creation apparently delivered to a working-class audience. Although the *Hexameron* did not specifically treat the garden in Eden, it was very important in the development of the paradise tradition, primarily because it was the immediate inspiration and model for St. Basil's anonymous follower's homilies on the first man and paradise; these, regularly grouped with St. Basil's works, in turn provided models for later writers. The *Hexameron* itself was the prototype of hexamerons from the patristic era to the Renaissance. From these developed the numerous literary works of the "celestial cycle," which tended more and more to focus upon the drama of paradise.[12] But St. Basil's influential work, though treating only the first five days of the Creation and seemingly the "unfinished hexameron," actually presents a complete and wondrous picture of the whole prelapsarian world as an earthly paradise.

The *Hexameron*, which was sometimes compared with the writings of Moses and Plato, is reverent and didactic, as well as realistic and "scientific." It is also highly lyrical in its sensitive description of the freshness and beauty of a pristine world. St. Basil told his listeners that he was leading them like strangers through the marvels of a great city, their first habitation, from which they had been expelled. He depicted a universe in which even the smallest plant pointed to the goodness, wisdom, and artistry of the Creator. Clasping tendrils taught love, and the union of the viper and the sea lamprey taught wedlock. Like Milton, he saw the variety, profusion, order, and vigor in nature. At God's brief command, arose "in a moment a vast nature, an elaborate system." Following the impulse of this first command, nature's power continued like a spinning top. He viewed with searching wonder the first perfection of a universe vast and majestic, yet made for man. "There was no failure," he said, "in this first vegetation; no husbandman's inexperience, no inclemency of the weather, nothing could injure it." Various classical paradises were suggested in the description of lofty mountains, thickly planted copses of towering firs, pines, and cedars, and fields of grain quivering in the wind like the sea — all watered by a great system of rivers and subterranean streams. In his description of the appearance of fruit trees, St. Basil envisioned a God who in his profusion created different paradises or special pleasure gardens, perhaps thought of as mountain retreats: "Immediately the tops of the mountains were covered with foliage" and "paradises were artfully laid out." In his portrayal of the vegetation, he told his listeners that "the rose was without thorns." This description was the ultimate source for Milton's climactic "and without thorn the Rose" in his depiction of the trees and plants of Paradise (IV, 255). Curious, sensitive, and observant, St. Basil reflected the science of his own day, much of which remained as the popular science of Milton's day. He explained evaporation, the sun's effect on plants, the sex of trees, and grafting. He noted that thick leaves protected tender fruit, while permitting the penetration of the sun's rays.[13] Combining religious exhortation and scientific information, St. Basil's *Hexameron* established a popular pattern for imitation and adaptation.

Pseudo-Basil's homily, perhaps written in accordance with St. Basil's ideas, presented a very sensuous picture of a historical paradise, but it also embodied a spiritual interpretation. Its mythic vision helped to crystallize in Christian literature the notion of a mountain paradise with a river irrigating all of Eden. As paradise was worthy of the hand of God, so it was also worthy to be the home of man, who was first created as an incorporeal spirit in the image of God before being formed of clay and placed in the garden. The rhetorical descriptions of classical paradises resound in the account of the summit garden, canopied by all the stars and surrounded by the purest air. "There were no strong winds, no storms, no hail, no disturbances, no violent thunderbolts, no winter ice, no spring dampness, no summer heat, and no autumnal dryness," but a climate perfectly temperate. The land was full of milk and honey, and waters making the land most fruitful flowed around the garden. Ever-blooming flowers and ever-bearing trees, high and lovely, abounded for pleasure and use. The animals were tame, and a variety of birds were delightful for their singing and chattering. Like St. Basil, this writer saw the vigor of nature producing a perfected land. "It is an injury," he said, "to compare paradise to anything in this life, since any similarity is so far from the original truth." However, he also felt that paradise had an allegorical meaning: it represented the realm of the virtues, with the East suggesting light and true knowledge.[14]

For the Basilian school, Adam in his paradise was a Christianized combination of a Neoplatonic spirit, a Stoic sage, and a Cynic philosopher — angelic, passionless, and content. Though St. Basil and the other Cappadocians did not accept with Origen the preexistence of the soul, they conceived of man in his first state as highly spiritualized, yearning for the supremely good and beautiful. For St. Basil, man was a "celestial growth," whose true country was the heavenly Jerusalem. God had bestowed upon Adam rationality, free will, and "the opportunity of taking his delight in all the unbelievable beauties of paradise." If he had persevered in virtue, a lucid aureole would have formed about him. Free from all passion, he lost paradise when he preferred fleshly beauty to intelligible beauty. St. Basil associated paradise with the monastic state, through which man could seek to regain the paradisal state. Adam had no house, ate fruits and vegetables, prayed, labored, and experienced no sexual passion. For Gregory of Nyssa, Adam was even more of a spiritualized Stoic. Beautiful and immortal, he was free alike from infancy and old age, from feeding and evacuation. Above all, he was passionless, and would have propagated by fission. Gregory Nazianzen considered Adam a "second angel." Pseudo-Basil spurned the luxuries of a fallen world and praised the true luxury of paradise, where man was free from the demands of the flesh and the enslavement of the passions.[15] Still under the influence of Greek philosophy, the Cappadocians envisioned man's original state as characterized not by any extraordinary intellectual achievements, but by an almost Godlike spiritual and moral perfection.

A synthesis of the traditionally accepted ideas of the Eastern fathers appears in the work of St. John of Damascus (c. 675–749), who was frequently cited during the Renaissance. Since man consists of both sense and mind, St. John thought of paradise as both physical and spiritual. Paradise was located in the East, higher than any place on earth, surrounded by the purest air, and flooded by light. "In truth," he wrote, "the place is divine, a meet home for him who was created in God's image: no creature lacking in reason made its dwelling there, but man alone, the work of God's own hands." St. John imagined Adam and Eve living a life of passionless, carefree, childlike innocence. Explaining that the pair learned of their own nature by partaking of the tree of knowledge, he said this knowledge was good for the mature, but for the innocent it was "like solid food to tender babes still in need of milk." Spiritually, he saw man's soul as a paradise inhabited by God. Every tree is "just Himself in Whom and through Whom the universe is maintained. But the tree of knowledge of good and evil was for the distinguishing between the many divisions of contemplation, and this is just the knowledge of man's own nature." [16]

A more comprehensive and creative Eastern synthesis of the literature of paradise appeared in the "Commentarius de paradiso" of Moses Bar Cephas, bishop of Massoul in Mesopotamia in the ninth century. This work, translated from Syriac into Latin by Andreus Maseus in 1569, was reprinted three times in the seventeenth century, was well respected by Renaissance exegetes, and was very possibly known by Milton. Seeking to analyze, sift, and reconcile earlier writing, Bar Cephas mixed Christian commentary, Greek ideas, and bits of myth and legend in an integrated, imaginative view of paradise. He reasoned that there must be one paradise which was both physical and spiritual because only thus could it delight both the body and soul of Adam. Bar Cephas rejected the view attributed to Ephrem Syrus and others that paradise was in the lunar sphere (fancy, he said, the four rivers falling from that height to the earth!), but he was certain that paradise was far loftier than any part of the inhabited earth; it was in another world far across the sea. Neoplatonism seems evident in the speculation that this land was of far finer and purer matter than our gross world, and popular Jewish tradition seems reflected in the portrayal of a gigantic Adam striding through the ocean to our distant world. Bar Cephas distinguished between Eden and paradise, which was far more lovely than the pleasant and spacious land surrounding it. As in *Paradise Lost*, a great river flowing through Eden rose in defiance of customary physical laws to irrigate a plateau paradise, and then fell precipitously down the slope. It then went under the ocean and reappeared and divided in our world. Bar Cephas praised the naked glory of Adam and Eve and, like Milton, imagined Satan overhearing their conversation about God's commandment. He thought that after the Fall paradise had continued to exist and had served as a home for the just until the Resurrection.[17]

The spiritual paradise was, for Bar Cephas, an inner life conducted in accordance with reason, temperance, and sanity, full of meditations of things divine and accompanied only by joy and exultation. "The earth of the mystic paradise was the soul and mind of Adam, of the man who stood there," he asserted. The trees and plants were meditations, the rivers were the cardinal virtues, and the tree of life was the Church.[18]

The Western Fathers: St. Ambrose and St. Augustine

In the West the early Christian fathers also were formulating conceptions of the earthly paradise and the original condition of man. Like the Eastern fathers, both Tertullian (150–230) and Lactantius (260–340) considered Adam and Eve to be innocent and immature; but, unlike their Eastern counterparts, they insisted on their free will. The most important Western contributions to the development of the paradise tradition were the works of St. Ambrose (339?–97), the militant bishop of Milan, and his great follower, St. Augustine (354–430), bishop of Hippo. Thoroughly familiar with both pagan literature and Greek exegesis, St. Ambrose continued to pour classical thought into Christian vessels. Facing the threat of Manichaean dualism, he developed the fullest and most explicit early patristic account of man's paradisal state, providing St. Augustine with all the essential materials for his more closely reasoned doctrine.

Both the classical and Christian traditions are reflected in St. Ambrose's conceptions of man's first state. Pagan ideas of the golden age and a state of nature shape his thinking about the paradisal state intended for man. He was sure that nature had poured forth all things for all in common. He also regarded the first man as innately endowed with a God-given natural law, superior to the written law and comparable to the innocence of children. He identified the Adamic paradise with the supraterrestrial paradise shown to St. Paul and promised by Christ to the penitent thief and, indeed, he closely associated it with Philo's paradise of the soul. Like the Cappadocians, he depicted Adam as a kind of angel who lived in a supernatural state of grace, breathed ethereal air, spoke face to face with God, and lived immortal without weariness or care — enjoying the most perfect state before the creation of Eve. The soul ruled the body and reason ruled the appetite in a state of harmony and happiness. Although Adam and Eve did not attain in paradise the intellectual and moral maturity intended for them, they were free and responsible creatures. In the commentary of St. Ambrose the literal paradise and the allegorical paradise often seem to melt into one another. He added a spiritual dimension to Philo's moral interpretation of paradise as a fertile soul in which Adam existed as mind and Eve as sense perception. Eve appeared to him as "the emotions of the first woman" and again, more abstractly, as "the emotions of the mind and heart," whereas the figure of the serpent represented sensual enjoyment. The beasts represented irrational faculties and even the birds were idle thoughts. The mind not only was intended to cultivate the paradise of the soul intensively, but it was to be a custodian of the work accomplished.[19] These spiritual, symbolic interpretations of St. Ambrose would appeal to some of the more mystical writers of the Renaissance.

Led to Christianity by St. Ambrose, St. Augustine provided succeeding centuries with the most penetrating and influential Christian interpretation of the thought of his time. During the sixteenth and seventeenth centuries he was claimed by both Catholics and Protestants. Milton cited him a number of times, once referring to St. Augustine's suggestion in *De Genesi ad Litteram* that God would have created another man in Eden instead of Eve if he had intended a purpose in marriage other than procreation.[20] For seminal discussions of the original condition of man, the nature of the Fall, and the pattern of Christian history, Milton and most of his readers would have looked to St. Augustine as a recognized authority.

St. Augustine struggled repeatedly with the questions posed by the first chapters of Genesis. How were the Creation and the paradise story to be interpreted and believed, and how was their meaning to be harmoniously related to a systematic Graeco-Christian philosophy? According to J. M. Evans, "nowhere is the essentially synthetic nature of his exegesis clearer than in his discussion of Man's unfallen condition." Avoiding both Pelagianism and Manichaean dualism, St. Augustine reconciled elements of the maximal and minimal conceptions of man's innocence and Fall in a systematic explanation that would dominate the Church's thinking on the subject for thirteen centuries. On the one hand, Adam enjoyed perfect health, absolute tranquillity of soul, and great intellectual gifts. On the other hand, he was a full-grown man, but not an angel, and he possessed only an inferior and conditional kind of immortality. While Gregory of Nyssa had envisioned an angelic first couple procreating nonsexually, St. Augustine thought that they would have procreated sexually at the proper time.[21]

Unable at first to accept Genesis literally and thrown for a time into the ranks of the Manichaeans, St. Augustine was charmed by the allegorical interpretations of St. Ambrose. In his early *De Genesi contra Manichaeos,* he met ridicule with allegory, though he did not entirely reject a literal meaning. For St. Augustine, paradise represented spiritual delights, and the East signified the light of wisdom. The tree of life planted in the center of the garden denoted the dominance of the soul over nature, and the tree of knowledge indicated the choice between spiritual joys and corporeal pleasures. As in the writings of the Cappadocians, Adam was regarded as childlike and superbly spiritual. Endowed with a transparent body, he had no need of physical nourishment and was to experience a purely spiritual union with Eve. Later, in *The City of God,* St. Augustine summarized the accepted allegorical interpretations and suggested that paradise might best represent the Church, with the four rivers symbolizing the gospels and the tree of life Christ.[22] But here his heart was more in the historical than in the allegorical interpretation.

St. Augustine left unfinished his first attempt to write a literal exegesis of the first chapters of Genesis. But in *De Genesi ad Litteram,* which elucidates his awareness of the difficulties in reconciling Genesis with human experience and Platonism, he asserted that these first chapters of Genesis gave an account of deeds, as does the Book of Kings; and in his later writings he treated paradise literally. He insisted more than had most previous writers upon the earthly characteristics of paradise and of Adam and Eve, but he assured Christians that "without any disturbance however of the Christian belief that there undoubtedly is such a paradise," they might be ignorant or uncertain of its real location and description. "Our first parents were indeed on earth," he wrote again, "in a well-wooded and fruitful spot, which has been named Paradise." As the Tiber was formerly the Albula, so the Nile and Ganges were formerly the Geon and Phison.[23]

St. Augustine bequeathed a comprehensive view of man's original righteousness and paradisal life to which centuries of later commentators continued to refer. Although he gloried in the perfect state of nature in paradise, his few statements about the possible role of grace in paradise have remained controversial. In his study of St. Augustine, Etienne Gilson has explained that "in this improper sense, even nature itself must be a grace, but a universal grace" which should be carefully distinguished from the grace enjoyed by some through the Incarnation. He said that in St. Augustine's conception Adam was adopted by God, was able to persevere in good, and possessed what today would be called sanctifying grace and actual grace. However, Adolf Harnack has asserted that the grace possessed by Adam, according to St. Augustine, "leaves the will free and really has no effect, but is merely a condition of the free decision for good, therefore not *irresistibilis*." St. Augustine also apparently felt that immortality was offered to man in a state of nature through another special grace.[24]

Though later writers still could not fully agree on the meaning of Augustine's conception of nature and grace, they did discover a clear and full presentation of his idea of the original righteousness enjoyed by Adam and Eve in paradise. The most important aspect of the life in paradise was the relation of the human soul to God. This relation was conceived partly in Platonic terms: the soul sought and loved God as the Supreme Being, the Supreme Good, and the Supreme Love. Upon this love of God and of the good was rooted the freedom of the will, which would be lost through a love of self. But St. Augustine's interpretation of the first man was also thoroughly Christian: Adam's body, though an animal body, was not a prison, but a good and integral part of him. Bound in love to God and to each other, Adam and Eve resembled Stoics in their freedom from all perturbations. "Their love to God," St. Augustine wrote, "was unclouded, and their mutual affection was that of faithful and sincere marriage; and from their love flowed a wonderful delight, because they always enjoyed what was loved." "Or did they perhaps desire to touch and eat the forbidden fruit, yet feared to die? . . . Away with the thought." Their avoidance of sin was tranquil. They experienced neither desire nor fear, sadness nor foolish joy, but true gladness. Indeed, without the Fall, the whole human race would have maintained this blessed lack of perturbation, he concluded.[25]

St. Augustine associated this paradisal peace of mind particularly with the will's domination of the mind and body, including the genitals. Perhaps drawing on his own long struggle with the passions, and pondering the Yahwist's statement that "they were naked, and were not ashamed," he constructed a complete statement of the body's perfect obedience to the will which continued to entrance exegetes and poets who dreamed of the lustless love of paradise. "By a garment of grace," the first couple, though naked, were not shamed by the "consciousness of their members warring against their will." Sexual intercourse would have been a "placid obedience to the will," and "the male semen could have been introduced into the womb of the wife with the integrity of the female genital organ being preserved." There would have been no blushes, no need for darkness or privacy, and no words would have become obscene. Such was the harmony that reigned within man before he disobeyed God and his members disobeyed him, bringing the torturing dualism of the spirit and the flesh. All the members worked in perfect health and harmony. In St. Augustine's paradise no languor made leisure wearisome, and no sleepiness interrupted the desire to labor.[26]

In this state of peaceful accord God instituted the harmony of marriage, with the injunction to increase and multiply. But for St. Augustine, this marriage was never consummated by intercourse in paradise. Although Scripture does not tell, he commented, of the time spent in paradise, it can be said that God had not yet commanded intercourse. For would not divine authority be awaited for this, when no concupiscence was good for flesh that could prove disobedient? Yet despite the Fall, St. Augustine, like many Renaissance writers, still rejoiced that the entire human race could trace its ancestry back to Adam and Eve. "God," he explained, "desiring not only that the whole human race might be able by their similarity of nature to associate with one another, but also that they might be bound together in harmony and peace by the ties of relationship, was pleased to derive all men from one individual." [27]

Renaissance writers generally accepted St. Augustine's statement of the perfection of knowledge and virtue in unfallen man. Striving to forge a Christian dogma from Platonic and Neoplatonic concepts, St. Augustine would not accept the recollected knowledge of a preexistent soul, but held that man had been naturally endowed by God with a moral and intellectual illumination by which he knew ideas or archetypes in the mind of God. This illumination, perfect in Adam in paradise, was darkened when man turned away from God. Developing the ideas of St. Ambrose, St. Augustine found man's conscience divinely illumined by the eternal, immutable natural law — the divine reason ordering all of nature — which is itself of God. He distinguished between the natural law, which appeared in the time of those still able to use their reason and free will, and the written law, which came into existence after man had become bound by the law of sin and death inherited from Adam. [28]

In opposing the Pelagian heresy, St. Augustine was stimulated to portray an Adam endowed with amazingly perfect intellectual attainments. Disputing the Pelagian contention that the human nature of Adam and his sons suffered no change due to his first disobedience, he added new glories to Edenic man in contrasting sharply the unfallen and fallen state. In his late dialogue with the Epicurean Pelagian Julian, who regarded Adam's mental powers as weak, St. Augustine marveled at Adam's superb understanding demonstrated in naming the species of living creatures. Pythagoras, he noted, had praised him who first gave words to all things as the wisest man. Along with his extensive knowledge, Adam possessed a memory and reason that functioned without error or delay. Indeed, he asked, what Christian doubts that Adam's mental powers surpassed those of the most gifted modern philosophers as the movement of birds surpasses that of tortoises? [29]

Similarly, in the controversy about the freedom of the will, both the Pelagians and St. Augustine looked back to paradise. For Julian, Adam and his descendants were equally able to sin and not to sin. The will, unaffected even by habit, was in a state of delicate balance, inclining neither to virtue nor to vice. But for St. Augustine and most later writers, Adam's will in innocence was confirmed in goodness by an inner rectitude and an established inclination toward virtue. Although there was a slight tendency toward evil in Adam, just sufficient to provide a trial, his virtue was effortless and saintlike, devoid of the struggles of temptation. Certain that man thus confirmed in goodness could suffer neither death, disease, nor discomfort, St. Augustine heaped scorn upon the "Pelagian paradise" of aches, pains, disease, and death.[30]

This paragon of human perfection was called to a life of pleasant, unwearying, and productive work with God and nature. Classical praise of agriculture is echoed in St. Augustine's idyllic description of man's willing, cheerful employment in the perfect climate. The Creator himself would be profoundly glorified when the man to whom he had given reason and the faculties needed for willing work came forward gladly with the offer of the aid of human labor. What is more wonderful, he asked, than reason joining with nature in the planting of seeds, the setting out of plants, and the transplanting of saplings? [31]

Not only did St. Augustine provide one of the most complete and luminous pictures of the first man and his life in paradise, but he developed the most thorough and influential view of the place of the paradise story in history. Most writers to the time of Bossuet accepted his twofold postulation of what would have happened if man had retained paradise and of what had happened and would happen since his expulsion. For St. Augustine, St. Thomas, and Milton, the historical paradise, itself the scene of its own loss, suggested both the history of the society that might have been and, by sharp contrast, man's almost inconceivable loss. The future inhabitants of paradise would have enjoyed all the delights of the external and inner paradise given to their first parents. There would have been a perfect society, a veritable City of God in which all would have been united in peace and love by their common love of God. "For there is nothing so social by nature, so unsocial by its corruption, as this race." In *The City of God*, St. Augustine insisted that God had so made Adam and Eve "that if they discharged the obligation of obedience, an angelic immortality and a blessed eternity might ensue, without the intervention of death," and they "would have lived eternally with their bodies." In this he opposed not only the Pelagian view that man had always been mortal, but the position of Porphyry and others that "bare, blessed souls" were more desirable than those dwelling within "healthy, well conditioned bodies." If man had continued sinless and "the number of the predestined saints should have been completed, there would have been bestowed that higher felicity which is enjoyed by the most blessed angels — a blessedness in which there should have been a secure assurance that no one would sin, and no one would die." In *De Genesi ad Litteram*, St. Augustine speculated that if it were not proper for men to become as angels, they might have attained a state inferior to that of angels but superior to that in which man was first made. If Elijah was translated in life to a better state, why could not Adam and Eve and others yield to future generations by translation? [32]

The continuing history set forth in *The City of God* concerned all as inhabitants either of the City of God or of the Earthly City. St. Augustine saw the pattern of history as a kind of Platonic idea in the mind of God, known to men by revelation and realized by men in time. History was universal and providential. In Adam,

St. Augustine said, were laid the foundations for the City of God, whose inhabitants would be associated with the good angels in their love of God and in their reward, as well as the foundations for the Earthly City, whose inhabitants would be associated with the wicked angels in their love of self and in their punishment. Rejecting the "evil imagination" or the angel "watchers" who consorted with women (Gen. 6:1–4) as the source of sin, St. Augustine looked unflinchingly to the disobedience in the garden as the origin of the world's evil. "For we were all in that one man," he asserted, "since we all were that one man, who fell into sin by the woman who was made from him before the sin." [33]

Like numerous Renaissance commentators, St. Augustine struggled with problems of time and chronology. How many years had elapsed since the Creation and the fateful events in paradise? One of his greatest contributions as a Christian historian was to reject completely the eternity of the world and historical cycles. History was a one-way straight course. Eden and Calvary were the great crises in history, but they were absolutely unique. St. Augustine dismissed as false and mendacious ancient historical accounts that contradicted the chronology of Genesis. He warned against being deceived, for example, by the Egyptians' assigning more than 8000 years to the empire of the Persians and Macedonians. Following Scripture, he was certain that not 6000 years had yet passed.[34]

Early Christian Poets

While early Christian theologians were developing doctrines concerning the life in paradise and the Fall, early Christian poets were converting classical rhetoric to the sensuous pictures of paradise and to the sensitive portrayals of Adam and Eve. With the new interest in hexameral literature and the "celestial cycle," the Renaissance welcomed new editions of the poetry of St. Ephrem Syrus, Claudius Marius Victor, Alcimus Ecdicius Avitus, and Blossius Aemilius Dracontius.[35] The paradise story offered poets a particularly fine opportunity both to combat dualism and Semi-Pelagianism and to turn the resources of classical literature to the service of Christianity. Like Milton later, they made poetry of the doctrine of original righteousness and drama of the doctrine of the Fall. Several of them also anticipated Milton in justifying the ways of God to man by presenting the great sweep of biblical history from the Fall to the Redemption. Familiar with classical descriptions of the ideal landscape (particularly those of Virgil), these Christian poets found in paradise the perfect theme for poetic exuberance and rhetorical display. Whereas commentators pointed to the truth behind pagan myth, the poets went further and showed the descriptions of a golden age to be true — "true, here only" — in paradise.

The appeal of the paradise theme is very evident in the fifteen hymns on paradise by St. Ephrem (b. 373), the Syrian "Lyre of the Holy Ghost." All were composed in a seven-syllable measure and set to the same melody. In a flood of lyricism, the poet envisioned paradise sometimes as a lofty mountain and sometimes as a kind of halo around the earth. He was aware of the great gulf between the incorruptible order of paradise and the corruptible order of the world. He also distinguished between an inner and outer paradise and a fore-paradise. The trees of paradise suggested fecundity as of a breast and the waters fell as from a goblet. The delicious perfumes were one of the main paradisal hierophanies. St. Ephrem associated paradise with the Church and celebrated it as the abode of the blest, the dejected, and the poor, who would live in houses of clouds hereafter.[36]

Latin works treating the paradise theme inherited much from the long classical tradition of the ideal life in the ideal setting. Perhaps the earliest Christian description of the earthly paradise occurs in *De Ave Phoenice*, long attributed to Lactantius. Although the poem does not concern explicitly the Edenic paradise or Christian themes, it was usually interpreted as dealing with these, and was often imitated in the vernacular. The poet told of a wooded grove atop a towering peak arising suddenly from a wide plain in the distant east. The tradition of the golden age is reflected in the picture of a land of perpetual spring, where there is no frost, or cloud, or rain, but a single fountain of life gushing forth once a month to water the grove. The inhabitants suffer neither fear, disease, senility, nor death. A description of the paradise in Eden occurs in the *De Judicio Domini,* attributed to Tertullian but probably composed in the sixth century. Giamatti has noted in this poem three motifs that become typical of characterizations of the Edenic paradise: the description emphasizes the wonderful fragrance of paradise, but also relies on Genesis for an account of the four rivers and of the jewels, particularly the emerald and carbuncle, found in the region of paradise.[37]

The development of the long Christian poem was to offer untold poets for centuries to come the chance to test their imaginative range and rhetorical skill in depicting the wonders of the earthly paradise. Important contributions were made by several Christian Latin poets of the fourth and fifth centuries: Aurelius Prudentius, a Spanish magistrate; Claudius Marius Victor, a rhetor of Marseilles; Alcimus Ecdicius Avitus, bishop of Vienne; and Blossius Aemilius Dracontius, a Carthaginian advocate imprisoned by the Vandal king.[38]

Strongly influenced by classical literature, Prudentius was himself one of the most influential of the early Christian Latin poets. He depicted paradise in his *Cathemerinon* (III, 101–10), a series of lengthy hymns for the Christian's day. Both in conception and phrasing these songs of praise mirror Virgil's Elysium. Motifs from Virgil, other classical writers, and Genesis converge in his description: "Then he bade man dwell in a leafy place, ranging over pleasant lawns where the scent of spring was unending and a swift stream in four-fold channel watered the many-coloured meads." His Adam and Eve appear to be innocent but immature, and Satan takes advantage of the untaught natural disposition of Eve. Opposing the Manichaean dualism in his *Hamartigenia,* Prudentius sought to establish the freedom of man's will by advancing an orthodox account of the origin of evil through Satan.[39]

The long Christian poem, exploiting the romantic and dramatic possibilities of the classical epic and the Old Testament, enjoyed its first flowering in the twilight glory of the vanishing Gallic schools of rhetoric. In the fourth century, Apollinaris the Elder of Syria and his son had transcribed the Old Testament into Greek epic verse, and Falconia Proba, the Christian daughter of a Roman consul, had composed a Virgilian pastiche on biblical subjects, transferring phrases from Virgil's Elysium to the description of the Edenic paradise. In his *Metrum in Genesim*, Hilary, bishop of Arles (first half of the fifth century), reflected Virgil's *Fourth Eclogue* and Ovid's *Metamorphoses* in his poetic interpretation of the first chapters of Genesis. The first great portrayal of the Edenic paradise by a Christian poet writing in the classical tradition is that of Victor, who anticipated Milton in his free adaptation of the classical literary epic and in his imaginative interpretation of biblical material. Genuine poetic feeling, rhetorical elegance, and a strong dependence on Virgil fuse in his creation of the Edenic paradise in his *Genesis* and *Alethia*.

In *Genesis*, Victor emphasized how God had brought together in the Edenic garden all the wonders of Nature found separately in other parts of the earth. The Virgilian voice is echoed in the reference to "nemoris paradisus amoeni." Victor looked to classical rhetoric to amplify the account in Genesis of the fruit trees and four streams. The fruit trees yield every kind of pleasant taste and odor. In the bosom of a high and sacred grove arises a fountain which divides into the four rivers. As these streams gently descend, some dwindle when they give up their water while others swell with increasing infusions. The sands of the Phison shine with gold, the glowing red of the carbuncle, and the radiant green of the emerald. No doubt, said Victor, the first parents dwelt there, and with them dwelt health, wisdom, grace, and a steadfast desire for the truth.[40]

In the digression on paradise in Victor's *Alethia*, or *Truth*, verbal echoes reverberate from Virgil's Georgics (II, 114–24) and his Elysium. The natural abundance of the golden age is poured forth in paradise, and the description of the fruit trees suggests the Garden of Alcinous. In the East extend the happy groves of paradise, girdled by a heavy forest. There is eternal spring, but also harvest. Each fruit that falls is replaced by another, delicious and beautiful, nourishing both mind and body by its savor and perfume. The earth shines with ever fresh starry blossoms of every hue. Like a divine ambrosia, the fragrance of cinnamon bursts forth from slender reeds. The sweetness filling the air exceeds that of Medean perfumes, the flowing hair of Archaemenius, Assyrian balsam, Mareotic spikenard, the soft Tarnessid twig, or the fragrant tears of the plant of Palestine. A gentle wind blends many fragrances into one nectar and awakes the forest to sing a hymn to God. Victor reminded his readers of the inner paradise signified by the outer and perhaps also of the millennial paradise in store for the blest. Glory, Grace, Wisdom, Love, Truth, and Peace, resplendent ideals of the soul, dwelt together in paradise before the Fall.[41]

In his conception of Adam and Eve, Victor was in fundamental agreement with much contemporary patristic thought. Seeking to refute the classical atomists, Victor adhered generally to a maximal interpretation of original righteousness. He gloried in Adam's creation by God, his dignity and wisdom. He emphasized free will, but seems to have avoided Semi-Pelagianism. The life of the first pair was highly spiritual. They apparently needed no food, and it was offered them only for their pleasure. Like most of the early Christian poets, Victor was restrained in his treatment of the pair's marital bliss. However, while picturing Adam and Eve as highly spiritual, Victor was in agreement with St. Augustine in assuming that the first parents had the opportunity to become more angelic. The *Alethia* presents the naming of the animals, the creation of Eve, and the temptation by a serpent who argues that he who has not learned the difference between good and evil does not really know the good. Although Victor gave little attention to the inner life of Adam and Eve before the Fall, he presents a moving account of their fear and uncertainty after their expulsion.[42]

Victor's descriptions of Eden provide another step toward Milton's Paradise. Transforming the ideal landscapes of Greek and Latin poetry into the true Christian paradise, he established the pattern and precedent for successors. Victor's miraculous fruits and scented plants anticipate Milton's "Groves whose rich trees wept odorous Gumms and Balme" (IV, 248), and his breeze-swept forest suggests Milton's "aires, vernal aires, / Breathing the smell of field and grove" that "attune / The trembling leaves" (IV, 264–66). His streams arising from a central fount and winding through paradise amidst gold and jewels reappear only slightly altered in Milton's Paradise, "Rowling on Orient Pearl and sands of Gold" (IV, 238). Victor's external paradise becomes a figure for the inner paradise, as it would repeatedly in later interpretations. Though they may become more angelic, Victor's Adam and Eve are gloriously endowed with the gifts of original righteousness. However, in Victor one does not yet find the power of nature and the power of love that would dominate Milton's Paradise.

Attracted by the success of Victor's work, another poet of fifth-century Gaul, Avitus, wrote his *Poematum de Mosaicae Historiae Gestibus Libri Quinque*, using the *Aeneid* as his model. In his introduction he said that his epic (published in 507) had been begun long before, lost during the siege of Vienne in 500, and then partly recovered. Since this work was studied in English grammar schools in Milton's day, its possible influence on *Paradise Lost* has long been disputed; yet three passages in *Paradise Lost* closely resembling passages in Avitus's poem indicate that Milton had read Avitus.[43] In any case, this early Latin poet, like Milton, expanded the Genesis account and invented striking characterizations and imaginative incidents in his epic on the twofold theme of the Fall and the Redemption.

The paradise of Avitus possesses all the traditional motifs derived from Virgil, Ovid, and other classical writers, but with some embellishments. Avitus was a highly self-conscious artist, never disdaining the adornment of metaphor, word play, and alliteration. Not only are there a temperate climate and blossoms and fruits at once, but the fragile blossoms do not even droop in the sun and a month brings to maturity fruits that would require a year elsewhere. No touch violates the violet and by a lasting grace a blush suffuses the face of the rose. Avitus trimmed his poem with the beauties of a fallen world only to show how far paradise exceeded these. The fountain, which feeds the Tigris, Euphrates,

Nile, and Ganges, is brighter than silver or sunlit ice and is encircled with a natural diadem of diamonds.[44]

This paradise abounds in dramatic contrasts. Adam, Eve, and Satan are true epic characters. Adam has a Godlike mind and all the virtues of a maximal interpretation of original righteousness. His marriage to Eve is celebrated with Hymen chanting angelic songs of blended harmony (I, 189–90) just as Milton's "heav'nly Quires the Hymenaean sung" (IV, 711). Adam and Eve rule the subject world with law and peaceful joy. However, as in *Paradise Lost*, the devil is inescapable in paradise. Much like Milton's Satan, he envies the innocent happiness of the first couple, and cries out "All is not lost, however, for pristine force of will survives" (II, 95–96). Eve succumbs to the serpent's blandishments and promise of deification, but not without genuine psychological conflict.[45]

The most distinguished early Christian poet in Africa, the imprisoned Dracontius, dramatized in his *Carmen de Laudibus Dei* the scenes in paradise as part of his scheme presenting the greatness of God, the universal order of nature, and the redemption of man. His paradise, set in the region of the Indies, is described in highly wrought rhetoric derived from characterizations of Elysium and the golden age. But the most important contribution of Dracontius to the poetry of the paradise tradition was his sensitive portrayal of the innocence of the first pair and the beauty and charm of Eve. Unlike Victor and Avitus, he gave a minimal interpretation of original righteousness and the first sin. Adam and Eve are like tame animals or lost children, full of wonder, enjoying simple pleasures and innocent affection. Much of the beauty of paradise is revealed through their fresh perception as they marvel at fields, groves, and banks of flowers. As in the first man's account to Raphael in *Paradise Lost*, the simpler Adam of Dracontius looks about him in wonder and asks what is man and for what purposes created. Although most of the early Christian poets scrupulously avoided the themes of paradisal love and of Eve's charms, Dracontius, like Milton, evidently felt that the beauty of Eve was an essential part of the beauty of paradise. He anticipated

Milton in comparing her to a classical deity. Borrowing from Ovid, he described her as like a nymph, with her snowy naked body, her lovely flowing hair, and blushing cheeks. But she is also childlike and innocent. The Adam and Eve of Dracontius do not possess the vast knowledge, understanding, and assurance of Milton's characters. They are fearful of the first sunset, but joyful to see the sun's radiance again in the morning.[46] Dracontius lacked the dramatic power of Avitus, but bequeathed tender portraits of a very human prelapsarian Adam and Eve to the early Christian poetic tradition.

The poetic creation of the Edenic paradise called forth some of the most sustained and most successful efforts of these early poets, who dedicated the wealth of classical rhetoric to Christian instruction by making the classical descriptions of the golden age, Elysium, and the ideal landscape a lasting part of the Christian tradition of the earthly paradise. Milton and other Renaissance poets could have been influenced directly or indirectly by all of these poets; and, as has been mentioned, some direct influence on Milton from Avitus is a strong possibility. In any event, neither Milton nor his readers could have escaped the traditional conceptions of paradise that these writers, turning theology into poetry, helped so much to create.

4

THE MIDDLE AGES

⁂ RENAISSANCE writers, particularly Protestants, generally derived their ideas of paradise more from the patristic exegetes
and poets than from the theological superstructures and fantastic
legends of the Middle Ages. This does not mean that they were not
familiar with various popular accounts of paradise and the theological commentary of St. Thomas and others, but they usually rejected with anger and contempt unhistorical allegory, Aristotelian
eternalism, and incredible fantasy, choosing instead to build upon
the rational and historical exegesis of Rashi, St. Thomas, and
their followers. Dante's great vision of the terrestrial paradise was
about as far removed as possible from the Renaissance quest for
an actual historical location. Milton showed less interest in the
medieval writers than in the fathers, but was one of the relatively few in seventeenth-century England who was familiar with
Dante.

The eclectic assortment of miscellaneous information left by
St. Isidore (560–636), bishop of Seville, was the most widely known
popular source of ideas about paradise during the Middle Ages,
and indeed was still frequently quoted in the seventeenth century. St. Isidore distinguished between the celestial paradise and
the earthly paradise, accepted both a literal and allegorical interpretation, and contributed to the fanciful medieval legends of

67

a faraway Eastern paradise. Like many, he translated the Hebrew "garden in Eden" as a *hortus deliciae,* a garden of delight, which should not be confused with the Fortunate Isles, although it, too, is in the eastern part of Asia. Perhaps following the suggestion of Tertullian, St. Isidore described paradise as surrounded by a wall of swordlike flames reaching almost to heaven. Allegorically, he followed the familiar interpretation of paradise as the Church and the four rivers as the four gospels.[1]

Like St. Isidore, the Venerable Bede (673?–735) summarized and passed on the lore and learning of his time. He believed in a real earthly paradise, from which the four rivers, including the Nile and Ganges, flowed under ground, but he was subject to the common enchantment of multiple allegorical interpretations. The four rivers signified baptism and the cardinal virtues; their heads signified not only the four Evangelists, but hot, cold, humid, and dry as well. The tree of life represented Christ, spiritual doctrine in the paradise of the church, and wisdom in the paradise of the body. The lands bordering the rivers also had allegorical significance. The Venerable Bede accepted and developed Philo's interpretation of Adam as reason and Eve as sense.[2] Other commentators such as Rabanus Maurus, Peter Comestor, and Rupertus of Deutz helped popularize similar interpretations.

Such influential theologians as Abelard, Peter Lombard, and St. Bonaventure contributed little that was new to the paradise concept. However, the fresh confrontations between the Greek, Latin, and Hebraic traditions brought new philosophical, mystical, and historical meaning to the paradise story, particularly in the works of John Scotus Erigena (810–80), St. Bernard of Clairvaux (1090?–1153), and St. Thomas Aquinas (1225–74).

The Spiritual Paradise:
Erigena and St. Bernard

Familiar with Plotinus, Origen, and the two Cappadocian Gregorys, Erigena brought to the Latin tradition a new emphasis on universals. For him, Man was an asexual Idea implicitly containing all men. The paradise of this Platonic Man was an Augustinian perfection of nature and grace, in which he was endowed with divine illumination. Sinning through separating himself from God, this man was divided into the sexes and then further divided into individuals. After the Resurrection, man was to return to the Paradise of his primary Idea.[3]

St. Bernard was also acquainted with Neoplatonic Greek philosophy and possibly with the works of Erigena himself. Gilson has emphasized his achievement of a harmonious synthesis, "a new theology which unites the Greek philosophy, based upon the relation of image to model, with the Latin theology based upon the relation of nature to grace." Man through grace can attain the lost resemblance between divine will and human will in which man loves God as he himself is loved. In this mystical union the senses slumber while the interior sense is "abducted" by God. This, like the cloister, is a paradise, but not the final paradise of the beatific vision. St. Bernard described his own mystical experiences as ineffable. He attributed this state to Adam at the creation of Eve and to Christ at the Crucifixion, when charity overcame the senses. The soul, whose true will is to love God, regains paradise when it regains the original state of a love of God.[4] Fusing the Greek and Latin traditions in the fire of his own spiritual experience, St. Bernard gave the consummate expression of the preeminence of love in any vision of paradise.

The Natural Paradise: St. Thomas

A mighty tide of new knowledge and changing attitudes cleared the way for the broad, philosophical, rational, and historical approach of St. Thomas, which would lead to the great commentaries of the Renaissance. He was faced not only with the conflicting Greek and Latin traditions synthesized by St. Bernard, but with the increasing tension between literal and allegorical interpretation, and with the new universe of Greek thought transmitted to the West by Arabic and Jewish thinkers.

While St. Thomas sometimes depended upon the old allegorical interpretation of the Bible, he also gave an important role to the new literal interpretation, as in his depiction of a natural

Edenic paradise. Among the first and ultimately most influential proponents of this new literal, linguistic, and historical exegesis were Rabbi Solomon Bar Isaac, known as Rashi (1040–1105) and Ibn Ezra (1092?–1167), Browning's Rabbi Ben Ezra. Rashi wrote: "I am only concerned with the plain sense of Scripture" and with facts that "explain the words of Scripture in a manner that fits in with them." Rejecting ideas of original righteousness, he imitated the Yahwist in depicting the garden state as essentially primitive.[5] Hugh of St. Victor and Andrew of St. Victor followed Rashi's rational and literal interpretation. By the thirteenth century both Dominicans and Franciscans, at Paris and at Oxford, were employing a sober rational approach.

The explosive potentiality of the tension between Christian theology and the rational methodology and scientific knowledge introduced into the West by the Arabic and Hebraic interpreters of Greek philosophy never materialized, but there were many attempts to combine the old theology and the new philosophy. The new knowledge of logic, mathematics, physics, and biology was utilized by William of Auvergne, Robert Grosseteste, Roger Bacon, and St. Thomas's encyclopedic master Albertus Magnus.

Grappling with the problems of the thirteenth century, St. Thomas formed a comprehensive, rational, Christian view of man's origin, nature, and destiny that was still widely accepted as highly authoritative in the seventeenth century, even by many English Protestants. Milton's only reference to him was the assertion in *Areopatica* that he dared to be known to think Spenser a better teacher than Aquinas. However, Milton accepted most of his ideas about the state of innocence. Aquinas was both cited for support and condemned as a representative of popery, but was generally treated with respect by such Anglican divines as Lancelot Andrewes, Joseph Hall, Jeremy Taylor, and John Bramhall. The nonconformists usually were less knowledgeable and less respectful of Aquinas, but Richard Baxter and John Norris approached him sympathetically.[6]

Although St. Thomas's discussion of paradise in his *Summa Theologica* is but a small part of the whole work, it provides one of the most lucid descriptions of original righteousness and a highly complete account of what the life in paradise would have been if Adam and Eve had not sinned. As an exegete St. Thomas was essentially traditional and sometimes conventionally allegorical: he claimed, for instance, that the tree of knowledge might signify free will and that Eve's creation from Adam signified the origin of the Church from Christ.[7] However, as a theologian he presented a logical and rational picture of the place of paradise in Christian history and theology. He scrupulously interpreted Adam and Eve and their future descendants in light of their human nature, which was distinct from that of angels or of animals; but he also studiously distinguished between the condition of man before the Fall, when he enjoyed the full gift of God's grace, and his condition afterward. His care, frankness, consistency, and precision gave added seriousness and significance to the place of paradise in a Christian theology which was forced to confront the tensions brought by a new world of philosophy.

Although Aquinas granted the possibility of a spiritual paradise, he insisted upon the existence of a real historical paradise, asserting that the historical truth of narrative must be the foundation of any spiritual explanation. He agreed with most of his contemporaries about the location of paradise. "The situation of paradise," he said, "is shut off from the habitable world by mountains, or seas, or some torrid region, which cannot be crossed." He speculated about the possibility of paradise being on the equinoctial line, but he rejected the idea that it might reach to the moon. He did admit, however, that underground rivers might flow from paradise. According to St. Thomas, paradise was not useless; it still existed and might be, as popular legend had it, the dwelling place of Elijah and Enoch.[8]

Aquinas viewed paradise as especially suited to man in a state of perfection, a creature between the angels and animals whose soul was adapted to govern his body. As paradise was made for man and man for paradise, he followed St. John of Damascus in excluding the animals before the Fall. Man was created not only in a state of perfect nature, but in a state of grace. Through

71

grace, his reason was subject to God and his body to his reason. Adam was without the passions which would impede the free use of reason. He had no passion with evil as its object, such as fear or sorrow, or of good not possessed, as concupiscence, but he did desire and hope for future good at the proper time. "Man was happy in Paradise," wrote St. Thomas, "but not with that perfect happiness to which he was destined, which consists in the vision of the Divine Essence."[9]

Did Adam know everything? Aquinas tried to define precisely what Adam did know as man, but as man in a perfect state. He did not comprehend the Divine Essence or the angelic Essence, but he had a more complete knowledge of angels than we because his inner knowledge was more certain and fixed. Adam possessed knowledge of natural things by divine infusion, but it was no different in kind from our knowledge. He had perfect knowledge of whatever truth man is naturally able to know. He possessed more truth by revelation than fallen man, and knew such supernatural truth as was necessary for him. But Adam did not know things which cannot be known by human effort and which are not necessary for the direction of human life, such as the thoughts of other men, future contingent events, and the number of pebbles in a stream.[10]

Milton's Adam and Eve approach the general patterns of St. Thomas's thought not only while awake but while asleep. Milton's account of Eve's dream and Adam's explanation (V, 28–128) is in essential harmony with the discussion of paradisal dreams in the *Summa*. Man would have dreamed in paradise, "adhering to images as to realities." In sleep the natural power of judgment is not free, so deception must be ascribed to a lower faculty. "A man is not accountable for what occurs during sleep; as he has not then the use of his reason."[11]

In his discussion of Adam and Eve, St. Thomas approached the literal, historical intepretation of paradise that would characterize Renaissance thought. Gone are the luminous, diaphanous creatures of the Cappadocians. He saw Adam and Eve as real human beings in a real garden: they would have eaten real fruit,

defecated, worked, and enjoyed sexual intercourse. Contrary
to some earlier commentators, Aquinas explained that man had
an animal life requiring food; indeed, man would have sinned
had he not eaten. He recognized that the Genesis account of the
tree of life resembled the Greek myth ridiculed by Aristotle and
he saw the difficulty inherent in the notion of a natural, corruptible plant producing a supernatural incorruption, but he adhered to Scripture and concluded that man could preserve and
renew his life indefinitely by partaking of the tree. He also maintained that it was unreasonable to suppose that there was no fecal
matter in paradise. "Wherefore," he said, "there was need for
voiding the surplus, yet so disposed by God as to be decorous and
suitable to the state." Man would have worked in paradise, dress-
ing and keeping the garden, but the labor "would have been
pleasant on account of man's practical knowledge of the powers
of nature." Though St. Thomas held that Adam and Eve had
been ejected from paradise before sexual union, he believed that
they would have enjoyed normal sexual relations, since coition
and the begetting of children were natural. Moreover, in their
state of perfection the "sensible delight would have been
the greater in proportion to the greater purity of nature and the
greater sensibility of the body." An unfallen reason would not
prevent pleasure, but would prevent the devotion of too much
time or importance to it.[12]

If Adam and Eve had remained in obedience in paradise, they
would have been joined by children born naturally in a state of
perfection and, in fact, by an entire and perfect human society.
Paradisal children would have been born in original righteousness and in sanctifying grace, but not confirmed in righteousness.
They would not have been born with full powers, for this
would have been unnatural. Since reason depends partly on corporeal organs, children would not have possessed full reason, and
as it is natural for man to acquire knowledge through the senses,
they would not have been born with a perfect knowledge. However, they would have learned early; their knowledge would have
been sufficient for their age and for continuing in righteousness,

and indeed more complete than what we have now by nature.[13]

As children matured and a society developed, there would have been inequalities in age, sex, and personal qualities. Due to free will, climate, natural laws, and diversity according to the stars, some would have been more righteous and more knowledgeable than others, but none would have possessed any defect. Aquinas agreed with Aristotle that social life was natural for man, and that it must exist under the direction of one superior in intelligence and virtue who would look after the common good. St. Thomas distinguished between postlapsarian servile subjection, in which a superior uses a subject for the superior's own benefit, and "another kind of subjection, which is called economic or civil, whereby the superior makes use of his subjects for their own benefit and good; and this kind of subjection existed even before sin. For good order would have been wanting in the human family if some were not governed by others wiser than themselves." Woman was naturally to be subjected to man, in whom discretion and reason were stronger. Furthermore, St. Thomas explained that in the state of innocence "the will of men would have been so ordered that without any danger of strife they would have used in common, according to each one's need, those things of which they were masters — a state of things to be observed even now among many good men."[14]

Several of the ideas of the state of innocence that St. Thomas synthesized in the *Summa* were widely accepted in the seventeenth century and appeared in *Paradise Lost*. Milton, like Aquinas, pictured Adam as potentially immortal, free from pain, with his reason subject to God and his body and passions subject to his reason. Although St. Thomas attributed this subjection to grace and distinguished between the gifts of nature and grace, Milton was never explicit or emphatic about the grace enjoyed by the first couple before the Fall. However, he considered one of the effects of the Fall to be "the loss of divine grace and of innate righteousness."[15] Neither Aquinas nor Milton rejected the spiritual meaning of paradise, but both stressed the natural life of Adam and Eve in a historical paradise. They pictured Adam and Eve eating, working, and enjoying sexual pleasures very much as do their descendants. Milton's conception of the nature and extent of Adam's knowledge was conceived in the scholastic pattern of St. Thomas. Adam's knowledge was infused; in relating to Raphael his naming of the animals, Adam recalls that "with such knowledge God endu'd / My sudden apprehension" (VII, 353–54). Adam's knowledge, which was limited, also became discursive as he learned new things. Though Milton was more interested in individual liberty than in a prelapsarian social order, he, like Aquinas, believed that the wisest and most virtuous should lead. He also thought that goods were to be held in common in the state of innocence (IV, 751–52).

The Legendary Paradise

While theologians were seeking to describe a historical paradise that was credible and natural, popular storytellers and chroniclers were depicting a paradise that belonged to a timeless world of fantasy, legend, and myth. Remnants of this medieval paradise were passed on to the Renaissance through such works as *Huon de Bordeaux* and the *Faustbook,* yet most of Milton's contemporaries impatiently rejected the fantasy of imaginary journeys to a mythic paradise in favor of the facts that would lead to the site of the actual paradise. The majority of the Renaissance commentators insisted that paradise had been destroyed. The Protestants, for example, regarded the belief in an existing paradise as popish error. The otherworldly glimmer of the medieval descriptions served as a foil to the natural beauty of the true paradise.

Although legends and popular accounts of the earthly paradise flourished, particularly in the later centuries of the Middle Ages, some of the imaginative possibilities in the paradise story had been developed long before this. Tales dating from the third or fourth century A.D. tell of the return to paradise of Adam's son Seth. Some Hebraic accounts of the early Christian era depict a sunlike Adam whose frame bestrid the earth, whose head reached the divine throne, and who was served wine by angels. The Jewish idea of an earthly paradise populated by Enoch and Elijah became a staple of medieval legend and was considered a serious possibility by Aquinas and later by Cardinal Bellarmine. This concept was supported by the Old Testament references to the translation of Enoch and Elijah (Gen. 5:24 and II Kings 2:11) and by the later Jewish references to the Edenic paradise as the abode of the righteous before resurrection (I Enoch 20:7 and II Enoch 8:1–6); it may also be reflected in the writings of St. Paul (II Cor. 12:1–4).[16]

The marvels of the earthly paradise were suggested to Europeans through the legends of Prester John and Alexander the Great. The curious Letter of Prester John to the emperor of Byzantium, a utopian document filled with exotic lore, first appeared in 1165 and circulated very widely throughout Europe. Prester John is represented as a Christian ruler whose realm is associated with India. Beyond it lies the earthly paradise. One of the rivers of paradise winds through one of his provinces "and there are found in it natural jewels, emeralds, sapphires, carbuncles, topazes, chrysolites, onyx, beryls, amethysts, carnelians, and several other precious stones." A manuscript account of the visit of the Patriarch John of India to Rome presented a similar description. Another version of the Letter tells of a spring arising near Mount Olympus, not three days' journey from paradise, whose wondrous waters, ever-changing in flavor, will enable any individual to live at the age of thirty-two all his life. In the *Iter ad Paradisum*, Alexander the Great travels through a mythic land of darkness, reaches the Well of Life, but is not permitted to enter the Land of the Blessed. In another story, Alexander sails for months up the Ganges to its source in paradise, which appears as a medieval walled city. It is, however, a timeless, otherworldly realm inhabited by the righteous awaiting judgment. It is a city of perpetual day, where neither hunger nor passage of time is ever felt, "ffor sic a melody of birdis sang."[17]

There were many other stories of those who approached paradise. Joinville in his *Histoire de Saint Louis* explained how the men of a Sultan of Cairo, seeking the source of one of the rivers of paradise, reported that they "had come to a great cliff of sheer rock" from which flowed the river. The earthly paradise of Sir John Mandeville, a late fourteenth-century compiler of other men's travels, emerges from a world of myth and archetype. He wrote that "beyond the land and the isles and the deserts of Prester John's lordship, in going straight toward the east, men find nothing but mountains and rock, full great. And there is the dark region, where no man may see, neither by day ne by night, as they of the country say. And that desert and that place of darkness dure from this coast unto Paradise terrestrial," which appears to be on the other side of the world. The author was not worthy to enter, but does relate what wise men say: paradise is the highest place in the world and almost touches the circle of the moon. "And this Paradise is enclosed all about with a wall, and men wit not whereof it is; for the walls be covered all over with moss, as it seemeth." An entry is closed with fire, and no mortal dares to enter. In the center is a well casting out four floods.[18]

Sometimes travelers, usually three monks, actually entered the timeless, jewellike, song-bathed paradise of the popular medieval imagination. Godfrey of Viterbo told of a group of monks who sailed from Britain to the end of the ocean, where they found a city of golden walls and edifices. Enoch and Elijah explain that here they heard angelic song, partook of celestial food, and enjoyed days lasting a hundred earthly years. One fourteenth-century Italian story tells of three monks who follow a stream that has borne to them a bough of gold, silver, and many hues. They come to the earthly paradise, situated on a mountain a hundred miles high, where they are admitted by a guardian angel and become entranced by the indescribably beautiful music of the wheel of heaven as it turns. Guided by Enoch and Elijah, they are spellbound by the song of angels and by the splendor of the tree of knowledge, a tree giving everlasting life, and the tree of salvation, from which came the wood of the cross. They see the four springs of the four great rivers, another spring whose waters turn the old to thirty, and a fountain five miles in breadth and length,

"full of many fish which sang day and night when they heard the
song of paradise." Then they view the tree of glory, whose
branches reach for a mile around, whose foliage is like golden
fig leaves and its fruit like highly wrought confections. The tree
is full of small, red-winged birds that "seemed to be hanging lan-
terns and sang together in one voice as though they were truly
angels of the celestial paradise." When the monks ask permission
to stay fifteen days, they learn that they have already been in
paradise for seven hundred years. In an even more vividly imaginative version, each tree bears a different fruit and each leaf on
a single tree is of a different shade. Flowers and precious stones
of every color abound. A delicious fragrance delivers one from
any wish to eat or drink. The sky is always pure and cloudless,
there is no night, and time is never measured.[19]

The popular chronicles and encyclopedic works of the late
Middle Ages usually provided a rather fanciful account of the
location and original life of paradise. The *Cursor Mundi* described a paradise whose sun was seven times brighter than ours
and whose moon was as bright as our sun. All life was of greater
strength. All creatures rendered service to Adam, whose four-
letter name indicated he would be king of the four corners of
the earth as God was lord of the heavens. But even here Satan
and Eve together overcame Adam with trickery. Caxton's *Mirrour
of the Worlde*, translated from Gossouin, presented a paradise
surrounded by evil beasts, hairy, omnivorous giants, and a wall
of flame. Adam had been a star pupil of God, for he "knewe alle
the seuen scyences lyberall entyrely, without faylling in a worde."
Before his sin he was immortal and afterward he was a combination of Solomon, Absalom, and Samson. Ranulph Higden in his
Polychronicon was somewhat more scholarly and rational, citing
St. Basil, St. Jerome, and St. Isidore in his discussion. He reacted
against tales of a paradise in a completely uninhabitable region,
"for nature wylle not suffre that, neither reason." He said that
"hyt is not to take to credence after some men of power and breve
intellecte, & also of lytelle experience, Paradise to be a region in
grete distaunce from the worlde habitable, eleuate un to the cercle

78

of the moone." Higden, who knew the earth was round from its shadow in an eclipse, explained that paradise could not be near the moon because vegetable life could not survive there and the element of fire would interfere. He believed nothing in paradise could die, "as testimony thereof Enoc & Eelias lyv yette there incorrupte." [20]

Ideas of the location of the earthly paradise as reflected in map or legend were usually imaginative, romantic, and unsupported. The most popular view was that beyond Islam lay the realm of Prester John and beyond this the terrestrial paradise. The Indies of Prester John were sometimes separated from the rest of the habitable world by the Indus and sometimes seen as divided into islands by the four rivers issuing from paradise. In many older maps paradise appeared in the east, at the top of the map, perhaps surrounded by flames and set directly under the moon. Some accounts of the voyage of St. Brendan led to the belief that paradise was in Cochin China, or Japan. Another popular notion was that paradise was on an island. In one account St. Brendan sought to find an island "just under Mount Atlas," which had been "the first home of Adam and Eve." Others favored Ceylon, and the tradition of a Ceylonese paradise lingered on into the Renaissance. The Canary Islands, occasionally associated with the Islands of the Blest, were also suggested as a possible site of paradise by Wynkyn de Worde and others. The Edenic paradise sometimes even blended with the Celtic paradise in the western sea, satirized in the Land of Cockayne. The idea of a paradise on the other side of the world, almost in a second world as implied by Moses Bar Cephas, became less popular in the later Middle Ages. [21]

In his studies of medieval myth and legend, Arturo Graf has noted many popular beliefs about paradise and has pointed out their relation to world myth. These beliefs may be found in biblical commentaries, versified Scripture, hexamerons, theological treatises, scientific tracts, chronicles, visions, legends, and poems. In the Middle Ages, paradise was usually thought of as on a mountain higher than all others, like the Indian Meru or

the Arabic Kaf, and this mountain was often identified with that
on which Noah's ark had rested. Peter Lombard and Albertus
Magnus repeated the old idea that the paradise mount almost
touched the sphere of the moon. Some writers believed one could
travel forty days across paradise, while others estimated that it
was only a few leagues in diameter. The exotic and magical trees
and plants of paradise, of every conceivable variety, resemble
those in the myths of India, China, and Persia. Storytellers told
of trees that ended forever all hunger, thirst, disease, or fatigue.
According to popular accounts, rivers of milk, oil, and wine
flowed through paradise. Some of the paradise rivers were said
to emerge in the outside world as streams or fountains, much as
in Indian and Persian myth.[22]

Visions of paradise appeared through diverse aspects of medieval life. Medieval art often depicted paradise as a mountain
with four streams issuing from it. The creation of Eve from
Adam's rib was shown, and Eve was portrayed as holding the apple or presenting it to Adam. The earthly paradise even figured
in what was perhaps a kind of charade. The Infante Dom
Pedro of Portugal noted that he played a game of "challenges,"
complete with costumes, at a party given in 1429 in Burgundy
for the Portuguese infanta, Isabel of Burgundy. One challenge
came from the deserts of India, he recalled, and another from
the terrestrial paradise. A simulated earthly paradise formed part
of the welcome in Henry VI's triumphal entry into London after
his coronation. In his poetic description of the festivities, John
Lydgate described a conduit from which "the watir ranne like
welles off Paradys," and was then turned into wine. Appearing
"lyke ffolkes off ffeyrye," Enoch and Elijah, accompanied by Bacchus, prayed for the king and wished him prosperity.[23]

The Renaissance would abandon the timeless fantasy and much
of the otherworldly beauty of an existing paradise in a faraway
land. However, the image of the inaccessible mountaintop garden,
with its luxuriant growth, rushing waters, and birdsong would
emerge afresh in *Paradise Lost*. Like the medieval chroniclers,

Milton and other Renaissance poets would continue to display Adam's original perfection, but with less quaint excess.

Medieval Gardens

A number of medieval poems describing gardens — both secular gardens and the Edenic garden — reflected both classical and Christian conceptions of an ideal landscape and an ideal life. The garden of love, which is represented best in the *Roman de la Rose*, contributed to characterizations of false paradises and of the true paradise as a garden of love. This idea appears in works as diverse as *Paradise Lost* and Loredano's *L'Adamo*. Medieval descriptions of the Edenic garden, which attained their final perfection in Dante's *Purgatorio*, carried the classical and early Christian motifs of Latin literature into the vernacular literature of the late Middle Ages and the Renaissance.

These secular gardens drew upon the epithalamic poetry of Statius and of Claudian, which associated physical love with a garden, but they were also often compared with the garden in Eden — the rhetorical touchstone of perfection — and they shared the beauties attributed to it. In his *Anticlaudianus*, Alain de Lille, the twelfth-century *doctor universalis*, depicted a garden and a temple of Nature as part of an allegory providing a Neoplatonic image of the creation of man. As in both Claudian and medieval accounts of the Edenic paradise, this garden is on a mountain that reaches almost to the sky. Like the Christian paradise, this one place receives all the bounty of Nature, is forever lovely in its eternal spring, and is far removed from our world. The palace of Nature, luminous with its gold and jewels, resembles those mysterious, dreamlike palaces and temples observed by those few chance visitors to the terrestrial paradise. Alain devoted his rhetoric to describing not only the plants and birds, but also the sensuous pleasure they afforded: the eyes are "consumed" and the ears "intoxicated" by the profusion of Nature. Another allegorical mountain paradise, the Mount of Ambition in Jean de Hauteville's twelfth-century *Architrenius*, soars almost to the stars, far above the Christian paradise that medieval commentators described as reaching to the sphere of the moon. Rushing down from this height is a great river, shining with gold and jewels.[24]

Habitually the courtly lovers of the troubadours and of poets like Guillaume de Machaut and Jean Froissart languish in gardens that are compared with or evoke the garden in Eden. In Guillaume de Lorris's portion of the *Roman de la Rose*, the Garden of the Rose is associated in various ways with the Christian paradise; this lost paradise also lies behind the description of the Good Pasture and the golden age in Jean de Meun's segment of the poem. The Dreamer's dream is ultimately the age-old dream of paradise. When the Dreamer was in the Garden of the Rose, he thought he was in the earthly paradise, for indeed, the garden seemed heavenly. He suggests that it is even better to be in the Garden of the Rose than in the Garden in Eden. This supreme garden of love, the realm of Lord Mirth, contains many elements often found in descriptions of the Christian paradise, but there are fundamental differences. Forbidding looking from the outside, this garden is surrounded by a wall with but a single gate. Within there is what appears to be the ideal landscape and the ideal life — exotic groves, clear streams, ravishing birdsong, and a life of ease and pleasure. The Dreamer sees the reflection of the rosebush which, as Patch has said, "by considerable forcing of correspondences may be taken as the substitute in this Paradise for the Tree of Life." Like Adam and Eve, Lord Mirth and Dame Beauty are unique, surpassing in appearance all those of the outside world. But this is the garden of Lord Mirth, not the garden of God. It is artificial, rather than natural, and its life is extravagant, rather than innocent. As a garden of vanity as well as a garden of love, it anticipates the enchanted gardens of the Renaissance and the gardens of Eden which become gardens of Eve; the fountain of Narcissus reminds one of the implied comparison of Eve and Narcissus in *Paradise Lost* (IV, 456–65). The Garden of the Rose is a false paradise. It is explicitly dismissed as a "fable" by Jean de Meun in his description of the true celestial paradise — fields of bliss where the righteous dwell with the

Lamb. This paradise is compared to Adam's Eden and to the golden age, a time when there were no seasons, no plow, no sweat of the brow, and no private property, a time that endured until Jupiter succeeded Saturn and ordained pleasure as the law of men.[25]

Although most of the medieval poems describing the Edenic garden are similar to earlier accounts and to each other, some of them, particularly the vernacular versions, possess new details and attitudes. Many of these poems transmit the image of the mountaintop paradise. Conventional Latin accounts occur in such twelfth-century works as the *De Mundi Universitate* of Bernardus Silvestris and the *Pantheon* of Godfrey of Viterbo. Alexander Neckham, a thirteenth-century grammarian and poet, writing in his *De Laudibus Divinae Sapientiae* of the divine wisdom in creation, pictured a paradise mountain whose peak almost touched the sphere of the moon. This paradise has escaped the floods of Noah and Deucalion, and is free from sterility and inclemency. In its Virgilian landscape Enoch and Elijah dwell forever in peace.[26]

In Federico Frezzi's *Quadriregio,* a thirteenth-century vernacular poem, the illustration of paradise is embroidered with various fantastic details which the Renaissance would ridicule and reject. Here one finds the tree of life with its roots in heaven and its branches on earth, the tree of knowledge stripped of its branches, and the grove where Adam concealed himself. Paradise itself is on a plateau so high that the ninth heaven and the Primum Mobile affect its pure atmosphere.[27]

Certain thirteenth-century vernacular descriptions of the Edenic paradise, like *L'Image du Monde* of Gautier de Metz and the *Weltkronik* of Rudolf von Ems, as well as other poems, contain many traditional elements. Giamatti, however, has noted two new, closely related characteristics: first, there is "the impression that the earthly paradise is absolutely unobtainable, that it is irrevocably lost," and then, because it is so remote, "it has more than ever become a landscape of the mind, a place in the topography of the soul." Divorced from the tradition of the

Church and Latin literature, these popular works express a sense of despair, longing, and spiritual alienation. Another indication of this mood is the presence of various animals which are not a part of the traditional poetic accounts of paradise; many of these are monsters, "phantoms of the popular imagination."[28]

Dante and the Earthly Paradise

The views of both Church doctors and medieval storytellers are reflected in Dante's description of the earthly paradise in the final seven cantos of the *Purgatorio*. This is the greatest of the medieval visions of paradise, as Milton's is the greatest of the Renaissance.[29] Dante's terrestrial paradise is atop the Mount of Purgatory on an isle in the sea of the southern hemisphere, directly opposite Jerusalem. The sea and the mount were formed when the soil fled from Satan, plunging from heaven (*Inf.* xxxiv). The Mount of Purgatory is first seen through the eyes of Ulysses, who recollects that after sailing for five cycles of the moon he sighted the mount, the loftiest he had ever seen, rising dimly from the sea in the distance. The ship was lost in a whirlwind when he tried to approach (*Inf.*, xxvi). Later Adam, "the first living soul," recalls the "mount high above the waters" (*Par.*, xxvi). In placing paradise on the other side of the world, Dante was upholding the tradition of Moses Bar Cephas, and in envisioning it on an island he was reflecting the views expressed in Peter Lombard (*Sent.*, bk. ii, dist. 17), the St. Brendan legend, and elsewhere.

After ascending the Mount of Purgatory, Dante passes through the purgatorial flames and regains the lost paradise and the lost innocence of Adam. In his ascent toward the celestial paradise, Dante stands on the ground lost by Adam and Eve:

Fain now to search within and round about the divine forest dense and living, which was tempering the new day to my eyes, without longer waiting I left the bank, taking the level ground very slowly, over the soil which on every side breathed fragrance. A sweet breeze that had no variation in itself smote me on the brow, not with heavier stroke than a soft wind; at which the branches, readily trembling, one and all were bending toward the quarter where the holy mountain casts its first shadow; yet not so swayed from their uprightness, that the little birds among the tops had to leave the practice of their every art; but, singing with full joy, they received the early breezes, which were keeping a burden to their rhymes, such as gathers from bough to bough through the pine forest on the shore of Chiassi, when Aeolus lets forth the Sirocco.[30]

Walking slowly through the "ancient wood" of the earthly paradise, Dante is barred by the dark but miraculously pure waters of the Lethe, which girds paradise on the left and then plunges down the mount and flows underground. Seized with wonder, he gazes across the narrow stream to see Matelda singing and gathering flowers of many colors. Matelda explains to him that the constant breeze in the pure air comes from the prime revolution of the universe. This mild wind causes the woods to resound and carries the "virtues" of the plants of paradise to various regions of the earth. Even in the earthly paradise, Dante weeps at the disappearance of Virgil, but is transported by the appearance of Beatrice. To him is revealed a heavenly pageant, which leads him to the tree of good and evil, now shorn of its leaves, and to the inexhaustible spring from which flow both the Lethe and Eunoe, whose waters make the penitent forget all sin but remember all good. When he has partaken of both streams, Dante is ready to leave the terrestrial paradise, renewed, pure, and "disposed to mount unto the stars."[31]

Dante's high Eden is of course preeminently the paradise within, enjoyed by our first parents during about six hours of original righteousness and by souls purified and redeemed. Dante departed from both tradition and Aquinas in placing the original earthly paradise on the soul's road from purgatory to the celestial paradise. Speaking to Dante of the intended life of "this place chosen for human nature as its nest," Matelda explains that "the supreme Good, which Itself alone is pleasing to Itself, made man good, and for good, and gave to him this place as earnest of eternal peace." Dante wonders how Eve, "where the earth and heaven were obedient," could not have remained devout, so that he might "have tasted those ineffable delights before, and for a longer time." But he understands these delights to be "the first fruits of the eternal pleasure," a foretaste of the celestial paradise. Indeed, Dante stated in the *De Monarchia* that man's first ultimate goal "is happiness in this life, which consists in the exercise of his own powers and is typified by the earthly paradise," and the second is the happiness of eternal life, as typified by the celestial paradise.[32]

A redeemed soul in Dante's earthly paradise is perhaps similar to Adam withstanding the test of obedience. Dante's will is in harmony with the divine will just as all his faculties are in harmony with one another; this reflects the traditional conception of the human will and reason in the state of innocence. Upon entering the terrestrial paradise, Virgil, who has been sent to Dante by the weeping eyes of Beatrice, tells Dante, "Free, upright, and sound is thine own will, and it would be wrong not to act according to its choice; wherefore thee over thyself I crown and mitre." He may sit in contemplation or wander through a pathless paradise at will. In paradise the soul possesses knowledge through reason, but may acquire revelation through faith. Human reason and knowledge, aided by divine grace and ecclesiastical authority, can guide the soul through Purgatory to the supreme happiness of the Adamic paradise.[33]

Milton made numerous references to the *Commedia* at a time when Dante's reputation was at a low ebb, even in Italy, and it is difficult to believe that Milton did not think of Dante when he created his own earthly paradise — recognizably on the same sacred ground but quite differently cultivated. There are similarities, however, due to both the well-established tradition and the convictions of the two poets. Upon entering the paradise of either poet, one is enraptured by the mingling of soft breezes, fragrance, and the singing of birds. The "unpierc'd shade" that "Imbrownd the noontide Bowers" in Milton suggests the grove in which the Lethe "moves along dusky under the perpetual shadow, which never lets the sun or moon shine there." In both, there is the varied flower-strewn classical landscape of eternal spring. Nature flourishes as nowhere else: For Milton, Nature in her prime pours forth a profusion tending to wildness, while for Dante paradise both nourishes plants unknown anywhere else and sends forth seedlike "virtues" to the rest of the world. Also in the work of both poets the classical paradises and the Edenic paradise are synthesized into new artistic wholes. According to Milton, Eden offers "Hesperian fables true" and Eve is more lovely than nymph or goddess; and Matelda tells Dante that "those who in old time sang of the Golden Age, and of its happy state, perchance, upon Parnassus, dreamed of this place." The Lethe and Eunoe are the life of Dante's paradise. Matelda moves along the Lethe "like the Nymphs who were wont to go solitary through the sylvan shades," and her eyes at times shine like those of Venus. In both poems, paradise is associated with Proserpina and the loss of eternal spring.[34] In both, the terrestrial paradise provides a glimpse into the nature of the celestial one. Man is in close relationship to God: Milton's Adam is informed by Raphael and Dante is enlightened by Matelda, Beatrice, and the Heavenly Pageant. For Milton and Dante, man is in harmony with God and nature, serves with love, and is free to govern himself by his reason.

Because the paradises of Milton and Dante seem to belong to different worlds, the similarities they bear are almost surprising. One can understand Dorothy Sayers's "impression — that whenever Milton feels Dante's influence he deliberately goes out of his way to repudiate it." [35] The differences in talent, faith, and purpose and the great cultural distance between the fourteenth and seventeenth centuries probably account for the distinctive power of these two images of paradise. In Milton one is overwhelmed by magnificence, while in Dante one is appreciative of the clarity of symbolic detail. More important, the direction of the spiritual movement in each alters the entire picture: Milton's Adam and Eve are on the brink of the Fall; Dante has ascended the Mount of Purgatory and is approaching the celestial paradise. Milton's Paradise is a prelude to earth; Dante's is a prelude to the beatific vision. Milton's Paradise is a field of temptation and trial; Dante's is the home of constancy, purity, and tranquillity. Eve and Satan threaten Milton's Paradise from within, but Matelda and Beatrice suggest the close link of Dante's terrestrial paradise to the celestial one. Most important, these two accounts of paradise belong to different worlds of the imagination. Milton's vision was of a time and place that had been lost, while Dante's vision was of the timeless life of the soul. Milton sought to re-create the historical paradise, while Dante followed the pattern of the imaginary visit to an existing paradise. Finally, Milton would have felt that his work was true in a sense that Dante's was not, for he was faithfully following the divinely inspired Scriptural account of God's first dealings with man in the beginning of the earth and of human society.

5

THE HISTORICAL PARADISE
OF THE RENAISSANCE

THE PARADISE of legend, vision, or even theology was not enough for the men of the Renaissance. A firm, reasonable, and enlightened belief in the historical paradise seemed the necessary foundation for Christianity itself. Faced with divisions within the Church, an increased rationalism in exegesis and in textual criticism, and expanding geographical exploration, both commentators and poets of the Renaissance sought the certainty of a natural paradise with a definite position in human history and a precise geographical location. Depending upon reason, observable evidence, and a literal interpretation of Scripture, they attempted to reconstruct man's beginnings in accordance with contemporary knowledge and historical method. The first steps were to demonstrate that man and the earth had been created by God and to establish an exact and consistent chronology beginning with the Creation, the life in paradise, and the Fall. To make vivid and credible man's creation and earliest history was the task to which Milton and the other poets of "the celestial cycle" dedicated themselves.

Orthodox Christianity had always accepted the truth of the paradise story, but in the sixteenth and seventeenth centuries the exegetes, historians, geographers, and poets utilized the new tools of a growing rationalism to investigate the historical interpretations of Genesis. This modern rationalism raised questions that seemed to threaten Christianity itself, but it also supplied elaborate answers to them. Under the influence of the linguistic, literal exegesis of Rashi, Nicholas of Lyra, and others, both Catholic and Protestant writers began to emphasize exactness, consistency, historical evidence, and credibility, and to devote their scholarly attention to the establishment of the biblical text and its exact literal meaning. They denounced allegory and such mystical interpretations as those of Sebastian Franck, though Erasmus, Luther, and others were willing to retain some symbolic interpretation. But the way was opened to increasing doubt and controversy about the authenticity of the text, the dating and inspiration of the Hebrew vowel points, seeming inconsistencies or absurdities in the biblical narrative, and even the Mosaic authorship of the entire Pentateuch.

Writers faced the necessity of harmonizing a literal interpretation with their belief in the divine inspiration of Scripture. The theory that Moses had "accommodated" the biblical text to the limited understanding of the primitive Hebrews was employed increasingly to reconcile Scripture with Renaissance reason and knowledge. Moreover, commentators did not hold that the Bible was uniformly inspired; Luther, for example, thought that error was possible in details. Many regarded Scripture as the embodiment of the Word of God which, though uniquely delivered in the past, was to be rediscovered by every generation through the continued inspiration of the Holy Spirit. The spiritual meaning, however, as Erasmus said, was to be interpreted in close relation to the grammatical and literal meaning.[1] Accepting the literal meaning of Genesis as inspired truth, both Renaissance commentary and *Paradise Lost* assumed the special powers of God, angel, and devil, but gave a realistic, rational account of paradise, the commandment concerning the tree of knowledge, Adam's work and his naming of the creatures, Eve's creation, and the speaking serpent.

While commentators labored over exhaustive discussions of the fine points of original righteousness, Milton and other poets

90

presented Adam and Eve and paradise itself. The lost paradise could exist only in literary re-creation: *Paradise Lost* was to be a vital, sensuous representation of the orthodox Renaissance belief about the Edenic paradise, a credible reenactment of supremely important historical events. The special creation of man and the very beginnings of time and history were to take on form and substance through the poet's vision.

The Writers and the Works

Who wrote about paradise? Biblical commentators — Catholic and Protestant, Anglican and Puritan — theologians, historians, geographers, authors of "mirror" literature, popular travel writers, political writers, philosophers, mystics, and poets. To the problems of paradise they sometimes devoted entire works, at other times only brief references; and, no doubt, many of the words appearing in print were heard in hundreds of pulpits. Writers of different nationalities, of widely divergent religious and political beliefs, shared many common assumptions about the importance of the first chapters of Genesis, though they often disagreed violently about their meaning, giving rise to some of the most heated controversies of the day. Milton knew the works or reputation of a large number of these writers, some of whom were historically important, and others obscure. Most of these writers' works have not been published since the seventeenth century, but their habits of thought and their frequently strong emotions live forever in their works.

The most ponderous discussions of paradise were found in the great folio Latin commentaries on Genesis. Arnold Williams, in his study of these Renaissance commentaries, has noted thirty-five Latin and six English commentaries on Genesis alone, and thirteen on the Pentateuch, not to mention those on the whole of Scripture. As Williams has said, Genesis meant to the commentators and their readers not only a single book of the Bible, but all of the "Genesis material" — the rabbinical lore, digests of previous commentary, pseudo science, and classical allusion that had accrued over two thousand years. The commentators usually

91

proceeded by disputation and question, examining such questions as these: What was the nature of paradise? Where was it? Why had it not been discovered? Did the tree of life give immortality? and Why was the tree of knowledge so called?[2]

Undoubtedly the best known of the commentators was the Spanish Jesuit Benedictus Pererius, a lecturer on rhetoric and on Scripture at the Collegium Romanum. His *Commentariorum et Disputationum in Genesin* appeared first in four separate tomes in the 1590s, and then in five complete editions in the seventeenth century. Other well-known Catholic commentaries were the *Commentarii in Quinque Mosaicos Libros* of Thomas Cardinal Cajetan, an early sixteenth-century Roman churchman and papal legate, and the *Commentaria in Pentateuchum Moysis* of Cornelius a Lapide, a Dutch or Flemish Jesuit who taught at Louvain and Rome in the early seventeenth century. His commentary had appeared in eleven editions before the publication of *Paradise Lost*. Protestants as well as Catholics depended heavily on such Catholic commentaries, especially that of Pererius. Milton was an exception among Protestants in never mentioning Catholic commentaries, but Williams claims that Milton's references to marriage and some other subjects indicate that he had dipped into the Catholic commentators.[3]

Three Protestant commentaries on Genesis that were well known and referred to by Milton were the *Commentarie of John Calvin, vpon the First Booke of Moses* (as translated by Thomas Tymme [1578]), *In Genesin Mosis Commentarius* (1609, 1614, 1716) of the German Calvinist David Pareus, a pupil of the commentator Hieronymus Zanchius, and the *Exercitationes* of Andraeus Rivetus, a French Huguenot who taught at Leyden, and was the last of the Renaissance commentators. Milton possibly knew Luther's commentary on Genesis, and did refer to some of his other works. Giovanni Diodati's *Pious and Learned Annotations upon the Holy Bible* appeared in three English editions in the seventeenth century. Milton knew Diodati, a most renowned Calvinist writer, who was the uncle of his friend Charles Diodati; Milton visited him daily in Geneva for a time in 1639, and referred to his works. Milton and most Protestant writers knew the theological works of Heinrich Bullinger, Zacharias Ursinus, and Caspar Olevianus, three architects of the Protestant conception of the protevangelium and the covenant of grace, as manifested to Adam in paradise. Harris F. Fletcher has said that Milton "was saturated" with Ursinus and with the Heidelberg Catechism as modified by Ursinus and Olevianus.[4] Another highly respected Protestant writer was Franciscus Junius, known for his exegesis and theological discussion, and his translation and annotation in the Tremellius-Junius Bible, the favorite Latin text of Milton and most Protestants.

English works dealing with the first chapters of Genesis took many forms. They were less comprehensive than the Latin commentaries and often written from a special perspective. Bishop Lancelot Andrewes, Bishop Joseph Hall, and Archbishop James Ussher, three defenders of the Established Church, whose views Milton reasoned against in his antiprelatical tracts, wrote about various aspects of man's beginnings in paradise. Milton composed an early Latin poem on the death of Andrewes, a celebrated preacher remembered for his guidance in the work on the King James Version of the Bible. A series of Andrewes's lectures on the first four chapters of Genesis, published posthumously in his *Apospasmatia Sacra*, were apparently delivered at St. Paul's in the 1590s and "taken by ear from [his] voluble tongue." Hall wrote of Adam in his *Contemplations*, and Ussher spoke of man's beginnings in his noted works on chronology and on divinity. Alexander Ross, Scottish-born schoolmaster and one of Charles I's chaplains, considered paradise in his *Exposition of the Fourteene First Chapters of Genesis* (1626) and his *Pansebeia: Or a View of All Religions in the World,* which was published in 1653 and went through numerous editions. Milton almost certainly used the latter study (which incidentally mentioned his divorce tracts) in his catalogue of the pagan deities in *Paradise Lost*.[5] Among the works of the eminent Hebrew scholar John Lightfoot, who left Christ's College about a year before Milton entered, were comments on Genesis — ". . . sometimes Profitable, and always Harmlesse."

Some of the most influential early Puritan leaders, such as Thomas Cartwright, John Preston, William Perkins, Richard Sibbes, and William Ames, wrote about the events in paradise, particularly God's covenants with man. The books of Hall, Preston, Perkins, and Sibbes were in use at Cambridge; and Milton probably also heard Preston and Sibbes deliver the "town sermons" there. In beginning work on *The Christian Doctrine*, Milton studied the *Medulla Theologiae* of Ames.[6] Sir Henry Vane, four years Milton's junior, developed his personal ideas about the state of innocence in *The Retired Mans Meditations*. Milton knew Vane as a member of the Council of State to which he was an assistant and addressed a sonnet to him. Other Puritans also wrote about the first chapters of Genesis; among the most important of these was the Separatist leader Henry Ainsworth, whose historical and typological interpretation of paradise appeared in his *Annotations* on Genesis. Although it is doubtful if Milton read all the Puritans' discussions of paradise, he and their readers could have known them as public figures. When Milton wrote *Areopagitica*, the Puritans John White and George Walker were members of the Westminster Assembly and Edward Leigh was a member of Parliament. White, the "Dorchester Patriarch," was instrumental in founding the Massachusetts Company, and had expounded the Bible chapter by chapter once through and half through again. No doubt he had twice preached on the substance of his *Commentary on the Three First Chapters of the First Book of Moses Called Genesis*. Walker, who wrote *The Creation*, was a pastor in Watling Street for thirty-seven years; he had been imprisoned in 1638 because of his charges against Archbishop Laud, and his case had been taken up in Parliament. Leigh, a colonel in the Parliamentary Army and a student of law, history, and divinity, assembled a useful compilation of the Hebrew and Greek words in Scripture and wrote two eclectic treatises in divinity.

Historians, authors of "mirror" literature, geographers, and travel writers usually dealt with man's beginnings and paradise in their disparate writings. Jean Bodin's *Method for the Easy Comprehension of History*, which postulated that history was fundamentally progress rather than deterioration, was well known in England. Milton makes frequent references to Bodin and owned a copy of his controversial *Heptaplomeres*, which included a skeptical discussion of the story of Adam and Eve. Enjoying even a wider reputation, of course, was Sir Walter Ralegh's popular *History of the World*, with its providential interpretation of history beginning with "Of Mans Estate in His First Creation" and "Of the Place of Paradise." Ralegh's *History* was familiar ground to Milton and has been considered an influence on *Paradise Lost*. Another work, read at Cambridge and thought to be an influence on Milton, was the *Omnium Gentium Mores* (English translation, 1611) of Johann Boemus, who might be called an early sociologist. Well-known volumes treating man's beginnings in connection with the controversy about the decay of nature included Louis LeRoy's *De la vicissitude ou variété des choses de l'univers* and George Hakewill's *Apologie*, both of which professed a belief in the possibility for progress, and the encyclopedic "mirror" works, Lambert Daneau's *The Wonderful Woorkmanship of the World* and John Swan's *Speculum Mundi*, which emphasized the corruption of the world through man's sin. Milton's Cambridge exercise *Naturam non pati senium* indicates that he had a knowledge of the controversy and that he almost certainly had read Hakewill. If he had ever looked into the books of Daneau and Swan, he did not have occasion to mention them. Nathanael Carpenter's *Geography Delineated Forth* (1625), the first English work on theoretical geography, blended Aristotle and Ptolemy with Gilbert and Mercator, but also considered the world to be in its old age. Milton, like many other Englishmen, knew Gerhardus Mercator and Abraham Ortelius and the popular little *Microcosmos* of Peter Heylyn, who was a royalist pamphleteer and, like Milton, blind in later life. One of the books most loved by Milton and many of his contemporaries was the *Purchas His Pilgrimage* of Samuel Purchas, who had been rector of the Milton family's parish of All Hallows for five months before his death in 1626.[7]

The Renaissance men, particularly in England, brought out separate tracts on paradise, some of which were brief and others more than three hundred pages. John Hopkinson, a teacher of Oriental languages, wrote one of the first of these tracts, entitled *Synopsis Paradisi* (1593), which was devoted to locating paradise in Mesopotamia. The most complete English tract was *A Treatise of Paradise* (1617) by John Salkeld, a former Catholic, a rector in Somerset, and the author of a work on angels. Salkeld, who depended heavily on Pererius, said that his aim was to "show the place, and demonstrate the grace, from which we fell" and to lead men to be grateful for the even greater felicity to which they are exalted through Christ. His tract tells of the size and nature of paradise, the state of work, generation, and knowledge in paradise, and the beauty of the serpent. While Salkeld's treatise was the most complete in England, Agostino Inveges's *Historia Sacra Paradisi Terrestris, et Sanctissimi Innocentiae Status* was the most comprehensive work of this kind in Western Europe. Inveges, a Sicilian priest, discussed the location of paradise, its physical characteristics, the exact time and place of the first parents' actions, and the life they and their descendants would have led if man had not fallen. He explains that he had taken his material from Scripture, councils, the fathers, theologians, expositors, rabbis, annalists, chronologists, and geographers. Another English tract was *A Discourse of the Terrestrial Paradise*, which was published a year before *Paradise Lost*, although the author, Marmaduke Carver, a rector of Harthill in the County of York, said that he had written it many years earlier for his own satisfaction. The main purpose of the discourse was to take issue with Junius and to show that paradise had been located in Armenia. Other treatises on paradise were written by Thomas Malvenda, Carlo Giangolino, and Bishop Huet. Milton would have known of Hopkinson through Ralegh's references to him in his discussion of paradise, but he did not mention any of these other authors.[8] A late seventeenth-century tract on paradise by Henry Hare, Lord Coleraine, quoted from *Paradise Lost* and dealt with the location and spiritual meaning of paradise.

The perspective from which each individual interpreted the first chapters of Genesis reflected in part his own intellectual interests and viewpoints: some focused upon the problems of the Creation; some studied the paradise story to gain insight into contemporary political problems; others discovered an enduring spiritual meaning in the paradise story. Both Machiavelli and Thomas Hobbes were concerned with the problems of Creation and the problem of original sin in relation to man's political institutions. Milton realized that their works called into doubt orthodox views of the Creation, and he acknowledged Hobbes to be a man of great parts, but "did not like him." Marjorie Nicolson has suggested that *Paradise Lost* was a reply to this great antagonist. The French Protestant Isaac de la Peyrère also called into question the biblical account of the Creation. His *Praeadamitae* (1655) maintains that men had existed before Adam, and, although Milton may or may not have been acquainted with La Peyrère's work, his theory was known in European literary circles as early as 1643, and the same idea also had been attributed to Giordano Bruno and Paracelsus. Among the many defenders of an orthodox belief in the Creation was Bartholomew Keckermann, a German reformed theologian and encyclopedic scholar, whose works were in favor at Christ's College and known to Milton. Other works defending an orthodox view were *The Primitive Origination of Mankind Considered and Examined According to the Light of Nature* of the eminent seventeenth-century jurist Sir Matthew Hale, *The Unreasonablenesse of Atheism Made Manifest* (1669) of Sir Charles Wolseley, and the *Origines Sacrae* (1662) of the youthful Edward Stillingfleet, who later became a bishop. Hale argued with lawyerlike skill and caution against the eternity of the world. Milton knew Wolseley as a member of the Council of State, a man with whom Cromwell frequently consulted. A related specialized work on the state of innocence was John Weemse's *Portraiture of the Image of God in Man*, which appeared in three editions between 1627 and 1636. Sister Mary Irma Corcoran has said that this book is "probably the volume of Protestant theology which offers the largest number of parallels to *Paradise Lost*." Milton most likely heard of Weemse, notable for his

Semitic learning, from his tutor Thomas Young, who had been at St. Andrew's when Weemse was there.[9]

Milton's concern with liberty in his political tracts, and even in his divorce tracts, reflects his broad interests and his knowledge of a number of political writers. Milton was familiar with Kecker-mann's treatise on political philosophy, as well as his other works. The Spanish Jesuit Francisco Suarez was known at Cambridge, and Ludovico Molina and Milton grappled with the same problems. Milton also was acquainted with the work of the prominent British political writers of the middle of the seventeenth century. In his divorce tracts, Milton adapted the political principles of the Scottish Presbyterian Samuel Rutherford and of the English Puritan John Goodwin, whose conception of the covenant was similar to Milton's. Underlying his ideas in *The Tenure of Kings and Magistrates* are arguments like those developed in the *Lex, Rex* of Rutherford and the *Jus Populi* of Henry Parker, a champion of contractual government. Milton also very possibly knew *The Power of the Crown in Scotland* of the Scottish humanist George Buchanan, to whom he has a number of references, and he was aware of the thought of the Levellers, who based their demands for political liberty upon both Genesis and Magna Carta. When the Leveller leader John Lilburne was committed to prison before the Council in 1649, Milton may have been present, and he was asked to reply to a pamphlet by Lilburne. He did not, however, perhaps because he was in sympathy with their ideas, if not their methods. Milton was also acquainted with the work of royalist writers whom he was challenging. There are apparent allusions in the *Tenure* to tracts by Henry Hammond and John Gauden, both Anglican clergymen and royalist apologists, and there are direct references to Hammond in the *First Defence*. Milton almost certainly knew the arguments of the *Sacro-Sancta Regum Majestas* of John Maxwell, a Scottish prelate famed for his learning, if only through Rutherford's reply. Maxwell traced kingship to Adam, but by far the most important writer to ground monarchy in Adam's God-given prerogatives was Sir Robert Filmer, although his *Patriarcha* was known only in manuscript un-

til after the Restoration. Nevertheless, in the period preceding
the execution of Charles, when Milton was mainly concerned
with conflicting political theory, Filmer published several tracts
that stated his basic ideas, which challenged Milton's essential
ideas. Milton also surely knew of Filmer's *Observations on the
Original of Government* (1652), which criticized the concepts of
the *Tenure* and the *First Defence*.[10]

Paradise was also taken into the province of philosophy and
science, as well as into the realm of the spirit. Probably Milton
had known Francis Bacon's *Advancement of Learning* since Cambridge and had consulted the work of Bishop John Wilkins.
Various Protestant groups gave a primarily spiritual and symbolic account of the first chapters of Genesis. The influence of
the German mysticism of Jakob Böhme and Sebastian Franck was
felt in seventeenth-century England and apparently touched Milton. Henry More, a leading member of the Cambridge Platonists,
followed Philo's allegorical interpretation of paradise in his *Conjectura Cabbalistica* (1654). Milton was a student with More at
Christ's College, and shared with him various common conceptions and antagonists. More's "conjectural cabbala" represented
an intellectual strain found in much seventeenth-century literature, including *Paradise Lost*.[11] Gerrard Winstanley, leader of
the Digger movement, mixed social and economic thought with
his symbolic interpretation of Genesis. Another kind of commentator on paradise was John Gregory, an Oxford orientalist,
whose works, full of curious lore and occult speculation, appeared
in four posthumous editions in the seventeenth century; some of
his observations on Genesis were translated into Latin and in-
serted in the *Critici Sacri* (1660).

The location of paradise was given more consistent attention
than any other question concerning it. Although no student of
Genesis could have known all the attempts to locate paradise,
no reader of any comment on Genesis could have escaped encountering the problem. Discussions of the location of paradise
occurred not only in the commentaries and separate tracts, but
in a variety of other works, such as those purporting to deal with

the origins of Antwerp, the rivers of the world, rhetoric, and Virgil's *Georgics*. Although only some of these accounts attracted large audiences, most of them were both serious and scholarly in their quest for paradise amidst conflicting arguments.

The subject of *Paradise Lost* was by no means an unusual one for a literary composition. During the sixteenth and seventeenth centuries there appeared at least 150 literary works treating aspects of "the celestial cycle," the story of the Creation and Fall and related events.[12] These testify to both the poetic appeal and the historical importance of paradise in this age. These imaginative works not only generally transcended the disputes of the prose commentators, but they also took on added significance because the authors and their readers were familiar with the complex problems of the nature, meaning, and implications of man's beginnings in the biblical paradise — problems that might lurk just behind the poetry.

A number of these works, some of which Milton knew, dealt directly with the Edenic garden and the life of innocence. Joshua Sylvester's *Du Bartas His Divine Weekes and Workes,* a favorite reading of the youthful Milton, was one of the most popular of these. This long hexameral poem, appearing in its first complete edition in 1608, was only one among scores of works derived from the *Semaines* of Guillaume Saluste, Seigneur du Bartas. Sylvester contributed many details to Milton's poetry. Another work that Milton probably had read was the youthful *Adamus Exul* (1601) of the Dutch scholar Hugo Grotius, whom Milton visited in 1638. Watson Kirkconnell has concluded that "internal evidence is convincing" in showing the influence of this Latin play on *Paradise Lost*. Milton may have known *L'Adamo* (1613) of Giambattista Andreini, actor, man of letters, and prolific playwright, but the play exerted no perceptible impact on *Paradise Lost*. Thomas Peyton's *Glasse of Time in the First Age* (1620), a doggerel "epic" in heroic couplets with long digressions on history and theology, would not have appealed to Milton. It is "at least plausible" that Milton had met Giavanno Francesco Loredano, founder of the most important literary academy in Venice, when

Milton spent a month there in 1638. At this time Loredano may have been writing his *L'Adamo* (1640), a prose romance which appeared in numerous Italian editions and was translated into English as *The Life of Adam* (1659). Milton most likely was not familiar with Troilo Lancetta's *La scena tragica d'Adamo ed Eva* (1644), a prose drama with rationalistic symbolism, Serafino della Salandra's *Adamo Caduto* (1647), part poetic tragedy and part morality play, or Samuel Pordage's *Mundorum Explicatio* (1661), a discursive English poem viewing the history of the world from an "external, internal, and eternal" perspective. Apart from Milton, the greatest poet of the Renaissance "celestial cycle" was Joost van den Vondel, a Dutch Catholic and the author of thirty poetic tragedies. Milton knew Dutch, and a number of close parallels suggest that he had a knowledge of Vondel's *Lucifer*, which encountered a storm of Calvinist protest when it was performed in Amsterdam in 1654. However, whether Milton was in any way indebted to Vondel's *Adam in Ballingschap*, which itself owed much to the *Adamus Exul* of Grotius, is doubtful.[13]

Creation

If one were to believe in the orthodox account of Adam and Eve in the garden, then one had to feel positive about the divine creation of the world and the single and special creation of man. Throughout the seventeenth century, many orthodox believers were troubled by Aristotle's idea of the eternity of the world, Lucretian atomism, and the new views of Descartes, Gassendi, and Hobbes. Not yet ready simply to dismiss these unacceptable classical concepts of creation, orthodox writers struggled to refute them by a classical logic which was rapidly becoming antiquated.

Aristotle and the Hebraic-Christian tradition were in direct opposition regarding the nature and origin of matter and man. The idea of the earth's eternity, developed by Ocellus Lucanus and Aristotle, had been defended at length by Proclus, a sixth-century Athenian Neoplatonist, Simplicius, Iamblichus, and others. Orthodox Christians held that God had created the world out of nothing as a miracle, thus manifesting the divine providence that was to shape human history. But Genesis, sometimes considered as presenting a dualistic view of God and matter, was not explicit about the Creation *ex nihilo*. In controversies about the nature of man and the world, Marcion and the Manichaeans expressed belief in a preexisting matter not created by God, yet almost all the fathers insisted that God had created the matter from which the world was formed. During the patristic period, the Aristotelian doctrine of the earth's eternity was opposed in *Quaestiones et Responsiones ad Graecos*, attributed to Justin Martyr, and in the works of Zacharias Mitytenensis and John Philoponus, which were directed against Proclus. In the thirteenth century this eternalism was revived in a confused blend of Proclus and Averroes, most notably by Siger of Brabant, who found a creation from nothing contradictory, although he believed in an eternal yet created world.[14]

Christians of the sixteenth and seventeenth centuries had difficulty in laying this Aristotelian ghost. Though almost no one believed in the earth's eternity as a practical reality, many strove to disprove it as a disturbing philosophical possibility that undermined Christian belief. Fashionable intellectuals and earnest philosophers debating the problem disputed about when time began and whether Aristotle's theory of privation could explain how decay was potential in an eternal world. Luther came immediately to the crux of the problem when he said that Aristotle "refuses to listen to anyone speaking about a first and a last man." Asserting that a blundering human reason could soar no higher than to the conclusion that the earth was from all eternity, Luther warned that "from this error there follows the dangerous error that the human soul must be mortal, for human speculation is incapable of conceiving of many infinite substances." Such popular works as Lambert Daneau's *The Wonderfull Woorkmanship of the World* and John Swan's *Speculum Mundi* attacked the theory. Daneau argued that it was "certain, that heauen began sometyme to mooue, from some one prefixed poincte and part of the circumference." Swan declared that Aristotle had maintained the world's eternity as a logical thesis, but not necessarily as truth. He noted the need for a beginning in history, and assured readers that there was no memory of any generation before those of Genesis despite the stories of the Egyptians and Scythians.[15]

One of the most complete Renaissance examinations of the problem of the world's eternity was Bodin's study of history. "If by the authority of philosophers and the force of reasoning," he said, "it could be clearly understood that the world was not ever-lasting, but founded by immortal God at a precise moment of time, we shall put greater trust in sacred history." He charged that this dangerous theory was held by such contemporaries as Abravanel, a Portuguese Jewish scholar, Sebastian Fox-Marcillo, a Spanish philosopher attempting to reconcile Plato and Aris-totle, and Cardinal Bessarion, the Greek Orthodox churchman who, by bringing Greek letters to Italy, helped revive the study of Greek philosophy during the Renaissance.

Nevertheless Bodin directed the brunt of his attack against Proclus, refuting such oft-disputed propositions as these: God could make the world everlasting and wished to do so, for only an ill-natured person hesitates to do good; to be transported from a state of quietude to one of activity indicates a change foreign to the constancy of divine nature; and, if the world is not de-clining, it did not have a beginning.[16] Bodin well illustrates the difficulty the Renaissance mind encountered in attempting to free itself from the patterns of the past.

In England in the seventeenth century, various writers still felt impelled to defend Genesis against the eternalist doctrine. Bishop Edward Stillingfleet in his *Origines Sacrae* (1662) accused Proclus and others of upholding the doctrine of the world's eter-nity in order to overthrow Christianity. The eminent man of law Sir Matthew Hale, in a book on human origins that he claimed was written some years before publication, summed up the atti-tudes of many. Admitting that his study might "seem a laborious Work to little purpose" since most Christians believe in creation, he said that most did not have "any serious deep conviction of the truth" based upon reason and natural evidence. According to Hale, "Many Christians in Name and Profession" think it below them to have faith in divine inspiration unless it can be supported by reason. Granting that the fact of creation could not be known with infallible certainty, he argued against the concepts of infinite time and infinite space and pointed out that the infinite population consonant with eternity was both lacking and indeed impossible. Sir Charles Wolseley, in demonstrating the "unreasonableness" of eternalism and of other doctrines which he felt led to atheism, admonished his readers: "We skirmish not like other ages to *retail single truths*; but the *whole* of *Religion* lies at stake with us!" He touched the nerve center of the controversy by focusing his argument on the necessity of a first man. Man begets man, "but where," he demanded, "is the first man, to beget, that was not begotten, nor brought forth in the common way of Generation?" It is self-contradictory to say he caused himself; therefore he must have been created by God. Similarly, the world, with its uneven generation and corruption, is dependent upon God and was created by God. Bishop John Wilkins also upheld the doctrine of the Creation, contending in his posthumous work on natural religion that the world's beginning was more credible than its eternity. As proof of this he cited the uninhabited areas of the earth, the lack of evidence of earlier people, and our knowledge of the rise of arts and sciences, even to the point of knowing inventors' names. Like Wolseley and Wilkins, Thomas Burnet attacked the Aristotelian concept of eternalism. In *The Sacred Theory of the Earth* (1684), he asserted that "this whole Book is one continued Argument against that Opinion" of Aristotle, and it shows the earth in its early and present forms to be transient and temporary.[17]

Genesis seemed threatened not only by Aristotle, but by Lucretian atomism and by all theories that postulated a fortuitous, spontaneous, or multiple generation of men. Although Christians accepted the classical tradition of the golden age as confirming their belief in paradise and in the expulsion, they rejected this other classical tradition, developed by Critias, Democritus, Epicurus, Lucretius, and Horace, which called into doubt God's single and special creation of man and which pictured human history as a rise from savagery rather than as a fall from felicity. In the world of the atomists, there could be no Adam.

Some Renaissance authors did not explicitly deny man's beginning in the biblical garden, yet they ignored this idea or relegated it to an irrelevant and unhistorical past and emphasized his rise from brutishness instead. The sixteenth-century sociologist Johann Boemus, in his study of the variety of human customs, discussed the theory that heat and moisture brought forth all living things. He explained that men, rising from "the rude simplicitie of the first worlde," finally "so laboured, beautified and perfeighted the earthe" that it seemed to be "the Paradise of pleasure, out of the which, the first paternes of mankinde (Adam and Eue)" were created. In a similar work, Loys Le Roy depicted man in a primitive state gradually developing talents and arts. He did not interpret human history as a retrogressive movement from Eden, but developed at length Plato's fable of the bungling Epimetheus who fashioned men with such lopsided diversity that they gradually perished until Prometheus brought fire. "Au commencement les hommes estoient fort simples et rudes en toutes choses peu different des bestes," he wrote. Machiavelli, influenced by Polybius, held that "in the beginning of the world, when its inhabitants were few, they lived for a time scattered like the beasts" before they gradually drew together, chose strong leaders, and formed governments. Later, Thomas Hobbes gave full development to a comparable picture of a primitive society of brutish men who continually clashed with one another in a "war of all against all" until they eventually were forced to establish governments as protection against their own fear of oppression.[18]

Bodin argued not only against the earth's eternity but against the theory that the earth itself had brought forth men of different races and nations. As examples of this error, he pointed out that Polydore Virgil had said that the Britons were indigenous and that Andreas Althamer, possibly following Tacitus, had stated that the Germans were not descended from any other race. He was confident that this Epicurean idea of men springing from the earth could be refuted by showing that all languages were

105

derived from Hebrew and that Homer and Aeschylus corrobo-
rated Moses. Haughty pride, he asserted, was demonstrated by
those who claimed they were autochthonous or earth-born.[19]

Descartes, often accused of advocating a mechanistic conception of man and the universe, described a supposedly imaginary
creation of a world out of chaos. This creation proceeded gradually according to the divinely established laws of nature, which
were immutable and constant. Descartes further reasoned that
just as God had created the natural law, He had also created
man's rational soul. But, despite his belief in the natural law,
Descartes expressly denied that he was a follower of Democritus.
He did agree with Democritus that sensible bodies arose from
the concourse of corpuscles of various figures, sizes, and motions,
but he criticized Democritus for not having shown how all things
arose only from this concourse of corpuscles.[20]

Epicurus, previously neglected by Englishmen, enjoyed a fashionable popularity after 1650, although atomistic conceptions of
generation were attacked in England throughout the century. According to Stillingfleet, "that which makes most noise in the world
is the atomical or Epicurean hypothesis." Criticizing both Descartes and Gassendi for holding that the universe had originated
from mechanical laws of matter and motion, he said that the
formation of mankind had "most shamefully puzzled" the atomists; he referred to Harvey's theory of the blood's circulation as
an argument for a Creator, and commended Henry More for his
discussions of the problem. The geographer Nathanael Carpenter
repeated many of Bodin's comments on different theories of the
origins of nations, and similarly declared that those, like Epicurus,
who "arrogantly boast themselves to be sonnes of the *Earth* . . .
strive to breake in sunder the bonds of society betwixt nations,
which *Gods word* and the Law of Nations binds us to obserue."
He explained that "the first inhabitants of the Earth were planted
in Paradise, and thence translated to the places neare adioyning."
Hale and Wolseley also denounced the ideas of Epicurus, Democritus, Lucretius, and Gassendi. Wolseley wrote that Epicureanism denied the divine providence in the world and therefore

106

denied God. In his "Atheists Catechism," he represented the atheist as telling his catechizer that the world was from "a casual hit of Atoms one against the another . . . as they were eternally dancing about in an infinite space." [21]

Most of those who disputed the Aristotelian and Lucretian conceptions of the world's beginnings wished to use evidence, reason, and Scriptural authority to show that all men were descended from Adam and shared the legacy of Eden. They often regarded classical myths as distortions of ancient truth and discovered widespread remains from Adam and Hebraic culture. They found biblical support in Genesis and in St. Paul's statement that God "hath made of one blood all nations of men for to dwell on all the face of the earth" (Acts 17:26), and they saw logic as well as beauty in the descent of all from one.

Calvin and Luther were among those who rejoiced in the fatherhood of Adam and the kinship of all. God could have filled the earth with men, Calvin explained, "but it was his will that we should proceed from one fountain, in order that our desire of mutual concord might be the greater, and that each might the more freely embrace the other as his own flesh." Commenting on the institution of marriage and other inheritances that man had received from paradise, Luther considered it most wonderful that all men should stem from one blood, but added that in disputations about man's origin we learn how awful is original sin, since the human race no longer knows its origin.[22]

The Bishops' Bible illustrates strikingly the origin of all in paradise. For eleven folio pages a genealogical table traces the line of descent from Adam and Eve. This is flanked by charts describing and dating the ages of the world and naming the kings of Israel, Syria, and Egypt and the emperors of Rome contemporary with Adam's descendants. At the top of the genealogical table appears a picture of Adam and Eve with the tree of knowledge and the serpent, and at the end of the table, preceding the text, is a full-page illustration of Adam and Eve and the tree surrounded by animals.[23]

Various kinds of knowledge and reasoning were employed by

107

other writers searching for extra-Scriptural reassurance to better understand man's past. Arguing for the descent of all from Adam and Eve, the French humanist Gulielmo Postellus reasoned that a multiple generation would be inadmissible for it would attribute a superfluous work to God and would be against the order of nature. Bodin found evidence of Adam's life and Hebraic culture everywhere. He traced "Janus" and "Elymaes," a word used by Xenophon for the Persians, to Hebrew words, and identified Cameses with Noah's son Cham and Saturn with Nimrod. Stillingfleet was confident that "the footsteps of Scriptural history" could be found even though the ancient history of the Egyptians, Greeks, and others had been corrupted into fables. He accepted the belief that Adam and Saturn were the same figure as both were called sons of heaven and earth, taught husbandry, and were deposed. He explained that "that power which Saturn had, and was deposed from, doth fitly set out the dominion man had in the golden age of innocency." The Greek deity's name, he said, was derived from *satar*, meaning to hide, just as Adam had hidden from God. Commenting on a passage in Tacitus's description of German beliefs, he wrote: "Either by *Tuisto* Adam is understood, who was formed of earth, and by *Mannus*, Noah; or by Tuisto God may be understood, and by Mannus, Adam." He further asserted that the name of the Cilician city Adana was derived from Adam.[24]

It was necessary not only to prove the existence of Adam, but to show that he was unquestionably the first man and the only man to be specially created by God. Challenging this belief were ancient records that told of ages before Adam, the questionable origin of the inhabitants of America and other recently explored lands, and even puzzling biblical passages. Although these ancient accounts were accepted by some such as Father Martini, a Jesuit missionary to China, the claims to antiquity made by the Egyptians, Chinese, Scythians, and Chaldeans were scornfully rejected by Ralegh, Hale, and Stillingfleet. They suggested that these records had been forged, corrupted, or completely misinterpreted. It was less easy to dismiss the American inhabitants, though there were many arguments to prove that they were descendants of one of Noah's sons. Just as centuries earlier Procopius of Gaza and Cosmas Indicopleustes had postulated that *if* the antipodes existed, there must have been a duplicate Adam and Eve, so at this time some believed in the independent origin of the Indians and other races. Bruno was said to have maintained that Adam was the father only of the Hebrews, and Paracelsus was reported to have believed in a second Adam and Eve, created in America.[25] La Peyrère openly defended a "first creation" ages before Adam. Troublingly enough, the unorthodox writers could also quote Scripture; they not only subjected the biblical account of man's origin to rational scrutiny, but they seized on passages that suggested the existence of men not fathered by Adam.

All of these challenges to orthodoxy appeared most boldly in La Peyrère's development of his pre-Adamite theory, which was also the focal point of his heterodox ideas about the authorship of the Pentateuch and about the transmission of original sin. His *Praeadamitae* and *Systema Theologicum* were published in the Low Countries in 1655 and an anonymous translation appeared in England the following year. Addressing himself to "this clear-sighted age" in his revolt against the accepted interpretation of Genesis, La Peyrère asserted that "to read, that which persuaded by your opinion, or forestalled with superstition, you dare, nor will not understand, is not to read at all." Comparing his discovery of new ages to Columbus's discovery of new worlds, he beseeched God that in this "better age" he would be spared the hatred heaped upon Columbus.[26]

La Peyrère's main thesis, supported by evidence, reason, and Scripture, was that God had created men continuously over the whole earth in the first creation, described in Genesis 1, and then had created Adam as the father of the Hebrews in the second and special creation, described in Genesis 2. La Peyrère extended the historical past to a primitive age long before that of the first parents. He cited not only ancient records, but the time necessary for the development of the astronomy, astrology, and other arts of the Egyptians and Chaldeans. He explained that there were many

nations, unknown to the biblical writers, which had not experienced Noah's Flood. He also sought to refute Grotius's attempt to
show that the American inhabitants were descended from venture-
some Norwegian seafarers who had settled in Iceland. Even the
Bible, he daringly concluded, was cumulative, with many statements copied from earlier records by various authors.[27]

Although La Peyrère used Scripture to authenticate his thesis,
he raised serious doubts about any literal interpretation of much
of Genesis. From Romans 5:12–14 he reasoned that men had lived
first in a state of nature, that the divine law initially had been
given to Adam rather than to Moses, and that after Adam's violation of the law, sin had been imputed spiritually, but not physically, to all other men before and after Adam. He also asked embarrassing questions. He wondered who had made Abel's tools,
whom did Cain fear, and how was the earth repopulated after
the Flood as rapidly as Genesis implied. Not only did La Peyrère
discover new ages before Adam, but he provoked further uncertainty by questioning the biblical account of the passage of time
after Adam's creation. He said that Adam and Eve had grown
up naturally outside paradise and then had been brought to
paradise, a part of the Holy Land, when Adam was old enough
to till and Eve was old enough to marry. He reasoned that Adam
could not have named the animals in a single afternoon, for not
even a month would have sufficed for such a task; he also indicated the impossibility of transporting animals from Africa and
America.[28]

La Peyrère's confidence in the clear-sighted tolerance of his
age was misplaced: he was kept in prison until he recanted. While
Isaac Vossius accepted his view of only a local flood and Thomas
Burnet was probably influenced by his interpretation of Genesis
in his *Archaeologicae Philosophicae*, more than thirty refutations
of his work appeared during the fifty years after its publication.
Stillingfleet, who perhaps encountered La Peyrère while working
on the second volume of *Origines Sacrae*, opposed his theory, defended the Mosaic authorship, claimed that he had already dis-
proven the antiquity of the Egyptian and Chaldean records, and

went on to denounce the pretence of nations claiming they were self-originated. Hale wrote that if La Peyrère "durst have spoken out he would have told us roundly and plainly that the eleven first chapters of *Genesis* were but fables." [29]

In England, Lord Herbert of Cherbury, often regarded as the first deist, was also skeptical of the biblical account of man's origins. He contended that one could accept as genuine truth only the universally held notions found in natural religions as well as in Scripture. "Quite wondrous matters" of Scripture, he said, sharpened the mind. He explained that the Christian might believe all that the Church said had happened "on this condition, however, that there be a common privilege of studying and arriving at conclusions about the consequence of acts said to have taken place from the earliest ages of the world, and that, although faith in the historical narrative remains the Church's prerogative, the liberty of passing judgment shall remain with mankind." [30]

Chronology

Confronted by Aristotelian eternalism, Lucretian atomism, the Egyptian records, and a growing contemporary bewilderment about man's origins, orthodox Christian writers sought security and reassurance in the establishment of a single exact chronology for the universal history of mankind. Because this chronology should begin with the beginning of the world, they endeavored with full seriousness to determine the exact year, day, and hour of Adam's entry and exit in the momentous drama of paradise. How could one be positive an event occurred if he did not know when it occurred? How could there be history without dates? But the problems of chronology were hopelessly snarled. It was necessary to reconcile Hebraic and non-Hebraic records, to resolve the chronological discrepancies in the Old Testament, and to ascertain the symbolic relationships between the Creation and world history and between the Fall and the Redemption which some men were certain were divinely ordained. Recognizing that the would-be historian stood lost and confused amidst conflicting claims and evidence, Bodin concluded, "Those who think they can under-

111

stand histories without chronology are as much in error as those who wish to escape the winding of a labyrinth without a guide." Ralegh, recognized in his time as a chronologist as well as a historian, testified to the crucial importance of this problem in his painstaking efforts to devise an acceptable system of dating. John Swan, who organized his treatment of natural history according to the days of the Creation, insisted, "In the account of Times, it is very necessary that there should be a proposed point or mark, from whence every reckoning may take beginning." [31]

Renaissance scholars were confident that they could discover this mark partly because both the world's beginning and its end seemed so close at hand. It is probably impossible for a modern man, straining to comprehend the billions of years in the earth's history, to sense the comparative nearness of Adam and the lost — almost just lost — paradise experienced by Milton and his readers. The assumption that the world would last 6000 years, a thousand for each of the days of the Creation, was almost universally accepted. The world's beginning seemed well within the memory of man. In the later decades of the seventeenth century, when the formidable ancient records were becoming more familiar, Burnet could still assert: "We have still the Memory of the Golden Age, of the first state of Nature, and how Mortals liv'd then in Innocency and Simplicity." The invention of the arts was within the knowledge of men, he said. Wolseley similarly observed that "we can not believe, but that *Adam* and *Eve* told the story of the worlds original to their posterity," and explained that the account could easily have been handed down, for Adam lived 243 years with Methuselah, who lived ninety-eight years with Shem, who lived fifty years with Isaac.[32] If man could thus remember his past, then surely he could and should know when this past had a beginning.

There were countless answers to this question of when the world had begun. Judaism placed the creation at 3750 B.C., but the Septuagint considered it to be approximately 5200 B.C. Most Renaissance writers would not accept so early a date since it would place their own time beyond the year 6000. One of the very few to reject this symbolic relationship between history and the Creation was John Harvey, who regarded it as cabbalistic and fantastic. More than a hundred writers contended that the date of the creation was between 3928 and 4103 B.C.[33]

Those seeking to establish a historical account of the early lives of Adam and Eve tried by appropriate reasoning to determine not only the year, but also the season, the date, and the hour of the crucial events in their lives. Most thought the world had begun in either the spring or the fall. Many Continental writers, believing in a correspondence between the Creation and the Annunciation, set Adam's Creation at March 25. Inveges speculated that Adam had been led into the garden at sunrise on March 25. He thought that about the seventeenth hour Adam alone had received the laws concerning the special trees of paradise, which had been created on the previous Tuesday. Inveges wondered exactly when and where Adam had received dominion over the animals, if all had been created then, and when, where, and for how long Adam had slept during the creation of Eve. Other writers, perhaps influenced by Jewish tradition, maintained that the world had come into being with the bounties of harvest time. The eminent Hebraist John Lightfoot decided that Adam had been created September 12, 3928 B.C. Speculating that the first day was probably October 25 or 26, Swan wrote, "For as the trees in Autumne being come to maturitie do then lose their beautie by the fall of their fruits and leaves; or as the yeare then slides away like the day at the setting of the sunne; even so mankinde, as soon as he began to be in a perfect state, kept it not, but fell away and lost his happinesse." Relating Christ's Redemption to the Creation, he said, "The fall therefore of man at the fall of the leaf, and the restoring of him at the reviving spring, do make a more perfect harmonie, then if for their circumstances of time we should cast them both into the spring." A London schoolmaster similarly described "the fall of Adam [as] being answerable to the fall of the leafe, because by his fall death was brought upon all." He interpreted Psalm 104 to signify that Adam entered paradise and began his labour about 6 A.M., "when we commonly goe to labour," some place near the gates of the garden.[34]

Exegetes also sought to determine how long Adam and Eve had remained in paradise. The majority concluded that Adam and Eve had not spent one night in Eden. To Luther it appeared that Adam had received the commandment concerning the trees before the creation of Eve, had partaken of the fruit about noon, and had been expelled shortly thereafter. A book instructing Christians how to read the Bible was most positive: "That *Adam* fell the day of creation, all must hold that loue not grosse ignorance." If he did not, what did he do on the Sabbath, readers were asked. And, if he did not fall then, "*Cain* was begotten in innocence; for it must needs be granted according to the institution and quality of nature; that day or the next night *Adam* knew *Eue* his wife, in which he was conceiued." Another view was that Eve had not eaten at all before partaking of the forbidden fruit "and doubtless she fell a Virgin." Archbishop James Ussher, the most renowned and widely accepted chronologist, who published his scholarly studies of chronology in the 1650s, fixed the beginning of time at nightfall preceding October 23, 4004 B.C. He concluded that after the first week, on the tenth day of the world (Tuesday, November 1), God apparently had brought Adam and Eve, newly married, to paradise. They seemingly were turned out of paradise the same day they were brought in, he said.[35]

Other writers thought that the first parents had preserved their innocence for a longer period. Some following medieval tradition assumed that there was a direct comparison between their stay in paradise and the Israelites' forty years in the wilderness, the Passion, Christ's forty days in the wilderness, or Christ's days on earth. Such writers went even further and found a correspondence between the Fall and the Crucifixion and between Adam's banishment from the earthly paradise and Christ's entrance into the heavenly paradise. The Flemish geographer Gerhardus Mercator supposed that Adam had remained obedient for several years, engaging in many conversations both with God and with the serpent. In his popular *Apologie*, George Hakewill admitted that he had given up the erroneous opinion that Adam had stood only one day. Anticipating the more thoroughgoing rationalism of La Peyrère, he concluded that the time was too short for all the events described in Genesis 2. The Somerset rector John Salkeld reasoned in his *Treatise of Paradise* that Adam had probably remained eight days in paradise. He thus perceived better what he had lost. Salkeld supported his position by pointing out the relationship between Adam's creation on a Friday and his Fall on the following Friday and Christ's conception and crucifixion, both on a Friday.[36]

Milton and "The Celestial Cycle"

In responding to the conflicting ideas, ancient and modern, about the origin of man, Milton did not simply accept the orthodox views. He gave enlightened attention to the problems of time, eternity, and creation, drawing widely upon classical, Hebraic, and Christian sources, and sometimes reaching unusual or unorthodox conclusions. However, in both his prose and poetry, he utilized all opportunities — indeed he created new opportunities — to reassert his belief in the origin of mankind through the special creation in time of Adam by God.

Milton had gained a thorough knowledge of the various views of the world's beginnings before he left Christ's College. He could have found the basis for most of his later ideas and interests in Johannes Magirus's physics text, in Christopher Scheibler's *De Deo*, and in Bartholomew Keckermann's *Systema SS. Theologiae*, and in similar works in use at Cambridge. Magirus devoted much of his work to problems of time and eternity and to an attempted reconciliation of Mosaic and Aristotelian conceptions of creation. In his second prolusion, Milton opposed the emphasis on Aristotle in the college curriculum. Though he denounced Aristotle's idea of the world's eternity, in another academic exercise, *Naturam non pati senium*, he also rejected the idea of the decay of nature, often used as an argument against eternalism. Among the books assigned while Milton was attending Cambridge were the *Omnium Gentium Mores* of Boemus and the works of Polybius. Milton owned a copy of Lucretius and was familiar with the thought of the classical atomists. He also had an interest in Bodin that probably started in Cambridge.[37]

Various references in Milton's prose reflect his response to unacceptable ideas which clearly opposed the Christian view of man's origins. In *Areopagitica* he noted that Proclus had produced "plaine invectives against Christianity" and that even the Bible brought in men "passionately murmuring against providence through all the arguments of *Epicurus.*" Again he asserted that "there is not that sect of Philosophers among the heathen so dissolute, no not *Epicurus,* nor *Aristippus,* with all his Cyrenaic rout" but would reject the spokesmen for prelacy, and he denounced a "philosophic phantasy as smacking of *Democritean* fabrications or the stories of nurses." Milton once illustrated a particular type of argument by referring to the attempt of Lucretius to demonstrate that the world had never been made. Milton shared his age's general disapproval of Machiavelli, but in his *Commonplace Book,* he cited without comment the discussion in *The Discourses* of the rise of governments from an early state of barbarism.[38]

While Aristotle, Epicurus, and their followers had spread error, the Bible, if read correctly, revealed the divine truth about the world's beginnings. Of this Milton was positive. It was "that book within whose sacred context all wisdom is infolded." Because of this belief, Milton's exegesis was not always disinterested; it was strained sometimes by a very strict dependence upon the word and at other moments by a very broad appeal to the spirit. It was often typological and sometimes figurative and symbolical. But usually his exegesis and commentary were within the Renaissance tradition of rational, linguistic, and literal interpretation. Like many of his contemporaries, Milton found a number of references to the Creation in various books of the Bible besides Genesis; these included Psalms 33, 104, and 148, Job 26 and 38, Proverbs 8, Amos 4, and II Peter 3. However, where Milton felt that Scripture was altogether silent, he was usually content to remain silent. Though he generally thought that important matters were clearly stated in Scripture, he did pursue divine truth through linguistic virtuosity. From an examination of many texts he concluded that "it appears that the idea of eternity, properly so called, is conveyed in the Hebrew language rather by comparison and deduction than in express words." He found the idea stated much more clearly in the Greek of the New Testament. He also examined the meaning of the Hebrew word for "beginning," and showed that the Hebrew, Greek, and Latin words for "create" meant to create from matter. Milton introduced arguments from both revelation and reason, and distinguished between them, as in his discussion of the generation of souls.[39] He also used reason, and sometimes choplogic, as a support to a literal reading or to his own interpretation rather than as an independent and inquiring guide in exegesis.

Milton insistently proclaimed the creation of all by God in time. Arguing against the tenets of atomism, he contended that "those who attribute the creation of everything to nature, must necessarily associate chance with nature as a joint divinity; so that they gain nothing by this victory, except that in the place of that one God, whom they cannot tolerate, they are obliged, however reluctantly, to substitute two sovereign rulers of affairs, who must always be in opposition to each other." While Lucretius had regarded history as an accident and the teleological argument as untenable, Milton stressed the omnipresent power of divine providence in a universe "ordained for a specific end." But God, the Creator of all else, and God only, was eternal, Milton concluded. His doctrine of creation was stated forthrightly: "CREATION is that act whereby GOD THE FATHER PRODUCED EVERYTHING THAT EXISTS BY HIS WORD AND SPIRIT, that is BY HIS WILL, FOR THE MANIFESTATION OF THE GLORY OF HIS POWER AND GOODNESS." In keeping with this single doctrine of the creation of all things both visible and invisible, Milton explained not only the special creation of man, but also the creation of the angels and heaven itself, and developed his unorthodox ideas of the Word and of God's creation of Christ and of all matter from himself rather than from nothing. Moreover, by his carefully defended theory of the

117

propagation of souls from father to son, Milton showed the historical truth and logical necessity of the creation of all mankind through the special creation of Adam. God would not be allowed to "rest on each successive sabbath, if he continued to create as many souls daily as there are bodies multiplied throughout the whole world, at the bidding of what is not seldom the flagitious wantonness of man." Indeed, "it was from one of the ribs of the man that God made the mother of all mankind, without the necessity of infusing the breath of life a second time."[40] By all the authority and reasoning that he could present, Milton set forth in his prose the certainty of his belief in God as the eternal Creator of all things and Adam as the one father of all men.

Through his poetry, too, Milton sought to establish the true doctrine of creation and to reject the false. Through the drama of his epics, God, Christ, Raphael, Abdiel, and Adam become the spokesmen for the true account of the origins of man and the universe, while Satan and the devils become the spokesmen for false myths which their erring followers still propagate in a fallen world. In Hell the fallen angelic singers "complain that Fate / Free Vertue should enthrall to Force or Chance," while the philosophical group, "in wandring mazes lost," anticipate the jumbled errors of both classical philosophy and Christian theology (II, 550–65). It is, however, in the great dialogues between Adam and Raphael in *Paradise Lost* and between Christ and Satan in *Paradise Regained* that the opposing ideas are most clearly and dramatically presented. Raphael begins by assuring Adam not only that God created the world in time, but that all heavenly events occur in time:

> (For time, though in Eternitie, appli'd
> To motion, measures all things durable
> By present, past, and future)
> (V, 580–82)

In Raphael's narrative of the great heavenly revolt, the indignant Abdiel reminds Satan that God through Christ the Word had made all things, including "all the Spirits of Heav'n." In a speech filled with the errors of the race he would later tempt to ruin, Satan replies,

> , strange point and new!
> Doctrin which we would know whence learnt: who saw
> When this creation was? rememberst thou
> Thy making, while the Maker gave thee being?
> We know no time when we were not as now;
> Know none before us, self-begot, self-rais'd
> By our own quick'ning power, when fatal course
> Had circl'd his full Orbe, the birth mature
> Of this our native Heav'n, Ethereal Sons.
>
> (V, 855–63)

Satan, boasting that the angels are not the sons of God, but the sons of fate and their native heavenly soil, voices the doctrines of all the atomists and historians who presented the belief that men first sprang from the earth. Lucretius explained that in the process of continuing change, Earth herself begat the human race, even supplying womb cavities and a juice like milk for the newly born.[41] Milton joined Bodin, Carpenter, and others who assailed the pride of those claiming to be "sons of earth."

Raphael's account of the creation of the visible universe and Adam's story of his creation and that of Eve come as an overpowering answer to the doctrine of Satan. This revelation of origins, this great Alpha, is imbued with all the awe, mystery, and splendor that was reflected in a fallen world's myths of the beginnings of the world and man. In Raphael's narrative God states that he can repair the detriment wrought by Satan, who was not self-raised but "self-lost,"

> and in a moment will create
> Another World, out of one man a Race
> Of men innumerable, . . . (VII, 154–56).

The Creator who sends the Word to "ride forth, and bid the Deep / Within appointed bounds be Heav'n and Earth," is unaffected by the "Necessitie and Chance" hailed by the race to be created. When it is Adam's turn to tell his life story to Raphael, he seems to answer Satan's question: "Rememberst thou thy mak-

119

ing? Adam could not know "himself beginning," but to his question, "How came I thus, how here?" he frames the answer: "Not of my self; by some great Maker then" (VIII, 277–78). Adam does remember the "shape Divine" that raised him and took him to the garden, and he similarly recalls that "Under his forming hands a Creature grew / Manlike, but different Sex, . . . (VIII, 470–71).

In *Paradise Regained*, Satan is the advocate of the Peripatetics, Epicureans, and Stoics. But Christ stresses the truth essential for man — which is also the subject of *Paradise Lost*:

> Alas what can they teach, and not mislead;
> Ignorant of themselves, of God much more,
> And how the world began, and how man fell
> Degraded by himself, on grace depending?
> (IV, 309–12)

Christ also espouses the argument that classical culture was derived from the Hebraic culture, an argument often to be used by Christians to help demonstrate the origin of all men in Adam:

> All our Law and Story strew'd
> With Hymns, our Psalms with artful terms inscrib'd,
> Our Hebrew Songs and Harps in Babylon,
> That pleas'd so well our Victor's ear, declare
> That rather Greece from us these arts deriv'd.
> (IV, 334–38)

Milton sought to place the creation of man within a credible sequence of celestial and terrestrial events, though he did not attempt to name exact dates and hours. In "On Time" and other earlier poems Milton apparently thought of time as beginning with the Creation and as concluding with the end of the world. However, in *Paradise Lost* Milton supported his belief in "the elder state" before the Creation by maintaining, through Raphael's first lesson to Adam, that "time, though in Eternitie," "measures all things durable." He also wrote that there was not sufficient evidence for the common opinion that time could not have existed before the world was made. Milton was perhaps depending on the argument developed by Hieronymus Zanchius that time was not only a measure of moving, as Aristotle had said, but could also be a measure of duration without motion.[42] On the basis of Scriptural revelation and reason, Milton envisioned the following order of events: creation of Christ or the Word, creation of the first matter, creation of heaven, creation of the angels, exaltation of Christ, the war in heaven, creation of the universe, creation of Adam and Eve, the Fall, and the expulsion from paradise. In *Paradise Lost* the events in the garden, and indeed all the events of human history, are framed by Raphael's history of the past and Michael's prediction of the "New Heav'ns and new Earth, Ages of endless date."

Milton's ideas of terrestrial chronology were similar to those of other defenders of a fundamentally orthodox position, and he was not unaware of the problems inherent in establishing chronology. He referred to chronological difficulties in *Of Prelatical Episcopacy* and in his *History of Britain*. He observed that the historical books of the Old Testament "appear sometimes to contradict themselves on points of chronology," but was certain that the law of Moses had been preserved in "an uncorrupted state." Milton thought that Moses had written Genesis as a prologue to his law and regarded his work as "a better and more ancient authority, then any heathen writer hath to give us." The descriptions of the pagan deities and heathen practices in the Nativity ode and *Paradise Lost* suggest that Milton discerned only error and deceit in the records of the Egyptians and other ancient peoples. Like most of his contemporaries, Milton felt the world was made to exist "for a few thousand years," yet he gave no specific date for the world's origin.[43]

Milton gave Adam and Eve more time in paradise than did most of the commentators. Although his main concern was to create the impression of a long span of perfect days, he also created the impression of historical accuracy by his references to time. His Adam and Eve apparently dwelt in Paradise for at least two weeks. Adam and Eve are seemingly well established in a domestic routine when Satan arrives; often they hear celestial voices on the midnight air and the day of Eve's creation is referred to as "that day I oft remember" (IV, 449). Satan, after fleeing Gabriel, spent seven days and nights circling the globe,

121

and "on the eighth return'd" (IX, 63–67). The Fall occurs the next day. Through Adam's narration of his first day to Raphael and the dramatic presentation of Adam and Eve beginning with Book IV, Milton specifically described three prelapsarian days, one postlapsarian "sleepless Night" (XI, 173), and the following day when the unnamed "hour precise" brought the end of Michael's predictions and then the expulsion from Paradise.

Milton, like many of the commentators, associated the Fall with the falling leaves of autumn. After his disobedience, Adam saw the winds "shattering the graceful locks / Of these fair spreading Trees" (X, 1065–67). Swan thought that Adam probably faced a hard winter after his expulsion,[44] and Milton's Adam hoped that God would teach

> by what means to shun
> Th'inclement Seasons, Rain, Ice, and Snow,
> Which now the Skie with various Face begins
> To shew us in this Mountain . . . (X, 1062–65).

Although Milton gave more attention to the problems of the world's beginnings than did the other Renaissance poets of paradise, many of these other poets, particularly Grotius, stressed the orthodox view of God's creation of mankind through Adam. Grotius, like Milton, expressed his ideas in both prose and verse. His literal, philological, and historical exegesis of Genesis reflected his Christian humanism. In an early work, first written in Dutch verse for sailors, he showed that all things were from God and were governed by God's law, never by chance. Defending the antiquity and veracity of Moses, he attempted to demonstrate the Hebraic origin of the culture and customs of the Egyptians, Phoenicians, and Greeks. In his *Dissertation on the Origin of the Native Races of America*, he accepted the belief in the descent of all from Adam and the universality of the Deluge. He also sought to prove that the Norse had settled much of America and that Yucatan, where the inhabitants practiced circumcision, had been populated not by the Jews, as many thought, but by Christianized Abyssinians. Like Milton, Grotius composed poems about Adam and Christ, the best known being his *Adamus Exul* and *Christus Patiens*. He wrote that his early play on Adam "elaborates the first grand historical event recorded in the inspired volume." In a dialogue comparable to that in *Paradise Lost*, Adam and an Angel discuss in wonder the creation of all by an eternal God. The Satan of Grotius is sometimes only a narrator, but he appears as a dramatic representative of Epicureanism when he warns Eve against "fond superstitions," tells her to trust "Nature, thy guardian and parent," and assures her that pleasure and her senses are her surest guides.[45]

Other poets of "the celestial cycle" showed a similar interest in giving the right view of creation. Sylvester in his translation of Du Bartas struck a passing blow to atomism: "Once All was made, not by the hand of Fortune / (As fond *Democritus* did yerst importune)."[46] In Andreini's *L'Adamo*, Adam immediately upon his creation recognizes before him the "heavenly Author of the Universe," and the newly created Eve also knows at once that she is "the handiwork of Him who made / From nought the Angels and the Empyrean." In Serafino Della Salandra's *Adamo Caduto*, Adam also realizes instantly that he has been formed by God's hands and in God's image. The protagonist of Vondel's *Lucifer* is not so consistent a dramatic character as Milton's Satan, but he sometimes similarly denies that God is the omnipotent Creator. He himself is like God, he says, in being "A Son of Light, a ruler," and his loyalty is to his "Fatherland" rather than to God. He knows it may be his "fate to fall," but he decides that he will "submit to chance."[47]

These poets in their own way joined their efforts with those of other men of the Renaissance who were trying to reconstruct a credible historical account of the beginnings of the world in accordance both with reason and with ancient and newly acquired knowledge. Many were disturbed by the continuing conflicts between Christian doctrine and ancient philosophy and between Old Testament chronology and pagan records. While most accepted the authority of Scripture, some in varying degrees doubted and rejected the orthodox interpretation of the biblical account of man's creation and his actions in Eden. The many poetic historians of these origins, sensitive to the problems in dispute around them, sought to provide their audiences, whether large and popular or fit but few, with a living account that would spurn the false and hold fast to the true. Some of these poets may well have influenced others, including Milton. However, it is more important to remember that they lived in societies which had comparable ideas and needs and that they wrote with very similar assumptions, aims, and ideals.

6

THE LEGACY OF EDEN

❧ SERIOUS study of man's creation and of the events in paradise seemed both necessary and natural to Renaissance scholars because of the legacy of man's original glory, as well as his burden of sin, which he had brought from paradise into the history of a fallen world. The inheritance from the "ruined millionnaire" (as T. S. Eliot called Adam in *East Coker*) had included not only the remnants of God's image in man, but God's covenant with man, the natural law, language, knowledge, work, marriage, the family, and the foundations of the Church and the state. All roads led back to paradise. The life in paradise, considered by many to be but a few hours, received more attention than any other period of history, for it was of incomparable value in showing what men, in their relationship with God and with each other, had once been, might have been, and had become. In searching studiously for the source of human history and institutions in paradise, Milton was only one of the many Renaissance writers who projected back to the lost paradise their own assumptions and aspirations.

Men bewailed the loss, but they also treasured the gain. "Ah, who can fitly describe the glory of the innocence that we have lost," asked Luther; yet he noted that we still must dress and keep the land, we still have sustenance and God's protection, we still praise and thank God, and we still retain "a small remnant of the blessed state of wedlock that Adam enjoyed (in the garden) that we through marriage are kept from impurity." Similarly, Bishop Lancelot Andrewes observed that man had received in paradise the two parts of his earthly vocation — labor in an occupation and the spiritual direction of his life. Milton found that Scriptural authority as well as "the wisdom and holiness of many of the heathen" gave evidence that "some remnants of the divine image still exist in us, not wholly extinguished by this spiritual death."[1] As Aeneas brought Trojan valor and virtue from Troy, so Adam and Eve took what was left of a perfect piety, a perfect liberty, and a perfect love with them when they were expelled from paradise.

This legacy from paradise might be understood and evaluated in different ways, but most accepted it as a heritage from the far happier state of original righteousness which had been described by St. Ambrose, St. Augustine, St. Thomas, Luther, and Calvin. Milton followed the essentials of this doctrine in his presentation of Adam in both *Paradise Lost* and *The Christian Doctrine*. This view of the legacy, however, is bounded by the opposing views of such humanists as Pico della Mirandola and Faustus Socinus. In his *Oration on the Dignity of Man*, Pico imagined God declaring to Adam in paradise that he would go forth with his own free will, "ordain for thyself the limits of thy Nature," and "fashion thyself in whatever shape thou shalt prefer." But Socinus, pursuing an unremitting rationalism to deny original righteousness, argued that Adam had possessed in paradise only the same mortality, intellectual limitation, and sensual domination that he left to his sons. Milton, indeed, warned against making Adam "as very an idiot as the Socinians make him."[2]

The Law, the Gospel, and the Covenant

No part of the heritage from Eden was more important or more precious than the law of nature, one of the first gifts bestowed by God upon Adam, and the gospel of Christ, given to Adam just before his expulsion from paradise. However, it was in terms of the two great covenants — the covenant of works and the covenant of grace — that a great many Protestant theologians examined both the failure of Adam and his sons to fulfill the law and the salvation of Adam and at least some of his sons through the mediation of Christ.

Natural law had become the necessary basis for the thought actions, and institutions of most of Adam's sons in Milton's age The eternal, immutable law of nature and right reason, which had been developed by the Stoics and Christianized as the divine law written in the hearts of men (Rom. 2:13–15), had been intact only in paradise. Yet those seeking to base their convictions and aspirations on the firm ground of paradise were sure that the remains of this law could be discovered and deciphered. With wide-angled vision, Richard Hooker saw that all law must be consonant with natural law which, as an expression of divine law, "comprehendeth all those things which men by the light of their natural understanding evidently know" or "know to be virtuous or vicious, good or evil for them to do." George Walker, a member of the Westminster Assembly, wrote in his history of the Creation that the divine law had been written in Adam's heart "so deeply that it remains in the heart of his corrupt seed in some measure, and cannot be quite blotted out." Ussher maintained that this law of nature had been chiefly imprinted on the hearts of Adam and Eve, but also had been uttered in Adam's ear in paradise for God had revealed to Adam marriage, the need to work, and the sanctification of the Sabbath. It was often assumed that Adam had received all the law later given to Moses.[3] Questions of the original nature and scope of natural law and its present clarity and sufficiency were repeatedly discussed by many writers, including Milton.

Milton discerned the law of nature to be the immutable but unwritten law of God "given originally to Adam, and of which a certain remnant, or imperfect illumination, still dwells in the hearts of all mankind; which, in the regenerate, under the influence of the Holy Spirit, is daily tending toward a renewal of its primitive brightness." Since natural law "is sufficient of itself to

teach whatever is agreeable to right reason, that is to say, whatever is intrinsically good," additional laws such as those concerning marriage and the special trees formed no part of natural law.
Under natural law, Milton said, partaking of the tree of knowledge would not of itself have been sinful. In *Paradise Lost* Milton
repeatedly and dramatically emphasized the special command
not to partake of this fruit, but the illumination of natural law
is reflected in the whole life of Adam and Eve in Paradise from
the time of Adam's first words in recognition of the goodness of
God and his works. For Milton as for St. Augustine, this God-
given law of nature leads to love and to delight. Love of God
is the wellspring of all law. Raphael, just before leaving Adam
and Eve, tells them all they need to know of Law:

> Be strong, live happie, and love, but first of all
> Him whom to love is to obey, and keep
> His great command (VIII, 633–35).

Raphael has just distinguished between passion and true love,
which "hath his seat / In Reason" and leads to heavenly love —
and "without Love no happiness" (VIII, 590–91, 621). Raphael,
like Spenser a better teacher than Aquinas, has told Adam of
Abdiel who knew that "God and Nature bid the same," that it
is true liberty to obey the worthiest and God's behests "worthiest
to be obey'd" (VI, 176, 185). The law of reason and nature, of
love and obedience, is also the law of happiness, for as Adam
tells Eve on the fateful morning,

> not to irksom toile, but to delight
> He made us, and delight to Reason joyn'd.
> (IX, 242–43)

Natural law in its primitive purity was lost with paradise, but it
still enabled Noah's descendants to live in love and peace until
Nimrod would "quite dispossess / Concord and law of Nature
from the Earth," usurping the dominion of God over man (XII,
28–29). Although the rule of reason and nature was written dimly
on many recalcitrant hearts, Milton still found it basic in defin-
ing the relationships between husband and wife, ruler and peo-

ple.[4] It could serve as a guide to the unregenerate, while regaining much of its paradisal clarity in the minds of the regenerate.

Not only law, but — more important — the gospel was revealed in paradise. The belief that the coming of Christ was made known in paradise and that Adam became a Christian was very old. These beliefs are based primarily on Genesis 3:15, the protevangelium or "first gospel," which was found in the words God addressed to the serpent: "And I will put enmity between thee and the woman, and between thy seed and her seed; it shall bruise thy head, and thou shalt bruise his heel." The passage probably originally explained and foretold the continuing hostility between the descendants of the first serpent and the descendants of the first woman, but both the Hebrew text and its interpretation have presented many difficult problems. From at least the early Christian era it was accepted as a messianic text by both Jews and Christians, and as recently as 1950 Pius XII found support in "the first gospel" for the bull declaring the assumption of the Virgin.[5] No scriptural text is more important for *Paradise Lost*.

Both the Jerusalem Targum and the Targum of Pseudo-Jonathan, which contained pre-Christian elements but was completed during the early Christian period, predict the coming of the messiah king in their vernacular explanations of God's curse on the serpent. But it was Justin Martyr, the first to formulate a Christian interpretation of Greek myths, who gave the world the first Christian interpretation of Genesis 3:15. Interpreting the serpent as the devil, he explained that "death was declared to come thereafter on the serpent through Him that would be crucified, but salvation to those who had been bitten by him and had betaken themselves to him that sent his Son into the world to be crucified." Treating as a novelty Tatian's heresy that Adam had not been saved, St. Irenaeus included the main elements of the Christian tradition of the protevangelium in his vigorous argument for a belief in Adam's salvation. He referred to the serpent as "biting, killing, and impeding the steps of man, until the seed did come appointed to tread down his head, which was born of

129

Mary." He even approached the treatment in *Paradise Lost* by picturing God as being compassionate toward Adam because he was truly penitent. He regarded Adam as representative of man in that if he is not saved, "the whole human race is still held in a state of perdition." [6] Neither Justin nor St. Irenaeus, however, dealt with the problem of Adam's understanding and acceptance of Christ.

Catholic writers tended more and more to consider Genesis 3:15 as the basis for their exaltation and adoration of the Virgin. Almost all writers followed St. Irenaeus in identifying "the woman" as Mary, not Eve. Moreover, while the Old Latin and the Septuagint had written "he will bruise," the Vulgate used the feminine pronoun *ipsa* ("she will bruise . . ."). St. Saphronius, patriarch of Jerusalem, sang praise to the Virgin "because through you your progenitors are saved." The constant theme in the hymns of St. Ephrem of Syria was that Mary was Christ's consort in saving man, including Adam and Eve. He also drew a touching picture of God revealing the Incarnation to a weeping and remorseful Adam and Eve.[7] The messianic interpretation of Genesis 3:15 was accepted by many other fathers and doctors, but it lacked the weighty approval of St. Augustine and St. Thomas Aquinas.

Apart from the protevangelium, a more popular tradition also held that Adam had received the message of salvation, either before or after his expulsion from paradise. The *Gospel of Nicodemus*, perhaps known in the second century, said that Seth went to paradise for oil for his dying father, was informed of the Redeemer by an angel, and returned to Adam with the message of salvation. This work is also apparently the source of the belief that Christ "harrowed" hell and led forth Adam as a representative of man. According to the Ethiopic *Book of Adam and Eve*, the *Spelunca Thesaurorum*, an apocryphal work attributed to St. Ephrem, and the *Cursor Mundi,* God revealed to Adam before the Fall the mercy that would be offered to man through Christ. In a play of the Chester cycle Adam sees a vision of the Incarnation during the creation of Eve.[8]

Protestants, however, based their belief in the revelation of the Redemption to Adam squarely on the Scriptural text of the "first gospel." For them, "the woman" was clearly Eve and "the seed" was Christ. Luther, Melancthon, and Calvin read salvation in Genesis 3:15, though Calvin's literal and grammatical exegesis led him to regard "the seed" as "all the faithful" or the Church. But the work which evidently first set forth the account of Adam's Christianization found in *Paradise Lost* was *Der Alt Glaub* (1537) of the Swiss Calvinist Heinrich Bullinger. While the earlier Catholic writers had used the protevangelium for theological discussion, moral allegory, and praise of the Virgin, Bullinger made it the foundation of a systematic history in which he traced step by step the development of Protestant belief as well as Christianity from the revelation in paradise. The work was translated into English by Miles Coverdale and his translation was republished in 1624 with the title *Look from Adam, and Behold the Protestants Faith and Religion . . . Has Continued from the Beginning of the World.* Bullinger maintained that the Christian faith was 2449 years older than the law and priesthood of the Jews and 2048 years older than the circumcision. Heathenism and idolatry began with Cham, he said. "And though this papistical religion," he concluded, "hath endured, prevailed, and triumphed certain hundred years, yet hath God always sent his faithful servants, and had a little holy flock of his own" as in the Old Testament era.[9]

Bullinger not only saw the protevangelium as the beginning of true Christian history, but he presented a clear, touching, and convincing account of the first parents' salvation through faith: "Forasmuch then as Adam and Eve had faith in God, and stood so toward God, that they knowledged themselves to be sinners, and trusted to be saved only through the blessed Seed, giving themselves over willingly unto the discipline and nurture, travail and trouble of the time; no man can say contrary, but it followeth that our first elders were christian." And, as Christians, they understood the full meaning of the promise. "God spoke it all to them himself, and wrote it in their hearts." Adam, he explained, knew in Christ "very godhead and manhood" and "saw on faith his passion and cross afar off." [10]

English Protestants felt that Adam had been saved by faith and pondered the question of how much he had understood of the prophecy concerning "the seed," and when he had understood this. One view, set forth in a sermon in 1645, and later in *Paradise Lost*, was that God "told Adam in plain tearms from the beginning, the end of the whole work of our salvation." Similarly, in Lightfoot's words, Adam "layeth hold upon the promise by Faith." Assuming, like most writers, the sacrifice of the beasts whose skins clothed Adam, Lightfoot said, "God teacheth him the rite of sacrifice, to lay Christ dying before his eyes in a visible figure." Others assumed that Adam comprehended that sacrifice showed an acknowledgment of sin and a turning to Christ for salvation, and that he taught this to his sons. However, to the question of how much Adam understood, the mystic John Saltmarsh answered "not much surely," for this was the "time of the hiding of this mystery." So much only was revealed, he said, "as man might rather consider himself *not destroyed* then *saved*, and rather not *damned* then *redeemed*." [11]

Much of Protestant Europe, however, understood man's redemption and indeed all the relations between God and man in light of an all-encompassing covenant or federal (from *foedus*, pact) theology. Mankind's relations with God through innocence, corruption, and regeneration were comprehended in respect to the covenant of works and the covenant of grace. The covenant concept, rooted in the thought of the Akkadians, Sumerians, and Hebrews, received little attention from either the early Christian writers or the medieval theologians. Calvinism, projected upon the world of Renaissance humanism, fostered the federal theology. Under the covenant of works established in paradise, Adam as federal head of the human race would receive eternal life only if he were wholly obedient; if he was disobedient, the end would be death for him and his heirs. Interpreting the Mosaic law as part of a covenant of works, some theologians held that after the Fall man, like Adam, would gain life if obedient to the law and death if disobedient; however, all agreed that perfect obedience was impossible for fallen man. Under a covenant of grace, man was granted salvation by the grace of God. Writers disagreed whether saving grace was given through an absolute covenant with the elect or through a conditional covenant with all who exhibited faith and repentance.

Bullinger, in his first attempts to formulate covenant doctrine, recognized only one covenant — the covenant of grace. "For it is but one covenant only," he wrote in his discussion of Noah, "ever the foresaid promise and end, made by God with Adam. Howbeit, the same covenant was afterward at certain times renewed by reason of certain occasions." For Bullinger, as for Milton, the Ten Commandments were not given as part of a covenant of works; rather the Israelites might have known that "the holy works which God requireth are not in their own power, for the which cause all the world hath great need of a mediator." [12]

The principal architect of covenant theology and of the influential Heidelberg Catechism of 1563 was Zacharias Ursinus, professor of theology at Heidelberg. Very important contributions to both were also made by Caspar Olevianus. For them, the covenant was the single controlling principle in the Old and New Testaments and in the life of man: it provided a pattern for living, a program for salvation, and a philosophy of history. They gave succeeding generations a basis for belief, but also for dispute. Was the covenant a promise or a pact? How many covenants had there been? Were they absolute or conditional? With whom were they made? Who were included? What exactly were the terms?

Ursinus was the first to write of a covenant of works made by God with Adam in paradise, but in his later work he developed only the conception of the covenant of grace. In his longer catechism, he referred to a "natural covenant" instituted by God with man at his creation, requiring perfect obedience and promising eternal life and threatening death. When Adam was unable to fulfill the first covenant, God established a covenant of grace with the elect in the promise of "the seed." In a work that was published in English several times, he wrote: "In special, the Covenant between God and man is a mutual promise and agreement, made by our mediatour, confirmed by othes and solemne tokens (which we call Sacraments), whereby God bindeth himself to remit their sins unto them that believe and to give them everlasting life, for and by his son, our mediatour, and men bind themselves to receeve this so great a benefite with true faith and to yeelde true obedience unto God." [13]

The continued thrust back to paradise is seen in the revival and development of the idea of the covenant of works which was made with Adam before the Fall. The highly respected Dutch scholar Franciscus Junius argued in 1584 that God had given man two covenants appropriate to his two conditions, integrity and corruption. The first, not specifically called a covenant of works, promised Adam and Eve supernatural life if they continued to worship, revere, and obey, and threatened them with death if they did otherwise. They were to partake of the tree of life, which was a sacrament of supernatural life, and to refrain from partaking of the tree of knowledge as a pledge of their obedience.[14]

Covenant doctrine was accepted in England not only by most of the Puritans, but by such Anglicans as Bishop Andrewes and Archbishop Ussher. Some of the early Puritans, such as William Perkins, thought that the covenant of grace had been established with the elect before the Creation, but that the covenant of works had been established only after the Fall. The Elizabethan Puritan leader Thomas Cartwright was apparently the first in England to write of a covenant of works given to Adam in paradise before the Fall. In "A Short Catechism" he asserted that the covenant craves of us "All such duties as are Requyred of Adame in his innocency, and requyred of all synce his faule." Almost all the seventeenth-century Puritans accepted the double covenant in some form. Milton was virtually alone in rejecting the covenant of works made with Adam. Regarding Adam as the federal representative of man, the popular Puritan preacher Richard Sibbes contended that "the communion and fellowship of man with God, was first founded on a covenant of works made with Adam in paradise. If he did obey, and did not eat of the forbidden fruit, he should have life both for himself and his posterity." But Adam fell, so "now by the first covenant of works, Adam and all his posterity are under a curse." After the breach of the first agreement, Sibbes explained, God raised Adam and established a second and better covenant, laying the foundation of righteousness in the seed of the woman. God has renewed this covenant from Noah to Abraham to Moses to Christ to the end of the world, he said. The Puritan John Preston, contrasting the two covenants as "a ministration of the letter" and "a ministration of the spirit" — "the good of all you hope for" — wrote that "God himself preaches the gospell to Adam and Eve" in promising the seed. In its summing up of covenant doctrine, the Westminster Confession regarded Adam as the federal head of the race, approved the double covenant, and considered the covenant of grace as the same covenant both in the time of the law and of the gospel.[15]

Many problems arose concerning man's relation to these two covenants both in paradise and under the law and the gospel. Various writers, including Milton, discussed the relation of the covenant of works to the two special trees and to natural law and its status after the revelation of the covenant of grace. Many writers were convinced that the two real but very distinctive trees in some way signified the covenant of works or the double covenant. If they were sacraments, they marked the first institution of sacraments and perhaps the beginning of the Church. They were variously and ambiguously designated as signs, symbols, seals, pledges, sacraments, and sometimes even as negative sacraments. The strict Calvinist William Ames described the tree of life as a "sacrament of life" and the tree of knowledge as a "sacrament of death." The "Dorchester Patriarch" John White went further than most of his contemporaries in asserting that the two trees represented the perfection in the life of both nature and grace promised by God and both the obedience and faith promised by Adam.[16]

Another problem was whether the covenant of works bound

Adam to obey only the commandment concerning the forbidden fruit or to obey natural law or other commandments as well. Arminius held that the covenant of works demanded obedience to natural law. Ussher believed this too, explaining that under this covenant "God commands perfection of godliness and righteousness" in keeping "all his commandments." Sir Henry Vane, a Cromwellian administrator and associate of Milton, asserted forthrightly that "when we speak of this Covenant in reference to the state of innocence, it is to be understood for the same thing with the law of nature, under which Adam was created." Salkeld noted that many considered it frivolous to interpret the covenant of works as referring only to the forbidden tree. However, Sibbes and even the youthful Thomas Hobbes spoke out for this view. Besides the obedience "which natural reason should dictate," Hobbes said, "God ruled over Adam and Eve but *by way of covenant,* that is to say, by the consent of men themselves." [17]

Writers also debated the extent to which this covenant of works originally made with Adam in paradise continued to remain in force after the Fall. Unlike Adam, fallen men did not and would not possess immortality under the covenant of works. In fact, many held that Adam's original sin was imputed to his posterity since he had been the federal representative of the race. The life of paradise had been lost by Adam's descendants precisely because they had been included in the covenant of works. As the "Larger Catechism" of the Westminster Assembly stated, "the Covenant being made with Adam as a publick Person, not for himself only but for his Posterity," all fell with him. The Westminster Confession itself explained that the law given to Adam as a covenant of works remained, though not as a condition. It "continued to be a perfect Rule of Righteousness, and as such was delivered by God upon Mount Sinai in the Ten Commandments." Giving particular attention to the continuation of the covenant of works, the Puritan divine William Pemble examined this covenant under two administrations, those of Adam in paradise and Moses at Sinai. After the light of nature grew dim, he wrote, God renewed this covenant in the Ten Commandments, promising the Israelites "to be their God, bestowing all blessings of life and happiness, upon condition that they would be his people, obeying all things that he had commanded." According to Pemble, the renewal of this covenant, designed to drive man to a dependence upon grace, did not abrogate the covenant of grace that had been renewed with Abraham.[18] However, with its Scriptural basis, the law of the covenant of works continued in its embodiment in civil codes binding upon all.

There was also warm debate concerning the origin and continuation of the covenant of grace. The most prevalent concept was that the covenant of grace had first been manifested at the time of the revelation of "the first gospel" and had remained in force both under the law and the gospel. Some, such as John Cotton, thought of the covenant of grace as beginning with God's promise to Abraham and his seed. Other common views were that God had entered into a covenant with Christ or with the elect in Christ before he had made the covenant of works with Adam, or that God had entered into a covenant of redemption with Christ as a basis for the covenant of grace, which had the Son as its mediator. The godly divines of the Westminster Assembly approved a covenant directly with the elect in the Confession, but a covenant "made with Christ as the Second *Adam*" in the "Larger Catechism." Saltmarsh maintained that Christ "articled with God for us, and performed the conditions for life and glory," but that the individual soul was in covenant with God when it felt itself under the promise.[19] Both a covenant of redemption and a covenant of grace were accepted in the rigid systemization of covenant doctrine at the end of the seventeenth century.

Another interesting question was that of exactly which of Adam's descendants were to be saved under the covenant. Those who were saved, beginning with Adam, were frequently seen as constituting the Church. All agreed that those who were saved showed faith and repentance, but there was no agreement whether the redeemed were saved because of this. Was the covenant an absolute and unconditional promise of salvation to the elect or was it a mutual pact offering salvation to anyone who put his faith in God and was truly repentant? Those believing in God's absolute promise regarded it as a covenant. The Westminster Confession represented God as "promising to give unto all those that are ordained unto Life, his holy Spirit, to make them willing, and able to believe." Saltmarsh, with the mystic's love of the mysterious, believed that salvation was given only to some, without any condition, because this was the more mysterious and therefore more appropriate to God. Cotton emphasized God's free grace aptly in assuring his readers that "a man is as passive in his regeneration as in his first generation." God gives faith; man does not choose to believe. In Cotton's eyes, the Arminians in giving the choice to man rather than to God had converted the covenant of grace into a covenant of works. However, those believing in the conditional covenant, including Milton, felt convinced that at the protevangelium God had offered salvation to Adam and Eve and to all their sons who chose to repent and accept Christ on faith. In the later sixteenth century, Robert Brown, the father of Congregationalism, defended with a dedicated vigor a turning from iniquity, an "upright and good profession," and "a promise of obedience" as conditions and parts of the covenant of grace. In the mid-seventeenth century, John Goodwin, well known as an Arminian, declared that reason as well as Scripture could prove the doctrine of universal redemption. If Christ died not for all without exception, then the covenant of grace was made with unknown persons. Nevertheless, he continued, it is contrary to the nature and intent of a covenant that the parties concerned should not be known or discernible from all other persons whatsover or that there should be any controversy regarding the identity of these persons. Richard Baxter, that most charitable of Puritans, described the covenant as "a mystical marriage of the sinner to Christ." Certain that Christ consents, the sinner consents, and the agreement is made. "The change," Baxter claimed, "is only in the sinner to whom the conditional promises become equivalents to absolute, when they perform the conditions." [20] Milton would have agreed.

Milton accepted the old belief that the Incarnation had been revealed in the protevangelium and that Adam had become a Christian. He also held the Protestant view that Adam had been saved by faith. Moreover, he saw these truths as part of covenant doctrine. The relation of Milton's thought to Arminianism can best be approached by examining his conception of the conditional covenant. Much of Milton's philosophizing in *The Christian Doctrine* and *Paradise Lost* shows his reaction to contemporary controversies concerning covenant doctrine and expresses an acceptance, rejection, or interpretation of this doctrine in the light of Scripture and his own convictions. While rejecting the covenant of works, he dwelt upon the profound meaning in the covenant of grace. It is through the covenant of grace that the "one greater Man" shall restore fallen man and that God's ways to man are revealed as both just and reasonable.

In *The Christian Doctrine* Milton wrote that the commandment concerning the tree of knowledge "does not appear from any passage of Scripture to have been either a covenant, or of works." In "an exercise of jurisdiction" God may issue a command "as a test of fidelity," but rewards and punishments attached to it do not make it a covenant. He also observed that since man needed no precept to enforce the law of nature implanted within him, it was not necessary that he "should be bound by the obligation of a covenant to perform that to which he was of himself inclined." Milton denied that the two special trees were sacraments and even avoided the words "sign" or "seal" used in the Protestant definition of a sacrament. The tree of knowledge signified "a pledge, as it were, and memorial of obedience." Although Milton followed Scripture in regarding the Hebrews as a "covenanted people," accepting Jehovah as their God, he did not write of the Mosaic law as part of a covenant of works, but as part of the divine design for bringing all men to God.[21]

Milton accepted with deep conviction the doctrine of a conditional covenant of grace extended to Adam and Eve and all of their descendants. Under this covenant, the law of nature in

139

the hearts of the regenerate was "daily tending toward a renewal of its primitive brightness." The covenant of grace was made manifest both under the law and under the gospel, itself a new dispensation of the covenant. This new "testament," written in the hearts of believers, is "ORDAINED TO CONTINUE EVEN TO THE END OF THE WORLD, CONTAINING A PROMISE OF ETERNAL LIFE TO ALL IN EVERY NATION WHO SHALL BELIEVE IN CHRIST WHEN REVEALED TO THEM, AND A THREAT OF ETERNAL DEATH TO SUCH AS SHALL NOT BELIEVE." [22]

According to Milton, we have Christ's own words ("had ye believed Moses ye would have believed me, for he wrote of me") to show that Moses referred to the gospel in the protevangelium, and in other passages. "THE COVENANT OF GRACE itself," Milton wrote, "on the part of God, is first declared Gen. iii. 15." "On the part of man, its existence may be considered as implied from the earliest period at which it is recorded that mankind worshiped God." He was apparently referring to the sacrifice of Abel and other instances of worship recorded in Genesis. "Even under the law the existence of a Redeemer and the necessity of redemption are perceptible, though obscurely and indistinctly." Through Moses the covenant of grace was foreshadowed in the redemption from Egyptian bondage. The Mosaic law, a law of works, was given to the Hebrews so that they and in time all nations might acknowledge their depravity and be led to the gospel — the new dispensation of the covenant of grace, announced obscurely by Moses and the prophets (especially Jer. 31:31–33) and afterward clearly by Christ and the apostles. The covenant of grace, Milton asserted, was represented by sacraments, whereby God gave token of saving grace through Christ's satisfaction and man testified to his faith and obedience. Under the law these testimonies included the rites of circumcision and the Passover and under the gospel they consisted of baptism and the Supper of the Lord. [23]

Seventeenth-century readers of *Paradise Lost* would have expressed surprise at Milton's avoidance of the covenant of works, disputed his view of the covenant of redemption, and either hailed his conditional covenant of grace as divine truth or condemned it as diabolical heresy. In any case, the covenant of works is rejected as surely in the drama and poetry of *Paradise Lost* as it is in the prose of *The Christian Doctrine*. Moreover, the covenant of redemption, though perhaps reflected in the dialogue between God and Christ in Book III, is not accepted, whereas the covenant of grace dominates the final three books, assuring man of the justice and mercy of God's ways.

The bond of love between the first parents and God in the early books of *Paradise Lost* becomes more radiant and moving as it is contrasted with the binding terms of the covenant of works. It is like the difference between the letter and the spirit. Milton's God demands obedience because he is God, not because he gives immortality. He does give immortality and other blessings freely, but not because Adam is obedient. Adam and Eve are obedient because they follow reason, love God, and are grateful, not because they are fulfilling conditions to obtain immortality. For Milton, the special trees do not signify a covenant promising immortality for obedience, but are chiefly physical realities. Neither God nor the unfallen Adam ever refer to the sole command as part of a pact by which Adam would receive eternal life for obedience or eternal death for disobedience. Adam and Eve feel they have "nothing merited" from God who is "As liberal and free as infinite" (IV, 415–18). Raphael cautions Adam to "retain / Unalterably firm his love entire"; Adam ironically is astounded by the suggestion that they could disobey or "possibly his love desert" (V, 501–2, 512–15). Raphael explains that God wants only the "voluntarie service" of angels and men (V, 529). Adam recalls that God had designated the tree of knowledge as a pledge not only of obedience, but of faith as well (VIII, 325). Satan knows this too. Since Adam's and Eve's relationship to God in Eden depends upon their faith and love, it is this faith and love that Satan seeks to undermine.

Only after the Fall does Adam once think erroneously of his relation to God in terms of a covenant of works:

> inexplicable
> Thy Justice seems; yet to say truth, too late,
> I thus contest; then should have been refusd
> Those terms whatever, when they were propos'd:
> Thou didst accept them; wilt thou enjoy the good,
> Then cavil the conditions? (X, 754–59)

But he remembers that he is a creature and God is the Creator, and the awareness finally dawns on him that "thy reward was of his grace / Thy punishment then justly is at his will" (X, 767–68).

In *Paradise Lost* there is one covenant — the covenant of grace — willed by God before the foundations of the world, revealed to man in the protevangelium, and assented to by Adam on the mount. However, the dialogue between God and Christ in Book III, like the covenant of redemption, provides a basis for the covenant of grace. Without compact, Christ was sent in the fullness of time "conformably to the eternal counsel and grace of God the father."[24] The Christ of *Paradise Lost* does not article, but

> as a sacrifice
> Glad to be offer'd, he attends the will
> Of his great Father (III, 269–71).

Nevertheless, others thought that a covenant existed when one person assigned a stipulated work to another with the promise of a reward upon its completion.

The covenant of grace is the most precious legacy that Adam takes from the lost Paradise into the fallen world. As the first divine revelation concerning the covenant of grace, the "first gospel" under the conditional covenant is not only a prophecy and promise, but an explicit assurance that anyone who meets the conditions will be saved. Unlike the absolute promise to the elect of a suprarational God, the conditional covenant may be understood by all and fulfilled by all. Milton's God was beyond human understanding, but his covenant was clear and comprehensible, eminently reasonable, and wholly dependable.

From the beginning, God wills that salvation shall be offered to all conditionally, that is, in the form of a covenant. God "will clear thir senses dark, / What may suffice" (III, 188–89). The language indicates that man's action is conditional, but that God's commitment is absolute:

> Though but endevor'd with sincere intent,
> Mine ear shall not be slow, mine eye not shut.
> And I will place within them as a guide
> My umpire *Conscience*, whom if they will hear,
> Light after light well us'd they shall attain,
> And to the end persisting, safe arrive.
> (III, 192–97)

"Hellish hate" wreaks destruction only in those "who, when they may, accept not grace" (III, 302). This covenant is God's answer to the "League" and "mutual amitie" that Milton's Satan, following a long tradition,[25] will seek with man (IV, 375–76).

Although in Genesis God delivers to the serpent the curse that contains the promise of salvation, in *Paradise Lost* Christ comes as "Mans Friend, his Mediator" and "his Ransom and Redeemer voluntarie" (X, 60–61). He comes as the "mediator" (this is the first time the word is used in *Paradise Lost*) of the covenant; his voluntary sacrifice is the basis of the covenant. The covenant is first declared in a close paraphrase of Genesis 3:15:

> Between Thee and the Woman I will put
> Enmitie, and between thine and her Seed;
> Her Seed shall bruise thy head, thou bruise his heel.
> (X, 179–81)

Milton's Adam and Eve differ from most of the figures imagined by the Protestant commentators for they do not understand at first the "mysterious terms" that, in Milton's rational interpretation, were "judg'd as then best" (X, 173).

The first couple's — and man's — regeneration begins immediately and continues through a close, reciprocal relationship between God and men. The promised grace is granted at once as Christ arrays man's "inward nakedness" with "his Robe of righteousness" (X, 221–22). "Prevenient grace" descends to Adam and Eve. God's "implanted Grace in Man" will bring forth fruits of prayer and repentance (XI, 1–25) that suggest the "Prayer, repentance, and obedience due" (III, 191) of God's earlier declaration of the conditions for salvation.

If the covenant declared in Genesis 3:15 is to be fulfilled, obviously Eve must bear children. In her finest moment, Eve takes the first step toward making this possible by seeking a reconciliation with Adam. She, indeed, shows remorse as a woman and prospective mother when she offers to forego the pleasures of sexual love and motherhood. But her proposals of birth control and genocide would make impossible forever the birth of "the Seed" and the redemption of man. In a work based on a historical interpretation of Genesis, this is an agonizing moment with the gravest implications. Fortunately, her proposals call forth in Adam's "more attentive mind" proposals that are the exact opposite and that are based on his faith in the promise of the "mysterious terms" which he is only beginning to understand. Adam's reason is also restored, "what may suffice," and he realizes the conditional nature of God's promise and their own responsibility. He tells Eve that "if thou covet death" such acts as she proposes will provoke God "To make death in us live." However, if they choose to follow the "safer resolution" based on God's promise, they will triumph over Satan through "the Seed." And "How much more, if we pray him, will his ear / Be open" (X, 1020–61). Adam's response is an echo of God's words (III, 191–97). Though unrecorded in Genesis, the couple's tearful repentance, sincere prayers, and faith in the divine promise become the first manifestation of the covenant on the part of man. After their orisons following a sleepless night, Adam and Eve find "Strength added from above" (XI, 138). Adam understands that prayer has inclined the divine will to mercy and feels assured that "the bitterness of death / Is past, and we shall live," and Eve marvels that she is "grac't / The sourse of life" (XI, 148–68).

The triumphant strain of the covenant of grace, offering redemption to all of Adam's sons, unifies and dominates the final two books of *Paradise Lost*. God instructs Michael:

Dismiss them not disconsolate; reveale
To *Adam* what shall come in future dayes,
As I shall thee enlighten, intermix
My Cov'nant in the womans Seed renewed;
So send them forth, though sorrowing, yet in peace.
(XI, 113–17)

The most important tidings brought by Michael are the terms of the conditional covenant. A reprieve from death is

Giv'n thee of Grace, wherein thou may'st repent,
And one bad act with many deeds well done
May'st cover: well may then thy Lord appeas'd
Redeem thee quite from Deaths rapacious claime.
(XI, 255–58)

This represents a treaty of peace between God and man. Michael tells of further alienation from God, but also of peace and salvation to come. Abel, struck down while offering a sacrifice with the piety and devotion expected on man's part, is the first to die through man's sin and the first to be saved under the covenant of grace. His "Faith approv'd," he will "Loose no reward" (XI, 458–59). Enoch is lifted up "to walk with God / High in Salvation" to show "what reward / Awaits the good" (XI, 707–10). Although Adam is shown Noah preaching "Conversion and Repentance" in vain (XI, 723–26), Book XI ends triumphantly, but tranquilly, with the colored bow "Betok'ning peace from God, and Cov'nant new." "Such grace shall one just Man find" that God, promising never to destroy the earth by flood again, makes his covenant that all things

Shall hold their course, till fire purge all things new,
Both heav'n and Earth, wherein the just shall dwell.

In the final book of *Paradise Lost* a wearied, guilt-stricken, and anxious Adam finally realizes how all men, under both the law and the gospel, will be offered redemption through the covenant of grace. The covenant is renewed with *"faithful Abraham,"* "trusting all his wealth / With God," in whose seed "all Nations of the Earth" shall be blest (XII, 133–34, 147–48). Under Moses, who is accepted as a mediator, the Hebrews become aware of the "destind Seed" through the "types and shadows" of sacrifice (XII, 231–34). The Tabernacle and the Ark with the "Records of his Cov'nant" are also established. Adam learns that the law is imperfect and was but given

> With purpose to resign them in full time
> Up to a better Cov'nant, disciplin'd
> From shadowie Types to Truth, from Flesh to Spirit,
> From imposition of strict Laws, to free
> Acceptance of large Grace . . . (XII, 301–5).

Though men abandon God, the divine covenant remains. Delivering the Hebrews from their deserved Babylonian captivity, God remembers mercy "and his Cov'nant sworn / To *David*, stablisht as the days of Heav'n," for of his line should be a King whose reign should never end (XII, 320–30, 346–47).

In explaining the triumph of Christ, Michael paraphrases three scriptural texts (Gen. 3:15, Rom. 16:20, and I John 3:8) which Milton cited as showing the declaration of the covenant of grace. Christ will crush Satan by destroying the devil's works in man (XII, 390–95). Those of all nations who believe will accept baptism in the "profluent stream," the outward sealing of the covenant of grace. "The Law of Faith / Working through love" belongs to the new dispensation of the covenant of grace,[26] written by the Holy Spirit on the hearts of believers (XII, 485–90). Adam, standing on the mount of Paradise "greatly instructed" and in "peace of thought," having finally understood how man is to be saved, accepts the covenant on the part of man as he declares his faith and repentance and acknowledges Christ as "my Redeemer ever blest" (XII, 560–73). With this "summe of wisdome," Adam goes into the world.

In rejecting the covenant of works, Milton differed from most of his British contemporaries and followed the earlier tradition of Bullinger and Ursinus. He disagreed with the Calvinists in his insistence on the conditional covenant of grace. His views, however, approached those of John Goodwin and of Baxter. Milton's Adam in the state of innocence lives with more dignity, faith, and love than would be possible under a covenant of works, and after the Fall he is able to accept the covenant of grace on behalf of all his sons, not merely the elect. Milton's God gives all freely to Adam and Eve in Paradise, and offers a salvation that all are free to accept after the Fall. Through the covenant of grace God's ways to men are seen to be reasonable as well as just and merciful.

In other literary interpretations of the story of paradise, the law, the gospel, and the covenant also figure prominently. In most of these, Adam and Eve immediately upon their creation recognize God as their Creator and realize the importance of loving and obeying him. In the works of Sylvester, Andreini, and Grotius, the redemption of man is promised to Adam before he leaves paradise. Sylvester apparently regarded the tree of knowledge as a sacrament signifying a covenant. However, only in the *Adamus Exul* of Grotius is there a clear presentation of a covenant of works and a covenant of grace beginning in paradise. God promises punishment for disobedience, but also promises immortality to Adam and his descendants if they continue to love God. "Thus the agreement with the parents made," God declares, "will like wise bless their due posterity" ("Sic et cum geminis pacta parentibus / Contingent similes foedera posteros"). After the Fall, the voice of God proclaiming the "first gospel" promises to send the "Saviour of mankind" and to "cherish sparks of former light, / Forerunners of salvation" in man. "Nor among such ills have I denied you comfort," God asserts, "raising you under the sacred covenant to a hope of salvation" ("nec malis solatium / Tantis negavi, vos sacro sub foedere / In spem salutis erigens").[27]

To Know and to Work

Knowledge of the redemption of man was the primary legacy that Milton's Adam took from Paradise; yet most commentators and poets, following Genesis 2, discerned in paradise the beginnings of man's knowledge of the natural world and of such practical arts as agriculture, and considered these to be of great importance. To know and to work — this is the nature of man as an individual. After the Fall, however, man retained only remnants of his former

147

knowledge, though he might gradually regain more of it, and labor that had once been delight was now toil.

The older commentators and storytellers had based their ideas concerning Adam's knowledge on his creation in the divine image, the concept of original righteousness, and the intelligence he must have had in order to name the animals and rule over them. Renaissance writers, with the exception of the Socinians, regarded Adam's knowledge similarly, sometimes debating whether the animals appeared before Adam in reality or in his imagination. While earlier writers had dwelt on Adam's knowledge and abilities with an unbridled imagination, the Renaissance writers usually imposed some rational limitations on Adam as a historical figure. Most agreed that he had a perfect generic knowledge of all natural phenomena, but they disagreed about his knowledge of such supernatural mysteries as the Incarnation. Renaissance interest in both occult lore and natural science colored interpretations of Adam's endowments in innocence. Adam's Hebrew was regarded as the well of language undefiled. Considerations of Adam's knowledge led naturally to discussions of the scope and history of all human knowledge. Most assumed that Adam's posterity would have been gifted with perfect wisdom, but some concluded that man would have continued to develop his language, skills, and knowledge to even greater heights. All, however, regarded Adam's infused knowledge as the beginning of human learning.

The Continental commentators generally thought that Adam understood the natures of all things terrestrial and sidereal, but they sometimes voiced doubts about his proficiency in geometry and physics. Benedictus Pererius, Spanish author of the most widely respected Catholic commentary on Genesis, considered Adam capable of comprehending all natural phenomena and all that was desirable in public or private life, including agriculture, music, architecture, and painting. Nevertheless, Pererius felt that because Adam was a human being, his understanding would in some ways be limited; he would not, for example, possess a knowledge of future contingencies, of individual members of a genus, of the secrets of God, or of the minds and activities of other individuals. Cornelius a Lapide, another well-known Catholic commentator, similarly held that Adam had an infused knowledge of all natural things and of such supernatural matters as the fall of the angels, the Trinity, and something of the Incarnation. The Huguenot Andraeus Rivetus maintained that Adam was gifted with only the knowledge necessary to live prudently, honor God, and govern the creatures — in short, knowledge merely of those things that immediately concerned him.[28]

The traditional view of Adam's learning was reflected by various English writers. Samuel Purchas wrote that "*Adam* was without studie the greatest Philosopher and the greatest Divine (except the second Adam) that ever the earth bare." Salkeld pondered the question of how the animals had been brought to Adam, but felt assured that Adam knew all natural things, the angels' fall, the Trinity, and the Incarnation, though not as man's redemption for sin. Andrewes conceived of Adam as the father of theology, grammar, rhetoric, agriculture, and every liberal science and mechanical art. By considering the animals' natures and giving them names, he said, Adam showed his judgment and eloquence, both qualities "agreeable to the nature of man."[29]

Besides these generally accepted ideas about the extent of Adam's knowledge, there were fantastic stories of Adam as author, magician, and alchemist, partly inherited from old Jewish and Christian tradition and partly new, which were accepted by the credulous, disputed by the scholarly, and ridiculed by the satirist. The encyclopedist Henry Alsted and others supported the popular opinion that Adam was the inventor of the alphabet and writing. Adam was regarded as having provided the basis for the Prometheus story, and his development of a variety of arts, including astrology, was discussed by Athenasius Kircher, Jacobus Salianus, and John Owen. His reputation as an author was prodigious. Two psalms attributed to Adam, one expressing his joy at the creation of Eve and the other his sorrow after his disobedience, appeared in Lyons in 1641. Kircher and Hadrian Reland reported that Adam had composed ten or more prophetic books foretelling the deeds of future kings and peoples. A cabbalistic work on magic,

149

supposedly transmitted to Adam by the angel Raphael, was rejected as unauthentic by the occultist Cornelius Agrippa, but was nevertheless published in Amsterdam in 1701. Martin Del Rio, a Belgian Jesuit with an eye for the occult, discussed the notion that Adam had written a book on alchemy in paradise.[30] And Ben Jonson, satirizing many of the popular beliefs of his time in *The Alchemist*, exposed the sublime credulity of Sir Epicure Mammon, who attributes works on alchemy to Moses and Solomon, and mused, "Ay, and a treatise penn'd by Adam — / O' the philosopher's stone, and in High Dutch" (II. i. 83–86).

During the seventeenth century, Adam's knowledge, thought, and perception were submitted to a scientific interpretation. Repeatedly, Francis Bacon emphasized the sharp distinction between the moral knowledge of good and evil, which led to the Fall, and the God-given natural knowledge, which might be legitimately regained by the industry of man. Bacon spoke of "a more ample greatness, a more perfect order, and a more beautiful variety" which man could find in nature before the Fall. The Scottish divine John Weemse said not only could Adam learn from observation and experience, but he could reason from the cause to the effect and from the effect to the cause. Joseph Glanvill, a follower of Bacon and one of the most ardent admirers of Adam's endowments, asserted that "the most refined glories of subcoelestiall excellences are but more faint resemblances" of Adam's powers. Indeed, Glanvill was sure that the first man's senses were so acute that he could perceive all of nature's actions. "*Adam* needed no Spectacles," he said. "The acuteness of his natural Optics (if conjecture may have credit) shew'd him much of the Coelestial magnificence and bravery without a *Galileo's* tube." "And 'tis not unlikely," Glanvill added, "he had as clear a perception of the earths motions, as we think we have of its quiescence." He probably also could see the "subtle streams" from the loadstone and the circulation of the blood beneath the skin. Consequently, Adam's knowledge, unlike our own, "was compleatly built, upon the certain, extemporary notice" of his comprehensive, unerring faculties.[31]

Though the rational commentators of the Renaissance dismissed the most extraordinary stories of Adam's accomplishments, they nevertheless were very serious in seeking in paradise the origins of the knowledge which, in accordance with God's provision, was handed down from generation to generation. Andrewes, for instance, explained that Adam's knowledge of divinity and of all natural things was transmitted to the house of Seth, from him to Noah, and so conveyed to the house of Shem, and thence continued in Abraham's family. Alsted, the teacher of Milton's friend John Comenius, in his *Synopsis Theologiae*, held that there had been in God's people an orderly scholastic succession from paradise to the present. Domestic or private schools had existed from Adam to Aaron and Moses, and then public schools, offering specialized doctorates, had followed. Indeed, the university itself, with its enclosed green and its campus for the soldiers of Christ, was regarded as a reinstituted paradise where scholars might seek to rectify the error of Adam and to guard and transmit knowledge.[32]

In their study of language, most of Milton's contemporaries found one of the most striking examples of this unbroken tradition. While Johannes Goropius, a Flemish physician and antiquarian, offered the conclusion that Adam had spoken High Dutch, most followed Origen and St. Augustine in assuming that Hebrew had been given to Adam by God in paradise and then had remained the only language until others were derived from it during the confusion of tongues at the Tower of Babel. Accepting this basic assumption, Renaissance philologists, never lacking in either industry or ingenuity, confidently traced European words to their Hebraic origins. Since Hebrew was read from right to left and the European languages from left to right, it was deemed quite legitimate to work out an etymology from either direction. Although there were disputes concerning the total inspiration of Hebrew and particularly the vowel points, Latin and English dictionaries tracing every word to a Hebrew root appeared as unshakable buttresses supporting the accepted view that language, the key to all knowledge, had continued from paradise to the present.

Despite the generally accepted ideas about the scope and perfec-

151

tion of Adam's knowledge, a number of diversely oriented writers believed that this knowledge was to increase gradually as human culture developed. Thomas Cardinal Cajetan, who shocked many by contending that Adam viewed the animals only in his imagination, also observed that the universal art of agriculture was the first disclosed to man because it was necessary for food, even in the state of innocence, and because in the natural order first comes agriculture, then the care of sheep, and finally the other arts. Even Pererius, who extolled Adam's intelligence, imagined Adam delighting in the study of new plants and animals produced by spontaneous generation or crossbreeding. According to Weemse, Adam's knowledge in paradise was obscure, compared to what it would have been. Adam possessed the "first principles" of all arts and sciences, whereby he might learn by observing the creatures and gain an *"experimentall knowledge."* Hobbes also contributed to the idea of a historical development from Eden. He remarked that the knowledge given to Adam to name the creatures was sufficient to lead him to more names, and then gradually to join these, "and so by succession of time, so much language might be gotten, as he had use for, though not so copious, as an orator, or philosopher has need of." Above all, said Hobbes, he did not learn such terms as "entity" and "quiddity." [33]

If man was to know, he was also to work. Though some earlier writers had considered the labor as spiritual cultivation and Bacon had deemed it "the work of contemplation," most Renaissance critics interpreted the gardening literally and felt that Adam's agricultural skill was part of his knowledge. From the beginning God had ordained that work was proper to the life of man. Hale, for instance, pointed out that God had created a paradise that needed to be worked. The myths of the golden age to the contrary, Pererius and Lapide saw the practice of agriculture beginning with man and the world. Luther reminded his followers that we must still dress and keep the land. John White, the "Dorchester Patriarch," thought that agriculture would have been the only employment of an unfallen race.[34]

While all commentators regarded the work in Eden as pleasant, some also regarded it as necessary. Although the Yahwist had not described the work as delightful, the Renaissance writers, following a long tradition, extolled it as affording joy, satisfaction, physical exercise, solace, recreation, and as a good way of keeping out of mischief. "All his delights," said Bishop Joseph Hall of Adam, "could not have made him happy in an idle life." Cajetan, Salkeld, and others regarded the work as essential for existence, and Inveges explained that the planting, transplanting, and grafting were all needed.[35]

Many also found in God's first instructions to Adam an enduring moral imperative, which operated even more strongly in the fallen world and provided the occasion for numerous homilies. Inveges thought that Adam had received the first law — the instructions to cultivate and keep the land — from an angel in a walk through the garden about the fourth hour. He raised the question of whether this law applied as well to Eve and her daughters. Calvin asserted that God "condemned all indolent repose" and had created men "to employ themselves in some work, and not to lie down in inactivity and idleness." Most English writers agreed. "Idlenesse and lawlesse liberty was not permitted to Adam in Paradise," one Puritan declared. Bishop Hall wrote that God had created Adam with "hands to worke, and worke fit for his hands," and White granted that it was "a very equall law" that man should work for what he would receive.[36]

The problem of knowledge was crucial for Milton. The problem of work was only slightly less important. His concern with both is reflected in his statement of the two goals of education: "to repair the ruines of our first Parents by regaining to know God aright," and to fit "a man to perform justly, skilfully, and magnanimously all the offices both private and publick of Peace and War." The truth possessed by the first parents before their ruin was the source of all real knowledge and the recovery of this shattered truth was man's most important labor. Milton regarded Adam's knowledge in paradise as an ideal and reacted violently against the Pelagian and Socinian interpretations that disparaged it. For Milton the contemplative life and the active life were

153

always one: work was the proper cultivation and use of knowledge. He referred to "the hardest labour in the deep mines of knowledge," and inquired what "a Nation so pliant and so prone to seek after knowledge" could want but "wise and faithful labourers, to make a knowing people." [37] Milton himself worked in his "great task-Masters eye," rejected sporting "with *Amaryllis* in the shade," and when he became blind asked, "Doth God exact day labour, light deny'd." He ultimately gave his own answer — *Paradise Lost*.

Avoiding extremes and novelty, Milton generally followed the commentators in his presentation of the characteristics and limitations of Adam's knowledge. However, the theoretical concept of knowledge in a state of original righteousness is transformed in the drama of a historical Adam whose knowledge relates him harmoniously to every aspect of his world and life. Milton realized that his poetry could only suggest to a fallen world the dazzling beauty of an unshattered Truth.

Both Adam and Eve were regarded as having been created with a knowledge and understanding appropriate to a state of original righteousness, but Adam was depicted by almost all the commentators and by Milton as preeminent in these virtues. Milton's Adam has an impressive array of the kinds of knowledge often attributed to him by the commentators. Although Adam has been given knowledge of the natures of all the creatures by "sudden apprehension," his knowledge is more closely related to his creation in the divine image than to his naming of the animals. He possesses infused knowledge, that acquired through the observation of nature and Eve, and knowledge revealed by God and Raphael before the Fall and by Christ and Michael afterward. He views the world neither as a hermeticist nor as a scientist, but as a creature of God. He is not a magician, a prelapsarian computer, or an intellectual showoff, yet he has a perfect knowledge of the natural world and of his own circumstances. He tells Raphael that he could speak immediately "and readily could name / What e're I saw" (VIII, 272–73) and that he understood almost immediately his creation and his destiny as the father of men. Adam also comprehends a great deal of astronomy and meteorology, the influence of the sun and stars on the earth, his gardening, human psychology, and dreams. He knows theoretically that unapproved evil can leave no blame (V, 117–19). Both Adam and Eve are, indeed, authors and composers, praising God in "various style" and "fit strains pronounc't or sung" of unmeditated "Prose or numerous Verse" (V, 146, 148–50). From God, Adam learns of his dominion over the creatures, his appointed work, and the institution of knowledge; and from Raphael, he receives revealed knowledge of the exaltation of Christ, the war in heaven, hell, the Creation, the Great Chain of Being, the love life and diet of angels, and the future of man if he continues in obedience.

Milton agreed with all the commentators that Adam's knowledge had fixed limits. Milton's Adam is seemingly not illumined with the divine archetypes mentioned by Augustine. In keeping with the views of Aquinas and many Renaissance writers, the unfallen Adam of *Paradise Lost* does not understand many divine mysteries such as the Incarnation. He does not really comprehend death ("what ere death is, / Some dreadful thing no doubt," IV, 425–26). Adam does not know his own future, and is therefore, as he recognized at his creation, happier than he realizes (VIII, 282); Eve is of course deceived in thinking good "had / And yet unknown, is as not had at all" (IX, 756–57). Adam is unaware of the secret thoughts of angels or of other individuals, though an extrasensory knowledge of Satan or of Eve might have prevented catastrophe. Even his natural perception is limited. Raphael might seem to be replying to such views as those of Glanvill when he tells Adam,

> God to remove his wayes from human sense,
> Plac'd Heav'n from Earth so farr, that earthly sight,
> If it presume, might erre in things too high,
> And no advantage gaine (VIII, 119–22).

Yet it is not how much or how little Adam knows in the state of innocence that is most important, but his sense of value. Before his ruin he recognizes all things to be in a harmonious relationship to each other because he sees them in relation to the true end of knowledge: "to know God aright, and out of that knowledge to love him, to imitate him." With this end, the root of all true knowledge, Adam is able to distinguish the greater good from the lesser good, the divine Truth from the human impression, the whole from the part, and thus he is able to comprehend the proper scope, the proper direction, and the proper use of knowledge. He is guided by Right Reason and possesses Right Knowledge. In this sense, Milton's Adam, as one who knows God and his creation aright and who loves true knowledge, is the philosopher pictured by many commentators from St. Augustine to Purchas.

In describing the first moments of humanity to Raphael, Adam explains that at first he did not know his origin but reasoned that he had been created by some great, good, and powerful Maker. His first question was "how may I know him, how adore" (VIII, 280). During the early hours of this first morning, Adam easily begins to distinguish between the infinity of God and the imperfection of man and also between the irrational beast and the rational man, made in the divine image. Adam's first speech in *Paradise Lost* (IV, 410–39) relates Eve, their dominion, their labor, and the special commandment to the goodness and generosity of God. His lectures to Eve are not to impress her, but to guide her to know herself in relation to God. When Eve asks why the stars are not put out when she goes to bed, Adam explains their continued appearance in relation to the orderly course of nature, the stellar influence on plants, "Nations yet unborn," and the angels; yet the underlying certainty in his answer is that none of God's works is in vain, and that all contribute to his "ceaseless praise" (IV, 660–89). When Eve awakes troubled by her dream, Adam explains the difference between fancy and true knowledge in order to bring Eve into harmony again with God and Paradise. In their morning hymn they perceive that all things praise God; their natural knowledge, response to beauty, and skill in verse and song fuse in this praise.

Much of Adam's discussion with Raphael focuses on the problem of knowledge and value. Recognizing his own limitations, Adam starts his questioning with the timid inquiry about angelic fruits in Book V; by the beginning of Book VII, however, he is emboldened to ask more of "Things above Earthly thought, which yet concernd / Our knowing" (VII, 82–83). He wants to learn more about the Creation "not to explore the secrets" but "the more / To magnifie his works, the more we know" (VII, 95–97). Raphael reminds Adam of the necessity for temperance in knowledge, the need to know what to know and what not to know. Those who seek to "calculate the Starrs," rather than to admire, will become lost in "Centric and Eccentric scribl'd o're the Sphere" (VIII, 80–83). Dismissing things remote, obscure, and subtle, Adam concludes that,

> to know
> That which before us lies in daily life,
> Is the prime Wisdom, what is more, is fume,
> Or emptiness, or fond impertinence,
> And renders us in things that most concerne
> Unpractis'd, unprepar'd, and still to seek.
> (VIII, 192–97)

This is not a renunciation of knowledge, but a value statement: the most valuable knowledge is to know what knowledge is the most valuable, and why.

Adam has a further question of value very near indeed — Eve. He has understood that the earth may be more excellent than larger and brighter bodies. He also realizes that "in the prime end of Nature," the instrument of God, inward faculties excel outward appearance, that he excels Eve, and that love excels passion. But as Adam himself perceives, he dismisses "higher" knowledge in Eve's presence by "attributing overmuch to things / Less excellent" (VIII, 565–66). Adam's knowledge does not fail him, though he ultimately fails to accept and direct his knowledge.

Eve comprehends less than Adam, but her problem is not so much that she lacks knowledge as that she has a short interest span and sometimes will not stop to think at all. She too realizes that to know God aright is the highest knowledge, but to know him through Adam is her happiest knowledge. After her first meeting with Adam, she understands "How beauty is excelld by manly grace / And wisdom, which alone is truly fair" (IV, 490–91). After she partakes of the apple, Eve's values are badly distorted. She no longer wants to know God aright, but selfishly to "keep the odds of Knowledge in my power" (IX, 820).

Following the Fall much of Adam's original knowledge is retained by him and his descendants, who even continue to learn and invent, yet the ability to judge all things in relation to a right knowledge of God is seriously impaired. Adam is at first lost in the serpentine writhings of his own psyche. Then, remembering the covenant of grace announced in "mysterious terms," he begins to regain the knowledge and love of God. Adam foresees how knowledge will be employed and misemployed in the future. He understands from his natural knowledge how he may produce fire, not by stealing it from the gods like Prometheus, but instructed by God through prayer (X, 1070–78). However, Adam, in regaining knowledge and love of God through his "Teacher" Michael, learns that natural and practical knowledge may become divorced from God and right values. The "just men," whom Adam views with "all thir study bent / To worship God aright, and know his works / Not hid," are opposed to the godless descendants of Cain who have fashioned tools on the forge and even the organ with its "resonant fugue." Moreover, the just men find "higher knowledge" debased in the presence of the "fair Atheists" who seduce them (X, 556– 627). Again, after the Flood, the few who live "With some regard to what is just and right" (XII, 16) are overcome by those who invent warfare and build a "Citie and Towre, whose top may reach to Heav'n" (XII, 44). Adam himself, having learned from the example of his Redeemer that the weak and meek can subvert the "worldly wise" and "worldly strong," leaves Paradise with "the summe / of wisdome" (XII, 568–76).

Milton's task in presenting the beginnings of human labor in the state of original righteousness was almost as formidable as that of presenting the beginnings of knowledge. Although the commentators repeatedly asserted that the work was pleasant, Milton had to make this pleasure dramatically convincing. He did this by keeping any actual labor in the background, despite Adam's and

Eve's frequent references to "our delightful task" and "our pleasant labour." When Adam and Eve first appear in Book IV, they are resting in the shade after no more labor "then suffic'd / To recommend cool *Zephyr*, and made ease / More easie" (IV, 328–30). In their next appearance, they are ready for repose from labor. After the discussion of Eve's dream and the morning prayer, they work — for eight and a half lines, most of which is a description of nature (V, 211–19). God then dispatches Raphael, but by the time the angel has completed his swift flight to earth, Adam is in his cool bower waiting for lunch. On the following fateful morning the couple separate, but do little gardening.

Milton's Adam and Eve depart from Renaissance commentary most in the kind of work they perform. Most writers thought that Adam's planting, sometimes even plowing, was necessary or at least very beneficial in producing a good harvest. True, God first gave Paradise to Adam to "Till and keep" (VIII, 320). However, since Milton conceived of Paradise as a wild plateau with an eternal spring and superabundant yield, rather than as a cultivated garden, his Adam and Eve need chiefly to lop, prune, and clear the luxuriant growth. In such a setting Adam seems to need a chain saw more than a plow.

More important than their gardening, the real labor of Adam and Eve is to found the human race. As Aeneas was to found Rome, so the first parents were intended to establish on earth the City of God, whose inhabitants would not only increase and multiply, but would know God aright and love him. Before placing Adam in Paradise, God hails him "First Man, of Men innumerable ordain'd / First Father" (VIII, 297–98). Similarly, Eve, even before she meets Adam, is told that she "shalt bear / Multitudes like thy self" (IV, 473–74). Repeatedly while viewing the superabundant growth of Paradise, they anticipate the hands that will assist them in the Lord's work in the future (IV, 628–29, 729–34; IX, 207–8, 246–47). The "Patriarch of Mankind" hears from Raphael in Paradise, as Aeneas hears from Anchises in the Underworld, of his continuing obligations and of the future of his race — but with the pointed warning "if ye be found obedient" (V, 501). Adam later learns of more difficult labors and of a more demanding future from Michael. Yet Adam and Eve, with true epic heroism, continue to perform their divinely assigned task with the favor of divine grace.

Although Milton does not sound the imperative of work as sternly as do some of the commentators, it is clear that Adam and Eve establish the basic pattern of daily life, labor and rest, though after the Fall the labor is more tiring and the rest periods considerably less frequent. As Adam explains to Eve,

> God hath set to men
> Labour and rest, as day and night
> Successive . . . (IV, 612–14).

> Man hath his daily work of body or mind
> Appointed, which declares his Dignitie,
> And the regard of Heav'n on all his waies (IV, 618–20).

Milton deviated from a strict and literal reading of Scripture and a great deal of exegesis in explicitly attributing to Eve as well as to Adam both the responsibility and dignity of labor. The references to the "younger hands" soon to assist suggest that children would also labor in Paradise. Despite the rest periods for food, conversation, and caresses, the day is for work, as the night is for sleep. The first pair are to arise "ere fresh Morning streak the East / With first approach of light" (IV, 623–24). They "haste" to work after the delay caused by Eve's dream. After the Fall, Adam resolutely accepts the toilsome labor to bring forth sustenance from a cursed ground: "Idleness had bin worse" (X, 1055). Beyond the gates of Paradise, Adam's vision of a field "Part arable and tilth, whereon were Sheaves / New reapt, the other part sheepwalks and foulds" (XI, 430–31) implies the continuance and development of human labor. The descendants of the "sweatie Reaper" Cain, without knowing God aright, nevertheless exploit knowledge granted through divine grace to expand the fields of man's work. It is not Cain, however, but the grand Hebrew patriarchs, Noah, Abraham, and Moses, who in their knowledge and love of God carry on the great labor of helping to establish the City of God on earth.

While in *Paradise Lost* the knowledge and work of Adam and
Eve blend with other aspects of the state of innocence in a harmonious, continuing whole, in the works of the other poets of
paradise the vision is often fragmentary. These poets may tell us
what Adam knew, yet they do not show his mind in action. Sylvester's Adam comprehends the good by experience and the bad, "but
not by proofe or yet infused." After the expulsion Adam tells Seth
of the heavens, creatures, and plants. In the drama of Grotius,
Adam can discuss the Trinity and God as the unmoved mover
when he speaks with an angel who explains to him the Creation.
Adorned with a laurel wreath, he can compose poetry and song.
Immediately upon his creation, the Adam of Andreini recognizes
God's infinity and his own finitude. During Eve's creation, he
dreams of the Trinity. As a kind of Edenic St. Francis, he politely
introduces himself to the animals and assigns them names. The
Adam of della Salandra is said to excel in the masculine virtues of
prudence, sanity, gravity, and wisdom. There is little emphasis on
knowledge in Vondel's *Adam in Ballingschap*, but here too Adam
understands the Trinity and is told of the Creation in an angelic
hymn.[38] These other poets had even more difficulty than Milton
in describing any actual work as part of the life of paradise.
Readers were assured that Adam's work was like play or dancing.
However, none of these writers risked detracting from his picture
of a carefree prelapsarian life by presenting Adam and Eve actually working.

Marriage, Religion, and Society

The origin of various social institutions was also found in paradise
by many writers. The first of these and the living root of the
others was marriage. God had clearly ordained marriage and, by
implication, the family in paradise (Gen. 2: 21–24). Some writers
discerned the first newly wed couple to be the beginning of certain
forms of worship or of the Church itself. Discussions concerning
the origin of the state focused on the problem of whether any kind
of government was appropriate to those in original righteousness
or only to the fallen. Milton discovered the ideals of marriage,

worship, and human society shining with pristine clarity in the lost paradise.

God himself had instituted marriage and had celebrated the first nuptials. Consequently, for Protestant critics, there could be no doubt that marriage was superior to the single life and to virginity. "There were never such Saints in the world, as were Saint *Adam* and Saint *Eve* in the estate of their innocencie and integrity," observed Andrewes, "yet were they married." Citing the original institution of marriage as an argument against the Catholic exaltation of virginity, the Puritan William Secker considered it "strange that that should be a pollution, which was instituted before corruption, or that impurity, which was ordained in the state of innocency." [39]

Although both Catholics and Protestants would have agreed that human love originated in paradise, all were less sure that sex had begun there. It was difficult to imagine a paradisal life with sex or without sex. Then, too, there were touchy questions. In a state of perfection Eve should have conceived, and yet Cain was certainly not born in innocence. Also, the first reference to Adam's knowing his wife was Gen. 4:1. A number of writers thought Adam and Eve had remained virgins, partly because of the short time spent in paradise. Pererius, for example, was not willing to grant that Adam and Eve had engaged in intercourse, but he assumed that if the state of innocence had continued, there would have been an equal number of boys and girls, none of course sterile and all to be married. Inveges concluded that Adam and Eve, after the consummation of their marriage, would probably have slept separately. He supposed they and their offspring would have engaged in normal intercourse with innocent pleasure, but without the lust and the frequency of the fallen world. Some Protestants were convinced that the marriage of Adam and Eve could not have been perfect in paradise without sexual life. Luther said it was as proper for Adam to cohabit with his wife as to eat with her, and Rivetus asserted that intercourse was of divine origin.[40]

What was the relationship between Adam and Eve in innocence and to what extent did it endure or change after the divine pronouncement that a husband should rule over his wife (Gen. 3:16)? It was generally agreed that before the Fall the woman's subservience to her husband was voluntary — she did what she wanted to do anyhow — while afterward it was involuntary. Marriage as first established by God continued as a pattern and ideal. From the beginning, a man and his wife were to be drawn together by mutual piety, praying for one another. From many pulpits, with little variation, one might hear listed the ends for which wives had been created: for procreation, for "lawfull Remedie agaynst whoredom," for comfort in sickness and affliction, and for taking care of household worries and troubles, including the education of children. Preaching on the establishment of marriage, Andrewes considered the marital tie as a union between hearts and bodies that was not to be broken. In his popular tract *A Wedding Ring Fit for the Finger*, Secker compared a man and his wife to "two candles burning together," "two fragrant flowers bound up in one Nosegay," two well-tuned instruments sounding together, and two springs joining in one stream.[41]

The married state and the family were also seen as providing the nucleus for the development of religious and social customs and institutions from the earliest times. Ernst Troeltsch has said that in both Catholic and Protestant doctrine the family, thought of as established in paradise or in the primitive state and confirmed and reordered after the Fall, is "the germ and the precursor of the Church" and the "archetype of all social organizations."[42] In the sixteenth and seventeenth centuries, both the desire to establish an accurate, unbroken history and the need to support or oppose a particular form of church or civil government led men to seek origins in the first man, the first marriage, and the first family.

In Ezekiel and in centuries of Christian writing, paradise and the Church had been symbolically associated. During the sixteenth and seventeenth centuries, some Protestant writers sought to explain the beginnings of the Church in paradise with Adam and Eve. Luther, in one of the most vivid descriptions of the establishment of worship and the Church in paradise, asserted

163

that "man should prove his reverence to God, and exercise himself, as it were, in divine worship" by abstaining from the tree of knowledge. With this tree, he said, God "built man a church to serve and praise Him for His gracious gifts." Imagining the tree in "a grove in which there were many trees of the same species," Luther thought that the "tree of the knowledge of good and evil would have been (Adam's) church, where he and his descendants would have gathered on the sabbath, and where after having partaken of the tree of life, he would have given praise and thanks to God for His many mercies." Pointing out that both the garden and the Jewish sanctuary (Ezek. 44:1) had eastern gates, Luther wrote that the garden would have been the temple of the world. One of Luther's followers considered the tree of knowledge to be a sign calling for reverence and worship of God. It would have been, he claimed, a temple where men would have gathered as they do at a divinely designated place of worship.[43]

Searching for a Scriptural basis for the establishment of the Church in the state of innocence, some English writers, both Anglican and Puritan, followed Luther in relating the beginning of the church to the commandment concerning the tree of knowledge; however, they went beyond Luther in also relating this to the covenant of works. Like Bullinger, others connected the first church to the "first gospel," the covenant of grace, and the sacrifice of the beasts whose skins clothed Adam and Eve. Andrewes felt that "the Almighty God had framed the estate Ecclesiasticall, which is his Church, by the Covenant made between God and man" regarding the forbidden fruit, and he imagined the tree as providing Adam with a pulpit from which on the sabbath he might preach sermons concerning the things represented by the two special trees. Similarly, Ussher regarded the trees as the "outward seals" of the covenant of works, so situated "that Adam before and in sight of them might resort to some special place to serve God in." Contemplating the church within, Vane said that Adam as the type of Christ was "the shadowy Temple and first Sanctuary wherein divine worship and service was to be performed according to the tenor of the first covenant." The establishment of the

164

Church was also based upon Genesis 3:15. Bishop John Overall's *Convocation Book*, which never achieved official status because of James I's disapproval, stated that God's promise of the seed laid the grounds for Christian doctrine and for the Church of Christ. Preston asserted that after God himself had preached to Adam and Eve in promising the seed, "the Church continued in the virtue of this promise, this preaching of the Gospell, until Abraham's time." Summing up the existing views, one writer found the origin of the Church "intermingled" and "intimated variously" in the accounts of Adam's creation in God's image, the sanctification of the sabbath, God's words concerning the trees, the promised seed, and the sacrifice of the beasts whose skins clothed the first pair.[44]

Figures as different as Alexander Ross, defender of the Establishment, and John Bunyan, defender of the unestablished, considered the Edenic garden as representative of the Church. Ross maintained that ordination, sacraments, and excommunication had existed for Adam and Eve. He thought that God had ordained Adam and some of his children, probably by the enduring custom of the imposition of hands. "God preached to Adam in Paradise and doubtless he preached to his children out of Paradise." The sacraments were also administered, Ross contended. He explained that "*Adam* and *Eve* for their disobedience were excommunicated out of Paradise, which was then the type of the Church." With preaching, sacraments, and excommunication, he concluded, "it follows there was then a Church and church government." Bunyan discerned that the Church was presented under the similitude of a garden in Genesis 2. He believed that the tree of life was a type of Christ and that Adam, who was to dress and keep the garden, was a figure of Christ as the "pastor and chief bishop of his Church."[45]

Views of the beginnings of civil government, within or outside paradise, were strewn as thick as autumnal leaves in Vallombrosa or as the fallen angels in Hell; indeed Milton might gladly have held these fallen angels responsible for many of these opinions. Various theories depended on conceptions of creation, natural law, the covenant, and marriage, but the pivotal issue was whether any kind of civil government had been instituted or would have been instituted in the state of innocence or whether it was a consequence of the Fall. In disputing magisterial prerogatives, writers repeatedly sought support either in Aristotle's ideal of man as a political animal by nature or in St. Augustine's view that government, a result of the Fall, would not have been appropriate when men were equal in the perfections of nature and grace. In Christianizing Aristotle, Aquinas distinguished between the directive service of the most virtuous which would have developed naturally in Eden and the coercive rule which developed after the Fall. Accepting government as natural and good, Aquinas and Dante thought of a universal state beside a universal Church, but under God; this vision was lost after Gregory XII denounced political government as the handiwork of Satan and Sin.

In the sixteenth and seventeenth centuries, Eden became a war-scarred battleground as polemicists disputed the origin of royal and magisterial prerogatives and of individual natural rights. What was the basis in divine revelation or in the earliest historical precedent for the promulgation and enforcement of laws in the state? No one doubted that God had given Adam dominion over the creatures, but had he given him dominion over other men? Even if the divine right of kings were accepted, could kings rule without the consent of the governed? Discussions of monarchy or of a social covenant led back to the unsettled question of when, where, why, and how government had first been formed. Both Luther and Calvin thought of government as beginning after the Fall. However, neither the Spanish Jesuits nor the natural rights philosophers such as Johannes Althusius could agree among themselves. Biblical commentators differed, but there was no clear, consistent Catholic or Protestant position. In England, there were not only the towering achievements of Filmer, Hobbes, and Milton, but the excited efforts of numerous dedicated pamphleteers.

The Spanish Jesuit Luis Molina, the German Calvinist Keckermann, and other writers following Aristotle considered the state to be an organic whole in which men would develop naturally and attain a harmonious relationship with others. Molina explained that in innocence the state would have sprung naturally from the family, and coercive power would have been unnecessary. In keeping with the usual position of the Spanish Jesuits, he assumed that a separate ecclesiastical power, representative of man's supernatural end, would direct the lay power. After the Fall, enough natural and supernatural knowledge remained with Adam to enable him to institute this directive ecclesiastical power. In short, Molina concluded that the Fall made much more necessary what would have developed anyhow. Keckermann, reflecting upon the "pulcherrimam quaestionem" of whether government would have existed without the Fall, argued that men in innocence would have been led to government by God, human instincts, and natural law. He said, "There would have been some political direction, even though it would have been quite different from that which now is." He saw a progression from husband and wife to larger families, to villages, cities, provinces, and kingdoms. Such Protestant commentators as David Pareus and Rivetus also asserted that civil government would have developed naturally from family relationships if man had not sinned. They agreed that there would have been voluntary acceptance of some civil order, with inferiors and superiors. According to Rivetus, as population increased, states would have developed with princes dedicated to the good of the people.[46]

In England too, writers reasoning from various premises concluded that paradise held the seedlings of utopian states. Taking issue with St. Augustine, Salkeld granted that there was "no burdensome dominion as now." "Yet questionlesse," he continued, "there should have been a kinde of order, subiection, and subordination, of children, inferiors, and subjects, to their parents, superiors, and political governours . . . by a voluntary and sweet subiection flowing from nature, and confirmed by grace." He based this conclusion logically on the assumption of a natural and inevitable inequality in "wisdom, knowledge, skill, magnanimitie and prudence" as well as in political aptitude. Looking simultaneously back to paradise and forward to the millennium in quest of a perfect society, Vane envisioned a perfect magistracy, exhorting the virtuous to virtue and preserving the good in their goodness. "We are not to conceive, as most are apt to do that man in his innocent and sinlesse nature, stood in no need of this office of Magistrate; for it is not only useful to restraine from unrighteousness and disorder occasioned by sin and the fall, but also to conceive and maintaine men in the good order and right disposition of things, wherein by their creation they were placed." Vane, however, insisted that this ideal magistracy would be concerned only with the outward man, not with Christ's inner government and the rule of conscience.[47] In paradise, then, might be found a precedent for magistracy, but also a touchstone to separate the bad magistrate from the good one.

This problem of the origin of government became focused on the pressing question of the origin of monarchy. Had monarchy been divinely ordained before the Fall, or after the Fall, or was it a consequence of the Fall? Writers wrung political significance from the first chapters of Genesis, the biblical accounts of the Hebrew kings, and the New Testament epistles, especially St. Paul's reference to "the higher powers" (Rom. 13:1–2). They also turned to Aristotle and to later classical historians and political writers. In England, William the Conqueror and Magna Carta were subjected to a new scrutiny. What was the basis for theories of kingship, the social contract, and natural law? What was divine and what was human in the establishment of government? What was the authority for a limited monarchy or for mixed government? Although Adam for centuries had been pictured as a king in his rule over the creatures, monarchy as an institution had usually been traced to Nimrod (Gen. 10:9–12). Most of the Renaissance commentators considered Nimrod not only as the first king but also as a tyrant. Some monarchists sought a firmer historical rooting for kingship in paradise, while other writers disputed the attribution of any regal powers to Adam. Inveges reflected some of the complexity of the problem. He characterized

Adam as "king of kings" under Christ and supposed that in paradise he had been assigned a guardian angel of a high order, probably Gabriel or Michael, since the heads of Church and state were to receive this honor and protection. He envisioned inequality and various kingdoms in an enduring state of innocence, but no palaces, crowns, or hereditary rule.[48]

In England in the early seventeenth century, a basis for monarchy was found in the powers given to Adam by God. In 1606 the English prelates agreed to the statement in Bishop Overall's *Convocation Book* that God had in effect given a "potestas regia" to Adam for his time and to the rest of the patriarchs and chief fathers successively before the Flood. Ralegh traced the development of royal power from Adam's lordship over his own children. Government developed through stages of filial obedience, he concluded, with the fathers of nations becoming the first kings.[49]

In the heated controversies of the 1640s, several writers conceived of Adam as the first king. John Maxwell, a chaplain to Charles I, in denying that the king derived sovereignty from the people through a social contract, depended heavily on "the higher powers" and maintained that the king derived his power only from God. Though aristocracy, democracy, and mixed government had developed after the Fall, God had originally ordained only monarchy, the one form of government rooted in unfallen nature. God had fixed government "in the person of Adam, before Evah or anyone else came into the world," but "that government was fixed in a governour before he had over whom to beare rule, is no paradox in Philosophy." All created things can subsist and continue only by order, by government, said Maxwell. He declared that after the Fall the kingship was "declared transmissible from Adam to the first borne." As the nation moved toward the execution of Charles, some moving pleas were made in his defense. John Gauden in his *Religious and Loyal Protestation* said that Charles's blood would cry out "as the blood of *Adam* would have done if *Cain* had slaine him being his father, instead of *Abel* his brother." Calling upon Puritan leaders "in the name, and in the bowels of *Jesus Christ*" to

169

review their principles, Henry Hammond asked whether Adam and his posterity, continuing in innocence, would not have been capable of positive precepts to order civil life and "whether in reason some one or more men should not have had superiority over all others, Parents over Children, and the like."[50]

The most cogent and influential arguments for Adam's kingship appeared in the writings of Sir Robert Filmer. *Patriarcha*, the fullest exposition of his political theory, was known in manuscript in 1642, but was not published until after *Paradise Lost*. However, in the period preceding the execution of Charles, Filmer's *The Anarchy of a Limited or Mixed Monarchy* as well as his other tracts were accessible. In all of these works, Filmer began with the assumption that any certain proof or credible account of government must originate with Adam. Although Filmer's explanation of monarchy depended on the acceptance of Genesis as a divine revelation, his method was to use the Bible as a consistent historical document, not as a quarry for separate texts to be laid together. His study showed that kingship from the world's beginning to the seventeenth century was not one jot less natural or less certain than fatherhood. Merritt Y. Hughes has written that the importance of Filmer's belief that the kings of his own time inherited Adam's lordship "was its truly representative character in the thinking of the time. It was one of the perilously self-consistent theories of royal absolutism against which the *Tenure* was a tough protest."[51]

In *The Anarchy of a Limited or Mixed Monarchy*, Filmer was replying in general to "all the arguments from pulpit and press representing the Kingdom of England as a limited or mixed monarchy" and in particular to the anonymous *Treatise of Monarchie*. Philip Hunton, the author of this work, had found the divine ordination of government in God's commandment to Adam to rule over his wife (Gen. 3:16), but had insisted that it was men's prerogative to determine the kind of government they desired. He argued that a monarchy "radically limited and fundamentally mixed" was founded as firmly upon divine authority as was any other form of government. Filmer's reply illustrates clearly the royalist strategy to reject the classical writers and to rely on Scripture. "It is a shame and a scandal for us Christians," he wrote, "to seek the origin of Government from the inventions or fictions of Poets, Orators, Philosophers, and heathen Historians, who all lived thousands of years after the Creation, and were (in a manner) ignorant of it." The true origin of government was with Adam, who was a king by divine appointment even before he had subjects. His power would have been directive, not coactive. While men living in innocence would not need moral direction, "yet things *indifferent* that depended meerly on their free will might be directed by the power of *Adam's* command." But Adam was decidedly not a constitutional monarch: "Neither *Eve* nor his Children could either limit *Adam's* power, or join others with him in the government, and what was given unto *Adam* was given in his name to his posterity." [52]

Patriarcha gained wide recognition as a very reasonable historical study which established the kingship of Adam and at the same time proved the logical impossibility of the individual natural rights assumed by writers as different as Hobbes and Milton. Though Adam's children of course held authority over their own children, still Adam as patriarch remained "Lord Paramount over his Children's Children to all Generations." The succeeding patriarchs also held "Royal Authority" over their descendants. "The Lordship which Adam by creation had over the whole world, and by right descending from him the Patriarchs did enjoy, was large and ample as the Absolute Dominion of any Monarch which has been since the creation," wrote Filmer. Showing no concern for the differences between royal power before and after the Fall, Filmer cited the patriarch's judging in capital crimes, their making war and concluding peace as signs of their sovereignty. Property was private and at the disposal of Adam and his legitimate heirs. As Peter Laslett has pointed out, *Patriarcha* implies the inferiority of women and the inequality of all humans, with sons subject to fathers, and younger brothers to elder brothers. [53]

Filmer used the argument for kingship to destroy the doctrine

171

of the natural freedom of mankind, "a New, Plausible and Dangerous Opinion," whose source was in paradise. In his *Observations concerning the Original of Government*, which included reflections on Hobbes and Milton, Filmer logically developed his case against natural rights: "If God created only *Adam*, and of a Piece of him made the Woman; and if by Generation of these two, as parts of them, all Mankind be propagated: If also God gave to *Adam* not only the Dominion over the Woman and the Children that should issue from them, but also over the whole Earth to subdue it, and over all the Creatures on it, so that as long as *Adam* lived no man could claim to enjoy anything but by Donation, Assignation or, Permission from him; I wonder how the *Right of Nature* can be imagined by Mr. Hobs . . ." Natural right, he said, could not exist unless all men had been created together, yet the Bible teaches that all men came by succession. Taking issue with Milton's contention that the people must consent to the rule of a sovereign, Filmer replied that subjects could no more consent to a ruler than sons could consent to a father.[54]

In opposition to those who held that monarchy or some other organized political system had existed actually or potentially in paradise, other political thinkers could not conceive of a government before the Fall, but assumed that men were first created with natural liberty and individual rights. This group emphasized the priority of the individual and contended that the authority of the state had been derived from individuals after the Fall. Some, like Althusius and Hobbes, had no real concern with a state of innocence, and many others, like Milton, found the origin and exemplary perfection of human liberty in the state of innocence.

Those accepting the Augustinian view that government was a consequence of the Fall were sure that men would have lived in peace as equals in a prelapsarian society. Because there were no problems of food, clothing, and shelter, there would have been no need for judges or governors. The Spanish Jesuit Francisco Suarez rejected the theory that Adam had been endowed with kingly powers at his creation. He maintained that "by virtue of his creation only and his natural right, one may infer simply that Adam possessed domestic — not political — power," since heads of new families would possess the same power. He held that under natural law men were free from all subjection save that of the family. George Buchanan, a leading humanist of sixteenth-century Scotland, discovered the origin of government in natural law, "a certain LIGHT" or "Heavenly Stamp," produced in man at his creation, and had argued that the people had the power to confer the government on whom they pleased. Many Continental monarchists reacted against the suggestion that monarchy would have originated in paradise. Efforts were made to refute the theory that monarchy would have been established in the state of innocence to deal with any who might violate this state.[55]

Nowhere was there a more violent reaction against the idea of Edenic restrictions than in England; and nowhere was there more vehement support of the Edenic origin of liberty and natural law. Groups as different as the Calvinists, Levellers, and Diggers saw external restrictions and the use of force as the fruits of sin. Because no external government would have existed before the Fall, men would have lived in peace and harmony by the inner government of their God-given natures. Those rejecting the belief in an Edenic government held that God had inscribed the law of nature in the first parents' breasts and had given them perfect freedom and enduring natural rights. It was argued that men still bore within them a natural law and natural liberty inherited from Adam, even though these were obscured by sin. Many believed that the regenerate Christian could regain in full measure this natural law and natural liberty impaired by the Fall. Similarly, by following the secondary law of nature, ascertained through the Old Testament and by reason, one might approach the partly discernible primary law known before the Fall. The Levellers and others hoped that by observing the secondary laws of nature men might regain the original natural rights which would assure them of elective magistrates and a renewal of the social contract. Thus the liberty of Adam, since he lived by Right Reason in paradise, was seen as the root both of the Christian liberty of the saint and of the natural political rights of all men.

Both royalists and conservative Presbyterians were alarmed by the clamor for natural rights. One royalist pamphlet warned Parliament that its doctrines would teach "some Wat Tylers Chaplaine to preach again on that text: When Adam *dolve* and Eve *span*, / Who was then a Gentleman?" In his *Gangraena* the Presbyterian Thomas Edwards noted with horror the view of numerous sectarians that all men as sons of Adam "notwithstanding the difference of Lawes and Governments, rancks and degrees, ought to be alike free and estated in their natural liberties, and to enjoy the just Rights and Prerogatives of mankind." [56]

The demand for natural rights derived from Adam was sounded from divergent quarters. Many groups opposed to one another rejected King Adam, but found Citizen Adam the first champion of natural rights. Rutherford, in replying to Maxwell, held that a prelapsarian society would not have been a monarchy, but a society governing itself without rulers. He distinguished between the paternal power Adam did possess and the political power he did not possess, and maintained that the power to establish kingships lay in the sovereignty of the people. The rational political theorist Henry Parker developed a conception of natural law and natural rights that became a cornerstone of Parliament's position in its relations with the king. Parker's thought was in many ways like Milton's. He held that government had become necessary only when the natural law inscribed in man's breast at creation was no longer sufficient to guide and restrain him. Adam and his sons had been endowed with freedom, and sovereignty continued to rest with the people. Parker in his *Jus Populi* insisted on making some distinctions: distinctions between a prelapsarian "order" and a postlapsarian "jurisdiction," between the divine element and the human element in government, and between the original constitution of power at man's creation and the restriction of it to a particular form or to a particular person. Men were not forced by any law of God to part with their freedom, and enjoyed perfect freedom, without trespass, in the choice of government. The power to protect the people has its source in the people and suffers no exhaustion. Parker rejected the "Oxford divinity" that based human

174

government on Adam's dominion over the animals and also the royalist theories that derived kingship from his power over his wife or children (Adam did not judge Cain).[57]

Among the groups that filled the conservative soul of Thomas Edwards with horror were the Levellers and the Diggers. In their demands for political rights, the Levellers pointed to reason, Magna Carta, English law, and English history, but ultimately they based their pleas on the proposition that all men derived a natural right and freedom from Adam's creation in the image of God. Protesting against his imprisonment by the Lords, the Leveller leader John Lilburne said that Adam and Eve were "the earthly, original fountain, as begetters and bringers forth of all and every individual man and woman, that ever breathed in the world since, who *are*, and *were* by nature all *alike in power, dignity, authority, and majesty*," none having dominion except by mutual agreement.[58] With his democratic interpretation of the creation in God's image, Lilburne gave much less emphasis than either Parker or Milton to the consequences of the Fall. The Diggers contended that in the beginning God had made the earth a common treasury. In a figurative reading of the first chapters of Genesis, the Digger leader Gerrard Winstanley interpreted the Fall to mean the loss of a rightful universal liberty and the establishment of private property by government.

The liberty of the individual — in marriage, worship and society — was the lifelong concern of Milton. Like his Renaissance contemporaries, he projected his own ideals and aspirations back to the lost paradise, which itself seemed to foretell the blessed state to which the regenerate might be renewed. He did not envision an established church or government in the state of innocence. The essence of the perfection of this state was the free exercise of Right Reason, the true basis of all human customs or institutions. The perfect marriage celebrated in paradise was the beginning and the center of perfect worship and of the perfect society. These convictions are explicit in Milton's prose works; they are deeply implicit in *Paradise Lost*.

175

In both *The Christian Doctrine* and the divorce tracts — those shocked tributes to a marital happiness lost before it could be gained — Milton sought to grasp the elusive inner secret of matrimony by examining its institution in paradise. Though exegetes for centuries had pondered the nature of woman's inferiority as a divinely transmuted male rib, Milton went beyond most in emphasizing a masculine superiority that stemmed from the man's creation directly in the image of God. Man through Adam possessed a dignity, a liberty entailing responsibility, which it was his duty to preserve. He could rule woman with love only when he could rule himself with appropriate self-esteem as the image of God. Whereas man is the image and glory of God, woman was created "in reference to the man," who in the Hebrew was her "lord" as well as her husband. Man's true dignity should be most evident in "this prime institution of Matrimony, wherein his native pre-eminence ought most to shine," but "just and natural privileges" must "be ally'd to inward goodnesse, and stedfast knowledge." Man must rule himself if he is to rule woman. Despite his dominance, he "receives her into a part of that empire which God proclaims him to, though not equally, yet largely, as his own image and glory." The man gives loving care and guidance; the woman gives help, solace, comfort, and good will. The "prime end and form of marriage" is "not the nuptial bed, but conjugal love and mutual assistance through life; for that must be regarded as the prime end and form of a rite, which is alone specified in the original institution." [59] It was God who had spoken of the help meet for Adam, and Adam who had spoken of flesh and bone.

Although Milton sought the foundations of Church government primarily in the New Testament and in the early Christian tradition, he found the bases of true worship in the natural dignity of man and in the institution of marriage. Showing that authentic church discipline was an inner discipline, Milton described a "pious and just honouring of our selves" as "this hill top of sanctity and goodnesse above which there is no higher ascent but to the love of God which from this self-pious regard cannot be far asunder." In the antiprelatical tracts and in *The Christian Doc-*

trine, Milton repeatedly proclaimed the God-given rights of all true believers to teach or exhort others. The Old Testament and the Jewish synagogue offered just precedents for this. These enduring rights were derived from the dignity and liberty of man, created in the divine image and endowed with an inner law. When the Puritan cause seemed all but lost, Milton insisted that church reform, as well as church government, must have recourse to the natural law first revealed to Adam.[60]

Milton followed the Puritan preachers and his own convictions in thinking that God had instituted marriage not only as a domestic and social relationship, but before all else as a religious relationship. Spiritual union in God sanctified marriage, and marriage was the seedbed of religious life. Milton wrote that "Piety and Religion is the main tye of Christian Matrimony" and that the wife was to give "help and society in Religious, Civil, and Domestic conversation." He cited evidence from the Old and New Testament to show that it was "necessary that the parties should be of one mind in matters of religion." This was also a favorite topic with Martin Bucer, as many of the sections that Milton quoted from him testify. The husband should instruct and incite the wife to all piety and she should be "truly a meet help to him," first of all in godliness, "especially furdering him in the true worship of God, and next in all the occasions of civil life." The couple must love each other "in the Lord, and in the communion of true Religion." [61]

In his political controversies Milton never doubted that all society, like marriage and religion, should be grounded in the natural freedom that Adam had enjoyed in paradise. The ideal had been the voluntary and harmonious spiritual union of the perfect marriage for the service and glory of God. In the dispute concerning the origin of government, Milton scornfully rejected the idea that any government could have existed in paradise. He adhered to the Augustinian position that inequality, coercive authority, and tyranny had developed after the Fall when men no longer ruled themselves by reason. However, the natural law given to Adam, the only just basis of all law, could never be abrogated,

177

nor could men lose to others their title to natural rights. Indeed, this original Edenic freedom was the natural basis of the Christian liberty that might be enjoyed by the regenerate. Interpreting the ideas of liberty developing in the seventeenth century as a continuing heritage from the state of innocence, Milton and many of his contemporaries clothed these natural rights in a paradisal radiance. At the same time they delineated more and more sharply the gulf that separated the present social corruption from the original purity and the envisioned reform.

In developing his own historical argument for natural rights in *The Tenure of Kings and Magistrates,* Milton challenged the historical argument for monarchy. As Filmer had traced to Adam's creation his right to rule over all succeeding humans, so Milton traced to Adam's creation the natural liberty given all to live by the natural law within. Milton characteristically began this tract on the nature and origin of government with the individual: men who were "slaves within doors" yielded to tyranny without, for "none can love freedom heartilie, but good men." [62] A government or a nation consists of individual men. After the Fall, men continued to possess natural rights which they exercised in the gradual formation of government:

No man who knows ought, can be so stupid to deny that all men naturally were borne free, being the image and resemblance of God himself, and were by privilege above all the creatures, born to command, and not to obey: and that they lived so. Till from the root of Adams transgression, falling among themselves to doe wrong and violence, and foreseeing that such courses must needs tend to the destruction of them all, they agreed by common league to bind each other from mutual injury, and joyntly to defend themselves against any that gave disturbance or opposition to such agreement. Hence came Citties, Townes, and Common-wealths. [63]

While the people retained their fundamental power as their natural birthright, they entrusted power to kings and magistrates. Because individual citizens continue to possess their rights and power, they can if necessary abolish or put to death a king. Indeed, covenants made after the Fall still "have ever the more general laws of nature and of reason included in them, though not express'd." [64]

If in the state of innocence there were to be natural rights but no external government, marriage would have been the only relationship instituted in this society. Since society, for Milton, was a collection of individuals rather than a new, organic whole, this marital relation was the only union within the society. Though marriage and worship preceded the state or even an ungoverned community, marriage was instituted to serve many of the same ends that the state established under natural law was to serve, for marriage offered the full realization of liberty and the test of liberty. Most important were the good and happiness of the individual, but these could not be obtained apart from the proper knowledge, love, and worship of God. Although families and tribes would spring from marriage, Milton distinguished sharply between fatherhood and kingship. While Filmer held that all succeeding Adam were born subject to him, Milton believed that each succeeding husband or father inherited a natural liberty from Adam.

In writing *Paradise Lost*, Milton accepted the challenge of making dramatically credible not only man's first disobedience, but also the happy beginnings of the full perfection that God had intended for man. With poetic imagination, he gave body and life to the conceptions of the state of innocence which had become the center of historical, theological, and political discussion. He presented man's first relations with God, man's first knowledge and work, and also the beginnings of marriage, religion and society. After engaging in heated controversy concerning man's original dignity and knowledge, the original purpose of marriage, right worship, and man's natural liberty, he, in his poetry, made these visible and present in the harmony and integrity of the life of Adam and Eve in Eden. He also showed how man had perverted the perfection of the Edenic life. The comments in *Paradise Lost* which echo the prose tracts do not signify that Milton is putting off his singing robes to turn polemicist. *Paradise Lost* is about

179

marriage, religion, and society—their happy beginnings, their corruption, and their renewed purity for the regenerate.

Like most of the Protestant writers, Milton glorified matrimony in *Paradise Lost*. As the bower of nuptial bliss is the center of Paradise, so marital love is the heart of the life of paradise, and the "happie nuptial League" (IV, 339) was to have been the core of all human activity. Though Adam and Eve together "seem Lords of all" (IV, 290), Adam's "absolute rule" required a subjection, lovingly acknowledged by Eve. Adam and Eve thank God for "our mutual help / And mutual love, the Crown of all our bliss / Ordained by thee" (IV, 727–29). Lonely Satan, who finds no solace with Sin, envies them, "Imparadis't in one anothers arms / The happier *Eden*" (IV, 506–7). Their "naked Majestie" reflects the "spotless innocence" of the pair who "thought no ill" (IV, 288–320). The Yahwist, in a primitive but yet fallen world, had envisioned with wonder a first man and first woman who were naked but not ashamed. Milton felt that the fallen might recapture some of the purity of the first and most perfect marriage, but he enlarged on the difference between the original perfection of marriage and its corruption. The reference to "Sin-bred" shame in the natural (IV, 315) shatters the paradisal idyll.

The passage embodying the hymn to wedded love (IV, 736–75) links Adam and Eve, who "lulld by Nightingales, imbracing slept," with "Saints and patriarchs" and succeeding couples who in marriage escaped "adulterous lust" and "Court Amours." "Hail wedded love" sounds almost like an answer to a Catholic "Ave." Here, as in his description of the Paradise of Fools, Milton, as the seer who saw the true paradise, cried out against what seemed Catholic error and hypocrisy. Milton also went beyond most Protestant commentators in hailing wedded sex in the state of innocence. Braving the Scriptural and theological difficulties, he insisted that the sexual love of marriage was in the beginning in paradise—and still remained—an ideal as natural and pure as marriage itself. Love, "mysterious love" with the "mysterious parts" and the "Rites / Mysterious," was "founded in Reason" and was the source of all endearing family relationships.

But the first and most enduring purpose of marriage was to provide a cure for loneliness, the only ill experienced by Adam in the prelapsarian Eden and the first thing that God found not good. Although in the divorce tracts Milton had written in disillusioned anger of the rational and spiritual companionship that remained the true basis of marriage, in *Paradise Lost* he touchingly dramatized the Genesis account showing Adam's realization of his lack before the creation of Eve. "In solitude / What happiness?" he asks (VIII, 364–65). He seeks fellowship, "fit to participate / All rational delight" (VIII, 390–91). A playful and tender God complies, and Adam prophesies that man and wife will cling together as "one Flesh, one Heart, one Soule" (VIII, 499). In a fallen world, loneliness is even more acute, as Adam himself understands in Book X when he feels that God has rejected him just as he has now rejected the wife for whom he had rejected God. But a fallen Eve is still able to follow her own God-given nature and fulfill the intention that a wife shall cling to her husband. Eve's action softens the force of the dire predictions of future marital difficulty that Adam has just made in bitter disenchantment with Eve (X, 895–908).

Milton did not follow the writers who explicitly speculated about the religious and social life that would have developed if innocence had endured, but he was vitally concerned both in his prose work and in *Paradise Lost* with worship and politics as they had developed in a fallen world. Like most of his contemporaries, he felt that in the creation of man and woman and in their first life in paradise were to be found the germ of a life that could have been. This life still remained as an ideal for the regenerate, and could be partly realized in a fallen world. As a polemicist, Milton had traced man's natural rights in the Church and state, as well as in matrimony, to his creation in the divine image. In *Paradise Lost* he portrayed the newly created unfallen Adam and Eve enjoying the dignity, sanctity, reason, and liberty which are the true bases of all religious and social life. Not only do Milton's Adam and Eve represent the family, but they also represent the original pattern of the true Church and society. In fact, so greatly did Milton emphasize the natural rights of the individual and abhor external restrictions that he seems to have conceived of the Edenic society of continuing innocence as an aggregation of Adams and Eves in happy nuptial leagues.

The religious life of Adam and Eve is the natural product of the marriage of free individuals. Their morning and evening prayers and their discussions of God's greatness and bounty are an inseparable part of the rhythm of their lives. Their own love leads them in gratitude to God, and to know God aright is to love him, thank him, and praise him. Their spontaneous prayers, spoken or sung while standing, reflect Milton's ideal of the inner dignity and sincere reverence of the individual before God. They need no external forms. That the couple pray as one is an indication of Eve's importance in the religious life and of the first parents' "one Flesh, one Heart, one Soule." After the Fall, tears of repentance are added to hymns of praise, but the pattern of their worship remains the same. It is never just a rigid form, but a transforming experience, for their prayers are welcomed with joy in Heaven.

There is no Establishment in Milton's Edenic society — least of all, prelates. Milton spoke with scorn of prelates who "run questing up as high as *Adam* to fetch their original, as tis said one of them did in publick." He would have vigorously rejected the claims of Ross. Although to know and to love God was to obey him, Milton did not, like Luther and Andrewes, see the commandment concerning the tree of knowledge as the establishment of the Church and religious service, nor did Milton think a sabbath had been instituted in paradise; nor, for that matter, did he think a sabbath had been divinely ordained for Christians. Adam and Eve worshiped whenever and wherever they pleased, without established forms and without external restraints, and their heirs would have continued to do so in a state of innocence. Adam's sons, inheriting the divine image, would have stood with him as equals before God. In their prayer the first parents look forward to the promised race "who shall with us extoll / Thy goodness infinite" (IV, 733–34). Even in the seventeenth century, the simple dignity, freedom, and sincerity of their worship might remain as a pattern. Finally, after the manifestation of the covenant of grace and the revelation of Michael, when Adam and Eve go forth to live "many dayes, / Both in one Faith unanimous though sad" (XII, 602–3), they possess the proper worship, the pure doctrine, the genuine evangelical love, and the knowledge of the covenant that Milton thought the true marks of the visible Church.[65]

The Edenic society of *Paradise Lost*, like the Edenic worship, was based on individual freedom. Milton's Adam, made in the divine image, enjoyed a dignity, happiness, and freedom that all of his sons would have possessed in a sinless society and which his godly sons could still enjoy. It would have been a highly individualistic society, with God and God's law as the only authority. All men, as Adam, would have been naturally free and independent, ruling themselves with reason, and knowing, loving, and obeying God. When they first appear, Adam and Eve move with majesty — a majesty originally intended for all — simply as the lords of God's creation and of themselves. Their "true autoritie" derives from their "filial freedom" as children of God (IV, 295–96). As even a tottering Eve can explain to Satan, with the exception of the single great divine command, "we live / Law to ourselves, our Reason is our Law" (IX, 653–54). For the Edenic society, the only danger lies within. There is complete security for so long — but only for so long — as the inhabitants follow reason, which is true liberty. Even in a fallen world, Adam's sons retain this independence and liberty insofar as they can rule themselves. The very essence of the first pair's life together in Paradise is freedom of choice in thought and action, but with this there is a personal responsibility to God, themselves, and each other.

In the society represented by Milton's Adam and Eve, the only bond or established relationship is matrimony. From the beginning, Adam has understood the ideal of individual liberty and personal responsibility as the true basis of society. He is shocked to learn from Michael of the tyranny of Nimrod, possible because neither conqueror nor conquered could rule themselves. He knows that all authority is from God, who has given man dominion over only beast, fish, and fowl:

183

that right we hold
By his donation; but Man over men
He made not Lord; such title to himself
Reserving, human left from human free.
(XII, 68–71)

Thus man was created and was to live, cherishing natural liberty
as his birthright. To liberty and reason, justice and temperance
would have been joined. Milton agreed with many commentators
that in the state of innocence all things would have been held
in common,[66] and in *Paradise Lost* he hailed wedded love as "sole
proprietie / In Paradise of all things common else" (IV, 751–52).
Then, with the family remaining as the single established social
unit, the generations spreading from Paradise apparently would
have lived very much as the few just men after the Flood, "With
fair equalitie, fraternal state," by families and tribes under paternal guidance (XII, 22–26). Descending from Paradise, Adam
and Eve leave behind forever a society in which each individual
was to rule himself, but they take their human dignity and natural
rights into a fallen world where men who can govern themselves
and choose aright are still free.

In the historical counterpoint of *Paradise Lost*, the ideals of
marriage, worship, and society established in Paradise — ideals
which the regenerate still seek to attain — are juxtaposed to the
distortions and corruptions of these ideals after the Fall. The first
and last two books, which present the devils' civilization threatening to corrupt man and then the fruits of this corruption, stand
in ominous contrast to the innocent beginnings in Paradise. Marriage will continue as the pure alternative to "adulterous lust,"
"casual fruition," and "Court Amours" (IV, 753–70), though
Adam also foresees all the pain and heartache of marriage (X, 897–
908). As the true marriage fosters true worship, so the unwise marriage relationship fosters idolatry and evil: the "uxorious King"
will build a temple to Astarte (I, 422–46). Michael tells Adam
how the God-fearing men from the hills will marry the "fair
Atheists," first invoke the pagan Hymen at weddings, and beget

a race of merciless warriors. *Paradise Lost* describes the continuing conflict on earth between the true religion and liberty inherited from Paradise and the idolatry and enslavement, internal
and external, inherited from Hell. Repeatedly, as is evident in
the great roll call of pagan deities in Book I and in Michael's
narrative, the few just men keep the faith in the face of paganism,
violence, and corruption. While succeeding patriarchs and their
families find salvation in following the faith of Adam, priests following Belial turn atheist (I, 490–96), fight among themselves,
and at last seize the sceptre in Israel (XII, 353–57). After the coming of the Savior, "persecution shall arise / On all who in the
worship persevere / Of Spirit and Truth." "Grievous Wolves" will
"force the Spirit of Grace it self, and binde / His consort Libertie"
and most "Will deem in outward Rites and specious formes / Religion satisfid" (XII, 507–34). Similarly, as reason yields to passions, individual liberty yields to the specious "full consent" and
expedient "public reason just" of Satan. Though the Jews found
their government upon divinely ordained laws, they sink again
into idolatry, and are subjected to the Babylonian captivity by
the sons of Nimrod (XII, 223–343). The legacy of Hell and the
legacy of Paradise — these reappear almost endlessly in human history, until the time when Satan shall be enchained and "the
Earth / Shall all be Paradise, far happier place / Then this of
Eden, and far happier daies" (XII, 464–66).

No other writer of the "celestial cycle" inquired into the nature
and history of marriage, religion, and society nearly so searchingly
as did Milton. None saw so clearly the relationships between these
in either an unfallen or fallen world. These poets vary in their
interpretation of the marital relationship of Adam and Eve, but
usually do not give a sense of their living together through work,
worship, conversation, and love. Sylvester gave little attention to
their love or marriage except to imply that they lived without
sexual relations and to wonder how they would have propagated.
In the *Adamus Exul* of Grotius, Adam tells of his loneliness without Eve, but Eve herself enters the drama only in connection

with the temptation. She offers Adam the fruit in the name of "the sacred contract of our matrimonial bond," but after the Fall she, like Milton's Eve, wishes to assume all the guilt. In Andreini's *L'Adamo* Adam and Eve lovingly explore paradise together and also "intertwine themselves" in "holiest embraces." However, in Giovanno Francesco Loredano's *L'Adamo*, Adam anticipates the weakness of his sons in his worship of Eve as a goddess. Vondel dwelt more upon the love and marriage of Adam and Eve than any of the other poets except Milton, and seemed particularly concerned about getting them properly wed before leaving them alone. They are married by the tree of life, with antiphonal odes by angels, Adam, and Eve, and with dancing by all. Vondel's Eve, like Milton's, can compose tender love lyrics. But instead of leading Eve to a nuptial bower after the wedding, Vondel's Adam goes off to talk with God in solitude.[67]

In the work of all these poets, Adam and Eve worship God in some way and receive some kind of dominion from him, yet none of these other poets presented Adam and Eve as worshiping together. Sylvester depicted a prelapsarian Adam as finding his "best and supreme delectation" in communion with God and a postlapsarian Adam as instructing Seth to worship with spiritual sincerity himself and to train his children to do so. The Adam of Grotius, alone or with angels, praises God with poetry and song. In Andreini, Adam and Eve praise God upon their creation; but Eve later, in turning her eyes to Heaven, feels she was "made for everlasting and celestial marvels." Vondel's Adam worships God alone. All of these poets used regal figures in describing the dominion of Adam and Eve over the earth, and they saw them as beginning some kind of society or rule. None emphasized their creation in the divine image and their endowment with reason and liberty as much as did Milton. Sylvester, observing that Adam himself could scarcely have unwound the "snarled clew / Of double doubts" concerning the state of innocence, at least raised the question of whether Adam would have left paradise to a son. He later considered Cain a "silly kingling." Grotius wrote that a wife was given to Adam so that heirs might succeed each other in ruling the imperial realm. In Vondel's drama, Gabriel and Raphael come to observe the "inauguration of Man's Kingdom" and to greet "the human king and queen." [68] But none of these other poets related the legacy of paradise to the course of history and the crises of his own time as thoughtfully as did Milton.

7

THE SEARCH FOR PARADISE

❧ WHILE Renaissance scholars and poets were seeking to understand man by studying the biblical account of his beginnings in a historical paradise, they also felt impelled to prove conclusively the historicity of these origins by identifying the exact location of this paradise. The vast scholarship expended in the search for the historical paradise provides the strongest evidence of the devotion and determination of the men of the Renaissance in their quest for the origins of human history. The belief in a paradise still existing somewhere just beyond the realm of Prester John had become increasingly less tenable. The exploration of the East and the New World had failed to reveal an existing paradise; yet the exegesis of the time demanded that the garden and rivers of Genesis be clearly identified. Although Milton and other poets retained some of the old mythic images in their conceptions of paradise, they also tried to describe it credibly as a historical site.

Like various other explorers, Christopher Columbus felt certain that he was approaching the earthly paradise. But he was probably one of the last to hold this belief. In recording his third voyage, Columbus described the western half of the world as "like the half of a very round pear, having a raised projection for the stalk . . . or like a woman's nipple on a round ball." However, he further wrote, "I believe it is impossible to ascend thither, because I am convinced it is the point of the earthly paradise, whither no one can go but by God's permission." [1]

The biblical paradise was not found by Columbus in the western hemisphere, or by other European explorers who brought back reports of India, Ceylon, Ethiopia, China, Japan, the New World, and many islands. Extolling the new advances in geography, many biblical commentators concluded that if paradise existed, it would have been found. Vadianus, a St. Gall humanist and follower of Zwingli, reflected the new rationalism in his discussion of paradise when he objected to those who restrained "themselves and others from the boldness of sifting and deciding, certain in view of Augustine's opinion that God can do this and all else even if the human understanding cannot follow." [2]

Confronted by this new geographical knowledge, the rational commentators of the Renaissance recognized the necessity of providing a literal, historical explanation of the garden described in Genesis. Ralegh, for instance, warned that it was necessary to search diligently to place paradise, or else the events Scripture recorded as occurring there would not be believed. Suppose, he suggested, that Christ had lived in an unknown region. Marmaduke Carver, a rector of Harthill, asserted that he had written his discourse of paradise to defend Scripture against Familists, Antinomians, Hobbians, Quakers, and other anti-Scripturists, "epidemically raging in these later times," who scorned paradise "as a mere *Utopia*, a fiction of a place that never was, to the manifest and designed undermining of the Authority and Veracity of the Holy Text." Even as late as the 1690s Thomas Gale, dean of York and a member of the Royal Society, could comment that if atheists and scoffers were not shown the exact location of paradise, they would "slide into a disbelief first of Genesis, then of the whole Bible, and lastly of all revealed Religion." [3]

There were various approaches to the problem of the missing paradise. Some Catholic writers clung to the old medieval view that an as yet undiscovered paradise still existed. Some travel writers and poets were fascinated with the notion that the Edenic paradise had been on Mount Amara in Ethiopia. For most commentators, however, there were two fundamental approaches to the problem. The first, developed by various humanists, contended that the paradise of Genesis had been the whole earth before the curse. The second, which was that of the majority of commentators, maintained that paradise had been some place near the scenes of later Old Testament history, but had been destroyed or greatly altered by Noah's Flood.

Luther illustrates well the difficulties encountered by a thoughtful man trying to reach a conclusion about paradise. According to his *Table Talk*, Luther had once explained: "I hold that the name Paradise applies to the whole world. Moses describes more particularly what fell within Adam's sight before his fall — a sweet and pleasant place, watered by four rivers." After Adam had sinned, he said, the earth lost its fertility. However, in his commentary on Genesis, Luther asserted that the theory that paradise was the whole earth was "manifestly wrong" and did not solve the problem of locating paradise. He also claimed that the location of paradise "seems a vain and unnecessary point about which to argue since it no longer exists." Nevertheless, he went on to propose that it had comprised Syria, Mesopotamia, Egypt, and part of the Red Sea, and would have been large enough for all of Adam's descendants.[4]

The Destruction of Paradise

The old idea of an existing paradise inhabited by Enoch and Elijah lingered on well into the seventeenth century, not only in popular tradition but in scholarly controversy. Protestants regarded this view as a popish error that endangered belief in the literal, historical interpretation of Scripture. In his description of the Flood waters sweeping away the Mount of Paradise, Milton was reflecting a Protestant position and opposing the view, held by Cardinal Bellarmine and some other Catholic writers, that the Flood had spared paradise and that the Edenic garden still existed in some undiscovered part of the world.

Despite new geographical discoveries, English maps of the earlier sixteenth century continued to picture an existing terrestrial paradise somewhere at the top, which represented the east in older maps. This legendary conception of paradise also continued to appear in popular works, such as the English *Faust Book* of 1592. Faust, standing on a high hill of the Caucasus, sees all of India and Scythia, a "cleare strike of fire comming from heauen vpon the earth," and a valley with four mighty waters springing forth and taking their course in different directions. No one is permitted to approach nearer.[5]

Many Catholic as well as Protestant writers assumed the destruction of paradise; in fact, the humanistic Pope Pius II was among the first to condemn the belief that paradise was to be given to the just on Judgment Day. Nevertheless, since the writers who defended its continued existenced were Catholic, Protestants were not reluctant to assail these writers' views as another example of popish error. Vadianus charged that for twelve hundred years the Catholic Church had paved the way for mistaken notions about paradise. The Huguenot Rivetus attributed the idea of a still existing paradise to four Catholic writers: Sixtus of Siena, Cardinal Bellarmine, the Belgian Jesuit Leonardus Lessius (who was at one time a student of Bellarmine), and Marius of Cologne. Purchas said it was an ignorance of geography that had led Bellarmine and Cajetan to suppose that Elijah and Enoch would abide in paradise until the coming of Antichrist. In the mid-seventeenth century, Edward Leigh, Puritan M. P. and army officer, wrote that "Bellarmine, and generally the papists will not admit that it was destroyed by Noahs Floud, and it is to maintain a false opinion," for they say that *"Enoch* and *Elias* are kept alive in this Paradise, which they say still remaineth." Taking issue with Bellarmine's statement that the Flood had spared the mountain of paradise, the Puritan Walker insisted upon a literal reading of Genesis 7:20 and asserted that the Flood had risen fifteen cubits above the highest mountains, sparing none. "Yea," he added, "if Paradise had been preserved safe from the flood, it had been needlesse and vaine labour for Noah to build such an huge arke. God might have saved him and all the creatures with him in the garden of Paradise." [6]

Various Catholic commentators, however, continued to hold that the Edenic paradise still existed, though it was yet undiscovered. Sixtus of Siena, in his *Bibliotheca Sancta* of religious errors, claimed that a belief in the destruction of paradise was against Scripture and the rule of right faith. Sixtus, a converted Jew, particularly castigated the errors of Augustine, bishop of Chisamensis, who had maintained that paradise had begun to lose its beauty after Adam's sin and had later been inundated and destroyed by the Flood, that Enoch and Elijah had not been translated there, and that "on account of the crime of man no part of that sacred place was remaining." Cajetan wrote as though paradise, though undiscovered, still existed. It was, he said, probably on a mountain, since streams originated there, but possibly flowed under ground afterward. The Flemish Jesuit Thomas Malvenda thought that paradise probably still existed some place in India; he argued, in fact, that "India" was derived from "Eden." [7]

The staunchest defender of an existing paradise, intact and habitable, was Roberto Francesco Bellarmino, noted for his controversies with Protestants on many questions. Cardinal Bellarmine could define clearly the "modern" view that a paradise in or near Mesopotamia had been destroyed in the Flood and that the cherubim with fiery swords no longer guarded the Edenic garden. Bellarmine, however, rejected this view on the basis that it was a new opinion and contrary to that of the fathers and scholastic doctors. He accepted the tradition that Enoch and Elijah existed corporeally in paradise, but asserted that no one in his right mind would say that the pair had been translated to Mesopotamia. Genesis 7, he explained, referred to the inundation of the mountains of the fallen world, but not to the mount of paradise. Finally, he refuted all the recent attempts to identify the four rivers described in Genesis 2. [8]

Milton, in emphasizing the destruction of paradise, reflected the solid Protestant opposition to the views of Bellarmine and other Catholic writers. At the same time he supported the literal, historical interpretation of the Scriptural account of Adam and

192

Eve and of Noah. Milton was also both helping to defend his location of the site of paradise and teaching a spiritual and moral
lesson. In accordance with his explanation of the various Scriptural references to Eden, Milton located paradise in Mesopotamia. But since no trace of paradise was to be found there, it
must have been completely destroyed — swept into what is now
the Persian Gulf by the waters which covered the entire earth.
Milton's first reference to the ruin of his Paradise, occurring as
Satan enters the garden on the fateful day of the temptation, is
ominous and proleptic:

> There was a place,
> Now not, though Sin, not Time, *first wraught the change,*
> Where *Tigris* at the foot of Paradise
> Into a Gulf shot under ground . . . (IX, 69–72).

After the Fall, Michael as a good teacher concludes his depiction of the destruction of the world of Adam's sons with his
account of the destruction of Adam's own world — Paradise. The
Ocean shall usurp

> Beyond all bounds, till inundation rise
> Above the highest Hills: then shall this Mount
> Of Paradise by might of waves be moovd
> Out of his place, pushd by the horned floud,
> With all his verdure spoil'd, and Trees adrift
> Down the great River to the op'ning Gulf,
> And there take root an Iland salt and bare,
> The haunt of Seales and Orcs, and Sea-Mews clang.
> To teach thee that God attributes to place
> No sanctity, if none be thither brought
> By Men who there frequent, or therein dwell.
> (XI, 828–38)

Milton's description makes it clear that he interpreted Genesis 7
to mean literally that the flood waters had covered the entire earth,
even the highest hills. The inundation of paradise was inevitable.
Milton's illustration of the Flood in *Paradise Lost* also shows his
opposition to those who maintained that somehow paradise had
been spared. Michael is explicit. The rain fell "till the Earth / No

more was seen," till "Sea cover'd Sea, Sea without shoar" (XI, 744–45, 749–50). The inundation rose above the highest hills, and it was then that the lofty Mount of Paradise was swept away (XI, 828–30). Milton's references to "the might of waves," the "horned flood," and "trees adrift" leave no doubt that he differed from those commentators who found Scriptural authority for the assumption that the rising waters had remained still and had therefore not greatly altered the terrain.

In the two passages referring to the destruction of Paradise, it is pointedly explained that this destruction was a consequence of man's sin. Michael tells Adam that no place (be it Paradise, a home, or a church) possesses true sanctity if men do not bring sanctity to it. Milton appears to be replying to those who, like Sixtus of Siena, condemned the belief that God had permitted the sanctity of paradise to be violated because of the sin of man. One wonders also if Milton recalled these lines from his youthful reading of Sylvester:

> But if thou list to guesse by likelihood
> Thinke that the wreakfull nature-drouning flood
> Spar'd not this beauteous place, which formost saw
> The first foule breach of Gods eternal law.[9]

Mount Amara

Mount Amara, as it was described by Spanish and Portuguese explorers, met the rational demand for a paradise with an exact location, but it also made real again the mythic image of the inaccessible mountain and the cascading river in an exotic land. Travel writers characterized it as an existing paradise, and poets were entranced by the suggestion that the towering Amara was the site of the original paradise. Milton dismissed the idea that Mount Amara was the historic paradise, but nevertheless pictured his Paradise as similar to Mount Amara.

Much of the basis and appeal of the conception of an Ethiopian paradise undoubtedly rested on the references to the Ethiopians in Homer, the Old Testament, and other early works. Purchas, for instance, wove these into his colorful account of Amara.

Homer spoke of "the blameless Ethiopians," placed their land near the Hesperides, and represented the gods as feasting there (*Il.*, I, 423–24, and *Od.*, I, 22). The land of Chus referred to in the description of the rivers in Genesis 2 was frequently identified as Ethiopia. The Ethiopian emperors supposedly had sprung from the union of Solomon and the Queen of Sheba (I Kings 10: 1–13), and through the conversion of the eunuch of Queen Candace (Acts 8:28), the Ethiopians had been among the first to embrace Christianity. Diodorus Siculus said the Ethiopians maintained that they were the first men and always lived godly, peaceful lives in the manner of the golden age. The Ethiopians were known as particularly beautiful and virtuous men through the works of Pomponius Mela, Dionysius of Alexandria, and others. In the Renaissance, the Ethiopians were still associated with a state of innocence. An Italian bishop recorded a story supposedly told by an old Ethiopian philosopher "from the most ancient memory of the Ethiopians." This memory was of a time when men remained nude, enjoyed an abundance of food, had a perfect knowledge of earthly and celestial matters, and lived in complete harmony with each other and with all the animals.[10]

The gradual transfer of the legendary realm of Prester John from India to Ethiopia helped prepare for the European interest in an Ethiopian paradise. For many centuries the Red Sea and Indian Ocean were minimized and India and Ethiopia were considered as parts of the same vast, mysterious realm. In the thirteenth and fourteenth centuries, Prester John was associated with the king of the Nestorian Christians in central Asia, and his territory was sometimes placed in Ethiopia, or "the third India." Stories of Ethiopian pilgrims and other accounts of a Christianized Ethiopia pointed to this region as the land of Prester John. Then about 1340, Friar Jordan of Severac not only considered Prester John an Ethiopian, but located the earthly paradise between the third India (itself sometimes identified with Ethiopia) and Ethiopia, since from this region descend the four rivers of paradise.[11] Both the search for the source of the Nile and the search for the terrestrial paradise led to the mountains of Ethiopia.

However, only with the Spanish and Portuguese exploration of Ethiopia in the sixteenth century was a particular location in Ethiopia found for an earthly paradise. Mount Amara, which deeply affected Milton and Coleridge and many lesser poets, rose into the European imagination as travelers returned and wrote colorful accounts that would be repeatedly adapted in travel literature and poetry. The first of these European descriptions of Mount Amara was given by Francisco Alvarez in his account of the Portuguese embassy in the years 1520 to 1527. Alvarez did not regard Amara as a paradise, and in fact reported that it was cold and uncomfortable, but his depiction included the essential features. The mountain looms above the valley, with one side "a rock cut like a wall, straight from the top to the bottom." The top, where the royal heirs dwell in palaces, is round and flat, but other peaks rise from it.[12]

Certainly the richest contribution to the haunting vision of an Ethiopian paradise was offered by Friar Luis di Urreta, a Spanish Dominican, in his history of Ethiopia. Urreta was probably the first to intimate that Mount Amara was paradise, and undoubtedly the first European to enlarge upon this idea. He penned the most complete and rhapsodic account of Amara as a paradise. Moreover — and perhaps most important of all — his description was the ultimate source of the discussions of Amara by Purchas and Peter Heylyn, which were transformed in the poetry of *Paradise Lost* and "Kubla Khan." Urreta's sources are very uncertain.[13] Throughout his work he strongly implied that Mount Amara was the original terrestrial paradise, but he avoided any explicit statement of such an unorthodox view. Steeped in the descriptions of paradise in the poetry of Lactantius, Avitus, and Marius Victor and in the speculations of St. Basil, St. Thomas, and St. Bonaventura, he saw these realized in the soaring splendor of Mount Amara. As a high mountain with "an eternal spring joyful and flowery," equal days and nights, and trees and plants found only there, Amara truly possessed the characteristics of paradise. Urreta said he would not be surprised if the Doctors "might call it Paradise" and concluded that "we could give it the name of

Paradise" — indeed, "Amara" in Ethiopian did mean "paradise." [14]

Urreta's description contains all the elements later found in Milton's references to Mount Amara and also many of the features of Milton's Mount of Paradise. The sons of the Ethiopian ruler, Prester John, are kept under guard on this impregnable mountain, with its walled plateau holding thirty-four palaces. Round, and about twenty leagues in circuit, Amara is situated in the midst of a great plain under the equinoctial line. The rock of this mountain, like a smooth and even wall "made by hand with a quadrant and a plane," rises so steeply that it appears to be a buttress holding up the sky. Overhanging rocks jut far out at the top. The mountain is so high "that there is about a day of climbing from the foot to the summit." There is one road of gradual ascent, cut into the rock, and a gate and a guard at the entrance and at the summit. From the plain at the top, "toward the south a hill, grandly rising, beautifies that entire plain and serves as a watchtower from which the human gaze can enjoy the furthest and most agreeable vistas that one can imagine." From this hill flows a fountain which feeds many streams that water the gardens before they plunge down the mountain, unite in a lake, and then form a river that empties into the Nile.[15]

Later writers built upon Urreta's description. Purchas, in his popular account "Of the Hill Amara," depended solely on Urreta, sometimes translating literally, sometimes selecting and condensing, and sometimes embellishing. He went beyond Urreta's explicit statements, however, in saying that "some" (perhaps meaning Urreta himself) took "this for the place of our Forefathers Paradise." Heylyn, in his condensed description of Amara in his *Cosmographie* (1652), apparently depended solely on Purchas. He wrote that "some have taken (but mistaken) it [Mount Amara] for the place of *Paradise*." [16] Although Milton may have remembered Purchas's description, he was probably using Heylyn as his immediate source in his lines on the Ethiopian paradise:

> Nor where *Abassin* Kings thir issue Guard,
> Mount *Amara*, though this by som suppos'd

197

> True Paradise under the *Ethiop* Line
> By *Nilus* head, enclosd with shining Rock,
> A whole days journy high, but wide remote
> From this *Assyrian* Garden . . . (IV, 280–85).

Here Milton not only shows that no other paradise might compare with the surpassing beauty of the "True Paradise," but he rejects any unorthodox idea of paradise as well. However, a few hundred lines later, he could apparently use specific details from the depiction of an actual Mount Amara to contribute to the mythic image of the Paradise Mount which was "True Paradise":

> the setting Sun
> Slowly descended, and with right aspect
> Against the eastern gate of Paradise
> Leveld his eevning Rayes: it was a Rock
> Of Alablaster, pil'd up to the Clouds,
> Conspicuous farr, winding with one ascent
> Accessible from Earth, one entrance high;
> The rest was craggie cliff, that overhung
> Still as it rose, impossible to climbe.
> Betwixt these rockie Pillars *Gabriel* sat
> Chief of th' Angelic Guards, awaiting night.
> (IV, 540–50)

Mount Amara also probably contributed to Milton's characterization of another side of Paradise where streams descend to form a lake (IV, 257–61), and to his general conception of the Paradise Mount, with its "verdurous wall," winding streams, and high hill from which Michael and Adam surveyed the earth (XI, 376–80). Although there had been many accounts of towering mountains, paradisal and otherwise, much of Milton's description, with its combination of the shining rock, overhanging cliffs, single winding ascent, and posted guard, was evidently derived ultimately from Urreta. Some of the elements, such as the illustrations of the overhanging rocks and the reflection of the setting sun, appeared in English in Purchas, but not in Heylyn.[17]

Other English poets, too, alluded to Mount Amara. Extolling the wonders of the true paradise, Sir John Stradling wrote that the "famous Hill *Amara* to this clime, / Is but a muddie moore

198

Plate 1. Title page of John Parkinson's *Paradisi in Sole* (1629),
a work on the cultivation of household gardens.

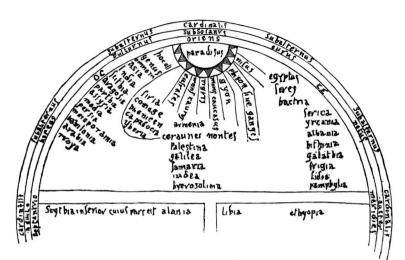

Plate 2. The *Mappa Mundi* from *De Statu Saracenorum*. Map illustrates the medieval belief that the Nile, Ganges, Tigris, and Euphrates flowed from paradise.

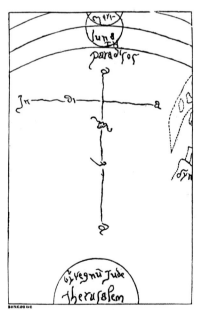

Plate 3. Fragment of *Mappa Mundi* of Paris.

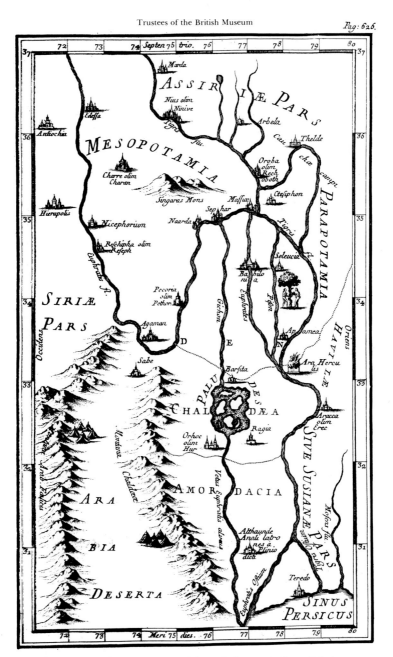

Plate 4. Map from John Hopkinson's *Synopsis Paradisi* shows
paradise in Mesopotamia in the region of Babylon.

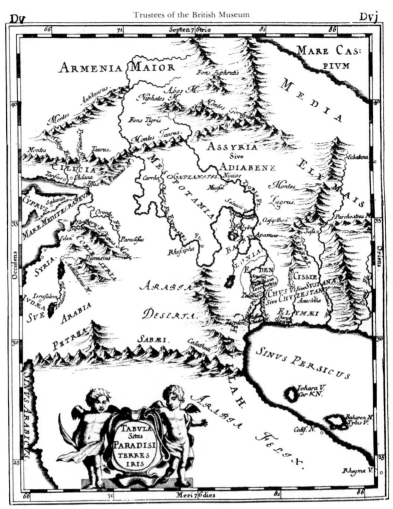

Plate 5. Map from Bishop Pierre-Daniel Huet's *Treatise of the Situation of the Terrestrial Paradise* illustrates paradise situated on "the great Meridional Branch of the great turning" of the Euphrates.

Plate 6. Fragment of the *Mappa Mundi* of Saint Severus. Map shows paradise rimmed by flames and surrounded by China and India. Reprinted from Eduardo Coli's *Il Paradiso Terrestre Dantesco* (1897).

Plate 7. Map from Mathieu Beroald's *Chronicum* shows paradise situated in Syria and adjoining territory. Adam and Eve and Israelites crossing the Red Sea are pictured.

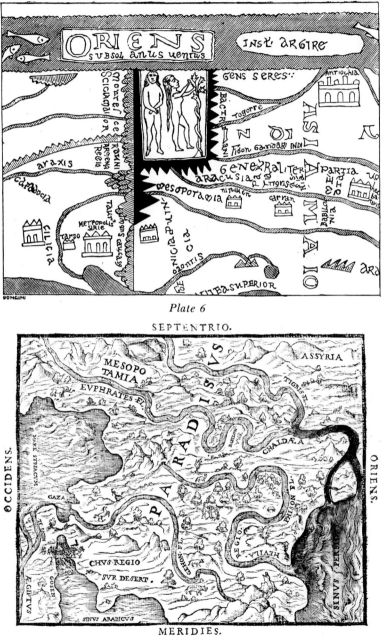

Plate 6

Plate 7

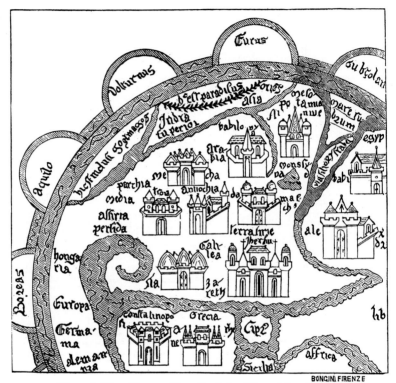

BONGINI FIRENZE

Plate 8. The *Mappa Mundi* of the Chronicle of Saint
Dionysius. Map shows paradise in the East,
surrounded by flames and bordered by India and Asia.

Plate 9. Title page
from Samuel Bochart's
Opera Omnia (1692)
showing Adam in paradise.

MUELIS
OCHARTI
PERA
MNIA

Apud CORNELIUM BOUTESTEYN, ET SAMUELEM LUCHTMANS.

Plate 10. Map from Tymme's translation of Calvin's
Commentaries on Genesis shows confluence of the
Tigris and Euphrates, where Calvin held that
paradise had been situated. This map also
appeared in the Bishops' Bible.

of dirt and slime," and Thomas Bancroft, though referring to Amara, would not accept it as paradise. Addressing "Dear Amara" in his roll call of theories of paradise, Thomas Peyton brought in the Queen of Sheba, Candace, Homer's feasting gods, and a crystal river purling down to the Nile.[18]

Nevertheless, at a time when the demand was for a rational, scholarly identification of the paradise of Genesis 2, it is not surprising that there was a reaction against the mythic wonders of Mount Amara; by the middle of the seventeenth century accounts of Ethiopia like those of Urreta were often refuted as romantic fable.[19]

Paradise as the Whole Earth

That paradise was the whole earth was another solution to the problem of the undiscoverable paradise, which was widely known, but generally regarded as dangerously unorthodox or absurd. Many exegetes, historians, and geographers stressed the need to refute this and other erroneous conceptions when they undertook yet another demonstration of the exact location in which human history had begun. Milton never mentioned this idea, but could not have escaped references to it in Ralegh and the Renaissance commentaries. He left no doubt that Adam and Eve had lost a paradise of limited area through a real expulsion. Calvin was one of the first to take issue with "authors who would extend this garden over all regions of the world," and he was succeeded by many other writers, both Catholic and Protestant. English readers probably encountered the notion most often through the condemnations of Purchas and Ralegh, who had attributed this idea to the Manichaeans.[20]

During the Renaissance, the discussions of earth as paradise were not only more frequent, but more literal, more explicit, and more fully developed than those of any earlier period. Those proposing it in some form were Vadianus, Johann Bronchorst, a professor of philosophy at various Protestant universities, Lodovico Nogarola, a count of Verona and a participant in the Council of Trent, Wolfgang Wissenburgus, a Swiss Protestant theologian, geographer, and mathematician, Goropius Becanus, a Flemish physician, antiquarian, and geographer, Ludovicus Fidelis, a Flemish professor of theology, and Juan de Pineda, a Spanish Jesuit noted for his advanced, rational exegesis.

These writers were seeking a literal, rational interpretation of Genesis 1–3 as the history of the beginnings of the human race. Some of the principal arguments for this interpretation were that the beauties ascribed in Scripture to paradise were also ascribed to the whole world; man was told to fill and rule the whole world; the whole earth was cursed after man's sin; the whole earth would have been needed for Adam's descendants if he had not sinned; and the important change suffered by man was a change of state rather than of place. For its opponents, this interpretation not only contradicted the description of the location of paradise in Genesis 2, but raised embarrassing questions about the intended Edenic society and about the expulsion.

Vadianus found the divine Word simple and clear. He showed that in Genesis 1:18–19 God had said to man, "Replete terram," and had given him every herb "quae est super faciem omnis terrae." "For," he wrote, "in so far as it says to fill the earth and rule over all living things below and upon the earth, it most clearly teaches that the whole existing earth (as it then was), with all kinds of enjoyments brought together, was to be the seat and garden for Adam and his posterity." Although Adam and Eve undoubtedly occupied a particularly delightful spot, he argued that this did not mean that the rest of the earth was without similar delights. The single river or fountainhead of paradise could be understood as the ocean by identifying the four rivers of paradise as the Tigris, Euphrates, Nile, and Ganges, flowing through a multitude of diverse regions. Bronchorst, Nogarola, and Fidelis developed similar ideas. However, Goropius, basing his argument on reason and on his interpretation of Scripture and ancient myth, offered the most fully developed theory of the earth as paradise. He quoted extensively from classical poets to show that they were speaking of this paradisal earth in descriptions of the golden age, the Elysian Fields, and the life of the

Phaeacians. Among his beliefs, he held that the four rivers, in watering the world, truly watered paradise.[21]

Some of these writers also reasoned that if man had not sinned, future generations would have deserved and needed the entire earth as a paradise in which to dwell. For centuries many commentators had supposed that all of Adam's descendants would have lived in paradise, but they did not calculate the increase in population of a race of immortals. These speculations on a prelapsarian population explosion raised questions about the adequacy of a limited Eden, and could have prepared the way for open doubt. If all the earth were not paradise, Fidelis asked, and Adam had not sinned, what would the rest of the earth have been — desert? He found it unthinkable that more of the earth would have been uninhabitable than habitable. According to Pineda, even if all the earth were habitable, if some dwelled within paradise and others without, there would have been an unmerited inequality in God's treatment of his beloved sons. He also wondered if those living two or three thousand leagues from paradise would have been provided with other trees of life or would have had the fruit transported to them. Assuming that men living in obedience and partaking of the tree of life could have lived three or four thousand years while continuing to have children, he envisioned a future in which no limited space would have been sufficient.[22]

Although these writers felt that both reason and Scripture supported the belief that the whole earth had been a paradise for man, they struggled with what their critics considered was the crucial issue — the difficult problem of the expulsion and the posting of the cherubim. Was the expulsion to be interpreted literally as part of a historical narrative or as a figurative representation of the theological concept of a change in man's condition? The expulsion could be interpreted as a change from place to place, from condition to condition, or both. Orthodox commentators explained the expulsion literally. Vadianus and Nogarola associated the expulsion with the loss of the tree of life, but suggested a figurative elucidation of the cherubim. Only Fidelis and Goropius followed the implications of the theory that paradise was the whole earth to

201

the extreme position of regarding the expulsion solely as a change in state. Goropius's Latin makes his point strikingly: "Eiectus itaque eodem mansit loco, sed dispari admodum conditione." "Ejected, he remained in the same place, but in a completely changed condition." [23]

Although Milton did not mention the idea of the earth as paradise, he scarcely could have avoided encountering it, since it appeared in histories, geographies, and countless commentaries on Genesis. To him it must have seemed a blatant misreading of Genesis 2, another unorthodox theory that increased the need for a credible presentation of the true paradise as a real place in an identifiable region. He was careful to give specific bounds in his own description of Eden.

Peyton's limping verses on the paradise story stumble in shock and scorn when he considers this idea:

> Fond, franticke men the sacred truth to reach,
> And Paradise o'er all the world to streach,
> The land of Eden of that spatious worth,
> To thinke it went quite over all the earth.
>
> . . . .
>
> That mans exile by cursed envious fate,
> Was nothing but the changing of his state.[24]

Theories of the Location of Paradise

Most of those searching for the paradise described in Genesis assumed that it had been destroyed. Only on this assumption could they argue for its historical existence and seek to identify its site. They rejected the idea of an undiscovered paradise, a paradise situated on Mount Amara, or one extending over the entire earth, as well as any theory like that of Postellus, who suggested the North Pole as the site of paradise.[25] Most writers placed paradise in the Near or Middle East not far from the other scenes of Old Testament history.

Despite this general agreement, however, there was disagreement about the exact location, particularly since no site really corresponded to the description of the rivers in Genesis. Nevertheless, the need to establish paradise as a historical reality made it necessary to establish it as a geographical reality. Armed with classical research, biblical scholarship, new geographical reports, and detailed maps, authors of commentaries and of special tracts on paradise disputed with one another concerning the original sites of paradise and Eden. Attempts to place paradise in Mesopotamia, Syria, the Holy Land, or Armenia brought countless discussions of the four rivers and the bordering lands referred to in Genesis 2. Carver recalled a dispute about the location of paradise that had occurred just after a sermon on the Creation.[26] The continued controversy about the site of paradise helped to focus attention on the many scholarly and creative works dealing with various aspects of the historical paradise.

All the attempts to identify paradise began with the description in Genesis: "And a river went out of Eden to water the garden; and from thence it was parted, and became into four heads." The four succeeding verses, sometimes considered a late addition to the Yahwist's original account, identified the four rivers as the Pison, encompassing the land of Havilah, where there was gold and the puzzling bdellium; the Gihon, encompassing Ethiopia; the Hiddekel, which went toward the east of Assyria; and the Euphrates. Thousands of pages were devoted to the explication of this passage, which was the key to the discovery of the lost paradise. Besides the numerous commentaries, various individual tracts on paradise, such as those of John Hopkinson, Carver, and Bishop Huet, were devoted to identifying the site of paradise.

Most writers began with certain assumptions and certain problems. They assumed that an actual earthly paradise had existed, that the biblical description of its location was accurate, that it had been destroyed, that its site nevertheless could be identified, and that this site was not far from the lands inhabited by Adam's descendants. The problems were to interpret the text properly, to throw all possible light on it through the resources of philology and biblical and classical learning, and then to find an actual site still identifiable as that of the destroyed paradise. The attempt to solve these problems became one of the most challenging intellectual exercises of the sixteenth and seventeenth centuries.

The obstacles barring the way to a solution were formidable. Those seeking paradise usually began with the Scriptural references to Eden, but these raised new questions. Three biblical passages after Genesis which concerned Eden (Ezekiel 27:23, II Kings 19:12, and Isaiah 37:12) linked it with Haran, Canneh, Gozan, Rezeph, and Telassar ("the children of Eden which were in Thelasar"), and a fourth reference (Amos 1:55) connected it with Damascus. Some commentators, however, identified two separate Edens in these references. Yet it was difficult to identify these places: Was the name Haran derived from Eden? What had been the bounds of Eden? and Where exactly in Eden had the garden been situated? But the rivers posed the most complex problem: Were the rivers described as in the time of Moses or at the beginning of the world? Was paradise irrigated by the one river flowing through it? Did the four rivers emerge from the paradise river in paradise immediately after leaving paradise, after a short distance, or after a long distance? What were the Pison and Gihon, and do they still exist? [27] And what exactly were the "heads" of the rivers? The ancients were examined closely for any clues leading to the identification of the four rivers. Many of the Renaissance discussions reflected the ancient accounts of a confluence of the Tigris and Euphrates near Babylon and of the separate early courses or "falls" of these rivers to the Persian Gulf. Although writers drew upon all available historical evidence, identification was still hazardous. Perhaps no other region could have offered so many possibilities and so little ground for certainty. The Tigris and Euphrates had long had very tortuous courses, affected by mountain ranges, earth movements, and lava flow. Not only were they fed by various tributaries, but they had abandoned old channels and formed new branch channels. The Tigris, particularly, had shifted its course many times. An abandoned channel might be the long lost Pison or Gihon.

Writing in the first decade of the seventeenth century, Pareus listed various theories of the location of Eden: the field of Baby lon, Mesopotamia, or Syria and Arabia in addition to Mesopotamia; the region around Damascus; upper Chaldea; Armenia, Assyria, and Egypt.[28] But his list was by no means exhaustive. Many of the arguments for a particular location were accompanied by carefully prepared maps, some of which confidently displayed an Adam and Eve in naked majesty standing near a confluence of four streams.

The most popular suggestion was that Eden was in Mesopotamia or some part of it, such as Babylonia or Chaldea. Augustinus Steuchus Eugubinus, an Italian ecclesiastic who served as bishop of Kisamos in Crete and as legate to the Council of Trent, Franciscus Vatablus, a French Hebraist and theologian, and Hieronymus Oleaster, a Portuguese commentator and a participant in the Council of Trent — all earlier sixteenth-century commentators — were often credited with the development of this thesis. Rejecting the old view that the Ganges and the Nile were two of the rivers, they emphasized a literal reading of Scripture and a common sense approach to geographical problems. Eugubinus noted that Ezekiel had linked Eden and Charan (or Haran), which was a real city in Mesopotamia. He also thought that the great river of paradise, from which the others branched off, was formed by the confluence of the Tigris and Euphrates. Vatablus carefully distinguished paradise from Eden, which he considered to be in the region of Mesopotamia and Arabia. He identified the Gihon as the lower Euphrates and the Pison as the Pasi-Tigris, a branch connecting the Hiddekel (Tigris) and the Euphrates. Oleaster, starting with the certainty of the Euphrates, reasoned that the other rivers must not be far distant. The Tigris was of course near. Of the other two rivers, there was more doubt, but he decided that they were less important and that they probably extended within the boundaries of Assyria.[29]

These accounts were for a long while generally better known than Calvin's discussion in his commentary on Genesis, published first in 1554 and translated into English in 1578. Calvin's primary purpose apparently was to remove the doubts of the perplexed. Quoting Strabo (Bk. XI) to show that the Tigris and Euphrates had united for some distance near Babylon to form the river and had then separated to flow into the sea, Calvin explained that he understood Moses to say that "Adam dwelt on the bank of the river, or in that land which was watered on both sides, if you choose to take Paradise for both banks of the river." However, it would make no great difference, he asserted, if Adam had actually dwelt above or below the confluent stream. Calvin struggled with the meaning of "heads," but provided a simple, straightforward explanation of the description in Genesis. "How the river was divided into four heads," he maintained, "is not difficult to understand. For there are two rivers which flow together into one, and then separate in different directions; thus it is one at the point of confluence, but there are two heads in its upper channels, and two towards the sea; afterwards they again begin to be more widely separated."[30] A map appearing in Tymme's English translation illustrates this clearly (see plate 10).

Many editions of the Bible also included discussions of the location of paradise and maps showing Eden. The account in the Bishops' Bible of 1568 appears to be a condensation of Calvin's commentary. A brief treatment of the problem in the Geneva Bible placed paradise on the Euphrates. A far more thorough investigation, which was highly respected, was that of Franciscus Junius in the popular Tremellius-Junius Bible of 1590. Purchas heartily recommended Junius as one who "hath largely and learnedly handled this matter," and praised particularly his comprehensive study of the ancient geographers. In minuscule Latin print, Junius traced the changing names of rivers and regions, and in marginalia equally minuscule his readers sometimes wrote lengthy observations. Junius sought clues in Ptolemy, Herodotus, Diodorus, Curtius, Strabo, Pliny, Dion, Marcellinus, and others to try to solve the mystery of the location of paradise. He rejected the proposal, made by Luther and Melanchton, that Eden or paradise had extended over large sections of Asia and Africa. Contending that the bounds of Eden were defined by the references to the four rivers and the lands they enclosed, he concluded that the garden was watered by the main stream of the Euphrates, from which the four

206

rivers later branched off successively. These often changed names, but from the ancient geographers he identified them. The first was the Perath, or lower Euphrates; the second was the Phison, known as the Pasitigris, Naharmalca, or Basilius; the third was the Gihon, known as the Naharsares or Baharsares; the fourth was the Chiddekel or Tigris. Paradise itself he located on the Euphrates in the section of Babylonia called Auranitis, a name supposedly derived from Audanitis or Edenitis. Maps appearing in the work of the French scholar Samuel Bochart show Auranitis in northern and west central Babylonia, bordering on Assyria, Chaldea, and Aram (see plate 9).[31]

Most other biblical commentators, Continental and English, struggled similarly with the problem of identifying the site of paradise. Both Pererius and Lapide placed paradise in the region where the Tigris and Euphrates had once joined for a short distance, and thought that the Gihon and Pison were derived from this river further downstream. Pareus assigned a similar location to paradise, but gave a different explanation of the four rivers. The popular commentary of Giovanni Diodati placed paradise in a great circuit made by the Tigris and Euphrates. Some English suggestions were that paradise had been east of Babylon, or around the coast of Mesopotamia, or where the Red Sea now is. In response to the objection that no site in Mesopotamia fit the biblical description, it was argued that the Euphrates had been deliberately diverted and that canals had been constructed.[32]

The first Englishman to write a tract devoted exclusively to paradise was John Hopkinson, whose *Synopsis Paradisi* was published posthumously in 1593. Hopkinson, referred to later by Ralegh as "our Hopkins," was a teacher of Oriental languages for twenty-two years. He, as well as others, developed the argument that paradise could not have been in the air or on a mountain near the moon because the temperatures would have been unendurable and because the earth could not have supplied a sufficient base for such a mountain. He also rejected the idea that paradise was in the region of Damascus, where Adam was believed to have been created, or that it was as spacious as Syria, Arabia, and Mesopotamia combined. Like Junius, he concluded that paradise had been in the region which was to become Auranitis in Babylonia. He was convinced that the changing names of this region had been originally derived from "Eden," and that this was the Eden referred to in various books of the Old Testament. He considered the Pison and Gihon to be two channels of the Euphrates, the Nahar Malca and the Moar Sares (see plate 4).[33]

Many English readers were familiar with Purchas's and Ralegh's speculations on the location of paradise. Recommending Junius's arguments for a paradise in Mesopotamia, Purchas was moved by the contrast between the region in its paradisal and present state. "It is more than probable, that here in these parts Paradise was, although now deformed by the Floud, and by Time consumed and become a stage of barbarisme." Purchas also regaled his readers with the story of the mountain in Ceylon which bore Adam's footprint, and with the legend of the paradise of "the Old Man of the Mountain" in northeast Persia.[34] Ralegh, too, was apparently influenced by Junius, with the difference that he emphasized the enduring character of Mesopotamia, rather than the changes, and brought to his popular account of paradise the fruit of his experience as an explorer.

Besides collating the biblical and classical references to Eden and adjoining lands, Ralegh argued for a Mesopotamian site for paradise on the strength of his own reasoning concerning geographic change and his own experience in tropical regions. For Ralegh as a historian, time seemed to increase knowledge without changing the face of the earth. He assumed that Moses, writing 850 years after the Flood, was describing a region that was still recognizable. The waters had evidently stood in a calm, since the Scriptures failed to report any wind and Josephus said that the pillars of Seth were still to be seen. While earlier Renaissance commentators had rejected the suggestions of Tertullian and Durandus that paradise might have been under the equinoctial line, Ralegh concluded that recent exploration had shown that the tropics were like paradise. The tropical character of Mesopotamia thus became another character in its favor. No one assigned to paradise a location that sounded more precise than Ralegh's — 35° from the equinoctial and 55° from the north pole. This placed it in the "lower part of the Region of Eden, afterward called Aramfluviorum, or Mesopotamia," which included portions of Shinar in the south and Armenia in the north. On Ralegh's map, paradise occupies a relatively large tract of land near the confluence of the Tigris and Euphrates. The four heads, he said, were not sources, but passages of the main stream to different lands.[35]

Later in the seventeenth century, two French ecclesiastics took issue with the arguments of earlier commentators. Bochart charged that the explanations of Junius and Hopkinson, though "extravagantly admired," were full of "flagrant errors." He rejected their conclusions concerning the rivers and asserted that the Naharmalca was actually an artificial canal. In a tract translated into English and Latin, Bishop Pierre-Daniel Huet contended that previous commentators had taken no notice of "the great Meridional Branch of the great turning" of the Euphrates, though the words of Moses expressly required this. The Euphrates, after running through the province of Eden, must have flowed from west to east, for it entered the garden "eastward in Eden," he concluded. Thus, "it is the most likely thing in the world, that paradise was placed on the easterly end of the southerly branch" of the great turning seen in Ptolemy's map.[36] An accompanying map placed paradise near Calneh (Korneh) (see plate 5).

Although the majority of those searching for paradise placed it somewhere in Mesopotamia, some maintained that it was further east, either in Syria or in the Holy Land itself. They found authority for this view in specific biblical references and in the assumption that much Old Testament history had taken place not far from the site of man's first blissful existence. This was also in keeping with the idea that Adam had been created on the plains of Damascus before he had been placed in the garden. Mathieu Beroalde, a French Calvinist and noted Hebraist, was one of the first to argue for a Syrian paradise. Like many, he reasoned that "eastward in Eden" had referred to an area to the east of Canaan or Judea. Syria, immediately to the east, was often regarded along with Arabia, Mesopotamia, and Persia as a part of the East. He discerned special significance in Amos 1:5: "I will break also the bar of Damascus, and cut off the inhabitant from the plain of Aven, and him that holdeth the sceptre from the house of Eden: and the people of Syria shall go into captivity unto Kir, saith the Lord." Noting that Eden, clearly a particular region, was linked with Damascus and the Syrians, Beroalde concluded that Eden, the site of paradise, was in Syria. He helped to solve the perplexing problem of the one great river branching into four by noting that a Hebrew singular frequently had a plural meaning. Paradise, a large tract with mountains, rivers, and plains, was watered by several rivers flowing into it, as well as from it, he explained. The distorted map accompanying Beroalde's account shows the Tigris and Euphrates too far east and Mesopotamia to the north of Syria. Paradise appears as a very large area extending to the north and east beyond the borders usually assigned to Syria (see plate 7).[37]

Though the association of Eden and Syria in Amos could not be rejected, many commentators dismissed this as an explanation of the site of the original earthly paradise. For example, *The Dutch Annotations*, which had been ordered by the Synod of Dort and approved by the English Parliament, distinguished between two Edens, one in Syria and the other in Telassar in upper Chaldea. It considered this second Eden the true location of paradise.[38]

The idea that paradise had been planted in the Holy Land was presented briefly by Michael Servetus, Inveges, and Salianus, but was developed chiefly by writers in the middle decades of the seventeenth century. That master of occult lore, John Gregory, was certain that the terrestrial paradise had been situated in the Holy Land because of the mystical relationship between this region and the celestial paradise. The argument for a Palestinian paradise was propounded much more fully by Eugène Roger in a popular work on the biblical geography of the Holy Land. Roger's somewhat old-fashioned notion was based much more upon early tradition and a typological interpretation of Scripture than upon linguistic or geographical research. Roger reminded his readers that the Armenians, Chaldeans, Abyssinians, Nestorians, and other Christians of the Orient had held paradise to be near Judea. Does not the Holy Land, he asked, have blooming trees, a temperate climate, and inaccessible mountains? Do not some hold Jerusalem to be the highest place on earth? He cited the old Jewish tradition that Adam and Eve had lived in the Holy Land after their expulsion. The earthly paradise had been destroyed by the Flood, he said, but it was believed that Noah had given the Holy Land to Shem as the noblest part of the earth. It was the land promised to the patriarchs because it was the most desirable. Roger even tried to reconcile his theory with the old tradition that Enoch and Elijah still dwelt in paradise. They were preserved invisible in some part of the Holy Land, from which they could conveniently emerge to dispute with antichrist at Jerusalem.[39]

Roger also depended on the old belief in a divinely ordained relationship between Adam and Christ, the tree of life and the tree of the cross, but he was much more specific about the exact location of paradise than most writers treating this tradition. Assuming that the tree of life and the tree of knowledge were near one another in paradise, Roger asked if it were not fitting that our reparation should begin where our loss had begun and that Christ should die, to give us life, on the site of paradise in the middle of the Holy Land, just as the tree of life had stood in the middle of the garden. Christ had shed his blood on Calvary, "which is the place where our first parents disobeyed God, since it is said that the redemption should occur in the place where the sin had been committed." "This makes me believe," he concluded, "that Paradise was in the Holy Land; and that the tree of the cross, true tree of life, has been planted in the same place where was that other tree of life of the terrestrial Paradise which was destroyed by the Deluge."[40]

Although maintaining that other men had been created before Adam, La Peyrère expressed the opinion that Adam had been carried to a paradise in the Holy Land when he was strong enough to till the soil. Johann Heidegger, a Swiss Protestant, also considered

the Holy Land to be the site of the original paradise. More specifically, he held that the region of Genesar (Gennesaret), later called
Galilee, was the first home of Adam and Eve. "Genesar" in Hebrew, he said, meant "hortus princeps," first or chief garden. The
Jordan was clearly the great river which had flowed through paradise. Believing that Adam and Eve had wandered only a short distance from paradise, he recalled the old tradition that Adam had
been buried on Calvary. The Silesian scholar Johannes Herbinus
suggested that the Sea of Galilee covered much of the area in which
the original garden had been planted. This theory that paradise
was in the Holy Land continued to receive attention in the eighteenth century.[41]

Another location given for paradise was Armenia. This idea
gained support in the middle of the seventeenth century and was
widely accepted well into the nineteenth century. This conception
was based partly on the observation that streams usually arose in
mountains, like those of Armenia, as well as on the assumption that
Seth's descendants had remained near paradise and that Noah's
ark had not been carried far when it came to rest on Mount Ararat
in Armenia. Both Pererius and Lapide had suggested Armenia and
Mesopotamia as logical locations for Eden and paradise. Johann
Vorstius, maintaining that Scripture clearly stated that the great
river arose in Eden itself, also contended that Eden and paradise
must be in Armenia.[42]

One of the most complete of the earlier arguments for an Ar-
menian paradise was offered by Carver in a tract published in
1666, but written twenty-six years earlier "for private satisfaction
only." Carver took issue with Junius, rejecting his interpretation
of the rivers and the derivation of "Auranitis" from "Eden." Because the Tigris and Euphrates were two of the four rivers flowing
from the great river, they must have a common source, he reasoned.
There Eden and paradise must be, since the great river arose in
Eden. He found the site of Eden in Armenia Major, on the south
side of Mount Taurus. He speculated that paradise might have
been transformed into a nitrous lake which Pliny had said was
located in this area.[43]

Descriptions of Paradise

Although locating paradise precisely was more important to the historical exegesis of the Renaissance than describing it, commentators also discussed the extent of paradise, its general terrain, streams, plants, and inhabitants. Earlier writers had envisioned a remote paradisal mountain, with deafening waters, jeweled trees, and palaces; the Renaissance commentators turned to both the letter and logical implications of Scripture to form a natural and credible picture of the scene of the first events of human history. Renaissance poets, however, in depicting earthly paradises, turned to the classical and medieval images of the ideal site.

Conceptions of the size of paradise were closely linked to theories of its location and estimates of its potential population if man had not sinned. Calculating the population increase with a race of immortals, most writers attributed somewhat vague but wide bounds to paradise and Eden. Various estimates were that the perimeter of paradise would have been twelve leagues, fifty leagues, or a hundred leagues. It would have been all of Mesopotamia, Mesopotamia and adjoining countries, or a large area in the Middle East. Most agreed that as the population increased, some men would have had to move to colonies elsewhere.[44]

All writers agreed that paradise was beautiful, fertile, and pleasant, and many felt that much of its charm lay in its diversity. As Genesis 2 combined references to the rivers, the garden, and man's first tillage, Scripture established much of the topography of paradise. Inveges thought paradise was an enclosed area containing mountains, valleys, and plains. It would have had at least three gates, and roads inside and outside the enclosure. Others, including Andrewes, considered paradise to be enclosed, and Luther noted that it had at least an eastern gate.[45]

All commentators also agreed that paradise was situated somewhere on at least one river and that it was well watered. Some still retained the idea of a mountain paradise. In a widely used rhetoric that Milton probably knew, the terrestrial paradise was described as a plateau with plains and hills abundantly watered by

213

streams cascading from a central fountain. However, most biblical commentators, following Scripture closely, thought paradise was on the bank of a river in a plain or valley. Calvin explained that Adam had dwelt on the bank, or possibly both banks, of the great river. Luther saw all four rivers as running through the garden, which was a very large part of the earth. For Pareus, the river was diverted into many streams which Adam might stroll along, navigate, or easily cross. Envisioning the four rivers issuing from paradise, Andrewes pictured the paradise garden as consisting of "three islands disjunct but meeting in one part." From his reading of Genesis 13:10, Lightfoot was certain that "the garden of the Lord" and indeed all of Eden had been watered by a river that overflowed once a year in the manner of the Nile and the Jordan.[46]

Both serious biblical commentators and more popular writers delighted in depicting the earthly paradise as a garden or park, artfully planted, and abounding in tame wildlife. They usually characterized paradise as always green, blooming, and fruitful, but they continued to discuss questions that had teased writers for centuries. Did paradise possess all kinds of trees and plants? Did these remain green all year? Did they bear fruit all year? Ralegh believed the trees and plants were tropical. Andrewes imagined paradise made beautiful with "herbs, flowers, plants, trees which were proper and special to that place alone . . . and that not in confused sort, but digested into a good seemly order." For another English writer the garden was "ordered in every respect as if it had been planted by art." The trees of life and of knowledge received special attention. Luther, Andrewes, and Gregory maintained that near these trees a special area had been reserved for religious service. White was sure the two trees had stood near one another, but Pererius said they could not have stood in the same place. Inveges suggested that both trees had stood in a conspicuous spot, possibly near the water, and that probably under one of these trees Adam had slept, Eve had been created, and the couple had been married. Adam and Eve were usually pictured as surrounded by animals living in peace with man and with one another, but it was debatable whether or not all animals had been admitted to the garden. In his fresh, realistic view of a historical paradise, Luther saw the animals sharing Adam's meal of fruits and herbs and observed that he was "sure Adam, before the fall, never wanted to eat a partridge." Even the beauty and friendliness of prelapsarian serpents were noted. John Parkinson, in his book on gardens, which he considered microcosms of paradise, began by picturing Adam as surrounded by the choicest herbs and fruits (see plate 1).[47] Truly, the garden in Eden remained the garden of gardens.

Commentators who debated "whether Eve's toes had corns" or whether Adam "did cut his beard spadewise or like a T" were satirized by John Hall. Yet, commentators, poets, and artists often tried to portray the first parents. Readers were assured that they were not "hairy nor wooly." Sir Thomas Browne concluded that they could not have had navels unless "the Creator affected superfluities, or ordained parts without use or office." Keeping in mind the great age of the patriarchs, many writers thought Adam was created at a ripe prelapsarian age of fifty to seventy. Expressing a popular opinion, Inveges asserted that Adam looked like Christ and that Eve looked like the Virgin Mary. Adam was handsome, mature, and eloquent. Eve, Inveges supposed, was about ten years younger, of medium height, somewhat slender, with blond hair, arched eyebrows, keen eyes, a slender nose, and red lips full of sweet words. Diodati claimed that the true cause of shame was in brutish motions and thoughts, not in the body's "pure naturall nakedness, which is a glorious pattern and masterpiece of God's works." And in a passage that Milton might have recalled, Purchas viewed Adam and Eve "in a naked Maiestie, delighting themselves in the enamelled walks of their delightfull garden."[48]

But a picture was worth a thousand words of seventeenth-century commentary. Shortly after the Restoration, while Milton was composing *Paradise Lost*, a model of the terrestrial paradise, along with reproductions of other scenes, was exhibited in London by Christopher Whitehead. According to a contemporary report, this "transplanted" paradise was a "most artfull and lively representation of the several creatures, plants, flowers, and other vegetables, in their full growth, shape, and colour." Adam appeared naming the animals, which ranged from the elephant to the mouse and from the crocodile to the glowworm, and Eve appeared, taking the apple from the serpent.[49]

Aside from the writers of "the celestial cycle," Renaissance poets described several distinctive kinds of earthly paradise. Assimilating the classical, early Christian, and medieval depictions of the paradisal site, they could paint in rich detail the Christian paradise, the enchanted garden or false paradise, and various allegorical and mythological gardens. This writing, too, formed a part of the Renaissance paradise tradition that was Milton's inheritance.

In his study of the earthly paradise and Renaissance epic, A. Bartlett Giamatti has shown the directions first taken by Renaissance poets in interpreting the meanings of paradise for a new age. A freshly conceived creation of the traditional Christian paradise appears in the third book of the *Parthenice Secunda* of Giovan Battista Spagnoli, known in English as Mantuan. At one time prior general of the Carmelites, this poet found his life in the Church, and depicted the Edenic paradise in his life and passion of St. Catherine of Alexandria. An angel visits the lost garden to gather food for the imprisoned saint. In writing of a paradise high on a mountain in the east, he preserved the paradise tradition of Christian Latin literature without depending on Ovidian allusion and Virgilian phrasing. Another paradise that flourished in the epics and romances of the Renaissance was the enchanted garden, which owed much to late classical and medieval gardens of love and the Renaissance interpretation of the golden age. In describing the distinctive character of these enchanted gardens, Giamatti has said, "The classic Renaissance garden presents what poets from Ariosto to Spenser will expand — the beautiful-seeming earthly paradise which in reality is a dangerous and deceptive place where man's will is softened, his moral fiber unraveled, and his soul ensnared. It is the garden where insidious luxury and sensual love overcome duty and true devotion." Like the golden age sites and the Christian earthly paradises, these gardens seem desirable but inaccessible. But two changes have occurred: "The place is no longer supposed to be morally beneficial, and it is no longer measured in 'literal' terms." The enchanted garden is the scene of an inner struggle between ease, pagan luxury, and sensuality on the one hand, and the true Christian life on the other.[50]

In England, the two most celebrated gardens in Spenser's *The Faerie Queene*, the Bower of Bliss (II, xii, 42–87) and the Garden of Adonis (III, vi, 29–54), illustrate clearly the enchanted garden or false paradise and the mythological garden embodying philosophical truth. Milton understood the Bower of Bliss as a false paradise. Writing of the virtue of the true Christian in *Areopagitica*, he praised Spenser as a better teacher than Scotus or Aquinas for bringing Sir Guyon with his palmer "through the Cave of Mammon, and the bowr of earthly bliss that he might see and know, and yet abstain." [51] One may "scout into the regions of sin and falsity" in pursuit of truth and virtue. The "baits and seeming pleasures" of vice, to which Milton had just referred, are those of "earthly bliss," which the "true wayfaring Christian" must distinguish from true wisdom and happiness. In both the true paradise and the false one there is trial whereby man can prove his virtue or fall. But while the natural beauty of Eden should lead man to know God aright, the artificiality and excess of the bower are calculated to deprive him of his self-knowledge.

The relation of the garden contrived by Acrasia to the garden planted by God is implicit in the description. The bower of earthly bliss is twice exemplified as a "paradise" (stanzas 58, 70). It is depicted by the traditional rhetorical formula:

> Thereto the heavens alwayes joviall,
> Lookte on them lovely, still in stedfast state,
> Ne suffred storme nor frost on them to fall,
> Their tender buds or leaves to violate,
> Nor scorching heat, nor cold intemperate,
> T'afflict the creatures that therein did dwell . . ."(51).[52]

It seems more "sweet and holesome" than Tempe, or Ida, or Parnassus, "Or Eden selfe, if ought with Eden mote compayre" (52). But it becomes increasingly evident that the bower is an unnatural perversion of the Edenic paradise:

217

The painted flowres, the trees upshooting hye,
The trembling groves, the christall running by;
And that which all faire workes doth most aggrace,
The art, which all that wrought, appeared in no place (58).

Here there is no eternal spring of love, but an enchanted garden
of debilitating sensuality.

There is, however, an underlying truth in the similarity between
the Garden of Adonis and the garden in Eden. The natural beauty
of Spenser's garden embodies the divine creative power and the
harmony of the life cycle. Virgil, Claudian, and the medieval
mountaintop paradise blend in the description, as Genesis and
Plato blend in the revelation of the garden's meaning.[53] The garden is "the first seminary / Of all things that are borne to live
and dye" (30). And there

All things, as they created were, doe grow,
And yet remember well the mighty word,
Which first was spoke by th' Almighty Lord,
That bad them to increase and multiply (34).

Images traditional in the description of the Edenic garden and
other earthly paradises reappear in Spenser's picture of the mountaintop plateau with its shaded grove:

Right in the middest of that paradise
There stood a stately mount, on whose round top
A gloomy grove of mirtle trees did rise,
Whose shady boughes sharp steele did never lop,
Nor wicked beastes their tender buds did crop,
But like a girlond compassed the hight,
And from their fruitfull sydes sweet gum did drop,
That all the ground with pretious deaw bedight,
Threw forth most dainty odours, and most
    sweet delight (43).

In "the thickest covert of that shade" is an arbor, "not by art, /
But of the trees owne inclination made . . ." (44).

In his description of the heavenly paradise in the Epilogue to
Comus, Milton revealed his assimilation of Spenser's depiction of

the Garden of Adonis. It is altogether likely that Milton would have recalled Spenser's garden again in composing his own description of Paradise. Indeed, Grant McColley has argued that the Garden of Adonis was an immediate source and that Milton moved backward in Spenser in writing his description of Paradise in Book IV of *Paradise Lost*. He cited the similarity of Milton's Paradise (IV, 132–49) to Spenser's paradise plateau with its shade trees dropping gum (43), its two walls (31), its eternal spring (42), and the forest's "stately theatre" (III, v, 39). The encircling trees are like a garland on Spenser's mount, while Paradise "crowns" the mountain in Milton's work. Both poets regard the garden's beauty as the product of nature, rather than of art.[54]

The continuing concern of English Renaissance poets with an earthly paradise — both the vision and the rhetoric — is evident in two of the mythological poems of Michael Drayton, written near the beginning and the end of his long and productive poetic career. His "Endimion and Phoebe" as well as his "Description of Elyzium" in "The Muses Elyzium" portray traditional images of paradise similar to those which appear in *Paradise Lost*. In this first poem, the earthly paradise is a grove surrounded by towering trees atop the mount of Latmus, which rises from a plain. From this grove arises a steep ascent of glistening marble. Trees are more glorious than those kept by the Hesperides, and streams with "straying channels" have silver sands strewn with "orient Pearle." Indeed, nature has here "imparadiz'd" all her pleasures.[55] The paradise of "The Description of Elyzium," the abode of the Muses, has a variety of trees and birds and all sorts of flowers throughout the year, and it is inhabited by the three Graces. The description of its wandering streams reflects a sense of potentially dangerous excess and irregularity comparable to that suggested sometimes by the landscape of Milton's Paradise. The rills stray in "wilde meanders," "playing many a wanton pranck."

> In Gambols and lascivious Gyres
> Their time they still bestow
> For to their Fountaines none retyres,
> Nor on their course will goe.

219

Those Brooks with Lillies bravely deckt,
So proud and wanton made,
That they their course quite neglect:
And seeme as though they strayde. . . .
(ll. 53–60) [56]

Milton's Paradise

Milton followed Genesis in placing his Paradise on a great river in the eastern section of Eden; he depended on other Old Testament references to Eden in describing its bounds:

Eden stretchd her Line
From *Auran* Eastward to the Royal Towrs
Of Great *Seleucia*, built by *Grecian* Kings,
Or where the sons of *Eden* long before
Dwelt in *Telassar* (IV, 210–14).

Milton differed from most of his contemporaries in situating his Paradise on the Tigris (IX, 71–73) rather than on the Euphrates or at the confluence of the two rivers. In his reference to the Tigris it is scarcely likely that he was thinking of the confluence of the two rivers, since the Tigris is yet to divide into four rivers south of Paradise (IV, 233). But where on the Tigris was Milton's Paradise? The reference to Seleucia helps to establish the eastern bounds of Eden, but does not place Paradise. Although Milton did not choose to designate an exact location, he perhaps envisioned his Paradise, the "Assyrian Garden" (IV, 285), as north of Seleucia. When he delivers his tortured address to the Sun, Satan is on Mount Niphates, "the Assyrian Mount," and is "in prospect of Eden, and nigh the place" where he must tempt man (III, 742; IV, Argument, 126). He reaches Paradise shortly after leaving Niphates, and later searches "From *Eden* over *Pontus*" (IX, 77), the Black Sea, for the creature best suited to his temptation.

In explaining the location of Eden, Milton was giving a geographic reality to a historic region in accordance with informed Scriptural interpretation. Eden's "Line" is apparently not a boundary, but a measure of distance. In determining the bounds of Eden, Milton, like the Renaissance commentators, found im-

220

portant clues in the biblical passages that linked Eden with Haran, Canneh, Gozan, Rezeph, and Telessar. Numerous places in the Middle East bore names like Haran. Milton's Auran, marking the western limit of his Eden, is the biblical Haran mentioned with Eden.

But where did Milton believe this Haran to be? There were three main possibilities. Hauran (Auran in the Vulgate), east of Galilee and about fifteen miles south of Damascus, was an eastern province in the district of Bashan, alternately part of Syria and Palestine. It is mentioned in connection with the northern and eastern boundaries of Israel (Ezek. 47:16–18). Seleucia lies on a fairly straight line east of Hauran, separated from it by the Syrian Desert. If Milton's reference is to Hauran, then his Eden extended eastward for about 450 miles. Most commentators, however, believed that Scripture distinguished between Haran and Hauran, but did not think Hauran was the place associated with Eden. Milton's description of Nimrod, "Marching from *Eden* towards the West" (XII, 40) to build the Tower of Babel, indicates that his Eden did not reach as far west as Hauran. Many writers concluded that the Haran mentioned with Eden was Haran (Harran), the city in northwest Mesopotamia to which Abraham journeyed from Ur, but Milton referred to this city as Haran (XII, 131), not Auran. Also, a line from Haran to Seleucia would run as far south as east. The third possibility was that Haran referred to Auranitis (believed derived from Eden), a district in the north and west of Babylonia. This view had been developed by Junius and supported by Hopkinson, Purchas, and others. An Eden running from the western boundary of Auranitis to at least as far east as Seleucia would extend for about a hundred miles. As Hauran, Haran, and Auranitis lie west of Seleucia, it is possible that Milton was deliberately providing a description of Eden that would be in accord with both Scripture and geography, no matter how Haran was identified. Nevertheless, it is probable that his Auran (IV, 211) is Auranitis. An Eden reaching from the lands along the Euphrates to the lands along the Tigris was generally accepted and would have seemed the most credible to the majority of Milton's readers. With this conception of a limited Eden, Milton could understandably place his Paradise "eastward" on the Tigris. Moreover, the account by Junius was regarded as authoritative and, as Harris F. Fletcher has said, the Tremellius-Junius Bible was "almost the standard Latin Bible of all Protestants" and "Milton's favorite Latin version." [57]

The eastern bounds of Eden are reasonably clear, but Milton's conception of the northern and southern limits and of the four rivers is conjectural. The eastern limits of Eden are suggested by the references to Seleucia, which lay about twenty miles southeast of modern Baghdad, and to the enigmatic Telassar. According to St. Jerome, Canneh and Seleucia had been situated on about the same site. The discussions of the location of paradise by Junius and others were filled with references to Seleucia. Some Renaissance maps also showed its "Royal Towrs." In his use of Telassar, Milton was following closely the biblical reference to the "children of Eden which were in Thelasar" (II Kings 19:12). But in seeming to identify Seleucia and Telassar ("Of Great *Seleucia* . . . / Or where the Sons of *Eden* long before" [IV, 212–13]), Milton probably had in mind the note on this passage in the Tremellius-Junius Bible which stated that Telassar, a city of Eden, was later called Seleucia. The borders of Eden apparently extend beyond the Tigris, for Adam and Eve leave Paradise by the eastern gate and are presumably walking eastward in Eden at the conclusion of *Paradise Lost*. Also, Milton's description of Nimrod's march indicates that Eden stretched some distance eastward from the Tigris.[58] Milton probably thought that Eden extended some distance to the north and south of Seleucia, but in the absence of Scriptural evidence, he was silent. Nor in his account is it at all clear how the Tigris divides into four streams. His apparent belief that the courses of these streams were no longer recognizable was consistent with his depiction of the Flood. Although Milton and his readers knew that thousands of pages of commentary had been devoted to the problem of the four rivers, Milton dismissed it:

> And now divided into four main streams,
> Runs diverse, wand'ring many a famous Realm

And Country, whereof here needs no account,
But rather to tell how, if Art could tell,
How from the Sapphire Fount the crisped Brooks. . . .
                                    (IV, 233–37)

Milton's obligation was rather, through the power of epic poetry, to authenticate once again the sacred ground and sensuous delight of the garden that God had planted for man "eastward in Eden." While the poet's Paradise can only suggest the historic paradise, this too must be real.

No aspect of *Paradise Lost* is more important to the whole than the description of the external Paradise. Without this, neither the life and events that occur there, nor the inner paradise of original righteousness, nor the loss of Paradise itself could be credible. Milton's Paradise is the fruit of the innumerable accounts of paradise in myth and legend, in classical literature, and in earlier Christian literature. For a fallen and secular world, it is paradise. Although the secret of the unique appeal of Milton's Paradise is impossible to explain, perhaps part of the answer is that Milton's Paradise, at once mythic and substantial, sublimely imaginative and painstakingly real, is simply always there, an inescapable part of all the actions, thoughts, and feelings of the characters who experience its beauty. The Mount of Paradise and the plateau garden become more solid and are more deeply experienced by the reader because they are seen not only through the eyes of the poet seer, but by different characters at different times and from different perspectives. Gradually, both the general appearance and diverse beauties of Paradise merge and form an enduring and harmonious whole, as some parts are seen repeatedly from dawn to nightfall and other parts are newly revealed.

Milton's mountain is the age-old archetypal paradise, but it is also freshly revealed as the one true and original Edenic garden. Milton's Paradise is a walled plateau on a great mountain, partly heavily wooded and partly craggy, through which plunges a great river. In this conception of paradise, Milton differed from most of the Renaissance commentators and the other Edenic poets. Milton's Paradise is in the same tradition with Mount Meru,

Kuen-Lun, the mountaintop garden of Siduri, and the "holy mountain of God" (Ezek. 28:14). Paradise was envisioned as a summit garden similar to that in *Paradise Lost* by Pseudo-Basil, Lactantius, St. John of Damascus, St. Ephrem, and Dante. In a description close to Milton's, Moses Bar Cephas explained how waters from a river flowing under paradise rose to irrigate the plateau garden. Milton's Paradise is also similar to Alexander Neckham's mount reaching toward the moon, Mandeville's summit paradise, enclosed with moss-covered walls, and Joinville's view of paradise as a "great cliff of sheer rock" from which flowed a river. The secular paradises of Claudian, Alain de Lille, and Jean de Hauteville loom behind Milton's sacred garden. But Milton's walled plateau garden, with its cascading streams, its own high hill, its guarded gate, and its single steep, rocky path of ascent, bears its most striking similarity to the description of Mount Amara in Purchas, which itself reflects the influence of the old mythic conception of the mount of paradise.

The Mount of Paradise is, like Mount Amara, "conspicuous farr" (IV, 545), rising steeply from the plains of Eden. If Milton's mountain is like Amara in size as well, it would be about twenty leagues, or at least sixty miles, in circuit. Adam and Eve are first seen by God "in the happy Garden plac't, / Reaping immortal fruits of joy and love" (III, 66–67). Raphael perceives Paradise from outer space as earth's highest mountain, "the Gard'n of God, with Cedars crown'd / Above all Hills" (V, 260–61). In his first view of the plateau garden, Adam understands well its general plan. He has been led by God up the mountain,

> whose high top was plain,
> A Circuit wide, enclos'd, with goodliest Trees
> Planted, with Walks, and Bowers . . . (VIII, 303–5).

After Adam has taken possession, the poet envisions the "enclosure green" as a "woody Theatre" surrounded, except on the east, by rank upon rank of ever taller trees. The beauty of this "rural mound or Silvan Scene" seems natural, but beyond the "verdurous wall" appear the mythical trees with "Blossoms and Fruits at once of golden hue" (IV, 132–49).

The great mountain is viewed from all sides at various times. Its beauties, like those of the garden, are diverse and full of contrast. On the north side, the swiftly flowing Tigris passes into a dark gulf beneath the "shaggy hill." On the south side, in a rather spectacular scene, the waters that arose to irrigate the garden unite again to plunge down a "steep glade" into the great river emerging from its "darksome passage" (IV, 223–32). On the west side, where Satan tried to ascend and where Adam was led up by God, there is a "steep wilderness," with "thicket overgrown" and with shrubs and entangling bushes "so thick entwin'd, / As one continu'd brake" (IV, 135–37, 174–77). On the eastern side the Mount of Paradise, like Amara, is "craggy cliff," with one winding path of ascent and the garden's single gate and its angelic guard at the summit (IV, 543–50). It is here "on th' Eastern cliff of Paradise" that Raphael lands and is welcomed by the angelic watch (V, 275–89). And at the end of *Paradise Lost* "our ling'ring Parents" are led down the eastern cliff to the plain, where they look back to see the angels with flaming swords and "the Gate / With dreadful Faces throng'd and fiery Armes" (XII, 637–44).

The garden's variety is ever present in the poet's vision and in the experience of the characters. What is seen seems only a suggestion of what is not seen. When Satan overlooks Paradise from the Tree of Life, the narrator reveals the fount and brooks, the flowers "Poured forth profuse on Hill and Dale and Plain," the groves of "rich trees," and "Betwixt them Lawns, or level Downs" with grazing flocks, or a "Palmy hillock," or an "irriguous valley." On "another side" are found "umbrageous grots and Caves," "murmuring waters" falling down a hillside, and a lake holding its "crystal mirror" to the myrtle-fringed bank (IV, 237–63). It was perhaps on this side that Eve first awoke after her creation. She recalled that she found herself "under a shade on flowers" where "a murmuring sound / Of waters issu'd from a Cave" to form a lake, in whose "wat'ry gleam" she admired her

image (IV, 450–65). The loveliness of Paradise is reflected in
Adam's determination to trim "Yon flow'ry Arbours, yonder Al-
leys green, / Our walk at noon" (IV, 625–27). Eve's enjoyment of
all the natural beauties of Paradise with Adam at her side is the
essence of her love lyric (IV, 639–56). Adam recalls how often
he and Eve have heard celestial voices "from the steep / Of echo-
ing Hill or Thicket" (IV, 680–81). He awakes to the sound of
"leaves and fuming rills" and "the shrill Song / Of Birds on every
bough," and is eager to go with Eve to see "how blows the Citron
Grove, / What drops the Myrrh, and what the balmy Reed" (V,
5–8, 21–23). The couple's morning prayer is a hymn to the natural beauties of Paradise. After Raphael alights on the eastern
cliff, he passes through "Groves of Myrrh," "A Wilderness of
sweets," and a "spicy forest" as he approaches the "cool Bow'r"
of Adam and Eve (V, 292–300). Eve goes forth to gather in Paradise "Whatever Earth all-bearing Mother yields" in any region
(V, 338–41). However, on the fateful morning the sensuous appeal of the almost lost Paradise is poignantly apparent. Eve has
wished to work alone "In yonder Spring of Roses intermixt / With
Myrtle" (IX, 218–19). Satan, seeking her through "Bowre and
Field," "By Fountain or by shadie Rivulet," discovers Eve,

> Veil'd in a Cloud of Fragrance, where she stood,
> Half spi'd, so thick the Roses bushing round
> About her glowed . . . (IX, 425–27).

Satan follows her through "many a walk . . . Of stateliest Covert, Cedar, Pine, or Palm" (IX, 434–35), and seeks to direct her
to the forbidden tree,

> Beyond a row of Myrtles, on a Flat,
> Fast by a Fountain, one small Thicket past
> Of blowing Myrrh and Balme (IX, 627–29).

Apart from the groves and fields, hills and fountains, Paradise
has certain highly distinctive features, such as the two special
trees, the central fountain, the high hill, and the Nuptial Bower.
Milton, like many commentators, thought of the Tree of Life
as "the middle Tree and highest there that grew" (IV, 195). Just

after Adam's creation, God shows him the Tree of Knowledge
"Amid the Garden by the Tree of Life" (VIII, 326). Milton created
a mountain Paradise, interpreting Scripture by the explanation
that the great river "Water'd the Garden" (IV, 230) by rising
through "veins / Of Porous earth" to gush forth as a fountain by
the Tree of Life and then to run with "mazy error" to visit each
plant (IV, 227–40; IX, 72–73). Milton's description is very similar to Caussin's, but is closest to the account of the stream that
originates on the high hill at the south end of Amara and then
descends and divides to water the whole plateau. Michael led
Adam to a very similar hill,

> Of Paradise the highest, from whose top
> The Hemisphere of Earth in cleerest Ken
> Stretcht out to the amplest reach of prospect lay.
>   (XI, 378–80)

All nature's wealth at once is found in the Nuptial Bower. Though
it may be compared to the sylvan retreats of nymphs and fauns,
it is more sacrosanct and more beautiful. Every animal of the
earth lives in Paradise in harmony with man, and not even an
insect or worm will violate the Bower. God himself has chosen
the place, and it is ready for Eve as soon as she is created (IV,
690–91; VIII, 510–11). The roof is "inwoven shade / Laurel and
Myrtle." There is "on either side / *Acanthus*," besides "*Iris* all
hues, Roses, and Jessamin," violets, crocuses, and hyacinths (IV,
693–702).

While commentators were seeking to identify the exact site of
paradise, Milton assigned a location to his Paradise in accordance
with Scripture and rational scholarship, but as a poet he sought
to create a poetic Paradise as real and as undeniable as the events
that had taken place in the Edenic garden. Milton's presentation
of Paradise almost certainly is not the result of different stages of
composition, but the reflection of a unified and considered conception. In *Paradise Lost*, more than in any other work, we are
given the actual experience of life in the original earthly paradise.

Milton's poetic achievement in creating his Paradise has recently received a great deal of perceptive and sensitive critical comment — comment which merits more attention than can here be accorded it. The diversity of critical views reflects the diversity within Milton's Paradise, and critics have shown how this diversity becomes part of a comprehensive unity. Some of this analysis has shown a concern with myth and archetype and the Miltonic conceptions of nature and the cosmos; some has explored the ambiguities of a landscape that complements an Adam and Eve not yet fallen but about to fall; some criticism, often in relation to these two concerns, has disclosed the untold resources of Milton's language and style, and some of course has dealt with other aspects of Paradise.

For Northrop Frye and others the myth of Eden embodies fundamental truths about the human mind and body and the world of nature. "Every act of the free intelligence," wrote Frye, "including the poetic intelligence, is an attempt to return to Eden, a world in the human form of a garden, where we may wander as we please but cannot lose our way." In the relation of Adam and Eve to Eden before the Fall may be seen the union of the free intelligence with "the totality of freedom and intelligence which is God in man." Isabel Gamble MacCaffrey has found throughout *Paradise Lost* the mythic relationships of light and dark, height and depth, and time and place. The mythic tendency to see any organic whole as like the human body also appears in the idea of nature as organism in Milton's Paradise. Referring to the classical allusions employed in describing Paradise and Eve, MacCaffrey asserted that "a broken image is reconstituted by fitting together the fragments that man has been able to collect in his myths, and at the same time the status of the image as the original of and superior to all the fragments is established." She also noted that the precariousness and vulnerability of Paradise was suggested repeatedly. Helen Gardner has written of the vital organism reflected in the natural landscape of Paradise, and has placed Milton's garden in a historical perspective. This historical paradise, though idealized, "is the world of nature as we know it." "It is the new concept of the garden as nature in miniature, where trees,

228

bowers, and fountains, lakes and waterfalls make up a landscape, a conception that comes to perfection in eighteenth-century garden parks and spread all over Europe as *le jardin anglais*." [59]

The tensions in Milton's Paradise between an unfallen and fallen world have claimed the attention of a number of writers, who have joined with this concern a fresh and sensitive study of style. Davis P. Harding, in his reflections on the influences of classical epic on *Paradise Lost*, has noticed that Milton, in his description of the scenes in the garden, "sought to implant in the minds of his readers a secret, furtive, tentative uneasiness" and employed an "elaborate and largely secret machinery to prepare our minds for the Fall." Considering *Paradise Lost* in its relations to the enchanted gardens of Renaissance epic, A. Bartlett Giamatti granted the great commonplace of Milton criticism — "that the garden in Eden reflects the innocence and perfection of Adam and Eve" — but also insisted that "if the garden is to be a true reflection of the first couple, it must reflect *all* that is within them; it must also include that potential for change, change for the better or change for the worse, which is part of their nature." Milton's fruit of "vegetable Gold" (IV, 220), as well as other references, recalls the "embracing vine" and grapes "of burnisht gold" in Spenser's Bower of Bliss (II, xii, 54, 55). Milton's "blissful Bower" (IV, 690) and his use of "blissful" and "bliss" (V, 292, 297) in referring to Adam's "Bow'r" (V, 300) "cannot help but recall, by echo, Spenser's Bower of Bliss." William G. Madsen, who has developed a typological approach to Milton, has written of Paradise that "this apparently Neoplatonic garden is indeed a forest of symbols, paradoxically typological and prophetic, not Platonic; they are a shadow of things to come." The rivers of Paradise do not represent the four cardinal virtues, "but in their movements they foreshadow the Fall and man's subsequent wanderings." The trees "weep" and "the steep wilderness" on the side of the mount of Paradise "foreshadows the wilderness of this world to which Adam and Eve must descend after their trespass." And Jon S. Lawry has said, "Although Eden is mounted upon poles of choice, it can be maintained as both a luxuriantly fertile and a quietly Horation 'happy rural seat of various view' (IV, 247), dear to classic and neoclassic hearts." [60]

While examining these and other aspects of Paradise, some critics have given particular attention to a searching study of Milton's language and style. C. S. Lewis analyzed Milton's method of seeming to describe Paradise when what he was really doing was arousing the reader's imagination. "We are his organ: when he appears to be describing, he is in fact drawing out the Paradisal Stop in us," especially in Book IV, 131–286. The reader is aroused by expectancy and a "serialism" that leads to ever purer air, ever increasing beauty. Arnold Stein has brought together archetype and ambiguity and Milton's "answerable style" in his discussion of Paradise. "It is an *image* of the archetype that he creates, a symbolic image in a dramatic situation that helps create the image and protect it at once — protect it by maintaining the ultimate impossibility of the *image* of the real archetype." His analysis provides numerous examples of Milton's subtle use of suggestion, sound, and rhythm in his description of Paradise. Milton's language may have a "simultaneous doubleness," and a phrase like "with mazie error," to characterize the streams of Paradise, argues "for the rightness in wandering — before the concept of error is introduced into man's world and comes to signify wrong wandering." In his perceptive reading of the morning hymn of Adam and Eve (V, 153–208), Joseph H. Summers has found in this example of "innocent man's perfect praise" a reflection of Milton's "grateful vicissitude," the continued and fruitful motion that is an intrinsic part of the beauty of an unfallen world. The sun that will "sound" the Creator's praise and fountains that "warble" as they flow are all aspects of a movement that is itself praise. J. B. Broadbent and Anne Davidson Ferry have examined Milton's use of language in evoking the state of innocence, but from different perspectives. In a phrase such as "vegetable Gold," and in similar wording, Broadbent has perceived a balance between nature and art and ultimately between reality and myth. Nature that behaves artistically symbolizes innocence. He also noted that Milton's language in describing Paradise was "not frigidly remote, though wonderful," for it was much like the language that travelers actually used for a brief period. Mrs. Ferry has argued that through "sacred metaphor," in which a word has both a concrete and an abstract meaning, like "Fruit" (I, 1), Milton expressed the unified vision of the narrator and the unity of the unfallen world, "a world now strange, awesome, distant but perfectly distinct." She has also discussed the way in which Paradise is presented in Book IV from the point of view of the epic narrator, not from that of either Satan or "Milton." Jackson I. Cope has shown the relation of Paradise to the total "metaphoric structure" of *Paradise Lost*, especially to figures of light and dark, ascent and descent. In the description of Paradise the "topography builds upward in lavish detail." Adam and Eve are "erect and tall / Godlike erect" (IV, 288–89). However, darkness and descent enter with the references to the declining sun (IV, 352, 597). In his study of "Milton's grand style," Christopher Ricks has cited many passages from the descriptions of Paradise. Milton's fluid syntax mingles sight, sound, and fragrance to suggest hyperbolical beauty. An "unexpected substantiality" often occurs, as in phrases like "flouring Odours" (V, 293). Milton's style expresses ambiguity in words like "luxuriant" and "luxurious" (IV, 258–60; IX, 208–09), and in a phrase like "liquid Lapse of murmuring Streams" (VIII, 263), he suggests the prelapsarian beauty of Paradise, but with "Lapse" he also anticipates the Fall.[61]

The range and subtlety of Milton's poetic description of Paradise were not displayed by any of the other writers of the "celestial cycle." But they, like Milton, wrote of the location and appearance of paradise. Those who specified a location placed paradise in the region of the Tigris and Euphrates. These writers conceived of paradise as on a plain or in a valley, rather than as on a mountain. Although none of these writers revealed a vision of paradise as integrated and sustained as Milton's, they followed scores of previous writers in recapturing for their age the beauties of the first garden.

These writers often followed the commentators in discussing theories of the location of paradise. Sylvester reviewed theories of its location, including the possibility that it was "on a Mountain neer Latona's shrine," regarded it as destroyed, but warned the "over curious" to "question not the site." Grotius devoted twenty-four lines to locating his paradise. Apparently influenced by Junius, he placed it in Auranitis and referred to the four rivers identified by Junius. Peyton set his paradise in Assyria, near Babylon. Samuel Pordage described paradise as once on the Euphrates, and Loredano wrote that the garden was situated in "Eden, an Orientall Region, which was a part of Mesopotamia." [62]

In their accounts of man's first home, the Renaissance writers depended both upon the mythic tradition and contemporary commentary. Much of the description in these poems of paradise came in a single virtuoso passage telling of an eternal spring with fragrant blossoms, abundant fruits, soft breezes, and birdsong. These paradises lack the jeweled trees and other-worldly quality of the medieval descriptions, and instead are quite habitable little settlements in a plain or valley by a great river. There are, however, distinctive features in some of these depictions of the earthly paradise. Sylvester reflected earlier descriptions of paradise in telling of a river with sands of pure gold and pebbles of precious stones, but nevertheless thought of his paradise as much like an artificial Renaissance garden, with smooth walks, bushes trimmed to represent beasts, and hedges in love knots, triangles, and lozenges. In Andreini's "L'Adamo," angels praise the beauty of "clear circling waters" and "legions of scattered flowers," while Adam is familiar with "lofty hills" and the "fair, blue prairie of the sea." In a moment of dramatic poignancy, just after Eve has partaken of the fruit and paradise is lost, Adam eagerly tells Eve of a newly discovered rivulet winding through a dense green grove, of a waterfall, and a fruitful valley. Peyton's paradise, walled in with rocky mountains and a volcano, has gates of precious stones and streams filled with ore. Loredano depicted a paradise, surrounded by a river; though it was subject to such natural phenomena as snow and hail, these brought no discomfort. In Vondel's paradise, apparently set in a valley watered by the four streams, very natural and commonplace sheep and cattle graze near shores gleaming with jewels.[63]

In these descriptions of paradise, as in *Paradise Lost*, biblical and classical images merge with the natural paradise of the Renaissance commentaries.

8

THE NATURAL PARADISE
THE CELESTIAL PARADISE
AND THE INNER PARADISE

❧ BOTH THE COMMENTATORS and poets of the Renaissance usually thought of the historical paradise as preeminently a natural paradise, an epitome of the purity and beauty of nature, but many writers were also convinced that this unparalleled natural beauty held symbolic significance. Almost no one would have doubted that this earthly paradise was the "type" of a heavenly paradise. A number of commentators and poets also interpreted it as representing some kind of an inner paradise. Although Milton's Paradise and Nature in her prime seem almost one, his natural Paradise provides a way of apprehending the celestial paradise and the paradises within man as well.

The Natural Paradise

For Renaissance commentators and Renaissance poets and painters, the most important sense in which the historical paradise could be understood was as an actual natural garden, the product and seat of nature. Since nature and natural laws provided standards in ethics, politics, aesthetics, and science, the Edenic paradise was regarded as almost synonymous with an uncorrupted nature. Stoic ideas, Renaissance humanism, the pastoral dreams of a golden age, documentary reports from newly discovered lands, and the efforts to describe the Edenic garden — all were clustered

234

around the Renaissance idea of nature. These vital relationships were reflected in the prophecy of the young humanist Ulrich Hugwald that man would return "to Christ, to Nature, and to Paradise."[1]

Images of the Edenic paradise and of newly discovered natural paradises mingled with one another. Montaigne, in his essay on the cannibals, wrote that they "are yet neere their originall naturalitie" and that they far exceeded the pictures of the golden age. Although most commentators were not primitivists, the radical Puritan William Walwyn saw Adam and Eve as enjoying a life very much like that of Montaigne's happy savages. Following the explorers, colonizers discovered new paradises in the unspoiled natural splendor of the New World. Ralegh considered the New World to be like paradise and paradise like the New World. Centuries before William Faulkner, the American South was pictured as a paradise — not to be lost, but to be possessed. The Roanoke colony was "this paradise of the world" and Maryland was advertised as a "Terrestrial Paradice," whose trees and plants spoke in "Hieroglyphicks of our Adamatical or Primitive situation" and still bore "the Effigies of Innocency according to their original Grafts." In popular belief, these sunny regions could produce all the wondrous things that Adam had possessed before the Fall.[2] In turn, these reports of a natural paradise influenced conceptions of the Edenic paradise.

Commentators had long disputed about what was natural and what was supernatural in Adam's paradise. Inveges reviewed these arguments and discussed at considerable length such questions as these: Did the trees of paradise bear their fruit all year, keep their leaves, and live for ever? Were there any harmful plants or animals in paradise? Was the rose really, as St. Basil had said, without a thorn? Did the tree of life and the tree of knowledge belong to known species? How could the fruit of the tree of life give immortality? In general, Inveges and most of his contemporaries were inclined to think of the plants and animals of paradise as natural, like those of the fallen world, but still superior to them. It was also believed that the special conditions prevailing in paradise could have been brought about by natural secondary causes.[3]

The thrust toward a natural interpretation of paradise was epitomized in the commentators' discussions in which they grappled with the problem of the two special trees and attempted to provide a natural and rational explanation of the trees that brought immortality, knowledge, and death. It was generally agreed that it was the act of disobedience, not the fruit of the forbidden tree, which had brought corruption and mortality to Adam and Eve. A common view was that the tree of knowledge had taken its name "from the event." Pererius described the tree of life as growing exactly like other trees and possessing a natural faculty to preserve man's body. However, British Protestantism offered a more forthright insistence on the natural. Many asserted that no corruptible food could make the body incorruptible and that Adam's immortality was the gift of God. Walker was particularly disdainful of any supernatural interpretation of the tree. "The fruit of a tree, which is pulled off, eaten, digested, and so changed from that which it was in a bodily nutriment by the operation of mans fleshly stomack, cannot in any reason be conceived to have naturall power in it to give that to man which its selfe had not, to wit, immortality and immutability." [4]

Moreover, while Catholics generally held that man, naturally mortal in the state of innocence, was miraculously sustained in immortality from without, Protestants usually maintained that man was naturally immortal in the state of innocence. Weemse said that of the three estates discussed in man by physicians, Adam enjoyed that in which "more nourishment remaines with the body, than goeth from the body." Like many, he found a natural beauty to be joined with a natural immortality. "The beauty which was in *Adam* before the fall," he wrote, "was that naturall beauty arising from that comlinesse and proportion of his body, wherein hee exceeded all the sonnes of men." [5] Others also praised the naked majesty of Adam and Eve as part of their natural perfection in the state of innocence.

The beauty and bounty of nature were celebrated by poets in

236

their imaginative descriptions of paradises of the New World as well as in their accounts of the Edenic paradise. Passages depicting the island paradise of Shakespeare's *Tempest* were almost certainly derived from the accounts of the Bermudas by Silvester Jourdan and William Strachey. Indeed, *The Tempest* and *Paradise Lost* are comparable in their complex revelation of the many faces of nature and of the relations between the natural and supernatural. Andrew Marvell, too, was haunted by the gleams of paradise reflected in the natural beauty of both the New World and the Old. A well-developed popular view of the Bermudas as a natural paradise appears in the easy clichés of Edmund Waller's "Battle of the Summer Islands." The islands are paradise, while England is an inclement fallen world. Although the islands are a real and inhabited land, where Nature's "lavish hand" helps the natives to pay their rent with tobacco and "with potatoes fat their wanton swine," they are also endowed with the age-old qualities of the mythic paradise:

> For the kind spring, which but salutes us here,
> Inhabits there, and courts them all the year.
> Ripe fruits and blossoms on the same trees live;
> At once they promised what at once they give.
> So sweet the air, so moderate the clime,
> None sickly lives, or dies before his time.
> Heaven sure has kept this spot of earth uncursed,
> To show how all things were created first.
>
> (I, 40–47)

Milton's only explicit comparison of the state of Adam and Eve with that of the natives of the New World comes after the Fall when the first parents have just donned their fig leaves (IX, 1114–16). But the arch-colonizer Satan, reconnoitering in Paradise, has discovered "In narrow room Nature's whole wealth" (IV, 207), a new world far surpassing in natural beauty and abundance any claimed by European explorers. In Milton's universe, Paradise and Earth, as distinguished from Heaven, Hell, and Chaos, are the realm of nature. The exuberant power and fresh loveliness of a primordial nature are more evident in Paradise

than elsewhere, but whereas the rest of the world is wholly natural, Paradise with its close relationship to Heaven also shares
in the supernatural.

Paradise is a naturalized image of Heaven, and Hell is a distorted imitation. While Heaven is radiant with the glory of God
and Hell has artificial lighting, Paradise is dominated by the
sun, which seems to Satan like "the God / Of this new World"
(IV, 33–34). Heaven resounds to the harmony of angelic choirs
and Hell boasts its marching bands and "partial song"; Adam
and Eve also hear celestial harmonies, but their natural music is
the birdsong of paradise. Heaven is animated by the adoration
of God, Hell by a cancerous disunity, and Paradise by the pre-
carious balance of human love. And while Heaven is eternity
and Hell is monotony, Paradise as the realm of nature is the realm
of time, human history, and moral struggle.

Nature, like a passionate and powerful Renaissance monarch,
strides through Milton's garden. Milton's Nature is so strongly
personified that she is almost another character as well as an endless source of creative energy bodying forth the omnipotence and
love of God. Nature has sprung from the womb of Chaos, and
apparently will sink again into the grave of Chaos (II, 911). The
elements themselves, that "mix and nourish all things," are "the
eldest birth / Of Natures Womb" (V, 180–83). Milton's Nature
"Powrd forth profuse on Hill and Dale and Plain" the flowers
of Paradise, "Wantond as in her prime, and playd at will / Her
Virgin Fancies." She "multiplies / Her fertil growth, and by dis-
burd'ning grows / More fruitful" (IV, 243; V, 296–98, 318–20).
She follows God's law (XI, 49), and "hath done her part" for
Adam (VIII, 561). And Nature, "Sighing through all her Works
gave signs of woe" when Eve partook of the fruit (IX, 783), and
"gave a second groan" when Adam fell (IX, 1001).

Though Nature yields her greatest abundance and variety in
Paradise, she remains essentially unchanged in the prelapsarian
and postlapsarian worlds. In Adam's garden, as in the gardens
of his sons, paths may be obstructed by overgrown branches and

by falling gums and blossoms. Tall plants may need props. Nature is "Wild above Rule or Art" (V, 297), but her own rule is growth. In Paradise and in a fallen world, the vitality of Nature must be complemented by human labor. As the lords of Nature, Adam and Eve must guide and restrain her in order to keep the garden as a habitable abode.

Paradise is "Natures whole wealth, yea more / A Heav'n on Earth" (IV, 207–8). As the Garden of God, it participates in the supernatural. Old mythic elements are retained poetically in the natural and historical paradise. Milton's Paradise enjoys a perpetual spring, though this and the later transition to the seasonal cycle are explained rationally in terms of the earth's axis and the sun's course (X, 668–87). Also, Milton's Paradise, like that of Moses Bar Cephas, is composed of elements far purer and more refined than those of the rest of the world. These purge off Adam as a distemper (XI, 50–57). Hearing the sentence of expulsion, Eve wonders "how shall we breathe in other Air / Less pure, accustom'd to immortal fruits?" (XI, 284–85). The two magic trees posed problems for Milton, as they had for most of the Renaissance commentators. Following Scripture and taking advantage of their poetic and dramatic appeal, he nevertheless interpreted them as natural trees. Milton agreed with the majority of Protestant commentators that Adam's immortality was the gift of God, not the effect of a fruit. Milton's God declares:

> I at first with two fair gifts
> Created him endowd, with Happiness
> And Immortalitie: that fondly lost,
> The other serv'd but to eternize woe (XI, 57–60).

Uncertainty and caution seem reflected in Milton's statement that the "tree of life, in my opinion, ought not to be considered so much a sacrament, as a symbol of eternal life, or rather perhaps the nutriment by which that life is sustained" [6] — but not given. Milton was apparently thinking of the view held by Walker and others that the tree of life was more naturally nutritious than other trees. In *Paradise Lost* Milton consistently added a rational and natural explanation to the Scriptural account of the tree of life. Satan perched on this tree, the middle and highest tree of the garden, to observe Paradise:

> nor on the vertue thought
> Of that life-giving plant, but only us'd
> For prospect, what well us'd had bin the pledge
> Of immortalitie (IV, 198–201).

This almost certainly means that Adam and Eve — not Satan — should have used the tree as a pledge or memorial of their obedience. Following Genesis, Milton's God removes Adam from the tree, but not to prevent his gaining immortality:

> Least therefore his now bolder hand
> Reach also of the Tree of Life and eat,
> And live for ever, dream at least to live
> For ever, to remove him I decree . . . (XI, 93–96).

Moreover, the cherubim are to guard the tree, not to keep Adam from a magic tree that produces immortality, but to prevent the devils from preying on all the trees and trying once again to delude man (XI, 122–25).

Milton's interpretation of the tree of knowledge is complex. In his prose he regarded it as a thing indifferent in itself, important only because it offered a test of obedience. In *Paradise Lost*, Milton went far beyond the other poets of paradise by providing a psychological explanation of the lapses that led to the Fall and of the consequences of disobedience. Yet in *Paradise Lost* the fruit also seems to retain some of its supernatural character. With skillful ambiguity, Raphael refers to "the Tree / Which tasted works knowledge of Good and Evil" (VII, 542–43). But it is really the tasting, not the fruit, that so works. Satan is the chief advocate of the idea that the fruit is magical. This is the basic premise of the temptation both in Eve's dream, as narrated in Book V, and in Book IX. The fruit, he says, has given him the power of speech and will make Eve a goddess. He speaks of knowledge "enclos'd" in the fruit, but suggests that this is not really from God. He induces

Eve to turn down to a supposedly magic tree rather than up to God. After Adam and Eve had partaken of the fruit, its force

> with exhilerating vapour bland
> About thir spirits had plaid, and inmost powers
> Made erre . . . (IX, 1047–49).

This explanation of the effects of the fruit, given in terms of the materialistic Renaissance psychology, fuses the forbidden fruit and the act of disobedience in a poetic description of growing spiritual corruption. Adam, when he arises to his first fallen day, realizes that they have obtained knowledge only of "Good lost, and Evil got" (IX, 1072).

Like all else in Paradise, Milton's Adam and Eve belong to the realm of Nature. Both in the external world and in their inner worlds, they are always participating in the life of Nature. They live in harmony with Nature, not as nature's children, but as Nature's lords. Milton would have agreed with Weemse and other Protestant commentators that their immortality and bodily perfection were natural, rather than the result of grace. Apparently the process whereby their "bodies may at last turn all to Spirit / Improv'd by tract of time" (V, 497–98) is also natural. Although they are independent of nature, they are moved by her. Adam feels Nature first as a "link" and then as a "bond" which draws him irresistibly to share his life with a fallen Eve (IX, 914, 956).

In none of the other literary interpretations of paradise is Nature so strongly personified, so dynamic, and so lavish as in *Paradise Lost*. Nowhere else does Nature so tend to wildness and need continued pruning. Yet most of the other poets described a paradise that was more strictly and consistently natural than Milton's. Apparently regarding the tree of life as a pledge, Sylvester thought it prevented "epidemick ills," insurrections and civil quarrels, "childish old age," and "powerful griefes" — assuring almost every blessing except immortality. However, he explicitly denied any supernatural power in the tree of knowledge:

> Not that it selfely had such speciall might,
> As mens dull wits could whet and sharpen so
> That in a moment they might all things know.[7]

241

In the paradise of Grotius, trees apparently blossom and bear fruit in the usual way and can decline and die. The tree of life denotes eternal life and the tree of knowledge presignifies twofold knowledge, but neither possesses any magical power. Even the Satan of Grotius bases his temptation on the sensuous appeal of the fruit, not on its magical powers. Andreini's Satan is his only character who represents the tree as magical. Although there is no actual violation of nature in Vondel's description of paradise (apart from one brook flowing with wine and cream), it is always God, not nature, who pours forth the bounty and God's angels who provide the wedding feast for a very spiritual, sometimes mystical, Adam and Eve.[8]

The Terrestrial Paradise
and the Celestial Paradise

Building upon centuries of Hebraic and Christian tradition, Milton and most commentators and poets saw the terrestrial paradise as resembling and foreshadowing the celestial paradise. Employing a typological interpretation of Scripture, they found in the Edenic garden of the first chapters of Genesis an anticipation of the heavenly paradise foretold and described in the last chapters of the Revelation of St. John. Milton himself was immensely sensitive to conceptions of both the earthly and heavenly paradises and to the relationships that bound them in Hebraic-Christian thought. The relationship between the two paradises is basic in *Paradise Lost*.

Protestants were more hesitant than Catholics to discover any allegorical or figurative meanings in Scripture, yet they tended more and more during the earlier seventeenth century to accept various kinds of spiritual meaning provided they were based on a firmly established literal sense. The one kind of spiritual meaning accepted by almost all Protestant commentators was the typological interpretation,[9] through which the terrestrial and celestial paradises were consistently linked.

Like the literal interpretation, the typological interpretation was a historical interpretation; indeed, sometimes it was regarded as the one real literal meaning. Milton stated, "No passage of scripture is to be interpreted in more than one sense; in the Old Testament, however, this sense is sometimes a compound of the historical and the typical."[10] The typological interpretation was a part of the legacy Adam took from Eden; Michael had maintained that the full significance of the covenant of grace would be revealed "From shadowy Types to Truth" (XII, 303). According to the typological interpretation, historical persons and events in the Old Testament are the shadows that New Testament events cast before them. This explanation was rooted in the typological relationship between Adam, the first man, and Christ, the second man, developed in the Pauline epistles. In various respects Noah, Isaac, Moses, Joshua, Samson, Jonah, and Melchisedec were types of Christ. The terrestrial paradise in which Adam fell was regarded as comparable to the celestial paradise into which Christ would receive the redeemed. Paradise lost was a shadow of paradise regained.

The relationship between the terrestrial and celestial paradises was almost as old as the idea of paradise itself, and was a part of many early mythic conceptions of paradise. In developing this connection in *Paradise Lost*, Milton depended not only upon the Renaissance commentators, but upon centuries of Hebraic and Christian tradition. His seventeenth-century readers would also have been familiar with the many promises and prophecies of a renewal of the lost paradisal felicity. The early Hebrews and Babylonians apparently shared the view common to many early religions that there were celestial models for the earthly paradise, earthly cities, earthly temples, and indeed for almost everything.[11] Descriptions of the lost earthly paradise influenced visions of a restored paradise and a restored Jesusalem. The old paradise, the new paradise, and the new Jerusalem merge in the description in Ezekiel 47:1–12 of the temple with its four rivers issuing forth to bring a future free from want and disease. In Isaiah, the peace and harmony of Eden will return as "the wolf shall dwell with the lamb," and "They shall not hurt nor destroy in all my holy mount" (Isa. 11:6–11). A new era will come with "a new heavens and a new earth" (Isa. 65:17, 66:22).

In the apocryphal and pseudepigraphal literature of the Old Testament, visions of a new paradise and a new Jerusalem, earthly or heavenly, shift and merge. In *The Book of Jubilees*, a miraculously translated Enoch is conducted "into the Garden of Eden in majesty and honor" (4:23). In *The Book of Enoch*, the tree of life is reserved for the righteous in a paradise that is sometimes celestial, sometimes terrestrial. A return to Edenic happiness is prophesied in *The Apocalypse of Baruch* (73:6–7), for there will be no more disease, pain, hatred, envy, lamentation, or death, but peace between men and animals, a consummation of the corruptible and a beginning of the incorruptible. There is also the promise that Jerusalem shall be restored forever (6:9). Full assurance of a new Edenic age is given in IV Ezra (II Esdras) 8:52–58: "For you is opened Paradise, planted the Tree of Life; the future Age prepared, plenteousness made ready; a city builded, a Rest appointed; infirmity extinguished, Death hidden, corruption forgotten, sorrows passed away; and in the end the treasures of immortality are made manifest." [12]

As early Christian writers had accepted the Jewish account of man's beginnings in paradise, they also accepted the messianic eschatology of the Jews and the belief in a new paradise and a new Jerusalem. In Christian typology, Adam was a type of Christ, Eve's creation a foreshadowing of the birth of Christ's spouse the Church, and the earthly paradise a form of the celestial paradise or the new Jerusalem of the Revelation of St. John. Almost all the references to heaven and to paradise in the New Testament are eschatological. Heaven is the final legacy of the righteous (as in Eph. 1:14) or a place to be prepared "in my Father's house" for the redeemed (John 14:2). Christ promises the thief entry into paradise (Luke 23:43). In popular belief, paradise was consistently thought of as in the third heaven. St. Paul speaks of being "caught up to the third heaven" and then finding himself in paradise (II Cor. 12:2–4), but it is not certain whether or not he identifies paradise and the third heaven.

The most influential conceptions of the paradise awaiting the righteous and of its relation to the Adamic paradise were derived from the Revelation of St. John, which was itself closely related to the *Book of Enoch* and the Jewish eschatological tradition. As in Isaiah, "a new heaven and a new earth" are promised (21:1). St. John sees the New Jerusalem descending out of heaven from God, 12,000 furlongs square, and resplendent with gold, jasper, and precious stones. God and the Lamb are the temple of the holy city. There is no more sun, for the Lamb is the light thereof (21:6–23). A great river flows from the throne of God. And, "In the midst of the street of it, and on either side of the river, was there the tree of life which bare twelve manner of fruits and yielded her fruit every month: and the leaves of the tree were for the healing of the nations" (22:2). It has already been promised: "To him that overcometh will I give to eat of the tree of life, which is in the midst of the paradise of God" (2:7). And, for the inhabitants of the New Jerusalem, there shall be no more death, sorrow, or pain (21:4).

Some of the early fathers saw the New Jerusalem very literally as a restored paradise. Irenaeus insisted that a real and terrestrial New Jerusalem would provide various mansions for the saints, according to their rank, after a literal bodily resurrection. "And it is right that when the creation is restored, all the animals should obey and be in subjection to man, and revert to the food originally given by God (for they had been originally subjected in obedience to Adam), that is, the productions of the earth."[13] The later fathers and the medieval doctors passed over the Apocalypse or interpreted it only allegorically, and not until the Reformation was it seriously studied in accordance with the historical and typological interpretation of Scripture.

Typological interpretation became highly systematized, detailed, refined, and popular. A correspondence between the terrestrial and celestial paradises would seem altogether expected to those who were certain that an orderly God had organized the universe through a complex system of correspondences. For commentators, the natural earthly paradise, with its rivers and tree

of life, was patterned on the heavenly paradise; it also foreshadowed the blissful heavenly paradise promised to the redeemed,
which itself was a renewed Eden. In the beauties of his own paradise, they felt, Adam saw suggested those of the celestial paradise
which he could attain through obedience. Fallen man was to return to the innocence and glory of Eden at the same time that
he gained a heavenly paradise through Christ. Writers commenting on Genesis 2 often cited references to the tree of life in the
Revelation and to paradise in Luke 23:43 and II Cor. 12:4,
while those commenting on the Revelation frequently turned
back to Genesis. Both on the Continent and in England, numerous commentaries on the Revelation appeared during the sixteenth and seventeenth centuries, but the most influential of the
new rational studies was the *Clavis Apocalyptica* (1627) of Joseph
Mead, a universal scholar whom Milton knew at Cambridge.[14]

In the eyes of diverse Continental commentators, the splendor
of Christ and the heavenly home of the redeemed were glimpsed
in the natural beauty of the Edenic paradise. Servetus, one of the
first of the reformers to interpret the Adamic paradise typologi-
cally, concluded that the two special trees, standing in a paradise
in the midst of the ancient world, were a figure of Christ, who
was the life and knowledge planted in the midst of our world.
He explained that the Promised Land, as a part of the Edenic
paradise and the birthplace of Christ, retained "a vestige and
shadow" of paradise and signified the restitution in a celestial
paradise. In his annotations, Diodati described the earthly paradise as "a figure of the Heavenly one" and the tree of life as "a
figure of Christs residing in heaven, which is the true celestial
paradise." He also foresaw that the "pure naturall nakednesse"
of the body in Eden would reappear at the resurrection "in glory
without any other ornament or garment but that of the image of
God." Views similar to these were expressed by the Catholic
commentators Pererius and Lapide.[15]

In England, both the bishops and the Puritan ministers explored the typological meanings of the earthly paradise. Andrewes
asserted that "this below was a shadow and nothing else but

quasi vestibulum." As from the first Adam we lost an earthly and temporal paradise, he said, so from the second Adam we will gain a heavenly and eternal paradise. "As man was the image of God," explained Joseph Hall, "so was that earthly paradise an image of Heaven." Of the typological significance of the tree of life, he declared strikingly, "Man saw his Saviour before him before he had need of a Saviour." One of the most complete examinations of the relationship between the two paradises was provided by the Separatist leader Henry Ainsworth. He wrote that "the pleasantness of [the terrestrial paradise] is made a figure of heaven," and that it "applied to the Church of Christ." The tree of life, he commented, signified for Adam "a spirituall life after in Heaven for ever" if he remained obedient, and was referred to in the description of "the Spirituall Paradise under the Gospell" in the Revelation. Also, in telling of the great river watering the Edenic garden, "Scripture speaketh of God's spirit and grace in his Church" (Rev. 22:1) and of "the river whose streams make glad the city of God" (Psalms 46:5 and John 7:38–39). Ainsworth noted, too, that the union of Adam and Eve set forth the everlasting mystical union of Christ and the Church.[16]

The similarity and correspondence between the terrestrial and celestial paradises were stressed by others. The view that the earthly paradise had been created in the image of heaven was related easily and harmoniously to the Renaissance belief in a system of correspondences linking the various realms of the universe and to the typological and eschatological interpretation of Scripture. "A little model of Heaven and a sign of the great Heaven" was Leigh's description of the Adamic paradise. Some pointed out that the heavenly paradise, like the earthly one, had "rivers of pleasure." Then Gregory, in his curious and comprehensive work on the significance of the East in Scripture, maintained that "the Garden of *Eden* was planted towards the equinoctiall East of the Holy Land," with the sanctuary in the eastern part of the garden. Corresponding to this, "the *speciall* Presence of God ever was and is in that part of the Heaven of Heavens which answereth to the Equinoctiall East of the Holy Land" and

247

the celestial paradise in "that part of Heaven where the *Throne of God,* and the Lambe is."[17]

Emphasizing the historical and typological approach, commentators found in the heavenly city of the last chapters of the Revelation the divinely ordained consummation of the human history that had begun in its "shadow," the Edenic paradise of the first chapters of Genesis. This heavenly paradise was a restoration of Eden, but was more glorious than Eden. The historicity of the "shadow" paradise gave assurance of the celestial paradise. A popular Puritan preacher interpreted God's making all things new to mean that he "would restore the world to that excellent estate wherein it was before *Adams* fall; and his elect to a state and condition far more excellent in heaven." Most were confident that more was to be recovered than had been lost. The new Jerusalem would have twelve gates — twelve angels admitting the inhabitants — while the earthly paradise had one passage to the tree of life, which was barred by the cherubim. The pure life-giving river flowing from the throne of God was contrasted with the river of corruption that flowed forth from Eden. The heavenly tree of life would be held in common by all, but the earthly tree was not to be touched after the Fall.[18]

The new heaven and the new earth, repeatedly promised in Scripture and in *Paradise Lost,* were generally given as natural and rational an interpretation as possible. Protestant critics usually looked for some kind of transformation rather than an annihilation of the earth, a purgation of the elements, or a cessation of celestial motions. A common view was that the heavens and earth would not be changed in substance, but in quality. More figuratively, the new heaven was interpreted as the Church's glory in heaven and the new earth as the glorious bodies of the saints, or both were interpreted as simply a new state of being leading to perpetual righteousness.[19]

Although much was revealed, there was still opportunity for debate, and explanations could be either highly literal or highly allegorical. One of the most perplexing questions was, What were the real qualities of the heavenly paradise foreshadowed by the earthly one? Junius and many others regarded the new Jerusalem and the new Church as one. All agreed that the paradise of the redeemed was spiritualized, but disagreed as to whether it was in the new heavens, the new earth, or both. There were two principal conceptions: the new Jerusalem represented the Church triumphant on earth after the conversion of the Jews, or the Church triumphant in heaven. In his "bare history of events," Mead reasoned that the new Jerusalem, surrounded as soon as Satan was unbound, must have existed before the end of the millennium, and that "after the new Jerusalem follows Paradise." Some of those who advocated Mead's views tended more and more to picture the redeemed as living in a utopian society. Others considered the new heaven and the new earth to be one harmonious kingdom. Most, however, regarded the final home of the saints as heaven or as a part of heaven known as paradise. The saints could be envisioned as passing from the new earth to a heavenly kingdom through a dissolution of their bodies and souls. To what end, it was asked, should the new Jerusalem descend out of heaven when all the elect shall be in heaven? While many of "the Millenaries" maintained that the saints would enjoy a bodily and earthly reign for a thousand years, another interpretation held that the "coming down from heaven" of the new Jerusalem should be understood as referring to its character, not to local motion. The "highest heaven," said Walker, will be the dwelling place of the saints, with Christ as their head.[20]

These beliefs concerning the celestial paradise and its relationship to the terrestrial one became a part of *Paradise Lost* and of other literary works treating the loss of Eden. Milton was the poet of the celestial paradise long before he was the poet of the terrestrial one that foreshadowed it. In fact, the celestial paradise is the most consistent theme in Milton's poetry, and is important in much of his prose. In *Paradise Lost*, the typological relationship between the earthly paradise and the heavenly paradise becomes basic to both the argument and the structure.

The fervor with which Milton writes of the regained paradise in his early works speaks for its appeal to his imagination. In the

Nativity ode, Milton sees a return to the golden age. In "At a Solemn Music," he imagines a restoration of the harmony that existed between heaven and earth before the Fall and envisions angels touching harps "With those just spirits that wear victorious palms." In "Lycidas," the pastoral landscape anticipates the "other groves and other streams" of "the blest kingdoms meek of joy and love" where Edward King will walk with "all the saints above." In Elegy III, Andrewes is welcomed to the shady retreats and shining landscapes of a celestial paradise, and at the end of *Comus* the virtuous are invited to follow the Attendant Spirit to the "broad fields of the sky." *Of Reformation* concludes with a vision of Christ proclaiming his "universal and milde *Monarchy* through *Heaven* and *Earth*," while the highest orders of saints "in supereminence of *beatifick Vision* progressing the *dateless* and *irrevocable* circle of *Eternity* shall clasp inseparable Hands with *joy*, and *blisse* in over measure for ever." [21]

In his later works, Milton was concerned with the sequence of events in the final establishment of the kingdom of glory. He tended to interpret these literally, but did not speculate as specifically as many about the exact nature of this kingdom. Espousing the "soul-sleeping" heresy, Milton expected no heavenly reward for the righteous until the end of the world. Christ "declares expressly," he wrote, "That there is not even a place appointed for the abode of the saints in heaven, till the resurrection" (John 14:2–3). After Christ's reign with his saints for a thousand years on earth will come the "destruction of the present unclean and polluted world itself, namely its Final Conflagration." It was uncertain and unimportant, he said, whether this would be a change in substance or not. The felicity of the heavenly paradise is the "perfect glorification" which consists in "eternal life and perfect happiness, arising chiefly from the divine vision." This will "be accompanied by the renovation of heaven and earth and of all things therein adapted to our service and delight, to be possessed by us in perpetuity." This is the new heaven and new earth referred to so often in *Paradise Lost*. Although Milton could virtually identify the celestial paradise with the new Jerusalem, this kingdom had its own discipline and degrees of glory. He did not, like some Puritan preachers, reject an earthly new Jerusalem, but he at least approached the views of Junius, Walker, and others in thinking that a special celestial paradise would receive the supremely blest. Citing Christ's words to the thief and St. Paul's experience, he wrote, "In this highest heaven seems to be situated the heaven of the blessed, which is sometimes called Paradise . . . where also God permits himself to be seen by the angels and saints." [22]

Paradise Lost reveals clearly how the old Jewish idea of a terrestrial and celestial paradise has become an indispensable part of the historical and typological interpretation of Scripture developed in the Renaissance. The typological relationships between Adam and Christ, the lost paradise and the regained paradise, are basic in Milton's presentation of the justice of God's ways and in the historical sweep of *Paradise Lost*. Repeatedly the earthly paradise is compared to heaven, and repeatedly a heavenly paradise is promised as a final abode. Thus, the earthly paradise is consistently seen as representing and foreshadowing the celestial paradise. Moreover, both paradises are described similarly, with dependence on classical descriptions of the Elysian Fields and of other paradises.

Paradise lost and paradise regained, the two major themes of *Paradise Lost*, are combined with the relationship between Adam and Christ in the familiar opening lines:

> Of Mans First Disobedience, and the Fruit
> Of that Forbidden Tree, whose mortal taste
> Brought Death into the World, and all our woe,
> With loss of *Eden*, till one greater Man
> Restore us, and regain the blissful seat. . . .

In the opening lines of *Paradise Regained*, Adam and Christ, the "happy garden" and the "recover'd Paradise" — that "Eden rais'd in the Waste Wilderness" — are similarly related. And near the end of *Paradise Lost*, Michael tells Adam how Christ will come

> to reward
> His faithful, and receave them into bliss,

251

Whether in Heav'n or Earth, for then the Earth
Shall all be Paradise, far happier place
Then this of *Eden*, and far happier daies.
(XII, 461–65)

Underlying these passages is the assumption that Adam was the type of Christ and that the earthly paradise at the beginning of history was the type of the heavenly paradise at the end of history. The final abode of the blest which Raphael promised Adam before the Fall, and which Michael promised Adam after the Fall, takes its name from the Edenic garden with which God first blessed Adam. The second paradise not only restores the felicity of the first, but offers a glory that could be attained only through Christ.

It has been disputed whether Raphael is giving a Platonic or typological interpretation when he asks,

though what if Earth
Be but the shaddow of Heav'n, and things therein
Each to other like, more then on Earth is thought?
(V, 574–76)[23]

Referring to the relationship of the earth to Heaven before the Fall, Raphael stresses the similarity in order to make his narrative more understandable and to warn that revolt against God could occur on earth as it had in Heaven. Actually, in the Hebraic tradition the terrestrial paradise is related both to a celestial pattern and to a garden of the righteous; and in some Renaissance commentary, including that of Pererius, Leigh, and Gregory, Platonic and typological interpretations merge loosely. However, although Milton's God evidently patterned Paradise on Heaven, the typological meaning of "shaddow" is the most important one in the context of *Paradise Lost* as a whole. For both Milton and his readers, Raphael's question must have implied that the prelapsarian earth, particularly Paradise, was a type of the celestial paradise to be given to the righteous.

Paradise and, indeed, the whole earth resemble the Heaven of *Paradise Lost*. Satan and Raphael, who know both Heaven and Paradise, are often moved to note how similar God's garden on earth is to the groves, bowers, and fountains of Heaven. Satan, who will see the saints claim what he has lost, is almost obsessed with the similarity. The sun, which dominates the natural paradise, first reminds Satan of Heaven (IV, 37–39). Adam and Eve are "to heav'nly spirits bright / Little inferior" (IV, 361–62). Just before undertaking the temptation, Satan, in a poignant inversion of values, thinks of the "Terrestrial Heav'n" as superior to the true celestial Heaven (IX, 99–103). For the imperialism of Hell, the earth is "a spacious World, to our native Heav'n / Little inferior" (X, 467–68). While Satan is tortured by the resemblances, Raphael can rejoice that God has "Varied his bounty so with new delights" which may still "compare with Heav'n" (V, 430–32). Not only does Raphael liken earth to Heaven in telling Adam of the war in Heaven, but he finds the newly created earth "like to Heav'n, a seat where Gods might dwell" (VII, 329) and "another Heav'n / From Heaven Gate not farr" (VII, 617–18).

In *Paradise Lost*, as in many commentaries, Paradise for its pleasantness is a figure or type of Heaven. Milton's Heaven, after which his God in many ways patterned Paradise and the earth, represents the heavenly kingdom promised the saints with the coming of the new heaven and the new earth. Milton's Heaven abounds in allusions to the Revelation and to other New Testament Books in which heaven and the new Jerusalem are depicted as the inheritance of the faithful. It is in many ways the Temple or Church which Renaissance commentators interpreted the New Jerusalem to signify. As the descriptions of Hell in books I and II foreshadow the hell on earth that will follow the Fall, so the descriptions of Heaven in book III and subsequent books foreshadow the new heavenly kingdom that will follow the general resurrection. This eschatological presentation of Heaven becomes evident as God, who knows past, present, and future as one, foresees the end of the realm of history before it has begun:

> Meanwhile
> The World shall burn, and from her ashes spring
> New Heav'n and Earth, wherein the just shall dwell . . .
> (III, 33–35)

Rejoicing in the promised Redemption, the hymning angels praise God and cast down "Thir Crowns inwove with Amarant and Gold." The allusion to amaranth, the unfading flower, relates the two paradises and links God's revelation of the new heaven and new earth with an apocalyptic description of Heaven:

> Immortal Amarant, a Flou'r which once
> In Paradise, fast by the Tree of Life
> Began to bloom, but soon for mans offence
> To Heav'n remov'd where first it grew, there grows,
> And flou'rs aloft shading the Fount of Life,
> And where the river of Bliss through midst of Heavn
> Rols o're *Elisian* Flou'rs her Amber stream;
> With these that never fade the Spirits elect
> Bind thir resplendent locks inweath'd with beams,
> Now in loose Garlands thick thrown off, the bright
> Pavement that like a sea of Jasper shon
> Impurpl'd with Celestial Roses smil'd (III, 353–64).

The tree of life in the earthly paradise and the fount and great river of the heavenly paradise (Rev. 22:1) represent here, as they did for most of the commentators, the salvation offered through Christ. The angelic "Spirits elect" that rejoice in man's redemption by the sea of St. John's apocalyptic vision (Rev. 4:6) foreshadow and almost become the saints to be redeemed through Christ. Man's ascent to Heaven is implied by the stairs and passage linking Paradise and Heaven (III, 509–37).

Even as Satan flies toward the earth to tempt man, the account of his journey looks toward his final defeat and the final triumph of Christ. The controversial Paradise of Fools (III, 444–97) is part of the eschatological view of *Paradise Lost*. This is the limbo assigned to those who will seek to be sure of the celestial paradise while taking their reward on earth. However, Satan also sees where

> underneath a bright Sea flow'd
> Of Jasper, or of liquid Pearle, whereon
> Who after came from Earth, sayling arriv'd,

254

> Wafted by Angels, or flew o're the Lake
> Rapt in a Chariot drawn by fiery Steeds.
> (III, 518–22)

In fact, Milton considered the translation of Enoch and Elijah to typify the perfect glorification that the saints would enjoy in eternity.[24]

The War in Heaven, too, seems to foretell the final triumph of the Redemption. Christ's going forth on the "third sacred Morn" (VI, 748) suggests his resurrection. As he returns victorious, "all his Saints" advance to meet him, "shaded with branching Palme" (VI, 882–85), as in St. John's apocalyptic vision. And the vision of Christ in Hebrews 1:3[25] seems reflected as he rode

> into the Courts
> And Temple of his mightie Father Thron'd
> On high, who into Glory him receav'd,
> Where now he sits at the right hand of bliss.
> (VI, 889–92)

The heavenly paradise represented by the earthly paradise is also heralded in *Paradise Lost* by the repeated allusions to the new heaven and new earth, allusions that epitomize the numerous apocalyptic promises of Scripture. This theme of a new heaven and a new earth harmonizes with the theme of the Seed and the covenant of grace in triumphant anticipation of the recovered paradise promised in the opening lines of *Paradise Lost*. The single kingdom of a terrestrial and a celestial paradise is promised Adam by Raphael on the condition of obedience:

> And Earth be chang'd to Heav'n, and Heav'n to Earth,
> One Kingdom, Joy and Union without end (VII, 160–61).

After the Fall, God pledges the final imprisonment of Satan:

> Then Heav'n and Earth renew'd shall be made pure
> To sanctitie that shall receive no staine (X, 638–39).

In words that accept the divine mystery of the earth's transformation, the angelic host hails Christ,

> Destin'd restorer of Mankind, by whom
> New Heav'n and Earth shall to the Ages rise,
> Or down from Heav'n descend (X, 646–48).

After the protevangelium, this promise is joined to that of salvation through faith under the covenant of grace. God decrees that "Faith and faithful works" will bring man to "second Life" and the new heaven and new earth. The trumpet that will "sound at general Doom" then summons the angels from the "waters of Life" to the synod of the blest in the way that future saints will be summoned at the world's end (XI, 63–80). Book XI closes with God's absolute promise: the covenant of faith is renewed, and all things shall hold their course

> till fire purge all things new,
> Both Heav'n and Earth, wherein the just shall dwell.

Finally Adam, when he has understood the mystery of the woman's Seed, learns how Christ,

> Now amplier known thy Saviour and thy Lord,
> Last in the Clouds from Heav'n to be reveald
> In glory of the Father, to dissolve
> *Satan* with his perverted World, then raise
> From the conflagrant mass, purg'd and refin'd
> New Heav'ns, new Earth, Ages of endless date
> Founded in righteousness and peace and love,
> To bring forth fruits Joy and eternal Bliss.
> (XII, 544–51)

None of the other Renaissance works focused on the Fall have the strong eschatological emphasis of *Paradise Lost*, but some interpret the earthly paradise as a figure of the heavenly one. For Sylvester, the terrestrial paradise was "the type of the upper Paradise." In *Psyche*, Joseph Beaumont wrote that "by perpetual interchange of hearts" Adam and Eve did "Fairly transcribe our blessed life above." Andreini's angels feel that Adam finds a heaven in the midst of earth, and his newly created Eve asks if earth has been changed to heaven. Vondel's Gabriel speaks of "The earthly Paradise (from Heaven named)" and looks for Adam

256

and Eve to rise from "Earth's courts of love" to "a fairer court in Heaven above."[26]

The Paradise Within

The natural external paradise typified the celestial paradise and provided the one way of apprehending a spiritual bliss that could be conceived of only as paradise. Some valuable recent studies have considered this inner paradise in relation to hexameral literature, the Augustinian tradition of meditation, and the tradition of the enclosed garden.[27] For Renaissance commentators and poets, the Edenic paradise was rich in spiritual significance and suggested various kinds of spiritual paradises, four of which, important in polemic, devotion, and poetry, were the inner life of Adam and Eve in innocence, the allegorical garden of virtues in the tradition of Philo, the "paradise within thee, happier farr" (XII, 587) of those justified by faith in Christ, and the innocence experienced and lost by each individual. The first three of these conceptions could be incorporated into the historical interpretation of Scripture and are an essential part of the design of *Paradise Lost*. The last conception, insofar as it called into question the historical interpretation, would have appeared dangerous to Milton and the orthodox commentators.

Conceptions of the inner paradise of Adam and Eve were based upon the familiar but still controversial ideas of original righteousness and of the nature of the divine image in man. The beauties of the external paradise were only a complement to the joys of the inner paradise. As the external paradise derived its beauty from the Creator and resembled heaven, so Adam experienced a divine illumination approaching that of the angels. Catholics and Protestants disagreed whether some of Adam's endowments in innocence were the product of nature or of grace, but almost all agreed that the divine image or likeness was reflected in his integrity, immortality, holiness, righteousness, justice, charity, knowledge, and wisdom. In one of the most complete seventeenth-century portrayals of God's image in man, Weemse explained that the divine image was expressed inwardly in the understanding, will, and affections, and outwardly in dominion. Weemse pictured an Adam, only a little inferior to the angels, who loved God above all else, exercised perfect freedom of choice, possessed all holiness requisite in man, and enjoyed a knowledge exceeding that of the greatest philosophers.[28]

Those who gave an allegorical interpretation to the garden in the manner of Philo conceived of it chiefly as a moral or spiritual state. Such allegorical interpretations differed from typological interpretations in that they were not a sense of Scripture, but simply an expression of universal philosophical and moral truths which could be attributed to Scripture. Though Philo's allegories were essentially abstract and unhistorical, some Renaissance writers, including Milton, combined elements of allegory with a literal and historical interpretation. Others, such as Henry More, were very skeptical about the literal interpretation, yet did not explicitly reject a historical reading. Many regarded paradise not so much as a place but as a state of moral perfection and spiritual exaltation in which man was free of earthly bonds and lived in the divine radiance.

The interpretation in which Adam represented reason and Eve passion and sensation, basic in Milton's characterizations of the first couple, was a literary commonplace in the Renaissance. The traditional Greek antithesis between reason and passion had become, chiefly through the influence of Philo, an accepted way of understanding the relationship of Adam and Eve and the loss of paradise. In his *Enchiridion*, Erasmus wrote: "Our Eve is fleshly passion, whose eyes were daily lured by that crafty serpent." Sir Thomas Browne suggested that the temptation of the man by the woman represented "the seduction of the higher parts by the inferiour and femine faculties." Similarly, Vane concluded that "in a mystical sense man was made Male and Female in the same person, through the setting up this two-fold exercise of life and operation of soul in him, sensual and rational."[29]

Two of the most complete and popular allegorical interpretations of paradise were those of Jakob Böhme, a German mystic, and Henry More, a Cambridge Platonist. All Böhme's work had been translated into English by 1662, and More's *Conjectura Cabbalistica*, first published in 1653, went through four editions. Böhme's study, full of alchemical figures, was mystical, mysterious, and highly individualized; More, citing Philo for support, was rational and skeptical, urbanely dismissing the literal in a search for congenial philosophical truth.

Böhme depicted an Adam with a spiritual body who dwelt simultaneously in Eden, which was on earth, and in paradise, which was in heaven. Adam possessed divine power, knew all tinctures and ruled over constellations. Spirit penetrated his earthly body "as fire does a hot iron" and the divine essence penetrated the essence of time "as sun penetrates fruit upon a tree." Adam fell and his spiritual body became gross when he loved himself in Eve, his feminine part, and hearkened to the "venomous imaginations" inspired by the devil. Böhme felt that all men in some sense had shared in Adam's experience. "I, in the essence of my soul and body," he wrote, "when I was not as yet I, but when I was in Adam's essence, was there, and did myself fool away my glory in Adam." But he also was assured that "we have yet that very first soul wherein the true understanding lieth." [30]

After discussing the site of a physical paradise, More observed: "Thus have we according to the Letter found Paradise which Adam lost, but if we finde no better one in the Philosophical and Moral Cabbala, we shall but have our labour for our travel." In his philosophical cabbala, More explained that Adam, at first "wholly *Ethereal*," was "placed in Paradise, that is, in an happy and joyful condition of the Spirit; for he was placed under the invigorating beams of the *divine intellect,* and the Sun of Righteousnesse then shown fairly upon him." The four rivers were the cardinal virtues. The tree of life, standing "in the midst of this Garden of mans soul," would have borne fruits of immortality. The tree of knowledge represented man's own will. Adam's soul descended into earth and he became a "downright terrestrial Animal," when his masculine part, "pure subtile intellectual Knowledge," was seduced by the inferior feminine faculty, sensation. In his moral cabbala, More emphasized that Adam's fall was not caused by "one single mistaken act," but by "disobedience at large and leading a life unguided by the Light and Law of God." [31]

A third kind of inner paradise was the joy of the soul which gave itself to Christ. This paradise was opened to Adam and his sons through their acceptance of Christ. Interpreting the rivers of Eden as symbolic of baptism, early Christian writers found this paradise in the midst of life, for in entering the Christian life through the waters of baptism, one crossed the rivers of Eden into paradise. Another important source of the conception of the spiritual life of the regenerate as a garden or paradise was the imagery of planting and cultivation found in the New Testament. Milton, in his discussion of regeneration, referred to Matthew 15:13 ("Every plant, which my heavenly Father hath not planted, shall be rooted up"), John 15:1–5 ("I am the true vine . . ."), and Ephesians 3:17. The parable of the sower, which appeared in three gospels (Matt. 13:1–23, Mark 4, and Luke 8:4–15), provided a popular text. Writers repeatedly turned to this biblical imagery to describe the new life and the growth of the soul united to Christ. Calvin was one of many who regarded the sacraments as "helps by which we may be ingrafted into the body of Christ." "The heart of a Christian is Christ's garden," wrote Sibbes, explaining that Christ's spirit, blowing upon his flowers, "makes them to send forth a sweet savour." A popular book on the parable of the sower said that the regenerate soul, forever longing to be more firmly rooted, sought "to conform to the image of *Adams* holiness in his innocency." The regenerate are Christ's husbandry, a part of his garden and his paradise, and they form the Church, "a new Paradise of God." The Digger leader Gerrard Winstanley, though sometimes dismissing the historical paradise, depicted sinners as standing outside paradise, barred by the flaming sword, "till God pull them unto himself in his own time and season." When the sword vanishes, "then the Father appears in manifestations of love, peace, and oneness, to the joy, life, liberty, and peace of the creature, which way soever he goes." [32]

In the fourth conception of an inner paradise, the paradise story is regarded as a drama enacted within each individual soul.

Although the mystical writers developing this idea did not consistently reject the historical interpretation, they did imply that it was uncertain or unimportant. This symbolic view of the Old Testament was developed by such sixteenth-century Continental writers as Sebastian Franck and Nicholas of Cusa, and by such seventeenth-century Englishmen as John Everard, Giles Randall, Winstanley, and others. For the orthodox defenders of an actual physical paradise and of a literal account of man's temptation, this symbolic interpretation seemed to imperil all sound Christian doctrine. Milton could have accepted this conception of an inner drama played in the soul of Everyman only as a subordinate aspect of the historical interpretation.

In Franck's *Forbidden Fruit*, paradise, with its wondrous trees, the serpent, the beast, the old dragon, and antichrist, is all within the human mind. "Therefore the fall of Adam happeneth dayly," he wrote; "dayly doth Adam in his posterity eate of the forbidden fruit." But everyone can regain the inner paradise through the promise of the protevangelium. We can "spitt out and vomitt up the knowledge of good and evil as poyson, and become as Adam was before his fall, Fooles, and innocent Turrtles, that we may eate of the Tree of Life and suffer the seed of the woman to be ingrafted in us." Franck proclaimed that "God alone and his omnipotent word is our Paradise" even as we are "the Temple of God and his Paradise." [33]

The theological implications of this interpretation of the inner paradise are evident in Bodin's *Heptaplomeres*, thought by the orthodox to be as dangerous as the fatal apple itself. One of the seven speakers discussing forbidden subjects says the story of Adam and the apple is fit only for children and the vulgar. He later declares that each is his own Adam and must suffer as Adam did if he abandons himself to sensuality and lightness. The next speaker takes the next logical step and denies original sin. The Old Testament patriarchs showed no original sin, he contended, and we ourselves remain free and responsible. [34]

Everard, Randall, and Winstanley knew the Continental mystics, but continued to develop the native mystical strain in English Puritanism. The inner paradise is at the heart of Randall's glowing translation of Nicholas of Cusa's *De Visione Dei.* "To see God the Father therefore and Jesus Christ his Son," he wrote, "is to be in Paradise and Glory and Joy everlasting, because hee that is without Paradise cannot have such a vision, seeing neither God the Father nor thou O Jesus are to be found without Paradise." As well as having translated *De Visione Dei,* Randall is probably the author of the strange *Divinity and Philosophy Dissected, and Set Forth, by a Mad Man.* Here he emphasized that we were to look on Scripture "with a spirituall eye, and then shall we see it as it is, for the looking on it as a history (and not as it is a sacred and holy mystery) makes so many false Religions." Surely, he said, Moses could not have written of the creation of the physical world, for "this externall world is one and the same for ever, for anything I could see or heare." Rather, he explained, "all Adams" appear free to stand or fall, but "thy subtle serpent carries thee into all mischief." Winstanley called upon the preachers not to "tell the peple any more, That a man called *Adam,* that disobeyed about 6,000 years ago, was the man that filled every man with sin and filth, by eating an apple. Rom. 5:19. For assure yourselves this *Adam* is within every man and woman: and it is the first power that appears to act and rule in every man." He regarded childhood as the condition represented by Adam's innocence, but asserted that each man had to make his choice between righteousness and evil upon entering an age of understanding.[35]

Some of these conceptions of an inner paradise corresponding to the external one became a significant part of the various literary interpretations of the paradise story in the Renaissance. In *Paradise Lost,* particularly, the poetic revelation of the inner paradise gives a spiritual depth, emotional intensity, and psychological credibility to the historical narrative. In all these works, the description of the external paradise helps suggest the extrabiblical bliss commonly attributed to Adam and Eve in their innocence. The Philonic tradition also influenced some of the portrayals of Adam and Eve, notably those of Milton, Lancetta, and Samuel Pordage. The inner paradise of the faithful Christian is more important in *Paradise Lost* than in the other works.

In *Paradise Lost*, the creation of man in God's image is the great fountainhead of the various conceptions of the inner paradise. From this flows "Truth, Wisdom, Sanctitude severe and pure" (IV, 293), and all the qualities of original righteousness with which Adam was endowed. Free of shame, Adam and Eve enjoy man's happiest life in "Simplicitie and spotless innocence" (IV, 318). Adam's direct creation in the image of God and Eve's creation from Adam form the basis of their marital happiness. Adam's rational superiority, as contrasted with Eve's more sensuous and emotional nature, is also a direct reflection of the divine image. When man falls through succumbing to the lower faculties, the divine image is darkened. But God promises to "renew / His lapsed powers, though forfeit and enthrall'd" (III, 175–76). With divine grace planted in his heart, man may once again through faith and obedience experience the happiness of an inner paradise, though abiding in a fallen world.

The inner paradise of original righteousness is the spiritual counterpart of the beauty of the garden before the Fall. In fact, for God, Satan, and the first parents themselves, the outer paradise and this inner paradise are virtually inseparable. The physical and the spiritual, the external paradise and the characters' experiencing of it, become corresponding parts of one whole. God beholds Adam and Eve

> in the happie Garden plac't
> Reaping immortal fruits of joy and love,
> Uninterrupted joy, unrivald love
> In blissful solitude (III, 66–69).

Immediately after the creation of Adam, God promises to conduct him to "the Garden of bliss, thy seat prepar'd" (VIII, 299). Entering Paradise, Satan "Saw undelighted all delight" (IV, 286). Barred from the inner paradise himself, he is tormented to see Adam and Eve "Imparadis't in one anothers arms, / The happier *Eden*" (IV, 506–7). If Adam and Eve do not know that they are happier than they know, they at least know that they are happy.

263

For them, Paradise is bliss and bliss is Paradise. Adam observes to Eve that God has "plac't us here / In all this happiness" (IV, 416–17) and later tells Raphael that they enjoy the utmost bliss imaginable (V, 516–18).

The inner paradise of innocence and the external paradise fuse to form a complex symbol of a spiritual state; and, the inner life of Satan and the devils fuses with the external features of Hell to form a comparable symbol. Both become a part of the historical sweep of *Paradise Lost*. The first parents' free choice will determine whether their descendants will inherit the inner life of Hell or of Paradise. While the devils suffer the deprivation of the light and life of God, Paradise is in close touch with Heaven and the first couple enjoy a glorious communion with God. While Hell is a wasteland surrounded by rivers of passion, Paradise is dominated by life-giving streams and the tree of life, the symbol of God's gift of immortality. Moreover, while Hell can suggest only the despair of an ever lower Hell gaping beneath, Paradise provides for Adam the hope of an ever higher paradise to be gained through obedience.

Dramatically and emotionally in *Paradise Lost*, the inner paradise of original righteousness is the paradise that is lost. Both God and Raphael have warned Adam that disobedience would bring a loss of happiness (VIII, 331–33; V, 521–23). After the Fall, the protevangelium, and the beginnings of regeneration, the expulsion comes to Adam and Eve as an anticlimactic surprise. Adam finds that the external paradise loses all its charm when the inner one is lost. As soon as he learns that Eve has tasted the forbidden fruit, he knows that he cannot live alone "in these wilde Woods forlorn" (IX, 910). Realizing that they have lost honor, innocence, faith, and purity, Adam desires only to "live savage, in some glade / Obscur'd" amidst an impenetrable forest (IX, 1074–75, 1085–87). Finally, the great inner storm of high passions sweeps away completely the inner paradise (X, 112–31), as the great Flood will sweep away the external one.

Milton's inner paradise of innocence is also related to the allegorical garden. Although insisting upon a historical paradise and

an Adam and Eve that were earthly human beings, Milton nevertheless utilized elements of the Philonic tradition. Like Philo and
his many followers, he showed an inner paradise lost through the
seduction of reason by passion and sensation, as revealed in the relations of Adam and Eve. In Philo, this allegorical interpretation is
essentially unhistorical; in *Paradise Lost*, too, it carries a timeless
moral truth, but its chief function is to make human and credible
the all-important historical events occurring in the actual Edenic
paradise.

In Milton's very real Adam and Eve, one can discover the timeless struggles within the garden of the human soul. Philo and his
Renaissance followers interpreted the creation of Eve while Adam
slept to represent the dominance of the emotions and senses when
reason was inattentive. Adam's first and seemingly innocent passion appears when, as in a trance, he sees the newly created Eve
(VII, 462–77). A rational Adam recognizes that his sensuous Eve
is "Bone of my Bone, Flesh of my Flesh, my Self / Before me"
(VIII, 495–96). Temptation comes first to Eve in the dream in
which Satan appeals to her vanity and tries to induce her to partake
of the luscious fruit (V, 28–94); Adam's explanation of dream psychology becomes a commentary on the relations between the reason and the lower faculties (V, 100–19). After her dream, Eve is no
longer content to remain inferior. Just before she partakes of the
fruit all her senses are aroused, and she becomes the very embodiment of sensuous desire.

> Fixt on the Fruit she gaz'd, which to behold
> Might tempt alone, and in her ears the sound
> Yet rung of his perswasive words, impregn'd
> With Reason, to her seeming, and with Truth;
> Meanwhile the hour of Noon drew on, and wak'd
> An eager appetite, rais'd by the smell
> So savorie of that Fruit, which with desire,
> Inclinable now grown to touch or taste,
> Sollicited her longing eye (IX, 735–43).

Philo's interpretation of reason's fall is humanized and refined in
Paradise Lost. Adam resolves immediately to join Eve in ruin not

because of sensuality, but because he cannot "forgo / Thy sweet Converse and Love so dearly joyn'd" (IX, 909). Reason abdicates and the inferior faculties, good in themselves if subjected to reason, assume dominion. Lust, however, follows, and the inner garden of virtues is swept away by the storm within. In his vision of the future, Adam sees that man's woe will continue, as "From Mans effeminate slackness it begins" (XI, 634).

Both the inner paradise of Edenic innocence and the allegorical garden of virtues are lost, but the inner paradise of the regenerate may be gained and possessed in a fallen world. This paradise of inner grace, like the external, natural paradise, is created by God. Like the celestial paradise, it is foreshadowed and suggested by the loveliness of the natural paradise. In *Paradise Lost*, when Adam goes forth into the world, he possesses the paradise within, "happier farr" than the external one he is leaving. Adam's descendants, too, may find happiness in this spiritual paradise, but more often will dwell in the spiritual hell brought to earth by Satan and his followers.

The garden symbolism of the New Testament, which was employed to describe regeneration, is linked with the natural, external paradise to form part of the pattern of *Paradise Lost*. Foreknowing man's disobedience and Fall, God first adumbrates the promise of the inner paradise of the regenerate when in his dialogue with Christ, he reveals that those who accept his Son and live "transplanted" in him shall receive new life and "As from a second root shall be restor'd" (III, 287–94). After they have lost their paradise of unfallen bliss, Adam and Eve unknowingly approach this "paradise within" when they resolve to confess their sin, express repentance, and hope for divine mercy and grace. God has removed the stoniness from their hearts and has made a new, regenerate flesh grow there. Presenting man's sighs and prayers to God, Christ pronounces this paradise of the regenerate to be far superior to the natural one:

> With Incense, I thy Priest before thee bring,
> Fruits of more pleasing savour from thy seed
> Sow'n with contrition in his heart, then those

> Which his own hand manuring all the Trees
> Of Paradise could have produc't, ere fall'n
> From innocence (XI, 25–30).

Commissioned by God to expel Adam and Eve from Paradise, Michael also comes to guide them to the paradise within. His revelation of God's justice and mercy, the Redemption and the covenant of grace, make possible Adam's entry into this inner paradise just before the descent from the mount. Michael is an excellent teacher, and Adam is an excellent student. His last speech to the angel (XIII, 553–73) sums up perfectly what he has learned. This knowledge and understanding have also gained him admission to the paradise within. Instructed by the example of Christ, whom he acknowledges as his Redeemer, Adam can depart, greatly renewed "in peace of thought." He has learned obedience to God, love of God, and an absolute dependence upon God's mercy and God's power to overcome evil with good. Michael gives Adam his final instruction for attaining the inner paradise:

> onely add
> Deeds to thy knowledge answerable, add Faith,
> Add vertue, Patience, Temperance, add Love,
> By name to come call'd Charitie, the soul
> Of all the rest: then wilt thou not be loath
> To leave this Paradise, but shalt possess
> A paradise within thee, happier farr.
> (XII, 581–87)

Michael's promise of this inner paradise of the regenerate comes most appropriately just after Adam's acceptance of Christ — the door to paradise in the Christian tradition — and just before the expulsion from the Edenic garden.

The interpretation of Genesis 2–3 as an unhistorical spiritual drama, repeated in the soul of every individual, does not appear in *Paradise Lost.* Milton could accept elements of this interpretation only insofar as they could be incorporated into the historical reading. Franck, Winstanley, and others considered this spiritual interpretation to be the most important sense, if not the only sense, of Scripture. For Milton, this was not a sense of Scripture, and therefore could not be a part of his poetic dramatization of Scriptural truth in *Paradise Lost*. In *Paradise Lost*, the Fall is unique. However, as a consequence of the Fall, Adam's descendants will continue to repeat its pattern in their own lives. In Michael's revelation of the future, Adam sees repeatedly the surrender to passion, the obscuring of the divine image, and the loss of true liberty. Moreover, although Milton's Adam and Eve are not themselves Everyman, they do provide moral examples and lessons applicable to Everyman.

Though less developed than in *Paradise Lost*, the same interpretations of the inner paradise appear in the other Renaissance works dealing with the paradise story. The happiness derived from the communion with God in innocence is often emphasized. Almost every characterization of Adam and Eve shows some influence of the Philonic tradition. In Salandra's *Adamo Caduto*, Adam and Eve clearly represent the interrelationships between the mind and the senses. But the two most highly developed allegorical interpretations are the prose drama of Troilo Lancetta and the epic rhymes of Samuel Pordage. Lancetta even provided a complicated chart showing the allegorical relationships. Paradise is "the habit of a tranquil mind"; Adam is "an untutored human spirit with free choice for good or for evil"; and Eve is "the sensual part which, when ill controlled, leads man into the Hell of disgrace." Depending heavily upon Böhme, Pordage explored the "Mysteries of the External, Internal, and Eternal Worlds." A very ethereal Adam, who flies, never sleeps, and is nourished only by divine love, falls when his will is broken off from the will of God. "*From Paradise* they go, or Paradise / Rather departs from them." [36]

Throughout the Renaissance works of the "celestial cycle" appear these four ideas of an inner paradise: the inner life of Adam and Eve in paradise, the garden of virtues, the happiness of those justified by faith, and the childhood innocence of each individual. All conceptions do not appear in each work. None of the other writers developed the paradise of Edenic innocence and the paradise of the regenerate as fully and sensitively as Milton.

9

THE FADING OF PARADISE

PARADISE LOST stands as the consummation not only of the Renaissance commentaries and the literary works of the "celestial cycle," but of centuries of biblical interpretation and imaginative speculation. As scholar and poet, Milton was uniquely endowed to draw upon these many currents of tradition in one great work. In the century after the publication of *Paradise Lost* in 1667, both theological writers and poets focused less and less upon the Edenic paradise of Adam and Eve as the historical site of the beginnings of the human race and of original sin. During this period there were no comprehensive commentaries on Genesis and no literary works bringing truth, seriousness, and imagination to the paradise story. Following the light of reason, scientists and historians turned further and further from Scripture in their study of the primitive earth and primitive man, while theologians raised searching questions about original sin and the Redemption, the central themes of *Paradise Lost*. Literary writers tended either to exploit the paradise story for urbane entertainment or to follow the polemicists in replacing the human drama of a historical Adam and Eve with abstract discussion.

Seven years after the publication of *Paradise Lost*, the Anglican divine William Sherlock could turn upon the old Puritan John Owen with frigid scorn in his denial of a personal relationship

between Christ and the saints and in his rejection of the imputation of Christ's righteousness to the redeemed. Attacking both the
idea of a conjugal union with Christ and a legal union with Christ,
with the Redeemer the surety, Sherlock protested that "we must
have done with *Metaphor* unless we will turn Religion into a
Romance." Men must be saved, he said, by their own personal
righteousness, not by the personal righteousness of Christ. Seemingly disoriented in a changing world, Owen asked, "But what doth
he intend?" He had written his own tract, he claimed, "when there
was the deepest peace in the mind of all men about the things
treated of therein, and when I had no apprehension of any dissent
from the principal design, scope, and points of it by any called
Christians, the Socinians only excepted."[1]

Although some writers still tried to identify the exact site of the
historical paradise, others ridiculed this quest or found the existing and inhabited paradises in newly explored lands more interesting. In the name of common sense, Samuel Butler denounced
the search for paradise as well as the efforts of Goropius, Sir
Thomas Browne, and others to reconstruct the lives of Adam and
Eve. His blockheaded Puritan knight erring, Sir Hudibras,

> knew the Seat of Paradise,
> Could tell in what degree it lies:
> And as he was dispos'd, could prove it
> Below the Moon, or else above it.
> What *Adam* dreamt of when his Bride
> Came from her closet in his side:
> Whether the Devil tempted her
> By a *High Dutch* Interpreter:
> If either of them had a Navel;
> Who first made Music malleable.[2]

Even though the search for the Adamic paradise seemed futile
and old-fashioned, Europeans still were delighted to find man's
pristine splendor perpetuated in the primitive paradises of
America, the Pacific Isles, and the East. To many, the American
Indians seemed like figures from a prelapsarian age. Describing
the idealized primitive society of Surinam, Mrs. Aphra Behn

found the natives, unclothed and unashamed, "so like our first parents before the fall." Extolling this life of pure nature without religion, laws, or organized government, she wrote that "these people represented to me an absolute idea of the first state of innocence, before man knew how to sin." But in the eighteenth century, primitive societies were more often associated with the classical golden age than with the biblical paradise, while the golden age was idealized for its own sake, rather than as a pale reflection of the Edenic garden. The ideal was not so much the original righteousness of Adam as the natural simplicity of primitive man. Moreover, knowledge of diverse societies undermined belief in the universal fatherhood of Adam and the universal taint of original sin.[3]

Critical Discussions

Under the banner of reason, scientists, historians, and theologians were revising, rejecting, and disputing the authenticity of Genesis and the fundamental doctrines of original sin and the Redemption. While the challenge to orthodoxy was increasingly open and radical, the defense remained vigilant and vigorous. Many of the crucial issues became focused for a time in the controversy about the theories of Thomas Burnet. However, a continuing devotion to natural religion and a faith in the rule of reason provided the most consistent threat to a Scriptural interpretation and to a theology that rested upon a belief in revelation.

In attempting to explain the paradisal state and its loss by secondary, natural causes, Burnet raised questions that would perplex and trouble succeeding generations. Contending that it was dangerous to oppose Scripture to reason in disputes about the natural world, Burnet developed his ideas in his *Telluris Theoria Sacra* (1681), in his translation *The Sacred Theory of the Earth* (1684), and in his *Archaeologicae Philosophicae* (1692), also later translated. Rationalizing the supernatural and regarding much in the first chapters of Genesis as only figurative, Burnet argued that the entire antediluvian earth, not just a limited area, had been paradisal. Rejecting the numerous scholarly discussions identify-

271

ing the exact site of paradise, Burnet ridiculed "the vain Temerity of modern authors; as if they could tell to an Acre of Land where Paradise stood." The belief in a Mesopotamian paradise he regarded as "a Conceit and Invention of some modern Authors" seeking assurance in an argument they could not well manage. On the contrary, Burnet wrote, "We might consider all that Earth as a Paradise, and *Paradise* as a *Garden*; and, as this Torrid Zone, bare of grass and trees, made a kind of Gravel-walk in the Middle, so there was a green Walk on either Hand of it, made by the temperate zones; and beyond those lay a Canal, which water'd the Garden from either side." He thought that "the whole earth was in some sense Paradisiacal" during the entire antediluvian era, but granted that one particularly paradisal region could have been known as paradise.[4]

Burnet did not mention any of the previous discussions of paradise as the whole earth, and perhaps deliberately wished to dissociate himself from the earlier writers because he felt that his own approach was fundamentally different and the only valid one. While the earlier writers had speculated about God's purposes and *why* he had made a particular kind of paradise, Burnet tried to demonstrate God's methods and to show *how* he had created a paradisal world. He believed he had found the key to man's early history in secondary causes rather than in final causes. He stated emphatically that to understand paradise, one must understand the natural causes prerequisite to a perpetual spring yielding abundance without labor. "For it is not any Region of the Earth that can be *Paradisiacal*, unless all Nature conspire and a certain order of Things proper and peculiar to that State." He explained that the eternal spring and natural abundance enjoyed by the primitive earth were caused by the earth's smooth surface, its oblong egglike figure, and its direct posture to the sun, assuring a perpetual equinox. "In this smooth Earth," he asserted, "were the first Generations of Mankind: it had the Beauty of Youth, and blooming Nature, fresh and fruitful, and not a Wrinkle, Scar, or Fracture on its Body; no Rocks, nor Mountains, nor hollow Caves, nor gaping Channeles, but even and uniform all over." With his figurative interpretation of the temptation, he envisioned changes as occurring only gradually until the time of the great Deluge when the earth's surface crumbled and its axis tilted as great stores of water burst forth from under ground.[5]

In *Archaeologicae Philosophicae*, Burnet scorned much in the literal interpretation of Genesis. He marveled how custom and preconceived opinion could lead men to believe "without the least Demur or Examination" accounts that they would never have accepted from the Greeks or the rabbis. He parodied the serpent's conversation with Eve and God's sentencing of the first parents after the Fall. Do you really believe, he also asked his readers, that angels stood for 1500 years guarding a garden? Like the ancient sages, he said, Moses spoke to the popular mind through fables and symbols.[6]

Burnet's works not only gave support to the development of natural religion and stimulated a long and lively debate about the physical characteristics of the primitive earth, but provoked a more popular response as well. One satire, while ostensibly a defense of orthodoxy, displayed a new irreverent tone. Burnet was credited with maintaining

> That all the books of Moses
> Were nothing but supposes;

And moreover,

> That as for Father Adam
> With Mrs. Eve, his madam,
> And what the serpent spoke, sir;
> "Twas nothing but a joke, sir.
> And well-invented flam, *etc.*[7]

During the late seventeenth and the earlier eighteenth centuries, scientists, historians, and theologians continued to debate the circumstances of man's beginnings. The mythic and miraculous almost disappeared. The older conception of a limited paradise, from which the first parents were expelled, became increasingly untenable because it could not be explained by natural causes. Similarly, the older universal, providential history, tracing all back to Adam and paradise, was superseded by histories more truly comprehensive and less biblical. Meanwhile, defenders of orthodoxy were confronted with probing questions concerning the literal interpretation of Genesis and the doctrines of original sin and the Redemption.

Burnet's critics continued to try to reconcile Scripture with not only reason, but the rapidly increasing scientific knowledge. However, like him and unlike earlier orthodox writers, they could not accept as scientifically credible any sharp distinctions between paradise and the rest of the world or between the prelapsarian and postlapsarian eras. They speculated about the life of Adam and Eve, but assumed that natural conditions in one place could not be understood either apart from their causes or apart from related conditions elsewhere in the world. With this approach, they found gradual change more probable than sudden change and the Deluge a more comprehensible and demonstrable explanation of the earth's ruin than the Fall and the divine curse on the earth. For them, the antediluvian era became an extension in time of the lost paradise. They were less concerned than the earlier writers with the traditional wonders of beauty, abundance, and unchanging climatic perfection, but were more interested in natural phenomena that could be understood by the laws of a postdiluvian world; in fact, their antediluvian earth assumed many of the features of the present earth. After much speculation, it was shown that the earth's axis and rotation must always have been as they are now.

John Woodward, a professor of science and a member of the Royal Society, thought that Burnet's primitive earth could not have existed and would have been most unparadisal if it had existed. His scientific approach to the earth as a whole led him to reject both the mythic conception of an eternal spring and Burnet's idea of the earth's unchanging relation to the sun. A lack of seasons, he explained, "would be so far from exalting the Earth to a more happy and Paradisiacal State, which is what he brought it in for, that 'twould turn it to a general *Desolation*, and a mere barren Wilderness, to say no worse. Such a *Heat* would be too *little* for some *Sorts* of *Vegetables,* and too great for others." "In brief," he concluded, "there would have been all the *Diversity, Uncertainty,* and *Disorder* in the Vegetable Kingdom that can well be conceived."[8]

Another prominent figure in the Burnet controversy, William Whiston, who succeeded Newton in the Lucasian professorship, assured readers that he would "at once keep sufficiently close to the Letter of Moses, and yet be far from allowing what contradicts the Divine Wisdom, Common Reason, or Philosophical Deduction." He tried to show that the earth, constructed very much like an egg, had been formed from the atmosphere of a comet. He assumed that the early earth had no diurnal motion. He disagreed with Burnet and held that the antediluvian world had mountains, seas, metals, and minerals; but he pictured it as having a particularly pure and subtle air, watered only by mists, without thunder, lightning, rain, or pestilential infections. The inhabitants were all long-lived vegetarians, he wrote, and there was a larger population before the Flood than the present earth would be able to supply with nourishment.[9]

John Keill, a Scottish mathematician and astronomer, disagreed with both Burnet and Whiston about the nature of the primitive earth. He maintained that God had created mountains, seas, and harbors, and had inclined the earth's axis from the beginning for man's benefit. He explained that the relation between the sun and the primitive earth described by Burnet would bring intolerable heat and cold to some regions. Criticizing Whiston's belief that the early earth had no diurnal rotation, he asserted that the cold would have been unendurable for Adam and Eve, while the heat "would have forced our first parents to seek shelter in Dens and Caves, which would have been in such a state, more convenient than the Garden of Eden."[10]

During the eighteenth century, man's conceptions of the primitive earth underwent very rapid and radical changes and at least approached contemporary views of geological time and evolution. The *Encyclopédie,* edited by Denis Diderot, stated that it was probable that the sea had covered uninhabited continents for several centuries. Depending upon the theory of accommodation in interpreting Scripture, the Comte de Buffon regarded the six days of the Creation as representing six epochs of thousands of years. He estimated, for instance, that the earth had required 74,000 years for cooling. In a passage that was later withdrawn, he also very cautiously suggested that, if it were not for the express statements of Scripture, one would be tempted to seek a common origin for horse and ass, man and monkey.[11]

The old universal history, like that of Ralegh, gradually disappeared. Standing at the end of the seventeenth century, Bossuet's universal history was the last great monument of Renaissance orthodoxy. Considering Moses as "the most ancient of historians" and "the most sublime of philosophers," Bossuet emphasized again the universal fatherhood of Adam, original sin, and the protevangelium. His presentation of the Fall, very much in the style of a novel, was the most imaginative and sensitive since *Paradise Lost*. But even Bossuet subordinated the historical interpretation to the study of religion in relation to the great revolutions that have begotten empires.[12]

After Bossuet, more and more historians, both in England and on the Continent, regarded Genesis as only one among many sources — and not a particularly reliable source — and the Hebrews as only one among many peoples. Lord Bolingbroke, in his letters on the nature and uses of history, shocked many of his contemporaries by asserting that the Old Testament had been "delivered to us on the faith of a superstitious people among whom the custom and art of pious lying prevailed remarkably." These works, he contended, had no authority in the ancient world until they were adopted by the early Christians. Attempting to trace objectively and empirically the development of religion itself, David Hume concluded that all records and remains showed that polytheism had been everywhere the most ancient religion. Hume contrasted the Adam of literature with a real, historical man. Milton's Adam, he said, perceived at once the glories of nature and turned to its Creator, "but a barbarous, necessitous animal (such as a man is on the first origin of society), pressed by such numerous wants and

276

passions, has no leisure to admire the regular face of nature, or make enquiries concerning the cause of those objects, to which from his infancy he has been gradually accustomed." The legacy of Eden had, indeed, vanished along with paradise. The article on Adam in the *Encyclopédie* stated that the word was included not as a proper name but, like Greek *anthropos*, as a designation of mankind. The article then provided a historical interpretation of the development of the concept of original righteousness.[13] In the *Social Contract*, Rousseau referred once to "Emperor Adam," sole ruler of his domain, but this reflects his interest in the independent development of political institutions in many different societies, not in the legacy of Eden. And Herder, in his *Ideas on the Philosophy of the History of Humanity*, saw the earth both as a star among stars and as an immense laboratory in which man, animals, and plants developed in accordance with fixed natural laws.

The orthodox, literal interpretation, however, suffered more telling attacks from the proponents of natural religion and the opponents of the doctrine of original sin. Like Burnet, the precursors of eighteenth-century deism subjected Scripture to the test of reason. Charging that Burnet had offended only "the blind Biggots of the old absurd Interpretation," Charles Blount confessed that original sin had been "ever a difficult Pill with me, my Reason stopping it in my Throat, and not having Faith enough to wash it down." He dismissed the lengthy arguments about the four rivers of paradise for a new reason — the rivers could not have been formed from perpetual springs, depending either upon rain or the sea, when paradise was created. Displaying his own fresh, clear-sighted reasonableness in commending the reasonableness of Christianity, John Locke found original sin unreasonable. The doctrine of the Redemption, he judged, was "founded upon the supposition of Adam's fall." But he found the death referred to in Genesis 2 and 3 to be only temporal death, not eternal misery and sin. According to Locke, the Scripture taught that men were rewarded or punished only for their own deeds.[14]

Fundamental questions were raised about God's Word and the

justice of God's ways to men both within the Church of England and among the nonconformists. Reared as a Calvinist, the polemical divine Daniel Whitby became one of the leaders in the assault on the doctrine of original sin. He proclaimed that there was not one word in Scripture to support either the "imaginary" and "exceeding cruel" covenant of works between Adam and God or any imputation of Adam's sin to his descendants. Such was plainly inconsistent, he contended, with the justice, wisdom, and goodness of God. Moreover, he maintained that almost all the bishops and "the great body of the clergy" were of his opinion.[15]

About two centuries after Bullinger had traced Protestantism back to paradise, Mathew Tindal argued that the religion of nature was "as old as the Creation." His work, a dialogue between a deistic teacher and a rather docile questioner, soon became a center of controversy. Natural religion was imprinted in men's breasts at creation, Tindal wrote, and the gospel was a republication of this religion of nature. Revelation, however, could never contradict reason. Tindal ridiculed the account of Eve and the snake, found original sin inconsistent with what reason showed to be the nature of God, and represented all sacrifice, including the sacrifice of the Redeemer, as unreasonable and inhumane.[16]

A scholarly defender of Tindal's position, Conyers Middleton, engaged in long, acrimonious controversies with Bentley, Dr. Daniel Waterland, and other orthodox writers. He marveled at the "strange variety of conceits which have been invented about the single article of a Paradise," and scoffed at the idea that God had created a paradise "which was no sooner made than forfeited, and like a *Theatrical Scene* changed in an instant, to a prospect of misery and barrenness." The story of the Fall he regarded as just another fable. While earlier writers had thought that pagan fables were a distorted reflection of Scriptural truth, Middleton suggested that Moses had based his account of the Fall on notions imbibed from the Egyptians in his youth.[17]

The liberal, influential nonconformist minister John Taylor rejected not only original sin, but also centuries of traditional belief about the life in paradise. While the Renaissance commentators had revered the fathers, Taylor blamed "dreaming, ignorant, and superstitious monks" for serious misconceptions. Examining Scripture without bias, he reported his findings without equivocation. He discovered no basis in reason or Scripture for the doctrine of original sin. But he went further toward demolishing the traditional conceptions of paradise and the Fall through his denial of original righteousness. Taylor wrote that "no Instance of his [Adam's] Virtue or Holiness is to be found in Revelation, from whence we can infer any extraordinary Principle of Righteousness and Holiness in him above his Posterity, even before he transgress'd." "From all this," Taylor concluded, "it appears to me, that the common Scheme of *Original Righteousness*, as well as that of *Original Sin*, is without any Foundation in Scripture, or the Reason and nature of Things."[18]

Those defending Scriptural authority, original sin, and the Redemption reiterated old doctrines, made some concessions, and occasionally offered new arguments. They seldom denied the claims of reason and natural religion in showing that revelation was consistent with both. They sometimes turned to the theory of accommodation and the literary form of Genesis to explain omissions, inadequate statements, and seemingly fabulous happenings such as Eve's encounter with the snake. However, even the defenders of a fundamentally historical interpretation tended more and more to lose sight of a human Adam and Eve in a tangible paradise in their devotion to reason and abstract argument. At the end of the seventeenth century, the defenders of orthodoxy clung tenaciously to the literal, historical interpretation or marshaled new knowledge to bolster an old faith. In his commentary on the Pentateuch, Bishop Richard Kidder granted that there was "a Mystery under the Letter," but insisted that "the Letter is to be preserved, and not to be questioned by any means." He referred readers to Ralegh for a discussion of the location of paradise. Putting a final reactionary touch on the historical interpretation, the nonconformist minister Samuel Clarke (1626–1701) thought it probable that the Hebrew letters and even the vowel points had been imprinted on Adam's soul in paradise. For such versatile thinkers as Richard Bentley and John Ray, science was the handmaiden of religion. They summoned a wealth of knowledge and reason herself to demonstrate the providence of God and the truth of his Word.[19]

In the eighteenth century, Bishop Thomas Sherlock, Pope's "plunging prelate," entered into a controversy with the deists by vigorously defending revelation and prophecy. He concurred that in the state of innocence, "natural Religion wanted no *other* assistance, and therefore *it* had no *other*." But after the transgression, "Then came in the *Word* of *Prophecy*; not in Opposition to *natural Religion*, but in Support of it." He maintained that the "first gospel" was a necessary *"rational Foundation"* for the first parents' future endeavors. Recognizing the "Difficulties which arise from the historical Narration of the Fall," Sherlock explained that Moses had had recourse to the "Common Usage of the *Eastern Countries*," parables and similitudes, in order to avoid a direct presentation of Satan. This, he said, might have led to dualism, and would have necessitated an explanation of the fall of the angels.[20]

Among others meeting the challenge of natural religion were Daniel Waterland and Bishop Joseph Butler. Waterland, esteemed for his learning, sought to argue for the authority of Scripture by showing the relationships of didactic, tropological, and anagogical readings to the literal meaning. Replying directly to Tindal, he asserted that to take away revelation was to take away the greatest support of natural religion. In discussing the credibility of the temptation, he revived the old suggestion that the serpent had appeared to Eve in the form of an angelic messenger. He met one of Tindal's queries by explaining ways in which Adam and Eve could have fastened together their fig leaves. Butler, in his scholarly demonstration of the analogy between orthodox Christianity and natural religion, helped to end the controversy with the deists. According to Butler, revelation is as credible as nature, for heathen moralists had inferred the Fall from their knowledge of primitive happiness and had perceived the natural conditions which the Redemption presupposes.[21]

The nonconformist Isaac Watts, noted for his hymns, regarded reason and revelation as two God-given lights, both illuminating the doctrines of original sin and Redemption. He logically deduced the state of original righteousness and then demonstrated the Fall by contrasting that state with man's present condition. He quoted from Milton's Michael in showing the human miseries that followed the Fall. He also claimed that man's reason suggests that "the habitation, in which a God of infinite goodness would place such a holy and innocent creature (Adam) *should be a very beautiful and magnificent building, furnished with all manner of necessaries and conveniences of life, and prepared not only for his safety and support, but also for his delight*." [22] In the middle of the eighteenth century, even for such an earnest and orthodox writer as Watts, paradise had become more like a plush resort hotel than the garden of God.

The Waning of the Celestial Cycle

In the century after the publication of *Paradise Lost*, there were far fewer imaginative interpretations of the paradise story than in the century preceding its publication. The writers who did treat the paradise story were no longer convinced that the most important events in world history had occurred in the Edenic paradise, and therefore their works lacked the earlier fusion of knowledge, faith, and imagination. Dryden and the other authors who adapted freely from *Paradise Lost* seemed more concerned with sophisticated entertainment than with sacred truth. Pope and others justified the ways of the universe to man in abstract argument rather than in dramatic epic.

Dryden's drama *State of Innocence* presents a more searching examination of the problem of free will than does *Paradise Lost*, but it does not re-create the beginnings of human history in the biblical paradise. Dryden's paradise is an elegant park rather than a sacred garden or a historic site. Trees surround a fountain, and "at the far end the prospect terminates in walks" (II. 2). Another scene presents the four rivers meeting in the middle of the garden, with the tree of life and the tree of knowledge on either side of a stream (IV. 1); yet most earlier commentators would not have felt that this arrangement was justified by the Scriptural and geographical evidence. Flowers fly from their stalks to strew the nuptial bower, while fishes leap above the streams to view the pomp of the marriage ceremony (III. 1).[23] The experience of paradise itself is not a constant part of the lives of Dryden's couple as it is of Milton's. Nor is his paradise the scene of the beginnings of law, knowledge, work, marriage, the family, religion, and society. Dryden's Adam displays a Cartesian rationalism rather than a divine illumination. He discusses free will, determinism, and original sin much more aptly than Milton's first man, but he does not know God aright. In Dryden's paradise there are no evening prayers or morning hymns of praise; there are no protevangelium and no covenant of grace. Dryden's Adam and Eve seem created in the image of Charles II's courtiers rather than in the image of God. They appear as novices at court rather than as the founders of the human race. They pass from comparative inexperience to experience very rapidly, but they never enjoy a state of innocence.

John Hopkins, characterizing his imitation of *Paradise Lost*, complete with "the primitive loves," as a Hercules in Petticoats, retained many of the incidents and much of the language of Milton's epic, but went much further than Dryden in converting the first parents into a pair of jaded lovers. Eve relates to Adam some of her first recollections:

> Now at the Bow'r arrived, Fond arts you us'd,
> And would enjoy, but bashfully I refus'd.
> Sweetly you pleaded, urg'd by am'rous Fires,
> And show'd your own, and Heightened my desires.
> I still deny'd, much Pleas'd to hear you Sue,
> Saw all your Longings, all your wishes knew.

The passage concludes with a rather displaced Miltonic echo:

> With gratefull Force which you did well Employ,
> You both took from me, and you gave me Joy.
> But a short while the transient Blessings stay,
> While in each others arms imparadis'd we lay.[24]

Madame Dubocage, a poetess of eighteenth-century Rouen, wrote an imitation of *Paradise Lost* in hexameter couplets, with alternating masculine and feminine rhymes. An illustration of Adam languishing on Eve's bosom preceded the text. The French poetess admitted that she had made changes, "guided by the desire to please my nation, in conformity to its taste."[25] A gleam of Urreta's description of Mount Amara shows faintly in her adaptation from Milton:

A l'orient d'Eden present à la vuë
Un roc, dont le sommet se couche dans la nuë;

In her "Jardins enchantés" the animals live in peace:

Aux approches du loup l'Agneau parôit sans crainte,
Le Tigre est sans fureur, et le Renard sans feinte.

Milton's "Hail, Wedded Love" becomes a hymn to "Tendre Himen." Adam and Eve are the happiest of lovers:

Le sôurire enchanteur, les entretiens charmans,
Tout ce qu'Auteur inspire à de jeunes Amans. . . .[26]

Other poets turned from a dramatic presentation to abstract argument. For example, there is no description of paradise and no reference to Adam and Eve in Sir Richard Blackmore's *Creation*. The historical paradise has faded away in this poem designed "to demonstrate the Existence of God from the Marks of Wisdom, Design, Contrivance, and the Choice of Ends and Means, which appear in the Universe." While Milton had shown the first man created in the image of God, Blackmore stated that man had been created by "an intelligent, Arbitrary Cause." Blackmore dwelt upon the woes of mankind, but without mentioning Adam's sin.[27]

John Byrom was a very facile, very minor, and very bad poet, but no eighteenth-century English poet dealt more perseveringly with Miltonic themes than he did. He possessed several copies of Milton, devoted himself to the study of *Paradise Lost*, and in a clever poetic dialogue defended Milton against William Lauder's charges of plagiarism. Never epic, dramatic, or even lyrical, Byrom's work was low-keyed and expository, reflecting the theological discussions of Bishop Sherlock, Middleton, William Law, and others. In his "Epistle to a Gentleman of the Temple," occasioned by two opposing treatises on the Fall, Byrom took from his friend Law the allegorical interpretation of Genesis that Law in turn had borrowed from Böhme:

> But, once convinced that *Adam* by his Crime
> Fell from *eternal Life* to that of *Time*:
> Stood on the Brink of *Death eternal* too,
> Unless created unto Life *anew*. . . .

In "On the Origin of Evil" he was at least sometimes succinct:

> So, by Abuse of Thought and Skill
> The greatest Good, to wit, *Free-will*,
> Becomes the *Origin* of Ill.

However, he felt that even in paradise evil was part of a harmonious plan. Byrom's "On the Fall of Man," beginning "Of mans disobedience while in Eden," is in some sense a reply to Milton. He developed the figurative interpretation that Adam through his transgression had exchanged the life, light, and spirit of God for the things of this world. Death was not the "loss of Being, but of Bliss." When "his Life of Paradise was fled . . . surely he was 'dead.' "[28]

Pope's *Essay on Man* was the most comprehensive religious or philosophical work of literature to appear after *Paradise Lost*. Both Milton and Pope expounded profound world views shared by numerous contemporaries in their efforts to express eminent living truths concerning man in relation to God, Nature, and the Great Chain of Being. Milton found these truths in the Scriptural history of the Fall and the Redemption, and expressed them through the dramatic action of epic, fusing history and imagination. Pope discovered essential truth not in Christian history, but in the conceptualized abstractions of a universal system that could best be explained through the pleasing rational discourse of the poetic essay. Yet, even though truth for Milton and Pope lay in different sources, and even though they lived at different times —

Milton writing after the publication of the Renaissance commentaries, and Pope after the appearance of the discussions of
natural religion by Tindal, Bolingbroke, and others — they still
voiced comparable aims. Milton attempted "to justify the ways of
God to man" and Pope determined to "vindicate the ways of God
to Man" (I, 16).[29] Both contrasted human pride and presumption
with the power and wisdom of God, and both represented God as
bringing good out of evil. But, where Milton saw providential history, Pope saw providential harmony. Milton's historical paradise
became Pope's metaphorical "Garden, tempting with forbidden
fruit" (I, 8). While Milton was interested in God's justice and
mercy, Pope was interested in God as an efficient planner and skillful architect. Milton found "a world of woe" resulting from the
Fall; Pope, although assuming man's degeneration from a pristine
state of nature, nevertheless attributed most of man's seeming im-
perfections to his position in a harmonious and orderly universe.
Milton and most of the earlier commentators and poets regarded
Adam and Eve as enjoying very superior faculties in a state of original righteousness. Pope thought such faculties, particularly the
kind of sensory perception described by Glanvill, as inappropriate
for man:

> Why has not Man a microscopic eye?
> For this plain reason, Man is not a Fly.
> (I, 193–94)

Before the Fall, Milton's Adam and Eve could have ascended on
the chain of being, but Pope felt that if man were "to press" on
superior powers, the entire chain might be broken (I, 241–47).
In *Paradise Lost*, passions lead to the Fall and are a consequence
of the Fall. Pope saw harmony in the "Two Principles of human
nature" as the passions, modes of self-love, inspire and impel while
the reason restrains and guides (I, 166–72; II, 54–92). Pope's God
moves in his own mysterious way in bringing good out of evil:

> Th' Eternal Art enducing good from ill,
> Grafts on this Passion our best principle.
> (II, 175, 76)

In tracing the origin of man and of human institutions, Pope never mentioned Adam and Eve and the Edenic paradise, but described a society comparable to the golden age. This is the closest that Pope comes to the conception of an external paradise:

> Nor think, in NATURES STATE they blindly trod;
> The state of Nature was the reign of God:
> Self-love and Social at her birth began,
> Union the bond of all things, and of Man.
> Pride then was not; nor Arts, that Pride to aid;
> Man walked with beast, joint tenant of the shade;
> The same his table, and the same his bed;
> No murder cloath'd him, and no murder fed.
> In the same temple, the resounding wood,
> All vocal beings hymned their equal God:
> The shrine with gore unstained, with gold undrest,
> Unbribed, unbloody, stood the blameless priest:
> Heaven's attribute was Universal Care,
> And Man's prerogative to rule, but spare.
> (III, 147–60)

Man's guide in this state was instinct and the creatures. From love sprang both benevolent patriarchy and monotheistic natural religion. Man found his greatest happiness in the love of God. Pope describes no temptation and no Fall, but he does depict a gradual degeneration that might be compared to the Fall and its consequences in *Paradise Lost*. Fear bred war, tyranny, polytheism, and superstition. Although most of the earlier commentators felt that sacrifice, a type of the Redemption, had been instituted in paradise when God clothed Adam and Eve with the skins of beasts, Pope followed Tindal and the Enlightenment in a shuddering condemnation:

> Altars grew marble then, and reeked with gore:
> Then first the Flamen tasted living food;
> Next his grim idol smeared with human blood.
> (III, 264–66)

For Milton, paradise could be regained only through Christ, and this celestial paradise could be enjoyed only at the end of time.

Pope, however, stressed man's role in regaining an ideal society. The "studious head or gen'rous mind," "Poet or Patriot," restored the light of Nature, and "If not God's image, yet his shadow drew" (III, 283–88).

But Pope, like Milton, felt that the inner paradise was the happier. Milton envisioned a spiritual happiness which could be enjoyed only by the regenerate Christian. Pope's nonsectarian paradise of moral virtue offered equal happiness to all who know

> where Faith, Law, Morals, all began,
> All end, in LOVE of GOD, and LOVE of MAN (IV, 339–40).

Milton's Adam entered the inner paradise when he acknowledged Christ. But Pope's inner paradise is open to any who is

> Slave to no sect, who takes no private road,
> But looks through Nature up to Nature's God (IV, 331–32).

In *Paradise Lost*, the grace that God planted in man brought forth faith. In the *Essay on Man*,

> Nature plants in Man alone
> Hope of known bliss, and Faith in bliss unknown.
> (IV, 345–46)

For both Milton and Pope, even if men had lost an earthly paradise, the inner paradise promised true happiness that could lead to the eternal bliss of a celestial paradise.

NOTES

NOTES

Introduction

1. *The Collected Works of C. G. Jung*, ed. Sir Herbert Read et al., trans. R. F. D. Hull (20 vols., New York, 1959), IX, pt. 1, 3–5, 81; Jolande Jacobi, *Complex Archetype Symbol in the Psychology of C. G. Jung*, trans. Ralph Mannheim (New York, 1959), pp. 37–39, 49–66. Bodkin, *Archetypal Patterns in Poetry* (London, 1948), pp. 137, 96–99. Eliade, *Myths, Dreams, and Mysteries: The Encounter between Contemporary Faiths and Archaic Realities*, trans. Philip Mairet (New York, 1960), pp. 57–76, and *The Myth of the Eternal Return*, trans. Willard R. Trask (New York, 1954), pp. 1–18. Brown, *Life against Death* (London, 1959), pp. 274–77, 98. Armstrong, *The Paradise Myth* (London, 1969), p. 103. In this "alternative" paradise tradition, Armstrong includes Shakespeare's *Tempest* and *The Winter's Tale*, Milton's *Paradise Lost*, and Coleridge's "Kubla Khan."

Eastward in Eden

1. *The Epic of Gilgamesh*, English version by N. K. Sandars (Baltimore, 1960), esp. pp. 95–102. See also Stephen Langdon, ed., *Sumerian Epic of Paradise, the Flood, and the Fall of Man* (Philadelphia, 1915), esp. pp. 5–10, 70–71. Morris Jastrow, Jr., *The Religion of Babylonia and Assyria* (Boston, 1898), pp. 549–51.

2. Albright, "The Goddess of Life and Wisdom," *American Journal of Semitic Languages and Literatures*, XXXVI (1920), 281. Graves and Raphael Patai, *Hebrew Myths: The Book of Genesis* (New York, 1964), pp. 79–80. Frazer, *Folk-Lore in the Old Testament* (New York, 1923), pp. 18–26, 6.

3. Humbert, *Études sur le récit du paradis et de la chute dans la Genèse* (Neuchatel, 1940), esp. pp. 48–66. *The Interpreter's Bible* (12 vols., New York, 1951–57), I, 492–500, 195. See also G. A. Barton, "*Abode of the Blest* (Semitic)," *Encyclopedia of Religion and Ethics*, ed. James Hastings (New York, 1951), I, 704–6.

4. See *The Interpreter's Bible*, I, 501–4.

MILTON'S EARTHLY PARADISE

5. Graves and Patai, *Hebrew Myths*, pp. 70–71. William F. Warren, a president of Boston University, lectured to his students on paradise and developed the thesis "that the cradle of the human race, the Eden of primitive tradition, was situated at the North Pole, in a country submerged at the Deluge." He supported this on grounds of general geogony, mathematical and astronomical geography, physiological geology, prehistoric climatology, paleontological botany, zoology, anthropology, and comparative mythology. *Paradise Found* (Boston, 1898).

6. Driver, *The Book of Genesis* (London, 1948), p. 56. Skinner, *A Critical and Exegetical Commentary on Genesis* (rev. ed., New York, 1925), pp. 94–95.

7. Barton, "Abode of the Blest (Semitic)," pp. 704–5; Skinner, *Critical and Exegetical Commentary on Genesis*, p. 58.

8. B. S. Childs, "Garden of Eden," *The Interpreter's Dictionary of the Bible* (New York, 1962), II, 24–25; *International Standard Bible Encyclopaedia*, ed. James Orr (Grand Rapids, Mich., 1960), II, 2246.

9. Mary W. Montgomery, "Garden of Eden," *Jewish Encyclopedia* (New York, 1916), V, 36–38; T. K. Cheyne, "Paradise," *Encyclopaedia Britannica* (11th ed., New York, 1911), XV, 751–52. Barton, "Paradise," *Jewish Encyclopedia*, IX, 515–17.

10. All references to Milton are to *The Works of John Milton*, ed. Frank Allen Patterson et al. (18 vols., New York, 1931–38). Scriptural quotations are from the King James Version of the Bible.

11. Barton, "Paradise," p. 518; Jastrow, "Adam and Eve in Babylonian Literature," *Journal of Semitic Languages and Literatures*, XV (1899), 202–8.

12. James H. Sims discusses Milton's descriptions of paradise and of Adam and Eve in relation to Scripture in *The Bible in Milton's Epics* (Gainesville, Fla., 1962), pp. 20–27.

"Such Pleasing Licence"

1. Giamatti, *The Earthly Paradise and the Renaissance Epic* (Princeton, N.J., 1966), pp. 15–82. Curtius, *European Literature and the Latin Middle Ages*, trans. Willard R. Trask (New York, 1953), pp. 185–200.

2. I am indebted to the discussions of the golden age and related conceptions in *A Documentary History of Primitivism and Related Ideas*, ed. Arthur O. Lovejoy and George Boas (Baltimore, 1935); Giamatti, *Earthly Paradise*, pp. 15–23, and Harry Levin, *The Myth of the Golden Age in the Renaissance* (Bloomington, Ind., 1969), pp. 3–31.

3. *Diodorus of Sicily*, trans. C. H. Oldfather (12 vols., London, 1960), I, 167–72. Horace, *The Odes and Epodes*, trans. C. E. Bennett (Cambridge, Mass., 1930), pp. 903–7. F. W. Hall, "Abode of the Blest (Greek and Roman)," *Encyclopedia of Religion and Ethics*, II, 696–98; De Witt T. Starnes, "The Hesperian Gardens in Milton," *Studies in English* (University of Texas), XXXI (1952), 42–51.

4. Giamatti, *Earthly Paradise*, pp. 26–27.

5. Alexander Sherman, *Homeric Essays* (Oxford, 1935), p. 259.

6. Most of these landscapes and gardens are discussed in Curtius, *European Literature*, pp. 180–95, and Giamatti, *Earthly Paradise*, pp. 33–50.

7. "Justin's Hortatory Address to the Greeks," trans. M. Dods, in *The Ante-Nicene Fathers*, ed. Alexander Roberts and James Donaldson (9 vols., Grand Rapids, Mich., 1950), I, 273–89. Levin, *Myth of the Golden Age*, pp. 32–33;

see also Douglas Bush, *Pagan Myth and Christian Tradition in English Poetry* (Philadelphia, 1968), pp. 1–31.

8. Levin, *Myth of the Golden Age*, pp. xvi–xvii, 32–34; Curtius, *European Literature*, pp. 215–19.

9. Giamatti discusses golden age sites, Christian paradises, and enchanted gardens in relation to the enchanted gardens of Renaissance epics, including *Paradise Lost*.

10. Davis P. Harding, *Milton and the Renaissance Ovid* (Urbana, Ill., 1946), pp. 20–23. Sandys, *Ovids Metamorphosis Englished, Mythologiz'd, and Represented in Figures* (London, 1632), p. 3; see also Henry Reynolds, *Mythomystes*, in *Critical Essays of the Seventeenth Century*, ed. J. E. Spingarn (3 vols., Oxford, 1900), I, 175–76.

11. Ralegh, *History of the World* (London, 1614), p. 86; see also Mathias Prideaux, *An Easy and Compendius Introduction for Reading All Sorts of Histories* (London, 1686), p. 6. This was first published in 1648. Carpenter, *Geography Delineated Forth* (London, 1625), p. 209.

12. See the discussion of the golden age myth in the Renaissance in Hiram Haydn, *The Counter Renaissance* (New York, 1950), pp. 492–501.

13. Guarini, *Il Pastor Fido*, trans. Richard Fanshawe (London, 1648), pp. 163–77. Spenser, *The Faerie Queene*, IV, viii, 30; *Poems of William Browne*, ed. Gordon Goodwin (London, 1843), I, 272. *The Works of Michael Drayton*, ed. J. William Hebel et al. (5 vols., Oxford, 1931–41), II, 363–64. *The Romance of the Rose*, trans. F. S. Ellis (3 vols., London, 1940), I, 21–22.

14. Bodin, *Method for the Easy Comprehension of History*, trans. Beatrice Reynolds (New York, 1945), pp. 296–98; Leonard F. Dean, "Bodin's 'Methodus' in England before 1625," *Studies in Philology*, XXXIX (1942), 160–66. *Letter Book of Gabriel Harvey*, ed. Edward John Scott (London, 1884), p. 86.

15. Milton, *The Doctrine and Discipline of Divorce*, III², 446.

16. See Starnes, "Hesperian Gardens in Milton," pp. 42–51, and Starnes and Ernest W. Talbert, *Classical Myth and Legend in Renaissance Dictionaries* (Chapel Hill, N.C., 1955), pp. 308–16.

17. The description of the fair field of Enna most familiar to the Renaissance is in Ovid's *Metamorphoses* (V, 385–91). A field of flowers was also described in the account of the rape of Proserpina in the Homeric *Hymn to Demeter*. Poets described this landscape repeatedly; see Charles G. Osgood, *The Classical Mythology of Milton's English Poems* (New York, 1900), pp. 19–20, and Giamatti, *Earthly Paradise*, pp. 36–37. George Wesley Whiting reproduces the description and illustration of the grove of Daphne from Ortelius, *Theatrum Orbis Terrarum*, in *Milton's Literary Milieu* (Chapel Hill, N.C., 1939), pp. 110ff. *Diodorus of Sicily*, II, 310–13.

The Early Christian Era

1. See Maury Thibaut de Maisières, *Les Poèmes Inspirés du Début de la Genèse à l'Époque de la Renaissance* (Louvain, 1931), pp. 17–29, and Stanislas Gamber, *Le Livre de la "Genèse" dans la Poésie Latine au Vᵐᵉ Siècle* (Paris, 1899), pp. 17–19.

2. See J. H. Hanford, "The Chronology of Milton's Private Studies," *PMLA*, XXXVI (1921), 251–314, and John Paul Pritchard, "The Fathers of the Church in the Works of John Milton," *Classical Journal*, XXXIII (1937), 79–87.

3. J. M. Evans, *"Paradise Lost" and the Genesis Tradition* (Oxford, 1968),

pp. 9–25, 59–99; Floyd V. Filson, *A New Testament History* (Philadelphia, 1964), pp. 327–28; Francis C. Haber, *The Age of the World: Moses to Darwin* (Baltimore, 1959), pp. 15–17.

4. Milton, *The First Defence*, VII, 79.

5. *Allegorical Interpretation of Genesis*, bk. i, ch. 14, and bk. ii, ch. 7, and *On the Creation*, ch. 56, in *Philo*, trans. F. H. Colson and G. H. Whitaker (10 vols. London, 1924–53), I, 175, 237, 125.

6. *On the Creation*, chs. 47–53, in *Philo*, I, 107–21.

7. *Noah's Work as a Planter*, bk. i, ch. 9, in *Philo*, III, 231. *On the Creation*, chs. 54, 59, and *Allegorical Interpretation*, bk. ii, ch. 8, in *Philo*, I, 121–23, 131, 241.

8. See Harry Robbins, *If This Be Heresy* (Urbana, Ill., 1963), pp. 61–63. Milton, *Of Reformation*, III¹, 34, 21. *Origen on First Principles*, trans. G. W. Butterworth (London, 1936), iv. 3. 288.

9. *Origen on First Principles*, ii. 11. 152.

10. Origen, *Contra Celsum*, trans. Henry Chadwick (Cambridge, 1953), iv. 39. 214–16. See R. P. C. Hanson, *Allegory and Event* (London, 1959), pp. 269–71.

11. Hanford, "Chronology of Milton's Private Studies," p. 279.

12. Thibaut de Maisières, *Les Poèmes Inspirés*, pp. 19, 30–40, 139.

13. St. Basil, *Hexameron*, trans. Blomfield Jackson, in *A Select Library of Nicene and Post-Nicene Fathers*, second series, ed. Henry Wace and Philip Shaff (14 vols., New York, 1890–1900), homilies v and vi, VIII, 78–82.

14. Pseudo-Basil, *De Paradiso*, in *Patrologiae Graecae*, ed. J. P. Migne (161 vols., Paris, 1857–81), XXX, cols. 63–70. *Patrologiae Graecae* will hereafter be cited as *MPG*.

15. St. Basil, *Hexameron*, homily ix, VIII, 102; St. Basil, *The Long Rules*, ii, iv, in *Ascetical Works*, trans. Sister M. Monica Wagner, in *Fathers of the Church* (New York, 1959), IX, 223–30, 41. George Boas, *Essays on Primitivism and Related Ideas in the Middle Ages* (Baltimore, 1948), pp. 28–33; Norman Powell Williams, *The Ideas of the Fall and of Original Sin* (London, 1927), pp. 267–71; Pseudo-Basil, *De Paradiso*, in *MPG*, XXX, cols. 44–45.

16. St. John, *Exposition of the Orthodox Faith*, trans. S. D. F. Salmond, in *Nicene and Post-Nicene Fathers*, second series, bk. ii, IX, 20–30.

17. Bar Cephas, *Commentarius de Paradiso*, in *MPG*, CXI, esp. cols. 491–99; see Grant McColley, "Milton and Moses Bar-Cephas," *Studies in Philology*, XXXVIII (1941), 246–51.

18. Bar Cephas, *Commentarius de Paradiso*, *MPG*, CXI, esp. cols. 583–602.

19. St. Ambrose, *In Psalmum David CXVIII Expositio*, and *De Excessu Fratris Sui Satyri Libri Duo*, in *Patrologiae Latinae*, ed. Migne (221 vols., Paris, 1844–80), XV, col. 1372; XVI, col. 1305. *Patrologia Latinae* will hereafter be cited as *MPL*. St. Ambrose, *Paradise*, chs. 1–4, 11, in *Hexameron, Paradise, and Cain and Abel*, trans. John Savage, in *Fathers of the Church* (New York, 1961), XLII, 287–303, 328–30; F. Homes Dudden, *The Life and Times of St. Ambrose* (Oxford, 1935), II, 613–15; Boas, *Essays on Primitivism*, p. 44; Williams, *Ideas of the Fall and of Original Sin*, pp. 300–1.

20. Milton, *The Doctrine and Discipline of Divorce*, III², 448.

21. Evans, *"Paradise Lost" and the Genesis Tradition*, pp. 93–95.

22. St. Augustine, *De Genesi contra Manichaeos*, bk. ii, ch. 9, in *MPL*, XXXIV, cols. 202–3; *The City of God*, trans. and ed. Marcus Dods (New York, 1948), bk. xiii, ch. 21, vol. I, 545–46.

23. St. Augustine, *De Genesi ad Litteram*, bk. viii, in *MPL*, XXXIV, cols.

371–72, 378; *On the Grace of God and on Original Sin*, trans. Peter Holmes, in *A Select Library of the Nicene and Post-Nicene Fathers of the Christian Church*, first series, ed. Philip Schaff (18 vols., Grand Rapids, Mich., 1956), V, 246; *City of God*, bk. xiii, ch. 18, vol. I, 540.

24. Gilson, *The Christian Philosophy of St. Augustine*, trans. L. E. M. Lynch (New York, 1960), pp. 148–50, 314–16; Harnack, *Outlines of the History of Dogma*, trans. Edwin Knox Mitchell (Boston, 1957), p. 376; St. Augustine, *City of God*, bk. xiii, ch. 20, vol. I, 544–45. See also *MPL*, XXXII, cols. 901–2.

25. St. Augustine, *City of God*, bk. xiv, ch. 10, vol. II, 20–21.

26. *Ibid.*, bk. xiv, chs. 17–26, vol. II, 33–45.

27. St. Augustine, *De Genesi ad Litteram*, bk. ix, ch. 3, in *MPL*, XXXIV, col. 395; *City of God*, bk. xiv, ch. 1, vol. II, 1.

28. St. Augustine, Epistle 157, in *MPL*, XXXIII, col. 681; Gilson, *The Christian Philosophy of St. Augustine*, pp. 130–31; Boas, *Essays on Primitivism*, pp. 103–4.

29. St. Augustine, *Operis Imperfecti contra Julianum*, bk. v, ch. 1, in *MPL*, XLV, cols. 1432–33.

30. *Ibid.*, bk. i, chs. 78, 91; bk. iii, ch. 154; bk. v, ch. 61, in *MPL*, XLV, cols. 1102, 1108, 1310–11, 1496. See Williams, *Ideas of the Fall and of Original Sin*, esp. pp. 340–41, 361–62.

31. St. Augustine, *De Genesi ad Litteram*, bk. viii, chs. 8, 9, in *MPL*, XXXIV, col. 379.

32. St. Augustine, *City of God*, bk. xii, ch. 27; bk. xiii, chs. 1, 19; bk. xiv, ch. 10 (vol. I, 519–21, 544; vol. II, 21–22); St. Augustine, *De Genesi ad Litteram*, bk. ix, ch. 6, in *MPL*, XXXIV, cols. 396–97.

33. Williams, *Ideas of the Fall and of Original Sin*, pp. 1–70. St. Augustine, *City of God*, bk. xii, ch. 27, and bk. xiii, ch. 14, vol. I, 520, 535–36.

34. St. Augustine, *City of God*, bk. xii, ch. 10, vol. I, 494–95.

35. Thibaut de Maisières, *Les Poèmes Inspirés*, pp. 17–29.

36. *Des Heiligen Ephraem des Syrers Hymnen de Paradiso und Contra Julianum*, ed. Edmund Beck (Louvain, 1957), pp. 5–60. See J. Danielou, "Terre et Paradis chez les Pères de l'Église," *Eranos Jahrbuch*, XXII (1954), 433–72.

37. Lactantius, *De Ave Phoenice*, ll. 1–28, in *Anthologia Latina*, pt. I, ed. A. Riese (Leipzig, 1869), pp. 188–89. Giamatti, *Earthly Paradise*, pp. 70–71.

38. For a discussion of these and other early Christian poets, see F. J. E. Raby, *A History of Christian-Latin Poetry from the Beginnings to the Close of the Middle Ages* (2nd ed., Oxford, 1953), pp. 15–19, 44–71, 75–85, 95–100; Giamatti, *Earthly Paradise*, pp. 67–83; Evans, *"Paradise Lost" and the Genesis Tradition*, pp. 107–42; and Watson Kirkconnell, *The Celestial Cycle* (Toronto, 1952), p. xiii, and "Descriptive Catalogue of Analogues." Giamatti also discusses Sollius Sidonius Apollinaris, Caelius Sedulius, Magnus Felix Ennodius, and Arator. Evans also discusses Valeria Faltonia Proba, Hilary of Arles, and Cyprianus Gallus. Kirkconnell includes English translations of parts of Avitus.

39. Curtius, *European Literature*, p. 200, n. 31, has pointed out the influence of Virgil's Elysium on Prudentius and Dracontius, and Giamatti, *Earthly Paradise*, pp. 72–76, has noted this influence on Prudentius and Victor. Prudentius, "Hymnus ante Cibum," in *Prudentius*, trans. H. J. Thomson (2 vols., London, 1949–53), I, 25–27, 251.

40. Victor, *Commentariorum in Genesin Libri Tres*, ed. C. Schenkl, bk. i, ll. 305–95, in *Corpus Scriptorum Ecclesiasticorum Latinorum* (Vienna, 1866

et seq.), XVI, pt. 1, 375–78. *Corpus Scriptorum Ecclesiasticorum Latinorum* will hereafter be cited as *CSEL*.

41. Victor, *Alethia*, ed. Schenkl, bk. i, ll. 224–304, in *CSEL*, XVI, pt. 1, 372–75.

42. See Evans, *"Paradise Lost" and the Genesis Tradition*, pp. 121–26. In reference to Victor's theology, Evans cites P. F. Hovingh, *Claudius Marius Victorius Alethia* (Groningen, 1955), introduction.

43. Kirkconnell, *Celestial Cycle*, pp. 505–6.

44. Avitus, *Poematum de Mosaicae Historiae Gestis Libri Quinque*, bk. i, ll. 210–57, in *MPL*, LIX, cols. 327–28; English translation in Kirkconnell, *Celestial Cycle*, pp. 6–7.

45. Avitus, *Poematum de Mosaicae Historiae Gestis*, bk. ii, ll. 35–276; Kirkconnell, *Celestial Cycle*, pp. 7–15.

46. Dracontius, *Carmen de Laudibus Dei*, bk. i, ll. 178–454, in *MPL*, LX, cols. 679–90; Isabel Clare Devine, "A Study of the *Laudes Dei* of Blossius Aemilius Dracontius" (Ph.D. dissertation, Columbia University, New York, 1945), pp. 26–55.

The Middle Ages

1. St. Isidore, *Etymologiae*, bk. xiv, ch. 3, *Differentiae*, and *Quaestiones in Vetus Testamentum*, in *MPL*, LXXXII, col. 496; LXXXIII, cols. 75, 216–17.

2. Bede, *Hexaemeron* and *In Pentateuchum Commentarii*, in *MPL*, XCI, cols. 43–44, 206–8.

3. Erigena, *De Divisione Naturae*, bk. iv, ch. 12, in *MPL*, CXXII, col. 799; see Gilson, *History of Christian Philosophy in the Middle Ages* (New York, 1955), pp. 133–34.

4. Gilson, *History of Christian Philosophy*, p. 164; Gilson, *The Mystical Theology of Saint Bernard* (London, 1940), pp. 86–118.

5. *Pentateuch with Targum Onkelos, Haphtaroth, and Prayers for Sabbath and Rashi's Commentary*, trans. M. Rosenbaum and A. M. Silberman (London, 1929), I, 10–14.

6. John K. Ryan, *The Reputation of St. Thomas Aquinas among English Protestant Thinkers of the Seventeenth Century* (Washington, D.C., 1948), *passim*.

7. *The "Summa Theologica" of St. Thomas Aquinas*, pt. I, trans. Fathers of the English Dominican Province (2nd and rev. ed., London, 1922), q. xcii, art. iii, and q. cii, art. i; IV, 278, 366.

8. *Ibid.*, q. cii, art. i, IV, 364–67.

9. *Ibid.*, q. xcv, art. i–iv, IV, 318–23; q. xciv, art. i, IV, 307.

10. *Ibid.*, q. xciv, art. iii, IV, 310–13.

11. *Ibid.*, q. xciv, art. iv, IV, 313–14.

12. *Ibid.*, q. xcvii, art. iii, IV, 339–40; q. cii, art. iii, IV, 370–73; q. xcviii, art. i–ii, IV, 345–49.

13. *Ibid.*, q. c, art. i–q. ci, art. ii, IV, 355–62.

14. *Ibid.*, q. xcii, art. ii; q. cvi, art. iii; q. xcviii, art. i; IV, 276, 330–31, 346.

15. Milton, *The Christian Doctrine*, XV, 205.

16. Howard Patch, *The Other World according to Descriptions in Medieval Literature* (Cambridge, Mass., 1950), p. 155. St. Thomas Aquinas, *Summa Theologica*, pt. I, q. cii, art. ii, IV, 369; Graves and Patai, *Hebrew Myths*, pp. 61–62, 70–71; Louis Ginzberg, *Legends of the Jews*, trans. Henrietta

Szold (7 vols., Philadelphia, 1919–38), I, 54–71; H. H. McArthur, "Paradise," *The Interpreter's Dictionary of the Bible*, III, 655–56.

17. Quoted from Boas, *Essays on Primitivism*, pp. 161–64; Lynn Thorndike, *A History of Magic and Experimental Science* (New York, 1923), II, 239–42. Mary Lascelles, "Alexander and the Earthly Paradise in Medieval English Writings," *Medium Aevum*, V (1936), 32–39, 89–91.

18. Jean Sire de Joinville, *The History of Saint Louis*, trans. Joan Evans (London, 1938), pp. 55–56. *The Travels of Sir John Mandeville*, ed. A. W. Pollard (London, 1915), pp. 199–200.

19. Patch, *Other World*, p. 159. Eduardo Coli, *Il Paradiso Terrestre Dantesco* (Florence, 1897), pp. 135–40.

20. *Cursor Mundi*, ed. Richard Morris, Early English Text Society, original series, vols. LVII, XCIX, CI (London, 1874, 1893), I, 42–51; Caxton, *Mirrour of the World*, ed. Oliver H. Prior, Early English Text Society, extra series (London, 1913), CX, 68, 153. Higden, *Polychronicon*, trans. John of Trevisa et al., ed. Churchill Babington (London, 1865), I, 67–75.

21. Coli, *Il Paradiso*, pp. 92–121; William H. Babcock, *Legendary Islands in the Atlantic* (New York), p. 35; Sabine Baring-Gold, *Curious Myths of the Middle Ages*, first series (London, 1866), pp. 228–36, and *Curious Myths of the Middle Ages*, second series (London, 1868), pp. 259–95.

22. Arturo Graf, *Miti, Leggende e Superstizioni del Medio Evo* (2 vols., Torino, 1892), I, 44, 16–18, 25–31.

23. References to the treatment of the earthly paradise in medieval art may be found in Patch, *Other World*, pp. 154–55. See also Lars Ivor Ringbom, *Paradisus Terrestris, Myt, Bild och Verklighet*, in *Acta Societatis Scientarum Fennicae*, n.s. (Helsingfors, 1958), English summary, I, 435–46. Francis M. Rogers, *The Travels of the Infante Dom Pedro of Portugal* (Cambridge, Mass., 1961), p. 73. *The Minor Poems of John Lydgate*, part II, ed. Henry N. MacCracken, Early English Text Society, original series (London, 1934), CXCII, 641–43.

24. Alain de Lille, *Anticlaudianus*, in *Anglo-Latin Satirical Poets and Epigrammatists of the Twelfth Century*, ed. T. Wright (London, 1872), II, 275–78; Giamatti, *Earthly Paradise*, pp. 48–56; F. J. E. Raby, *A History of Secular Latin Poetry in the Middle Ages* (2nd ed., 2 vols., Oxford, 1957), I, 17; Patch, *Other World*, pp. 178–79, 181.

25. Giamatti, *Earthly Paradise*, pp. 56–60; Patch, *Other World*, p. 204. *The Romance of the Rose*, I, 21–23. C. S. Lewis writes of the relation of the Garden of the Rose to the earthly paradise in *The Allegory of Love* (New York, 1958), pp. 119–20. Patch, *Other World*, p. 200. *The Romance of the Rose*, III, 177–92.

26. Neckham, *De Laudibus Divinae Sapientiae*, bk. vi, ll. 35–54, in *De Naturis Rerum Libri duo . . .* , ed. Wright (London, 1863), XXXIV, 441.

27. Frezzi's description is quoted in Graf, *Miti*, appendix I, pp. 197–217. See also Patch, *Other World*, p. 187.

28. Included in Graf, *Miti*, appendix I, are the paradise descriptions of Gautier de Metz and Rudolf von Ems, and also those from two Dutch poems, the *Spieghel Historiael* by Jacob van Maerlant and *Der leken Spieghel* by Jan Boendale. Giamatti, *Earthly Paradise*, pp. 80–83.

29. Irene Samuel, *Dante and Milton* (Ithaca, N.Y., 1966), pp. 184–97, has discussed the relation of Milton's Eden to Dante's *Commedia*. Milton knew and admired the *Commedia*, and "from Dante's Earthly Paradise Milton drew far more than phrases and descriptive details." However, in its paradigmatic

function, Milton's paradise has even more in common with Dante's *Paradiso*. "What Milton's Earthly Paradise chiefly shares with Dante's," she writes, "is the concept of a place from which man might rise naturally to Heaven." There are also differences in approach. In Dante, light or vision leads to love and then to happiness; in Milton, obedience and love are always the best guide to knowledge.

30. Dante, *Purgatorio*, xxviii, 1–21, in *The Divine Comedy of Dante Alighieri*, trans. Charles Eliot Norton (rev. ed., Boston, 1902), II, 213–14. Subsequent references are to this edition.

31. *Ibid.*, xxviii–xxxiii, II, 214–59.

32. *Ibid.*, xxviii, 91–93, II, 216–17; xxix, 22–27, II, 221. Dante, *Monarchy and Three Political Letters*, trans. Donald Nicholl (New York, 1954), bk. iii, ch. 16, p. 92.

33. Dante, *Purg.*, xxvii, 137–42, II, 212. See Dorothy L. Sayers, *Further Papers on Dante* (New York, 1957), pp. 46–47, 50.

34. Milton, *P. L.*, IV, 264–68; Dante, *Purg.*, xxviii, 1–33, II, 214. Milton *P. L.*, V, 294–95, IV, 249–51; *Purg.*, xxviii, 139–41, 64–66; xxix, 1–6; ii, 219–20, 215. *P. L.*, IV, 268–72; *Purg.*, xxviii, 49–51, II, 215.

35. Sayers, *Further Papers on Dante*, p. 167.

The Historical Paradise
of the Renaissance

1. For discussions of biblical interpretations in the Renaissance, see Don Cameran Allen, *The Legend of Noah: Renaissance Rationalism in Art, Science, and Letters* (Urbana, Ill., 1949), pp. 39–79; Roland H. Bainton, "The Bible in the Reformation," in *The Cambridge History of the Bible*, ed. S. L. Greenlaw (Cambridge, 1963), II, 1–37; Frederic W. Farrar, *History of Interpretation* (London, 1886), pp. 307–54.

2. Williams, *The Common Expositor: An Account of the Commentaries on Genesis, 1527–1633* (Chapel Hill, N.C., 1948), pp. 3–19.

3. *Ibid.*, p. 35. Williams's "Check List of Commentaries" identifies commentators and provides bibliographic information.

4. *Ibid.* Two other well-known Protestant commentaries on Genesis were those of Hieronymus Zanchius and Peter Martyr. Milton referred to other works by these authors, but not to these commentaries. William Riley Parker, *Milton, a Biography* (2 vols., Oxford, 1968), I, 181. Milton's references to authors may be found in the *Index* to the *Works* (Columbia edition). Unless otherwise stated, biographical information about Renaissance writers is from the *Schaff-Herzog Encyclopedia of Religious Knowledge*, the *Dictionary of National Biography*, or other standard reference works. Fletcher, *The Intellectual Development of John Milton* (2 vols., Urbana, 1956–61), II, 95–96.

5. Williams, *Common Expositor*, pp. 68, 109; Paul A. Welsby, *Lancelot Andrewes, 1555–1626* (London, 1958), p. 6. See Grant McColley, "The Epic Catalogue of *Paradise Lost*," *ELH*, IV (1937), 180–91, and Kirkconnell, *Celestial Cycle*, pp. 615–16.

6. Fletcher, *Intellectual Development*, II, 592, 640; Parker, *Milton*, 42, 293. Other English works written in the later sixteenth and earlier seventeenth centuries and dealing as a whole or in part with the first chapters of Genesis were: Gervase Babington, *Certaine Plaine, Briefe, and Comfortable Notes, vpon Euery Chapter of Genesis* (London, 1592); Thomas Cooper, *A Briefe*

NOTES

Exposition of Such Chapters of the Olde Testament as Usually Are Redde in the Churche at Common Praier on the Sundayes (London, 1573); Nicholas Gibbens, *Qvestions and Disputations concerning the Holy Scripture* (London, 1601); Thomas Hayne, *The General View of the Holy Scriptures; or the Times, Places, and Persons of Holy Scripture* (London, 1640); George Hughes, *An Analytical Exposition of the Whole First Book of Moses* (London, 1672, published posthumously); Arthur Jackson, *A Help for the Understanding of the Holy Scripture* (London, 1643); Elnathan Parr, *Grounds of Divinitie* (London, 1651; 1st ed., 1620); Mathias Prideaux, *An Easy and Compendious Introduction for Reading All Sorts of Histories* (London, 1686; 1st ed., 1648); John Richardson, *Choice Observations and Explanations upon the Old Testament* (London, 1655); Francis Roberts, *Clavis Bibliorum, the Key of the Bible* (London, 1649); Edward Vaughan, *Ten Introductions: How to Read, and in Reading, How to Understand . . . the Holie Bible* (London, 1594); William Whately, *Prototypes, or the Primarie Precedent Presidents out of the Booke of Genesis* (London, 1640); and Andrew Willet, *Hexapla in Genesin* (Cambridge, 1605).

7. Dean, "Bodin's 'Methodus,'" pp. 160–66; L. I. Bredvold, "Milton and Bodin's *Heptaplomeres*," *Studies in Philology*, XXI (1924), 399–402. George Wesley Whiting in *Milton's Literary Milieu* has found Milton indebted to Ralegh for his conception of the location of paradise and for various other ideas. Fletcher, *Intellectual Development*, II, 335, 568; II, 350, 343; Whiting, *Milton's Literary Milieu*, p. 97. Parker, *Milton*, I, 31, 255.

8. Salkeld, *A Treatise of Paradise* (London, 1617), p. 2. Hare's *The Situation of Paradise Found Out: Being an History of a Late Pilgrimage unto the Holy Land, with a New Apparatus Prefixt, Giving Light into the Whole Design* was published anonymously in London in 1683. Although Hare sometimes addresses his readers in a cajoling tone, the work is fundamentally a serious work of piety and is primarily concerned with the spiritual meanings of paradise. The "Apparatus," the only part of the book dealing with the earthly paradise, reflects a knowledge of the previous century of scholarship and carries four passages of the description of Paradise from *Paradise Lost*.

9. Parker, *Milton*, I, 584; Nicolson, "Milton and Hobbes," *Studies in Philology*, XXXIII (1926), 405–33. David Rice McKee, "Isaac de la Peyrère, a Precursor of the Eighteenth-Century Deists," *PMLA*, LIX (1944), 456–85. Fletcher, *Intellectual Development*, II, 147–49, 151, 159, 176, 182, 198, 210, 341, 345. Parker, *Milton*, I, 449, 537. Sister Mary Irma Corcoran, *Milton's Paradise with Reference to the Hexameral Background* (Washington, D.C., 1945), p. 125. Fletcher, *Intellectual Development*, I, 144.

10. Fletcher, *Intellectual Development*, II, 188. Arthur Hesselberg, "A Comparative Study of the Political Theories of Ludovico Molina, S. J., and John Milton," *Dissertation Abstracts, Catholic University of America* (Washington, D.C., 1952), pp. 1–25. Arthur Barker, *Milton and the Puritan Dilemma* (Toronto, 1942), pp. 108–9. Ernest Sirluck, "Introduction," *Complete Prose Works of John Milton* (New Haven, Conn., 1953–   ), II, 130–31; Merritt Y. Hughes, "Introduction," *Complete Prose Works of John Milton*, III, 121; see also III, 408, n. 7; III, 90, 110; III, 36; III, 104–5, 191, 195; III, 69–70; Parker, *Milton*, I, 410.

11. Fletcher, *Intellectual Development*, II, 563. Grant McColley, "Milton's Dialogue on Astronomy: The Principle Immediate Sources," *PMLA*, LII (1937), 728–62. Margaret L. Bailey, *Milton and Jakob Boehme* (New York,

1922). Marjorie H. Nicolson, "Milton and the *Conjectura Cabbalistica*," *Philological Quarterly*, VI (1927), 1–18, and "The Spirit World of Milton and More," *Studies in Philology*, XXII (1925), 433–52.

12. Kirkconnell's *Celestial Cycle* provides the most complete catalogue of analogues to *Paradise Lost*, as well as texts of the most important works or of the most relevant portions of these and English translations. Much of the following information is from the catalogue of analogues.

13. George Coffin Taylor, *Milton's Use of Du Bartas* (Cambridge, 1934). In the introduction to *The Life of Adam (1640)* (Gainesville, Fla., 1967), Roy C. Flannagan and John Arthos discuss the circumstances which may have led to a meeting between Milton and Loredano. Flannagan and Arthos consider L'Adamo "probably the most comprehensive fictional treatment of the Fall before Milton." They suggest that it may have helped to provide Milton with an impetus to write *Paradise Lost* and they point out a number of parallels, at least one of which could be more than tradition or coincidence. George Edmundson, *Milton and Vondel* (London, 1885), has made the largest claims for the influence of both Vondel's *Lucifer* and his *Adam in Ballingschap* on *Paradise Lost*. Reviewing the evidence for Milton's knowledge of *Lucifer*, Kirkconnell, *Celestial Cycle*, pp. 627–31, concluded that "there are enough close resemblances to make his familiarity with Vondel reasonably assured." However, he thought that any influence of *Adam* on Milton was much less probable.

14. C. M. Walsh, *The Doctrine of Creation* (London, 1910), pp. 91–100. Gilson, *History of Christian Philosophy*, pp. 389–92.

15. See Victor Harris, *All Coherence Gone* (Chicago, 1949), pp. 185–87. See also Don Cameron Allen's discussion of the controversy about the world's eternity in "The Degeneration of Man and Renaissance Pessimism," *Studies in Philology*, XXXV (1938), 202–27. *Luther's Commentary on Genesis*, trans. J. Theodore Mueller (2 vols., Grand Rapids, Mich., 1958), I, 3–4. Daneau, *The Wonderfull Woorkmanship of the World*, trans. Thomas Tymme (London, 1578) pp. 31, 76–77. Swan, *Speculum Mundi* (Cambridge, 1635), pp. 1–2.

16. Bodin, *Method for the Easy Comprehension of History*, pp. 304, 309–13.

17. Stillingfleet, *Origines Sacrae, or a Rational Account of the Grounds of Natural and Revealed Religion* (2 vols., Oxford, 1836), II, 12, 18. Hale, *The Primitive Origination of Mankind, Considered and Examined according to the Light of Nature* (London, 1678), pp. 1–3, 110–18, 129, 180. Wolseley, *The Unreasonablenesse of Atheism* (2nd ed., London, 1669) pp. 10, 38, 49–54. Wilkins, *Of the Principles and Duties of Natural Religion* (8th ed., London, 1722), pp. 56–64. Burnet, *The Sacred Theory of the Earth* (5th ed., London, 1722), pt. I, p. 54.

18. Boemus, *The Fardle of Facions*, trans. William Watreman (London, 1555), reprinted in *The Bookworm's Garner*, vols. III–V (Edinburgh, 1884), I, 14–18, 29–30. Le Roy, *De La Vicissitude ou Variété des Choses en l'Univers* (Paris, 1598), esp. pp. 51–54. *Discourses of Nicolo Machiavelli*, trans. Leslie J. Walker (New Haven, 1950), I, 212. Hobbes, *Leviathan*, pt. I, ch. 13, in *The English Works of Thomas Hobbes, of Malmesbury*, ed. William Molesworth (11 vols., London, 1839–45), III, 110–16.

19. Bodin, *Method for the Easy Comprehension of History*, pp. 334–38.

20. Descartes, *Discourse on Method Etc.*, trans. John Veitch (London, 1946), pp. 34–36, 223–24.

21. Thomas Franklin Mayo, *Epicurus in England (1650–1725)* (College Sta-

tion, Texas, 1934), p. xi and *passim*. Carpenter, *Geography Delineated Forth*, pp. 206–8. Stillingfleet *Origines Sacrae*, II, 34–39, 55–58. Hale, *The Primitive Origination of Mankind*, pp. 246, 253. Wolseley, *The Unreasonablenesse of Atheism*, p. 197.

22. Calvin, *Commentaries on the First Book of Moses Called Genesis*, trans. John King (Edinburgh, 1847), I, 97. *Luther's Commentary on Genesis*, I, 58–59.

23. *The Bishops' Bible* (London, 1585), sig. Biff. Both Milton and his father could have known the Bishops' Bible (Fletcher, *Intellectual Development*, II, 103).

24. Postellus, *De Orbis Terrae Concordia Libri Quatuor* (Paris, 1544), p. 65. Bodin, *Method for the Easy Comprehension of History*, pp. 296–97, 339–40. See also Prideaux, *An Easy and Compendious Introduction for Reading All Sorts of Histories*, p. 6. Stillingfleet, *Origines Sacrae*, II, 205–6.

25. Hale, *The Primitive Origination of Mankind*, pp. 184–85; Stillingfleet, *Origines Sacrae*, I, 2–10; II, 137; McKee, "Isaac De La Peyrère," pp. 467–69. Andrew Dickson White, *A History of the Warfare of Science with Theology* (2 vols., New York, 1897), I, 104; McKee, "Isaac De La Peyrère," p. 467, and Georg Horn, *De Originibus Americanis* (Hague, 1653), p. 8.

26. La Peyrère, *A Theological Systeme upon that Presupposition that Men Were before Adam* (London, 1655; actually published, 1656), pp. 276, 130; *Men before Adam* (London, 1656), pp. 19–20.

27. *A Theological Systeme*, pp. 169–82, 200–18, 271–77.

28. *Men before Adam*, pp. 6–13, 16, 442–43. La Peyrère, *A Theological Systeme*, pp. 249–53; 136–45.

29. White, *History of the Warfare of Science with Theology*, I, 255. Stillingfleet, *Origines Sacrae*, II, 137; Hale, *Primitive Origination of Mankind*, p. 185.

30. Lord Herbert of Cherbury, *De Religione Laici*, ed. and trans. Harold R. Hutcheson (New Haven, 1944), p. 99.

31. Bodin, *Method for the Easy Comprehension of History*, p. 303. Swan, *Speculum Mundi*, p. 28.

32. Burnet, *Sacred Theory of the Earth*, pt. I, pp. 54–55. Wolseley, *The Unreasonablenesse of Atheism*, p. 70.

33. Harvey, *A Discoursive Probleme concerning Prophesies* (London, 1588), pp. 15–16. I am indebted in this section to C. A. Patrides, "Renaissance Estimates of the Year of Creation," *Huntington Library Quarterly*, XXVI (1953), 315–22.

34. Patrides, "Renaissance Estimates," p. 319. Inveges, *Historia Sacra Paradisi Terrestris et Sanctissimi Innocentiae Status* (Palermo, 1649), pp. 113, 47, 105, 126, 141. This work is also referred to in an Italian translation, but the only copy that I have been able to find is the Latin edition in the Biblioteca Nazionale di Palermo. Lightfoot, *Works* (London, 1684), I, 692. Swan, *Speculum Mundi*, pp. 36–40. Hayne, *The General View of the Holy Scriptures* (2nd ed., London, 1640), pp. 15–25.

35. *Luther's Commentaries on Genesis*, I, 20, 41–42. Vaughan, *Ten Introductions*, sigs. Eiii–Eiiii. Richardson, *Choice Observations and Explanations upon the Old Testament* (London, 1655), sig. B3. Ussher, *The Annals of the World* (London, 1658), pp. 1–2.

36. Graf, *Miti*, I, 53–54; Juan de Pineda, *Los Treynta Libros de la Monarchia Ecclesiastica, o Historia Vniversal del Mvndo* (Barcelona, 1620), pt. I, bk. I, vol. I, p. 18; Willet, *Hexapla in Genesin*, p. 54. *Historia Mundi or Mercator's Atlas, Containing His Description of the Fabricke and Figure of the World*,

enlarged by Iudocus Hondy; trans. W. Saltonstall (London, 1635), p. 48. Hake-will, *An Apologie or Declaration of the Power and Providence of God in the Government of the World* (London, 1635), pp. 2–3. Salkeld, *A Treatise of Paradise*, p. 227.

37. Fletcher, *Intellectual Development*, II, 172–73, 188–97; II, 286, 325, 332.

38. Milton, *Areopagitica*, IV, 302, 312. *The Reason of Church Government*, III¹, 274; *Prolusion* I, XII, 135. *Ars Logicae*, XI, 37; *Commonplace Book*, VIII, 197.

39. Milton, *The Reason of Church Government*, III¹, 181–82. *The Christian Doctrine*, XV, 37; XIV, 45–47; XV, 9–11, 17–19, 43–47.

40. Milton, *The Christian Doctrine*, XIV, 27, 43; XV, 41, 45.

41. Lucretius, *On the Nature of Things*, trans. W. E. Leonard (London, 1916), pp. 219–21.

42. Milton, *The Christian Doctrine*, XV, 35; Arnold Williams, *The Common Expositor*, p. 42.

43. Milton, *Works*, III¹, 88; X, 31. *The Christian Doctrine*, XVI, 277; *The Reason of Church Government*, III¹, 181–82. *The Christian Doctrine*, XV, 3.

44. Swan, *Speculum Mundi*, p. 35.

45. Grotius, *De Veritate Religione Christianae* (London, 1821), pp. 1–21. *Bibliotheca Curiosa*, no. 3, ed. and trans. Edmund Goldsmid (Edinburgh, 1884), pp. 7–20. Kirkconnell, *Celestial Cycle*, pp. 118–37, 168–69.

46. *Bartas, His Devine Weekes and Works (1605)*, trans. Joshua Sylvester, facsimile reprint with introduction by Francis C. Haber (Gainesville, Fla., 1965), p. 2.

47. Kirkconnell, *Celestial Cycle*, pp. 230–31; 292–93; 373–74.

The Legacy of Eden

1. *Luther's Commentary on Genesis*, I, 51–52. Andrewes, *Apospasmatia Sacra, or a Collection of Posthumous and Orphan Lectures* (London, 1657), p. 84. Milton, *The Christian Doctrine*, XV, 209.

2. Mirandola, *Oration on the Dignity of Man*, trans. Elizabeth Livermore Forbes (Lexington, Ky., 1953), p. 3. Socinus, *Praelectiones Theologicae*, in *Opera Omnia* (Amsterdam, 1856), I, 531–40. Milton, *Tetrachordon*, IV, 94–95.

3. Hooker, *Of the Laws of Ecclesiastical Polity* (London, 1958), I, 182. Walker, *The History of the Creation* (London, 1641), p. 18. Ussher, *A Body of Divinity*, trans. and ed. Hastings Robinson (London, 1841), pp. 151–52. See references in Inveges, *Historia Sacra*, p. 116.

4. Milton, *The Christian Doctrine*, XVI, 101; XV, 117. See C. A. Patrides, *Milton and the Christian Tradition* (Oxford, 1966), pp. 85–88, 184–86.

5. Dominic J. Unger, *The First-Gospel: Genesis 3:15* (St. Bonaventura, N.Y., 1954), p. 72. This provides the most complete study of the protevangelium and also a very extensive bibliography.

6. *Ibid.*, pp. 6–7. Justin, *Dialogue with Trypho*, trans. M. Dods, in *The Ante-Nicene Fathers*, I, ch. 91, 245. St. Irenaeus, *Against Heresies*, iii, 23, in *Ante-Nicene Fathers*, I, 457–58.

7. Quoted from Unger, *First-Gospel*, pp. 6–7, 139, 143–48.

8. These works have been pointed out and discussed in John E. Parish, "Pre-Miltonic Representations of Adam as a Christian," *Rice Institute Pamphlet*, XL, 3 (1953), 1–24, and John M. Steadman, "Adam and the Prophesied

Redeemer (*Paradise Lost*, XII, 359–623)," *Studies in Philology*, LVI (1959), 214–25.

9. These references and many others have been pointed out and discussed in C. A. Patrides, "The 'Protevangelium' in Renaissance Theology and *Paradise Lost*," *Studies in English Literature*, III (1963), 19–30. This is the conclusion of Parish, "Pre-Miltonic Representations," p. 13. *The Old Faith*, in *Writings and Translations of Miles Coverdale*, Parker Society Publications, vol. XIII (Cambridge, 1844), pp. 34–35, 82.

10. Bullinger, *The Old Faith*, pp. 25–27.

11. Quoted from Patrides, "The 'Protevangelium,'" p. 26. *The Marrow of Modern Divinity*, with notes by Thomas Boston (Pittsburgh, 1830), p. 46. This work, first published in London in 1645, has been doubtfully attributed to Edward Fisher. Saltmarsh, *Free-Grace, or the Flowings of Christs Blood Freely to Sinners* (London, 1645), pp. 111, 113.

12. Coverdale, *The Old Faith*, pp. 32, 34.

13. Ursinus, "De Lege," *Summa Theologiae*, in *Opera Theologica* (3 vols. in 1, Heidelberg, 1612), I, 10, 14. Ursinus, *The Svmme of Christian Religion*, trans. Henrie Parrie (Oxford, 1587), p. 254.

14. Junius, *Theses Theologicae*, in *Opuscula Theologica Selecta*, ed. Abraham Kuyperus (Amsterdam, 1882), pp. 183–84.

15. Perkins, *A Golden Chaine* (London, 1591), ch. 19. *Cartwrightiana*, ed. Albert Peel and Leland H. Carlson, Elizabethan Nonconformist Texts, vol. I, (London, 1951), p. 159. Sibbes, *The Faithful Covenanter*, in *The Complete Works of Richard Sibbes, D.D.*, ed. A. B. Grosart (7 vols., London, 1862–64), VI, 3–4. Preston, *The New Covenant, or the Saints Portion* (London, 1629), pp. 317–20, 365. *The Westminster Confession*, VII, 2–4, in *A Collection of Confessions of Faith . . . in the Church of Scotland* (Edinburgh, 1719), pp. 36–37.

16. Ames, *The Marrow of Sacred Divinity* (London, 1643), pp. 52–54. See also Arthur Jackson, *A Help for the Understanding of the Holy Scripture* (London, 1643), pp. 9–10. White, *A Commentary upon the Three First Chapters of the First Book of Moses Called Genesis* (London, 1656), bk. II, pp. 37–39.

17. Disputation XXIX, *The Works of James Arminius*, trans. William Nichols (3 vols., London, 1825–75), II, 369. Ussher, *A Body of Divinity*, p. 152. Vane, *The Retired Mans Meditations* (London, 1653), p. 58. Salkeld, *A Treatise of Paradise*, p. 307. Sibbes, *Works*, VI, 3; *The English Works of Thomas Hobbes*, II, 227–28.

18. *Larger Catechism*, q. 22, in *A Collection of Confessions*, p. 176. *Westminster Confession*, XIX, 2, 37. *Vindiciae Fidei, or A Treatise of Justification*, in *The Works of William Pemble* (4th ed., Oxford, 1659), pp. 215–16.

19. Cotton, *The New Covenant of Grace* (London, 1655), pp. 30, 171. Perry Miller discusses the common New England view that the covenant of grace began with God's promise to Abraham in Genesis 17. *The New England Mind: The Seventeenth Century* (New York, 1939), p. 377. *Westminster Confession*, VII, 3, and *Larger Catechism*, q. 31, in *A Collection of Confessions*, pp. 36, 183. *Opera Omnia Johannis Coccei* (8 vols., Amsterdam, 1673), VII, 35; Owen, *The Doctrine of Justification by Faith* (Philadelphia, 1841), pp. 200–5. Saltmarsh, *Free Grace*, pp. 126, 128–29.

20. *Westminster Confession*, VIII, 3, in *A Collection of Confessions*, p. 26. Saltmarsh, *Free Grace*, pp. 152–53, 203. Cotton, *The New Covenant of Grace*, pp. 48–49, 55. Brown, *An Answere to Master Cartwright His Letter* (London, 1583), sig. Ci. Goodwin, *Redemption Redeemed* (London, 1811, reprinted

from edition of 1651), pp. 588–89. Baxter, *The Saints Everlasting Rest*, in *The Practical Works* (4 vols., London, 1707), III, 63. The views of Brown and Baxter were indicated in John F. New, *Anglican and Puritan* (Stanford, 1964), pp. 51, 92–93. See also Leonard J. Tinterud, "Origins of Puritanism," *Church History*, XX (1951), 37–57.

21. Milton, *The Christian Doctrine*, XV, 112–17. Milton did not include any discussion of a postlapsarian covenant of works in *The Christian Doctrine*. Although he did not explicitly deny that the Mosaic law was part of a covenant of works, he apparently wished to avoid interpreting it in this way. He regarded the essentials of the Mosaic law as comprehended in natural law, which he said was not part of a covenant of works. Milton wrote that the Mosaic law was intended for the Israelites alone and was given to lead them and ultimately others to acknowledge man's depravity and to have recourse to the promised Savior (XVI, 103). The Mosaic law included a promise of temporal life for obedience and a curse for disobedience (XVI, 103). However, Milton did not regard commandments with rewards and penalties attached as constituting a covenant (XV, 115). Also, Milton apparently thought of all true covenants as conditional, and indicated that man must exercise some free will in entering a covenant (XV, 215). All agreed that it was impossible for any man to fulfill the conditions of the covenant of works. Milton followed the Old Testament in regarding the Jews as a covenanted people, even before Sinai, and he followed St. Paul (Heb. 7:22; 8:6) in referring to the covenant of grace as a "better covenant" (XVI, 115; *P. L.* XII, 302). In one statement only in *The Christian Doctrine*, Milton associated postlapsarian covenants and works. In arguing that the entire law, not the ceremonial alone, had been abolished under the covenant of grace, Milton wrote that the Gentiles " 'were aliens from the commonwealth of Israel, and strangers from the covenant of promise,' which promise was made to the works of the whole law, not to those of the ceremonial alone" (*"abalienatis nempe a civili statu Israelis, et extraneis quod ad pactorum promissionem*, promissio autem facta est totius legis operibus, non caeremoniis tantum," XVI, 128–29). This biblical passage used a plural form and the word *pactum*, rather than *foedus*, the word Milton used in his rejection of the *foedus operum* made with Adam in paradise. He was referring to Eph. 2:12: "That at that time ye were without Christ, being aliens from the commonwealth of Israel, and strangers from the covenants of promise, having no hope and without God in the world." Elsewhere Milton apparently interpreted the "covenants" to include or to signify the covenant of grace (XVI, 105).

22. *Ibid.*, XVI, 101, 113, 153–57.

23. *Ibid.*, XV, 117; XVI, 99, 103–4, 113, 165.

24. *Ibid.*, XV, 233.

25. Origen wrote, "The serpent made of old a pact with Eve" (*MPG*, XIII, col. 516). Bullinger said that Adam made a bond with the devil (*The Old Faith*, p. 17).

26. Milton, *The Christian Doctrine*, XVI, 99; XVI, 113–19.

27. Sylvester, *Bartas*, pp. 278–79. Kirkconnell, *Celestial Cycle*, pp. 156–57, 212–13, 214. I have here given a more literal translation than that of Kirkconnell.

28. Pererius, *Commentariorum et Disputationum in Genesim Tomi Quattuor, Tomus Primus* (Mainz, 1612), pp. 178–92. Lapide, *Commentaria in*

NOTES

Pentateuchum Moysis (Antwerp, 1630), p. 74, col. 2. Rivetus, *Operum Theologicorum quae Latiné Edidit, Tomus Primus* (Rotterdam, 1651), p. 94.

29. *Purchas His Pilgrimage* (London, 1613), p. 11. Salkeld, *Treatise of Paradise*, pp. 185–96. Andrewes, *Apospasmatia Sacra*, pp. 206–8.

30. For these and other popular beliefs concerning Adam, see *Codex Pseudepigraphus Veteris Testamenti*, ed. Johann Fabricius (Hamburg, 1713), I, 1–33.

31. *The Advancement of Learning*, and *De Augmentis Scientiarum*, in *The Works of Francis Bacon*, ed. James Spedding et al. (15 vols., London, 1868), VI, 138, VIII, 440. Weemse, *The Portraiture of the Image of God in Man* (London, 1636), p. 75. Glanvill, *The Vanity of Dogmatizing* (London, 1661), p. 1–8.

32. Andrewes, *Apospasmatia Sacra*, p. 208. Quoted from George H. Williams, *Wilderness and Paradise in Christian Thought* (New York, 1962), p. 194. *Ibid.*, esp. pp. 156–57.

33. Cajetan, *Commentarii . . . in Quinque Mosaicos Libros*, in *Opera Omnia* (Leyden, 1639), I, 20. Pererius, *Commentariorum et Disputationum*, p. 178. Weemse, *Portraiture*, pp. 66, 91–92. *The English Works of Thomas Hobbes*, III, 18–19.

34. *The Advancement of Learning*, in *Works of Francis Bacon*, VI, 137. Hale, *The Primitive Origination of Mankind*, p. 317. Pererius, *Commentariorum et Disputationum*, p. 145; Lapide, *Commentaria in Pentateuchum Moysis*, p. 72, col. 2. *Luther's Commentary on Genesis*, I, 51. White, *A Commentary upon the Three First Chapters*, bk. II, p. 54.

35. *Contemplations on the Historical Passages of the Old and the New Testaments*, in *Works of Bishop Joseph Hall* (London, 1634), p. 777. Cajetan, *Opera Omnia*, I, 20; Salkeld, *A Treatise of Paradise*, p. 128. Inveges, *Historia Sacra*, p. 120.

36. Inveges, *Historia Sacra*, p. 120. Calvin, *Commentaries on the First Book of Moses*, p. 125. Elnathan Parr, *Grounds of Divinitie* (London, 1651), p. 29. Hall, *Works*, p. 777. White, *A Commentary upon the Three First Chapters*, bk. II, p. 54.

37. Milton, *Of Education*, IV, 277, 280. Milton, *Areopagitica*, IV, 347, 341.

38. Sylvester, *Bartas*, pp. 280–81, 376. Kirkconnell, *Celestial Cycle*, pp. 117–21, 157; 229–30, 233, 240; 304; 435–38.

39. Andrewes, *Apospasmatia Sacra*, p. 229. Secker, *A Wedding Ring Fit for the Finger* (London, 1658), p. 16.

40. Pererius, *Commentariorum et Disputationum*, pp. 166–67. For a discussion of the treatment of marriage in the Renaissance commentaries of Pererius and others, see Williams, *The Common Expositor*, pp. 88–89. Inveges, *Historia Sacra*, pp. 153–54, 166, 175–80. *Luther's Commentary on Genesis*, I, 56. Rivetus, *Operum Theologicorum*, pp. 106–7.

41. See, for example, Pererius, *Commentariorum et Disputationum*, p. 133, and Salkeld, *A Treatise of Paradise*, pp. 129–30. See, for example, Thomas Cooper, *A Briefe Exposition of Such Chapters of the Olde Testament as Usually Are Redde in the Churche at Common Praier on the Sundayes* (London, 1573), p. 95. Andrewes, *Apospasmatia Sacra*, pp. 225–26. Secker, *A Wedding Ring*, p. 23.

42. Troeltsch, *The Social Teachings of the Christian Churches*, trans. Olive Wyon (2 vols., London, 1931), II, 544, 651.

43. *Luther's Commentary on Genesis*, I, 47, 51–52, 88. Munsterus, in *An-*

305

notatia ad Pentateuchum . . . sive Criticorum Sacrorum Tomus I, ed. John Pearson (Frankfurt, 1695), col. 33.

44. Andrewes, *Apospasmatia Sacra*, pp. 197, 165. Ussher, *A Body of Divinity*, p. 153. Vane, *The Retired Mans Meditations*, p. 50. *Bishop Overall's Convocation Book MDCVI, concerning the Government of God's Church and the Kingdoms of the Whole World* (London, 1690), p. 4. Preston, *The New Covenant*, pp. 365–67. Francis Roberts, *Clavis Bibliorum, the Key of the Bible* (2nd ed., London, 1649), p. 13.

45. Ross, *Pansebeia, or a View of All Religions of the World* (2nd ed., London, 1655), p. 2. *The First Ten Chapters of Genesis*, in *The Works of John Bunyan*, ed. Henry Stebbing (4 vols., London, 1862), III, 379.

46. Molina, in *Extracts on Politics and Government*, trans. George Albert Moore (Clearfield, Pa., 1951), pp. 1–12. Keckermann, *Systema Disciplinae Politicae* (Hanover, 1613), pp. 9–13. Pareus, *In Genesin Mosis Commentarius* (Geneva, 1614), col. 245; Rivetus, *Operum Theologicorum*, pp. 42–46.

47. Salkeld, *Treatise of Paradise*, pp. 125–28. See also Hughes, *An Analytical Exposition*, p. 22. Vane, *The Retired Mans Meditations*, pp. 387–93.

48. Williams, *The Common Expositor*, pp. 222–23. Inveges, *Historia Sacra*, pp. 109–10, 192–95.

49. Overall, *Convocation Book*, p. 2. Ralegh, *History of the World*, pp. 178–80.

50. Maxwell, *Sacro-Sancta Regum Majestas: Or, the Sacred and Royall Prerogatives of Christian Kings* (Oxford, 1644), pp. 33, 83–84, 78, 85; see Sirluck, *Complete Prose Works*, II, 130–32. Gauden, *The Religious and Loyal Protestation* (London, 1648), p. 8. Hammond, *To the Right Honourable the Lord Fairfax and His Councell of Warre: The Humble Address of Henry Hammond* (London, 1649), pp. 8–9.

51. Hughes, *Complete Prose Works*, III, 70.

52. Filmer, *The Anarchy of a Limited or Mixed Monarchy* (London, 1648), p. 1. Hunton, *Treatise of Monarchie* (London, 1643), pp. 1–3. Filmer, *The Anarchy of a Limited or Mixed Monarchy*, pp. 1–13.

53. Filmer, *Patriarcha* (London, 1680), pp. 12–13. Laslett, ed., *Patriarcha and Other Prose Works of Sir Robert Filmer* (Oxford, 1949), p. 12.

54. Filmer, *Patriarcha*, p. 12. Filmer, *Observations on the Original of Government* (London, 1679), pp. 1–2, 26.

55. A clear statement of this view is found in Alfonsus Tostatus, *Commentaria in Genesim* (Venice, 1728), p. 101. Tostatus was a well-known Spanish commentator of the late fifteenth century. *Selections from Three Works of Francisco Suarez, S. J.*, trans. Gwladys (*sic*) Williams et al. (2 vols., Oxford, 1944), II, 374. Buchanan, *De Jure Regni apud Scotos, or a Discourse concerning the Due Privilege of Government in the Kingdom of Scotland* (London, 1721), pp. 178–79. See George Kirchmaier, *De paradiso, ave paradisi manucodiata, imperio antediluviano, et arca Noae*, in *Fascis IV, Exercitationum Philologico Historicarum* (Lyons, 1700), pp. 95–97. The first edition was published in Wittenberg in 1662.

56. Quoted from Sirluck, *Complete Prose Works*, II, 7. Edwards, *Gangraena*, part III (London, 1646), p. 17.

57. Rutherford, *Lex, Rex: The Law and the Prince* (London, 1646), pp. 3, 10, 43–45, 142. Parker, *Jus Populi* (London, 1644), pp. 2–9, 31–34.

58. Lilburne, *Regall Tyrannie Discovered* (London, 1647), pp. 6–7. Approximately the same statement occurs in two other tracts by Lilburne, *A*

Protestation Against the Lords, and Appeale to the House of Commons and *Free-mans Freedome Vindicated.*

59. Milton, *Tetrachordon*, IV, 73–76; *The Christian Doctrine*, XV, 121, 177.

60. Milton, *The Reason of Church Government*, III¹, 260. *The Christian Doctrine*, XVI, 239–45, 325; *The Readie and Easie Way to Establish a Free Commonwealth*, VI, 113–18, and *passim*.

61. Milton, *Tetrachordon*, IV, 101. *The Christian Doctrine*, XV, 153. *The Judgement of Martin Bucer*, IV, 27, 47–48.

62. Milton, *The Tenure of Kings and Magistrates*, V, 1.

63. *Ibid.*, V, 8.

64. *Ibid.*, V, 35.

65. Milton, *The Reason of Church Government*, III¹, 196. *The Christian Doctrine*, XV, 117; XVII, 177–79, 81–85; XVI, 219–49.

66. Milton, *Tetrachordon*, IV, 170–71.

67. Sylvester, *Bartas*, pp. 292–93. Kirkconnell, *Celestial Cycle*, pp. 137, 181–85; 240–41. Loredano, *The Life of Adam (1640)*, reprinted from the English translation of 1659, with an introduction by Roy C. Flannagan with John Arthos (Gainesville, Fla., 1967), pp. 20–21. Kirkconnell, *Celestial Cycle*, pp. 45–62.

68. Sylvester, *Bartas*, pp. 284, 376. Kirkconnell, *Celestial Cycle*, pp. 139–47; 157; 229–31, 242; 472. Sylvester, *Bartas*, pp. 294, 366. Kirkconnell, *Celestial Cycle*, p. 103; 444.

The Search for Paradise

1. *Select Letters of Christopher Columbus*, trans. R. H. Major (London, 1870), pp. 136, 141.

2. Vadianus, *Epitome Trium Terrae Partium, Asiae, Africae et Europae Compendiarium Locorum Descriptionem* (Zurich, 1534), p. 184.

3. Ralegh, *History of the World*, p. 33. Carver, *A Description of the Terrestrial Paradise* (London, 1666), "To the Reader," and sig. A3. Gale, "Introduction," Pierre-Daniel Huet, *A Treatise of the Situation of Paradise* (London, 1694), sig. A2.

4. *The Table Talk of Martin Luther*, ed. Thomas S. Kepler (New York, 1952), p. 79; *Luther's Commentary on Genesis*, I, 45–49.

5. E. G. R. Taylor, *Tudor Geography, 1485–1583* (London, 1930), pp. 8–13. *Faust Book*, p. 46. Quoted from Philip Palmer and Robert More, *The Sources of the Faust Tradition* (New York, 1936), p. 190.

6. Pius II, *La discrittione de l'Asia et Europe* (Venice, 1544), p. 380. Vadianus, *Epitome*, p. 183. Rivetus, *Operum Theologicorum*, pp. 198–99. Purchas *His Pilgrimage*, p. 14. Leigh, *A Systeme or Bodie of Divinitie* (London, 1654), p. 293. Walker, *The History of the Creation*, p. 240.

7. Sixtus, *Bibliotheca Sancta* (2nd ed., Cologne, 1576), p. 370. Cajetan, *Commentarii*, in *Opera Omnia*, pp. 18–20. Malvenda, *De Paradiso Voluptatis* (Rome, 1605), pp. 161–62, 268–78.

8. Bellarmine, *De Gratia Primi Hominis*, bk. i, ch. 12, in *Opera Omnia* (7 vols., Cologne, 1617–20), IV, 51–57.

9. Sylvester, *Bartas*, p. 277.

10. *Diodorus of Sicily*, II, viii, 89–93. *Dionysii Alex. (Periegesis) et Pomp. Melae Situs Orbis Descriptio Aethici Cosmographia C. J. Solini Polyhistor*

(Paris, 1577), pp. 45–46, 70–71, and *passim*. Francesco Patritio, *Della Retorica* (Venice, 1562), pp. 5b–6a.

11. Boies Penrose, *Travel and Discovery in the Renaissance, 1420–1620* (Cambridge, Mass., 1952), pp. 11–13. *Mirabilia Descripta per Fratrem Jordanum*, in *Recueil de Voyages et de Memoires, par la Société de Géographie* (Paris, 1839), IV, 56, 556–57.

12. Alvarez, *Narrative of the Portuguese Embassy to Abyssinia during the Years 1520–1527*, trans. and ed., Lord Stanley of Aldersley (London, 1881), pp. 140–44.

13. Urreta attributed much of his information about Amara, but not the idea that it was paradise, to Juan de Baltasar, who he said had lived there many years. He wrote that Philo had maintained that if a terrestrial paradise existed, it was on this mountain, and claimed that Rabbi Samuel Hierosolymitanus and Amatus Lusitanus had similarly praised Amara. I have found no written accounts by Juan de Baltasar, or any specific reference to Amara in Philo. The rabbi is almost certainly Simson (ben Samuel) Jeruschalmi, who lived in Jerusalem in the middle of the fourteenth century. Urreta could have consulted a collection of precepts and verses published in 1597, but some of Jeruschalmi's work remains in manuscript. *Catalogia Librorum Hebraeorum in Bibliotheca Bodleiana*, ed. M. Steinschneider (Berlin, 1852–60), col. 2639. I have not been able to consult these works. R. J. de Castel Branco (1511–68), known as Amatus Lusitanus, was well known as a traveling physician and botanist. In the works of Amatus that I have been able to consult, I have found only the statement that the Ethiopians live long and retain their strength and health. *Curationum Medicinalium Centuriae Septem* (Barcelona, 1648), p. 463.

14. Urreta, *Historia ecclesiastica, politica, natural, y moral, de los grandes y remotos Reynos de la Etiopia, Monarchia del Emperador llamado Preste Juan de las Indias* (Valencia, 1610), pp. 96–100.

15. *Ibid.*, pp. 92–94.

16. *Purchas His Pilgrimage*, p. 843. Heylyn, *Cosmographie in Foure Books* (London, 1677), IV, 53.

17. Milton almost certainly did not know Urreta in the original. However, scholars have disputed whether passages apparently derived from descriptions of Amara were based on Purchas, Heylyn, or both. Robert Ralston Cawley presents persuasive evidence that Milton depended directly on Heylyn in *P. L.*, IV, 280–84. *Milton and the Literature of Travel* (Princeton, 1951), pp. 23, 67–70. Milton's dependence on Purchas has been discussed in Grant McColley, *Paradise Lost* (Chicago, 1940), p. 156, and E. M. Clark, "Milton's Abyssinian Paradise," *Studies in English* (University of Texas), XXIX (1950), 129–50.

18. Stradling, *Divine Poems* (London, 1625), p. 27. Bancroft, *Two Books of Epigrammes* (London, 1639), F1, L3. Peyton, *The Glasse of Time*, in *The First Age* (New York, 1886), p. 71. The first edition was published in 1620.

19. See Vincent Le Blanc, *The World Surveyed*, trans. Francis Brooke (London, 1660), p. 212.

20. See Joseph Duncan, "Paradise as the Whole Earth," *Journal of the History of Ideas*, XXX (1969), 171–86. See *The Antiquities of the Jews*, bk. i, ch. 1, in *The Works of Josephus*, trans. William Whiston (Loeb, 4 vols., New York, 1884), I, 77, and *Adnotationes Elucidatoriae in Pentateuchon*, MPL, CLXXV, col. 39. Calvin, *Commentaries on the First Book of Moses Called Genesis*, I, 113–14. *Purchas His Pilgrimage*, p. 13.

NOTES

21. Vadianus, *Epitome*, pp. 183–87. See Bronchorst, *Bedae, Viri Literatissimi Opuscula . . . cum Scholiis in Obscuros Aliquot Locos* (Cologne, 1537), sig. 2d; Nogarola, *Dialogus qui Inscribitur Timotheus, Sive de Nilo* (Venice, 1553), pp. 18–23; Fidelis, *De Mundi Structura* (Paris, 1556), pp. 288–89. Goropius, *Origines Antwerpianae* (Antwerp, 1569), pp. 481–82, 495–98.

22. Fidelis, *De Mundi Structura*, p. 289. Pineda, *Los Treynta Libros de la Monarchia Ecclesiastica o Historia Universal del Mvndo*, pt. I, bk. I, vol. I, 16–17.

23. Vadianus, *Epitome*, p. 192; Nogarola, *Dialogus*, pp. 20–21. Goropius, *Origines Antwerpianae*, p. 482.

24. Peyton, *The Glasse of Time*, p. 73.

25. Postellus, *Cosmographicae Disciplinae Compendium* (Basel, 1561), p. 25.

26. Carver, *A Discourse of the Terrestrial Paradise*, "To the Reader," sigs. A3–A4.

27. All of these questions are posed, for instance, in Agostino Torniello, *Annales Sacri et Profani ab Orbe Condito ad Eundem Christi Passione Redemptum* (Cologne, 1622–26), 1, 19.

28. Pareus, *In Genesin Mosis Commentarius*, cols. 334–35.

29. Eugubinus, *Recognitio Veteris Testamenti ad Hebraicam Veritatem* (Venice, 1529), pp. 22–28. Vatablus, in *Annotationes ad Pentateuchum . . . sive Criticorum Sacrorum Tomus I*, col. 57. Oleaster, *Commentaria in Mosi Pentateuchum* (Lisbon, 1556), pp. 59–60.

30. Calvin, *Commentaries on the First Book of Moses Called Genesis*, I, 119–22.

31. *Purchas His Pilgrimage*, p. 14. Junius, *Testamenti Veteris Biblia Sacra, sive Libri Canonici Priscae Judaeorum Ecclesiae a Deo Traditi* (Geneva, 1590), pp. 5–7. Bochart, *Geographia Sacra*, in *Opera Omnia* (3 vols., Leyden, 1692), I, frontispiece and map facing col. 77. This was first published in 1646.

32. Pererius, *Commentariorum et Disputationum*, pp. 111–13; Lapide, *Commentaria in Pentateuchum Moysis*, pp. 66–67. Pareus, *In Genesin Mosis Commentarius*, cols. 324–35. Diodati, *Pious and Learned Annotations upon the Holy Bible* (3rd ed., London, 1651), sigs. D1–D2. Willet, *Hexapla in Genesin*, pp. 29–30. Cooper, *A Brief Exposition*, p. 94. Nicholas Gibbens, *Qvestions and Disputations concerning the Holy Scripture* (London, 1601), pp. 59–60.

33. Hopkinson, in *Thesaurus Antiquitatum Sacrarum*, ed. Blasio Ugolino (Venice, 1747), VII, DCXII–DCXXVI.

34. *Purchas His Pilgrimage*, pp. 14, 458, 317.

35. Ralegh, *History of the World*, pp. 34–36, 38–39, 47, 64.

36. Bochart, *De Serpente Tentatore* and *Dissertatio de Paradiso Terrestre*, in *Opera Omnia*, I, col. 834; II, col. 12. Huet, *A Treatise of the Situation of Paradise*, pp. 161–62.

37. Beroalde, *Chronicum, Scripturae Sacrae Autoritate Constitutum* (Geneva, 1575), pp. 80–87.

38. *The Dutch Annotations upon the Whole Bible*, trans. Theodore Hoak (London, 1657), sig. B3.

39. Servetus, *Christianismi Restitutio* (Nuremberg, 1791, reprinted from the edition of 1553), pp. 373–74; Inveges, *Historia Sacra*, p. 15; Jacobus Salianus, *Annales Ecclesiastici Veteris Testamenti* (Cologne, 1622), p. 35. *Gregorii Opuscula: Or Notes and Observations upon Some Passages of Scripture, with Other Learned Tracts* (London, 1650), p. 78. Roger, *La Terre Saincte* (Paris, 1646), pp. 7–11.

309

40. Roger, *La Terre Saincte*, pp. 11–12.

41. La Peyrère, *A Theological Systeme*, p. 142. Heidegger, *Historia Sacra Patriarchum* (Amsterdam, 1667), I, 142–43. Herbinus, *Dissertationes de Admirandis Mundi Cataractis* (Amsterdam, 1678), pp. 147–51. In a digression from his commentary on Virgil's *Georgics* (1636), the Jesuit Nicolas Abram also placed paradise in Palestine. See, for example, Jean Hardouin, *Nouveau Traité sur la Situation du Paradis Terrestre* (La Haye, 1730).

42. Pererius, *Commentariorum et Disputationum*, p. 101; Lapide, *Commentaria in Pentateuchum Moysis*, p. 67, col. 2. Vorstius, *Dissertatio de Paradiso*, in *Thesaurus Antiquitatum Sacrarum*, VII, DCCIX–DCCX.

43. Carver, *A Discourse of the Terrestrial Paradise*, sig. A3, pp. 4–5, 47–49, 152.

44. See Tostatus, *Commentaria in Genesim*, p. 85, col. 1; *Luther's Commentary on Genesis*, I, 45–49; Malvenda, *De Paradiso Voluptatis*, p. 195; White, *A Commentary upon the Three First Chapters*, p. 48; and Salkeld, *A Treatise of Paradise*, pp. 31–33.

45. Inveges, *Historia Sacra*, pp. 15–37. Andrewes, *Apospasmatia Sacra*, p. 174. *Luther's Commentary on Genesis*, I, p. 8.

46. Fletcher, *Intellectual Development*, II, 215–16, 255, 581, 631, 643, 657. Nicolas Caussin, *De Eloquentia Sacra et Humana* (Paris, 1630), pp. 724–25. Calvin, *Commentaries on the First Book of Moses Called Genesis*, I, 122. *Luther's Commentary on Genesis*, I, 48. Pareus, *In Genesin Mosis Commentarius*, p. 361. Andrewes, *Apospasmatia Sacram*, p. 156. Lightfoot, *Works*, I, 690.

47. See Inveges, *Historia Sacra*, pp. 39–41. Andrewes, *Apospasmatia Sacra*, p. 156. Jackson, *A Help for the Understanding of the Holy Scripture*, p. 9. *Luther's Commentary on Genesis*, I, 47; Andrewes, *Apospasmatia Sacra*, p. 165; *Gregorii Opuscula*, p. 78. White, *A Commentary on the Three First Chapters*, p. 38; Pererius, *Commentariorum et Disputationum*, p. 103. Inveges, *Historia Sacra*, pp. 58, 145, 153–55. *Luther's Commentary on Genesis*, I, 20, 77, 84. Parkinson, *Paradisi in Sole, Paradisus Terrestris* (London, 1904, reprinted from edition of 1629), p. 2.

48. *Minor Poets of the Caroline Period*, ed. George Saintsbury (Oxford, 1906), II, 187. Parr, *The Grounds of Divinitie*, p. 28. Browne, *Pseudodoxia Epidemica*, bk. v, ch. 5, in *The Works of Sir Thomas Browne*, ed. Geoffrey Keynes (Chicago, 1964), II, 345. See Willet, *Hexapla in Genesin*, p. 31. Inveges, *Historia Sacra*, pp. 90–92, 153. Diodati, *Pious and Learned Annotations*, sig. D2. *Purchas His Pilgrimage*, p. 20.

49. I. H., *Paradise Transplanted and Restored, in a Most Artfull and Lively Representation* (London, 1661), pp. 1–4.

50. Giamatti, *Earthly Paradise*, pp. 134–37; 126–27.

51. Milton, *Areopagitica*, IV, 311.

52. References are to *The Complete Poetical Works of Edmund Spenser*, ed. R. E. Neil Dodge (Boston, 1908). For discussions of these gardens, see *The Works of Edmund Spenser: A Variorum Edition*, ed. E. Greenlaw et al. (11 vols., Baltimore, 1932–57), vols. II and III.

53. See Josephine Waters Bennett, "Spenser's Garden of Adonis," *PMLA*, XLVII (1932), 46–78, and "Spenser's Garden of Adonis Revisited," *Journal of English and Germanic Philology*, XLIV (1942), 46–51.

54. McColley, "Milton's Technique of Source Adaptation," *Studies in Philology*, XXXV (1938), 61–110. See esp. pp. 69–71.

NOTES

55. *The Works of Michael Drayton*, I, 129–30.
56. *Ibid.*, III, 248–51. The *Index* of the Columbia Milton lists some apparent allusions to one section of "The Muses Elyzium."
57. Fletcher, *Intellectual Development*, I, 191; II, 292.
58. George Wesley Whiting has suggested that Milton followed Ralegh's assumption that Nimrod had come to Babylon from east of Mesopotamia, yet most commentators held that he had come from the north. *Milton's Literary Milieu*, pp. 48–52.
59. Frye, *The Return of Eden* (Toronto, 1965), p. 31. MacCaffrey, *Paradise Lost as "Myth"* (Cambridge, Mass., 1959), pp. 122–23, 144–56. Gardner, *A Reading of Paradise Lost* (Oxford, 1965), pp. 35, 77–79.
60. Harding, *The Club of Hercules: Studies in the Classical Background of Paradise Lost* (Urbana, Ill., 1962), pp. 69, 80. Giamatti, *Earthly Paradise*, pp. 299, 308–11. Madsen, *From Shadowy Types to Truth: Studies in Milton's Symbolism* (New Haven, 1968), pp. 102–3. Lawry, *The Shadow of Heaven: Matter and Stance in Milton's Poetry* (Ithaca, N.Y., 1968), p. 71.
61. Lewis, *A Preface to Paradise Lost* (Oxford, 1942), pp. 47–50. Stein, *Answerable Style* (Minneapolis, 1953), pp. 53, 62, 66–67. Summers, *The Muse's Method: An Introduction to Paradise Lost* (Cambridge, Mass., 1962), pp. 71–86. Broadbent, *Some Graver Subject: An Essay on Paradise Lost* (New York, 1960), pp. 174–85. Ferry, *Milton's Epic Voice: The Narrator in Paradise Lost* (Cambridge, 1963), pp. 92–93, 113–15, 51–61. Cope, *The Metaphoric Structure of Paradise Lost* (Baltimore, 1962), pp. 111–12. Ricks, *Milton's Grand Style* (Oxford, 1963), pp. 93–95, 110–12.
62. Sylvester, *Bartas*, pp. 276–77. Kirkconnell, *Celestial Cycle*, pp. 97, 99–101. Peyton, *The Glasse of Time*, p. 76. Pordage, *Mundorum Explicatio, or the Explanation of an Hieroglyphical Figure* (London, 1661), pp. 28–29. Loredano, *The Life of Adam*, p. 9.
63. Sylvester, *Bartas*, pp. 288–89. Kirkconnell, *Celestial Cycle*, pp. 230, 234, 252. Peyton, *The Glasse of Time*, pp. 76–78. Loredano, *The Life of Adam*, pp. 8, 9. Kirkconnell, *Celestial Cycle*, pp. 435, 446.

The Natural Paradise, the Celestial Paradise, and the Inner Paradise

1. Quoted from Norman Cohn, *Pursuit of the Millennium* (New York, 1961), p. 258.
2. Winstanley, *The Power of Love*, in *Tracts on Liberty in the Puritan Revolution, 1638–1647*, ed. William Haller (3 vols., New York, 1933), II, 279–80. See A. S. P. Woodhouse, ed., *Puritanism and Liberty* (London, 1938), p. 55. Quoted from Charles L. Sanford, *The Quest for Paradise: Europe and the American Moral Imagination* (Urbana, Ill., 1961), pp. 83–84. Louis Wright, *The Colonial Search for a Southern Eden* (Tuscaloosa, Fla., 1953), pp. 21–22.
3. Inveges, *Historia Sacra*, pp. 41–62, 70. See Torniello, *Annales Sacri et Profani*, p. 22.
4. Pererius, *Commentariorum et Disputationum*, p. 105; see also Torniello, *Annales Sacri et Profani*, p. 25. See Willet, *Hexapla in Genesin*, pp. 27–28. Walker, *History of the Creation*, p. 243.
5. Weemse, *The Portraiture of the Image of God in Man*, pp. 30–31, 38.
6. Milton, *The Christian Doctrine*, XV, 117.
7. Sylvester, *Bartas*, pp. 278–80.

8. Kirkconnell, *Celestial Cycle*, pp. 117, 156, 171, 247–49, 437–39, 443–44, 447, 460.

9. The importance of typological interpretation in Renaissance exegesis and in Milton's works has been emphasized by Barbara Kiefer Lewalski, *Milton's Brief Epic* (Providence, R.I., 1966), esp. pp. 167ff, and by William G. Madsen, *From Shadowy Types to Truth*. For a useful study of symbolical interpretation of Scripture in the sixteenth and seventeenth centuries, see Madsen, pp. 18–53.

10. Milton, *The Christian Doctrine*, XVI, 263.

11. See Martin Rust, *The Interpreter's Bible*, XII, 533.

12. *The Apocrypha and Pseudepigrapha of the Old Testament,* ed. R. H. Charles (2 vols., Oxford, 1913), II, 19; esp. II, 205, 207, 212, 224, 275–76, 236–37; II, 518, 484; II, 592–98.

13. St. Irenaeus, *Against Heresies*, bk. iv., chs. 35–36, in *Ante-Nicene Fathers,* I, 566–67.

14. See Ernest Lee Tuveson, *Millennium and Utopia* (Berkeley, 1949).

15. Servetus, *Christianismi Restitutio*, pp. 373–75. See also Cornelius Jansen, *Commentariorum in Suam Concordiam . . . Partes IIII* (Louvain, 1576), p. 1076. Diodati, *Pious Annotations*, sigs. D1, D2. Pererius, *Commentariorum et Disputationum*, p. 100; Lapide, *Commentaria*, p. 69, col. 1, and p. 70, col. 2.

16. Andrewes, *Apospasmatia Sacra*, p. 161. Hall, *Contemplations*, in *Works,* pp. 777–78. Ainsworth, *Annotations upon the Five Bookes of Moses* (London, 1627), pp. 10–13.

17. Leigh, *A Systeme, or Bodie of Divinitie*, p. 293. See Parr, *The Grounds of Divinitie*, p. 28, and White, *A Commentary on the Three First Chapters*, bk. II, p. 33. *Opuscula Gregorii*, pp. 72, 78.

18. Arthur Dent, *Ruine of Rome* (London, 1650), p. 302. See Patrick Forbes, *An Exqvisite Commentary vpon the Relevation of Saint John* (London, 1613), p. 256, and Hezekiah Holland, *An Exposition, or a Short, Restfull, Plaine, and Perfect Epitome of the Most Choice Commentaries Upon the Revelation of St. John* (London, 1650), pp. 173–74.

19. See Dent, *Ruine of Rome*, p. 379; Holland, *An Exposition*, pp. 171–72; and Forbes, *An Exqvisite Commentary*, pp. 240–41.

20. Junius, in his annotations in the Geneva Bible (Amsterdam, 1644), p. 264. See Richard Bernard, *A Key of Knowledge* (London, 1617), p. 336. Mead, *Clavis Apocalyptica: Or the Key to the Apocalypse*, trans. E. N. H. (Dublin, 1831), pp. 58–59, 63, 65. See Thomas Brightman, *The Revelation of St. John* (Amsterdam, 1644), pp. 276–77. Holland, *An Exposition*, pp. 157, 173. Walker, *History of Creation*, p. 58.

21. Milton, *Of Reformation*, III¹, 78–79.

22. Milton, *The Christian Doctrine*, XV, 223; XVI, 359–79. *The Reason of Church Government*, III¹ 185. *The Christian Doctrine*, XV, 31–33.

23. See Madsen, *From Shadowy Types to Truth*, esp. pp. 85–113.

24. Milton, *The Christian Doctrine*, XVI, 337; *P. L.*, XI, 665–71, 700–10.

25. Merritt Y. Hughes in the notes to his editions of Milton's works has pointed out Milton's dependence upon this passage. He has also called attention to many other echoes from Scripture in the description of Heaven.

26. Sylvester, *Bartas*, p. 276. Beaumont, *Psyche*, stanza 252; Kirkconnell, *Celestial Cycle*, p. 353; 230–31; 443, 444.

27. See Sister Mary Irma Corcoran, *Milton's Paradise with Reference to the Hexameral Background*, ch. IV. Louis L. Martz has written that "in their cen-

312

tral imagination Traherne and Milton share the Augustinian vision of a Paradise within, the vision that Vaughan also sought, and the vision that the Cambridge Platonists were seeking during the same era, . . ." (p. 35). Many believed that the image of God in the soul was not wholly lost, but hidden beneath the ruins of the Fall. The inner paradise could be regained by uncovering and developing the inner forms of truth and good. *The Paradise Within: Studies in Vaughan, Traherne, and Milton* (New Haven, 1964), esp. pp. 33–35.

Stanley Stewart has shown that the enclosed garden, derived from the Song of Solomon and associated with paradise, may represent the individual regenerate soul, protected by its wall from the wilderness outside and shaded from the sun of divine justice. The enclosed garden often represented the Virgin Mary, the new garden created by God after man had lost the Edenic garden. Stewart has included a number of illustrations, some showing a walled garden with Adam and Eve. *The Enclosed Garden: The Tradition and the Image in Seventeenth-Century Poetry* (Madison, Wis., 1966), esp. pp. 38–42, 51–62.

28. Weemse, *Portraiture of the Image of God in Man*, esp. pp. 65–66, 110, 162, 254.

29. *The Enchiridion of Erasmus*, trans. and ed. Raymond Himeleck (Bloomington, Ind., 1963), p. 75. Browne, *Pseudodoxia Epidemica*, bk. i., ch. 1, in *Works*, II, 20. Vane, *The Retired Mans Meditations*, p. 52.

30. Böhme, *Mysterium Magnum, or an Exposition of the First Book of Moses Called Genesis*, trans. John Sparrow, ed. C. J. Barker (2 vols., London, 1924), I, 104–19, 125–31; I, 53.

31. More, *Conjectura Cabbalistica* (London, 1653), pp. 127; 37–38; 40–50; 23.

32. Milton, *The Christian Doctrine*, XVI, 3, 11. Calvin, *Tracts and Treatises on the Doctrines and Worship of the Church*, trans. Henry Beveridge (Grand Rapids, Mich., 1958), II, 336–37. Sibbes, *The Bruised Reed and the Smoking Flax*, in *Works*, I, 75. Thomas Taylor, *The Parable of the Sower and the Seed* (London, 1621), pp. 317, 329, 393, 384–85. Many instances of the use of garden symbolism in describing regeneration are cited in Rachel Hadley King, *George Fox and the Light Within* (Philadelphia, 1940), pp. 76–77. Winstanley, *The Saints Paradise* (London, 1648), pp. 45–48.

33. Franck, *The Forbidden Fruit*, trans. John Everard (London, 1640), pp. 136, 4–5.

34. Bodin, *Colloquium Heptaplomeres de Rerum Sublimum Arcanis Abditis*, ed. Ludovicus Noack (Paris, 1857), pp. 296–97; 306–7.

35. *The Single Eye* (London, 1646), p. 138. *Divinity and Philosophy Dissected* (Amsterdam, 1644), pp. 12–13, 29–37. *The New Law of Righteousness*, in *The Works of Gerrard Winstanley*, ed. George H. Sabine (Ithaca, N.Y., 1941), pp. 196, 212.

36. Lancetta, *La Scena Tragica d'Adamo e d'Eva* (Venice, 1644), facing p. 1. Pordage, *Mundorum Explicatio*, esp. pp. 59–61, 68–69, 72.

The Fading of Paradise

1. Sherlock, *A Discourse concerning the Knowledge of Jesus Christ, and Our Union and Communion with Him* (London, 1775), pp. 24, 142–56, 281–87, 295–98. Owen, *A Vindication of Some Passages in a Discourse concerning Communion with God, from the Exceptions of William Sherlock*, in *Works*, ed. Thomas Russell (21 vols., London, 1826), X, 352, 342–43.

2. Butler, *Hudibras*, ed. A. R. Waller (Cambridge, 1905), pt. I, canto I, p. 8.

3. Behn, *Oroonoko*, in *Shorter Novels, Jacobean and Restoration* (London, 1949), II, 149. See Henri Baudet, *Paradise on Earth*, trans. Elizabeth Wentholt (New Haven, 1965), esp. pp. 25–50.

4. Burnet, *The Sacred Theory of the Earth* (5th ed., London, 1722), pt. I, p. xix; pt. I, pp. 350–51; pt. I, pp. 370–71; pt. I, p. 240.

5. *Ibid.*, pt. I, pp. 234, 51, 264–66; pt. I, p. 89. Burnet, *Archaeologicae Philosophicae*, trans. Foxton (London, 1729), pt. I, pp. 5, 8, 23, 67–70; *The Sacred Theory*, pt. I, pp. 371–77.

6. Burnet, *Archaeologicae Philosophicae*, pt. I, pp. 5–7, 23, 67–70.

7. John Hunt, *Religious Thought in England* (3 vols., London, 1873), II, 222.

8. Woodward, *An Essay toward a Natural History of the Earth and Terrestrial Bodyes, Especially Minerals* (3rd ed., London, 1723), pp. 271–72, 297, 300.

9. Whiston, *A New Theory of the Earth* (6th ed., London, 1755), pp. 2, 41–59, 234–37, 243–60.

10. Keill, *An Examination of Dr. Burnet's Theory of the Earth* (2nd ed., London, 1734), pp. 45, 52–53, 61–63, 73.

11. "Terre," in *Encyclopédie ou Dictionnaire Raisonné des Sciences, des Arts et des Métiers*, ed. Denis Diderot (36 vols., Lausanne and Berne, 1781), XXXII, 234–36. Buffon, *Oeuvres Complètes*, ed. Pierre Flourens (Paris, 1853–54), IX, 89, 97, 154; William Cecil Dampier-Whetham, *A History of Science and Its Relation with Philosophy and Religion* (New York, 1929), p. 201.

12. Bossuet, *An Universal History from the Beginning of the World to the Empire of Charlemagne*, trans. Ephilstone (New York, 1821), pp. 14–15, 124–32.

13. Bolingbroke, *Letters on the Study and Use of History*, esp. pp. 72–76. Hume, *The Natural History of Religion*, ed. H. E. Root (Stanford, 1957), pp. 23–24. "Adam," in *Encyclopédie*, I, 481–83.

14. Blount, *The Oracles of Reason* (London, 1693), "Preface," pp. 12, 35. Locke, *The Reasonableness of Christianity* (London, 1850), pp. 3–12.

15. Whitby, *Six Discourses* (Worcester, Mass., 1801), pp. vii, 71–75.

16. Tindal, *Christianity as Old as the Creation* (London, 1731), esp. pp. 40, 80–81, 165–69, 229.

17. Middleton, *Miscellaneous Tracts* (London, 1752), pp. 127, 148, 151.

18. Taylor, *The Scripture-Doctrine of Original Sin Proposed to Free and Candid Examination* (2nd ed., London, 1741), p. 167.

19. Kidder, *A Commentary on the Five Books of Moses* (2 vols., London, 1694), I, 1, 9. Quoted from Hunt, *Religious Thought in England*, II, 324. Bentley, *The Folly and Unreasonableness of Atheism* (London, 1693–96), and Ray, *The Wisdom of God Manifested in the Works of the Creation* (London, 1691).

20. Thomas Sherlock, *The Use and Intent of Prophecy* (2nd ed., London, 1726), pp. 57–69.

21. *Scripture Vindicated*, in *Works of the Reverend Daniel Waterland, D. D.* (10 vols., Oxford, 1823), VI, 14–15, 22–23, 30, 37. Joseph Butler, *The Analogy of Religion* (New York, 1961), p. 256.

22. Watts, *Ruin and Recovery of Mankind*, in *Works* (9 vols., Leeds, 1800), III, 373–78.

23. Dryden, *State of Innocence*, in *Works*, ed. Sir Walter Scott (18 vols., Edinburgh, 1821), V, 132, 149; V, 135.

24. Hopkins, *Milton's Paradise Lost Imitated in Rhyme in the Fourth Sixth and Ninth Books* (London, 1699), pp. 11–12.

25. Dubocage, *Le Paradis Terrestre. Poème imité de Milton* (London, 1760), p. 2.

26. *Ibid.*, pp. 28, 20–22.

27. Blackmore, *Creation* (2nd ed., London, 1712), pp. xxxii–xxxiii, 261, *passim*.

28. *The Poems of John Byrom*, ed. Adolphus William Ward (5 vols., Chetham Society Publications, n.s. vols. 29, 30, 34, 35, 70, Manchester, 1894–1912), I, pt. II, 178, 184; II, pt. I, 161–62; II, pt. II, 475; III, pt. II, 79–81.

29. Quotations are from *The Poems of Alexander Pope*, ed. Maynard Mack (London and New Haven, 1950), III, pt. I.

INDEX

INDEX

Aaron, 151
Abdiel, 118, 128
Abel, 110, 140, 145, 169
Abelard, 68
Abraham, 135, 137, 145, 151, 165, 221
Abram, Nicolas, 41, 310
Abravanel, 103
Absalom, 78
Abyssinians. *See* Ethiopians
Acrasia, 217
Adam: associated with Saturn, 20–24, 27, 108; as first man, 25, 56, 102, 107–8, 276; symbolic meaning of, 46, 68–69, 261–62, 284; as Cynic, 48; as Stoic, 48–49; original perfection of, 48–50, 52, 53, 125–26, 147–52, 236, 279; in Jewish tradition, 50; work of, 57, 73, 126, 152; not first man, 97, 108–11; lack of original perfection, 126; dominion of over animals, 166; and origin of monarchy, 168–72; and origin of natural rights, 172–75; dwelling place of, 206; creation of, 209; relation to Christ, 211, 243–44; as mankind, 277; temptation and fall of, 277–78; mentioned, *passim*
Adam (literary character): original perfection of, 74, 78, 154–57, 161; in legend, 75; as first man, 84; work of, 161; and origin of monarchy, 186; immortality of, 239; re-

lation to Christ, 251–52; symbolic meaning of, 256; contrasted with historical man, 276–77; mentioned, 4, 15, 17, 31, 46, 118, 119, 120, 125, 141, 142, 143, 144, 145, 146, 147, 150, 158, 159, 160, 179, 180, 181, 182, 183, 184, 185, 193, 194, 198, 225, 226, 227, 243, 255
Adam and Eve: historical importance of, 6, 9, 72; of Hebrew writers, 9, 13; tasks of, 11; marital relations of, 11, 55–56, 73, 114, 126, 162–63; original perfection of, 11, 40–41, 51–52, 54–57, 71–72; temptation and fall of, 11–12, 80, 113–14, 273; symbolic meaning of, 43–45, 52, 68, 247, 258–60, 264–66; as first parents, 107–8, 112; and problem of chronology, 113–15; expulsion of, 114; and natural law, 127–29; salvation of, 131; and beginning of Church, 163–65; dwelling place of, 200; description of, 215–16; like primitives, 235, 270–71; mentioned, 41, 54, 58, 69, 74, 80, 82, 95, 101, 105, 109, 205, 211, 212, 236, 286
Adam and Eve (literary characters): postlapsarian condition of, 16; marital relations of, 16, 24, 31, 63, 180–81, 185–86, 282–83; original perfection of, 30, 61, 63, 65–66, 85, 253; temptation and fall of, 63,

319

ernment in, 167–72; ideals of natural rights in, 173; model of paradise in, 215; garden description in, 217–20; ideas of heaven in, 246–47; mentioned, 29, 67, 109, 111

Enkidu, 10, 16

Enna, Field of, 23, 36

Enoch, 14, 71, 76, 77, 79, 80, 83, 145, 190–92, 211, 244, 255

Enoch, Book of, 244–45

Ephrem Syrus, St., 39, 50, 60, 130, 224

Epicureanism, 123

Epicurus, 104–6, 116, 120

Epimetheus, 31, 105

Erasmus, 90, 258

Erigena, John Scotus, 68–69

Ethiopia, 194–96, 199

Ethiopians, 25, 122

Eugubinus, Augustinus Steuchus, 205

Euphrates River, 64, 206–10, 212, 220–21, 231–32

Evans, J. M., 53

Eve: symbolic interpretation of, 71; creation of, 80, 149, 244; work of, 153; Adam's kingship over, 171; mentioned, *passim*

Eve (literary character): creation of, 16–17, 31, 63; and classical goddesses, 31–32, 240; original perfection of, 155, 157–58; in relation to Adam's knowledge, 156–57; mentioned, *passim*

Fall, *passim*

Faulkner, William, 235

Faustbook, 75, 191

Ferry, A. D., 230–31

Fidelis, Ludovicus, 200–1

Filmer, Sir Robert, 98–99, 166, 170–72, 178–79

Flannagan, Roy, 300n13

Fletcher, Harris F., 93, 222

Flood, 158, 169, 184, 190–93, 208, 211, 222, 264, 273–75

Fortunate Islands, 19, 22, 40, 68. *See also* Blest, Islands of the

Fox-Marcillo, Sebastian, 103

Francis, St., 161

Franck, Sebastian, 90, 99, 261, 267

Frazer, Sir James, 11

Freud, Sigmund, 7–8

Frezzi, Frederico, 83

Froissart, Jean, 82

Frye, Northrop, 228

Gabriel, 121, 169, 187, 256

Gale, Thomas, 189

Galileo, 150

Ganges, 54, 65, 68, 76

Gardner, Helen, 228

Gassendi, Pierre, 101, 106

Gauden, John, 98, 169

Gautier de Metz, 83

Geon River, 207–8

Giamatti, A. Bartlett, 19, 21, 61, 83, 216, 229, 293n9, 295n39

Giangolino, Carlo, 96

Gihon River, 54, 207–8

Gilbert, William, 95

Gilgamesh Epic, 10, 14

Gilson, Etienne, 54, 69

Glanvill, Joseph, 150, 155, 285

God: creation of Eve, 16–17; justice of, 40; promise of to man, 58; as creator, 101–8, 117–20, 122–23, 147, 267, 275; speaks to serpent, 129; speaks to Adam, 130, 132; speaks to Adam and Eve, 131, 165; relations with Adam and Eve, 141–43; and covenants, 142–47; ordains work, 152–53; Adam's knowledge of, 155–58; ordains marriage, 161–62; in relation to social order, 166–75 *passim*; leads Adam to paradise, 224; relation to man, 236, 242, 263, 266–67, 281; reflected in nature, 238; presence of, 247–48; patterns paradise on heaven, 252; foresees heavenly paradise, 253; mentioned, *passim*

Godfrey of Viterbo, 77, 83

Golding, Arthur, 27

Goodwin, John, 98, 138, 146

Goropius, Johannes, 151, 200–2, 270

Gospel of Nicodemus, 126

Graf, Arturo, 79

Graves, Robert, 10

Greeks, 39, 108, 122

Gregory XII, Pope, 166

Gregory Nazianzen, 46, 49, 68

Gregory of Nyssa, 41, 46, 49, 53, 68

Gregory, John, 99, 210, 214, 247, 252

Grosseteste, Robert, 70

Ulysses, 23, 84
Urreta, Friar Luis di, 196, 197, 198, 199, 283, 308n13
Ursinus, Zacharias, 93, 133, 146
Ussher, Archbishop James, 93, 114, 127, 134, 136, 164

Vadianus (Joachim Von Watt), 189, 191, 199, 200, 201
Vane, Sir Henry, 94, 136, 164, 168, 258
Vatablus, Franciscus, 205
Venus, 24, 32, 87
Victor, Claudius Marius, 22, 39, 59, 61, 62, 64, 65, 196
Virgil, 20, 21, 22, 25, 26, 32, 33, 60, 61, 62, 64, 83, 85, 86, 100, 216, 218
Virgil, Polydore, 105
Von Watt, Joachim, 189, 191, 199, 200, 201
Vondel, Joost van den, 101, 123, 161, 186, 187, 232, 242, 256
Vorstius, Johann, 212
Vossius, Isaac, 110

Walker, George, 94, 127, 191, 236, 239, 249, 251
Waller, Edmund, 237
Walwyn, William, 235
Warren, W. F., 292n5

Waterland, Daniel, 278, 280
Watts, Isaac, 281
Weemse, John, 97, 98, 150, 152, 236, 241, 257, 258
Westminster Assembly, 94, 127, 136, 137
Westminster Confession, 135, 136, 138
Whiston, William, 275
Whitby, Daniel, 278
White, John, 135, 152, 214
Whitehead, C., 215
Whiting, G. W., 299n7, 311n58
Wilkins, Bishop John, 99, 104
Williams, Arnold, 91, 92
Winstanley, Gerrard, 99, 175, 260, 261, 262, 267
Wissenburgus, Wolfgang, 199
Wolseley, Sir Charles, 97, 104, 106, 112
Woodward, John, 274
Worde, Wynkyn de, 79

Xenophon, 14, 108

Yahwism, 153, 180
Young, Thomas, 98

Zanchius, Hieronymus, 92, 120
Zohar, 15
Zwingli, Ulrich, 189